Since Ryo Shishido and Chotaro Ohtori did so well in the Valentine's Day poll, I put them on the cover. I'm thinking about doing something a little special for the next volume's cover, so keep an eye out for it!

— Takeshi Konomi, 2006

About Takeshi Konomi

Takeshi Konomi exploded onto the manga scene with the incredible **THE PRINCE OF TENNIS**. His refined art style and sleek character designs proved popular with **Weekly Shonen Jump** readers, and **THE PRINCE OF TENNIS** became the number one sports manga in Japan almost overnight. Its cast of fascinating male tennis players attracted legions of female readers even though it was originally intended to be a boys' comic. The manga continues to be a success in Japan and has inspired a hit anime series, as well as several video games and mountains of merchandise.

**THE PRINCE OF TENNIS
VOL. 34
SHONEN JUMP Manga Edition**

**STORY AND ART BY
TAKESHI KONOMI**

Translation/Joe Yamazaki
Touch-up Art & Lettering/Vanessa Satone
Design/Sam Elzway
Editor/Leyla Aker

VP, Production/Alvin Lu
VP, Publishing Licensing/Rika Inouye
VP, Sales & Product Marketing/Gonzalo Ferreyra
VP, Creative/Linda Espinosa
Publisher/Hyoe Narita

Printed in the U.S.A.

Published by VIZ Media, LLC
P.O. Box 77010
San Francisco, CA 94107

10 9 8 7 6 5 4 3 2 1
First printing, November 2009

www.viz.com

PARENTAL ADVISORY
THE PRINCE OF TENNIS
is rated A and is suitable
for readers of all ages.
ratings.viz.com

THE WORLD'S
MOST POPULAR MANGA

www.shonenjump.com

SHONEN JUMP Manga

テニスの王子様

THE PRINCE OF TENNIS

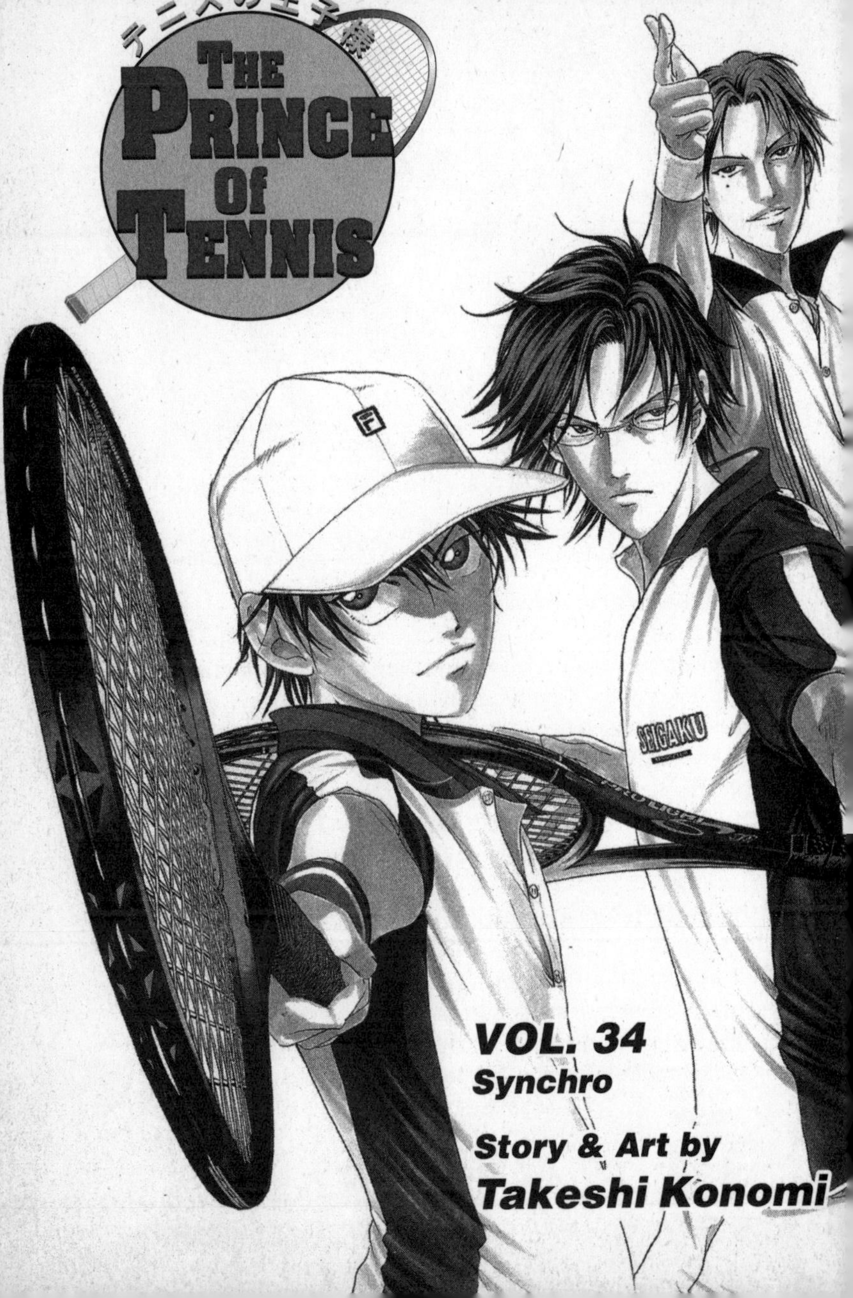
SEIGAKU
PRO LIGHT

VOL. 34

Synchro

Story & Art by

Takeshi Konomi

ENNIS CLUB

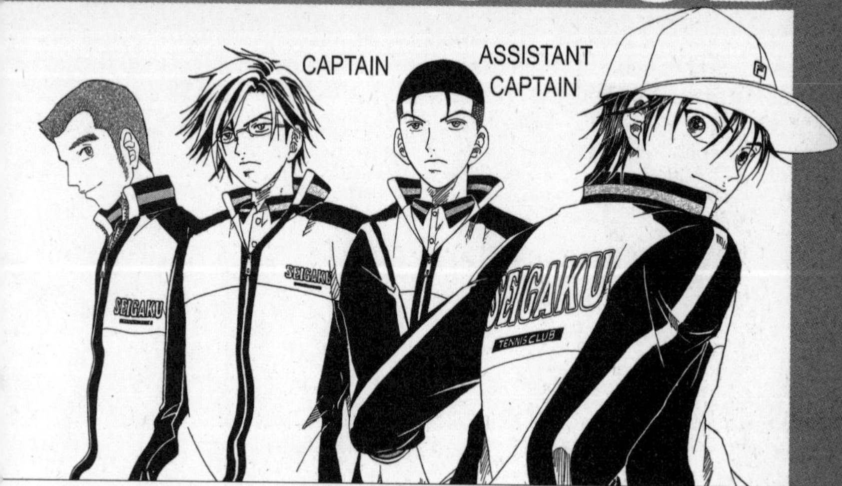
CAPTAIN
ASSISTANT CAPTAIN
SEIGAKU
SEIGAKU
SEIGAKU
TENNIS CLUB

• TAKASHI KAWAMURA • KUNIMITSU TEZUKA • SHUICHIRO OISHI • RYOMA ECHIZEN •

STORY & HARACTERS

Seishun Academy student Ryoma Echizen is a tennis prodigy, with wins in four consecutive U.S. Junior Tennis Tournaments under his belt. He became a starter as a 7th grader and led his team to the District Preliminaries! Despite a few mishaps, Seishun won the District Prelims and the City Tournament, and earned a ticket to the Kanto Tournament. The team came away victorious from its first-round matches, but captain Kunimitsu injured his shoulder and went to Kyushu for treatment. Despite losing Kunimitsu and assistant captain Shuichiro to injury, Seishun pulled together as a team, winning the Kanto Tournament and earning a slot at the Nationals!

With Kunimitsu recovered and back on the team, Seishun enter the Nationals with their strongest line-up and defeat Okinawa's Higa Junior High in the opening round to face Hyotei in the semifinals. Seishun are up by two wins to one as Eiji and Shuichiro clash against Ryo Shishido and Chotaro Ohtori in No. 1 Doubles! And now the game has reached match point at tie-break!

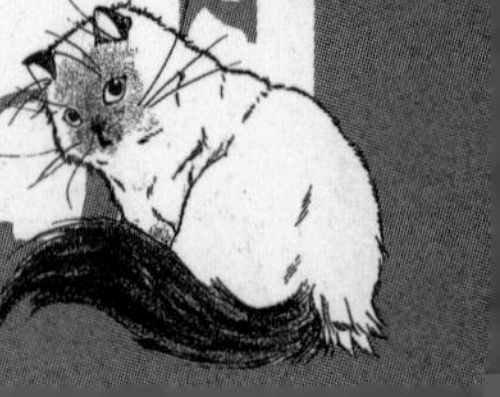

SEIGAKU T

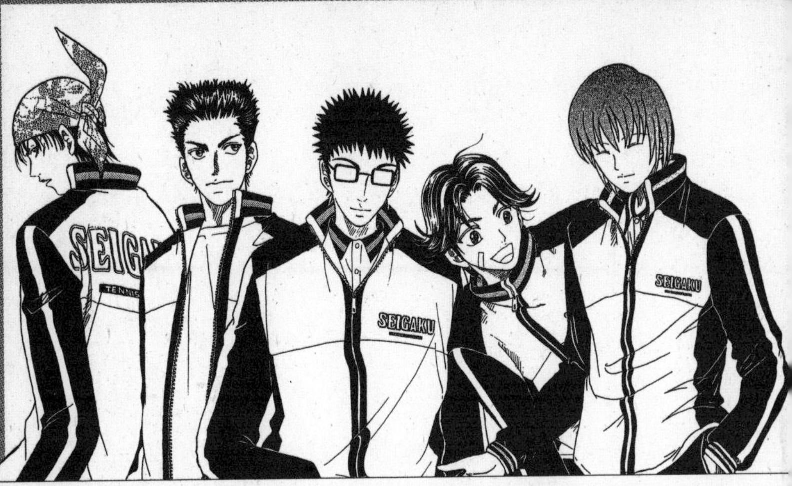

SEIGAKU
TENNIS
SEIGAKU
SEIGAKU

• KAORU KAIDO • TAKESHI MOMOSHIRO • SADAHARU INUI • EIJI KIKUMARU • SHUSUKE FUJI •

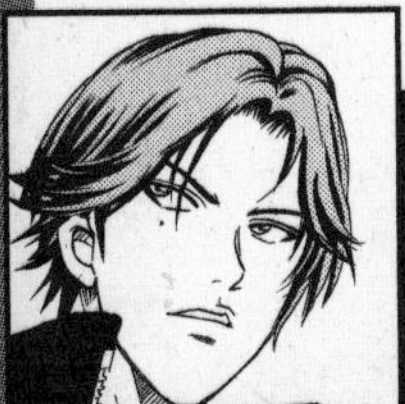

HYOTEI ACADEMY
KEIGO ATOBE

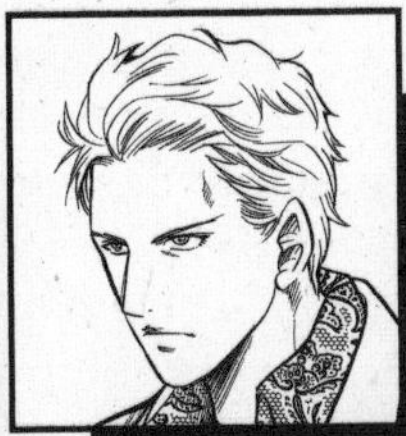

HYOTEI ACADEMY TENNIS COACH
TARO SAKAKI

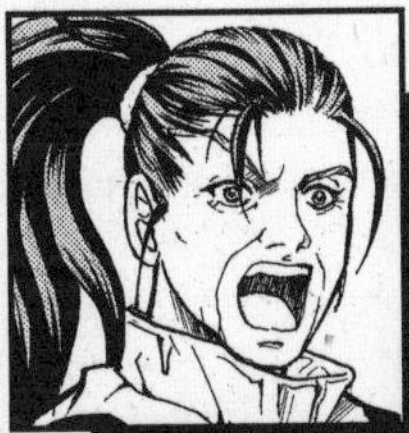

SEISHUN ACADEMY TENNIS COACH
SUMIRE RYUZAKI

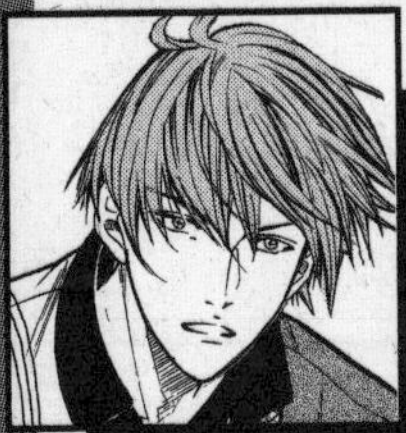

HYOTEI ACADEMY
WAKASHI HIYOSHI

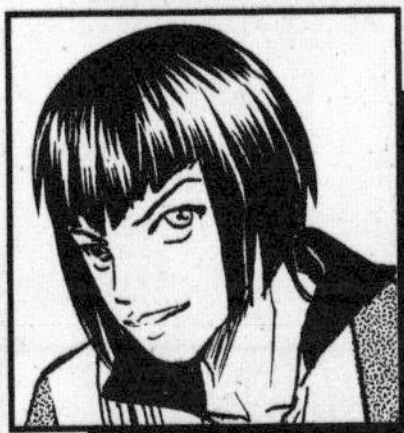

HYOTEI ACADEMY
GAKUTO MUKAHI

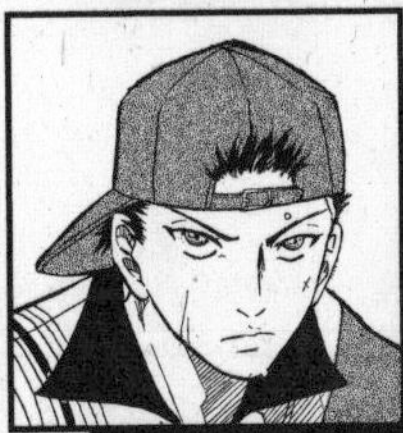

HYOTEI ACADEMY
RYO SHISHIDO

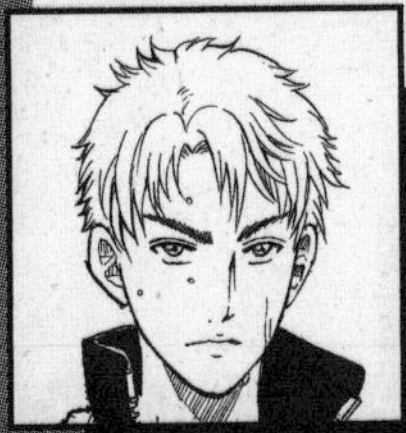

HYOTEI ACADEMY
CHOTARO OHTORI

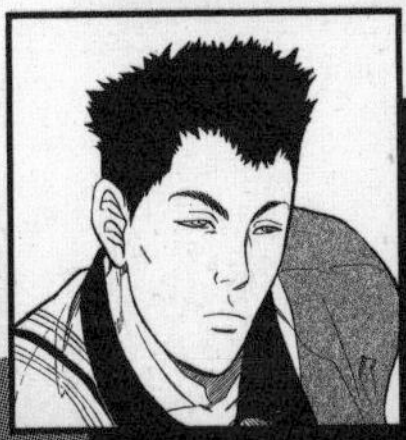

HYOTEI ACADEMY
MUNEHIRO KABAJI

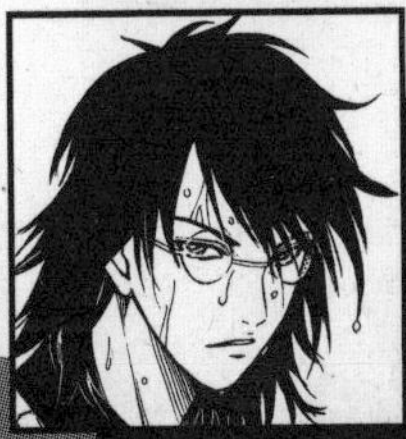

HYOTEI ACADEMY
YUSHI OSHITARI

CONTENTS

Vol. 34
Synchro

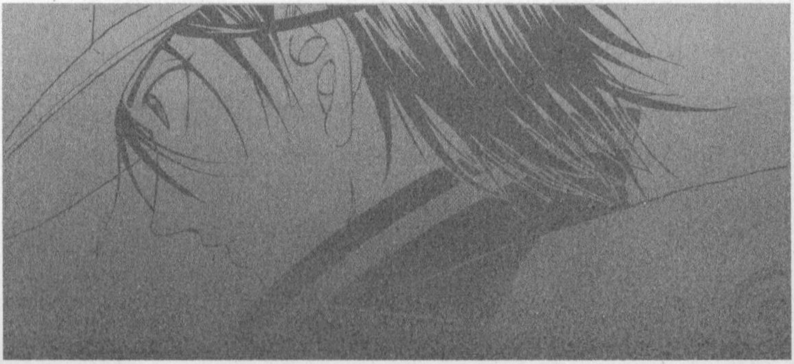

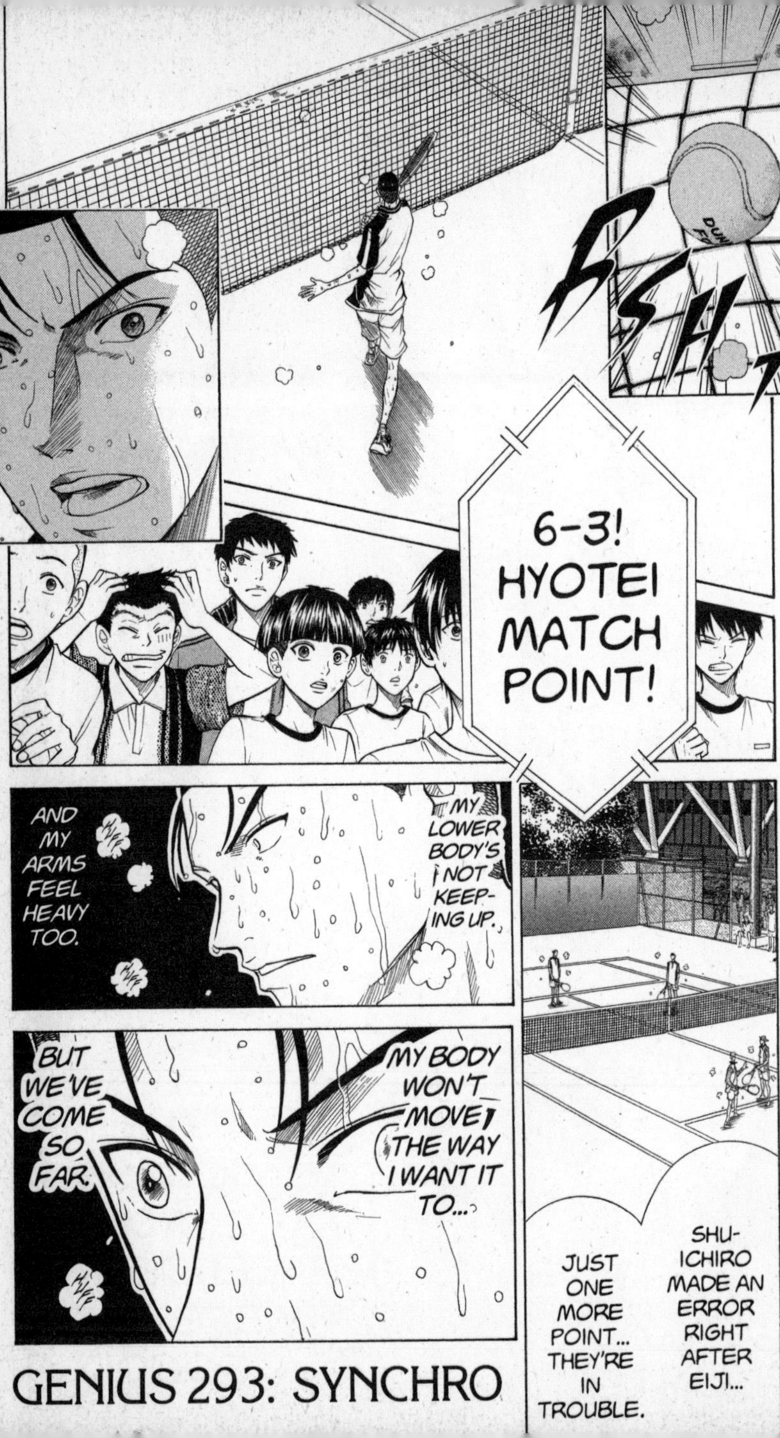
RSHHT
6-3! HYOTEI MATCH POINT!
SHUICHIRO MADE AN ERROR RIGHT AFTER EIJI...
JUST ONE MORE POINT... THEY'RE IN TROUBLE.
MY LOWER BODY'S NOT KEEPING UP.
AND MY ARMS FEEL HEAVY TOO.
MY BODY WON'T MOVE THE WAY I WANT IT TO...
BUT WE'VE COME SO FAR.

GENIUS 293: SYNCHRO

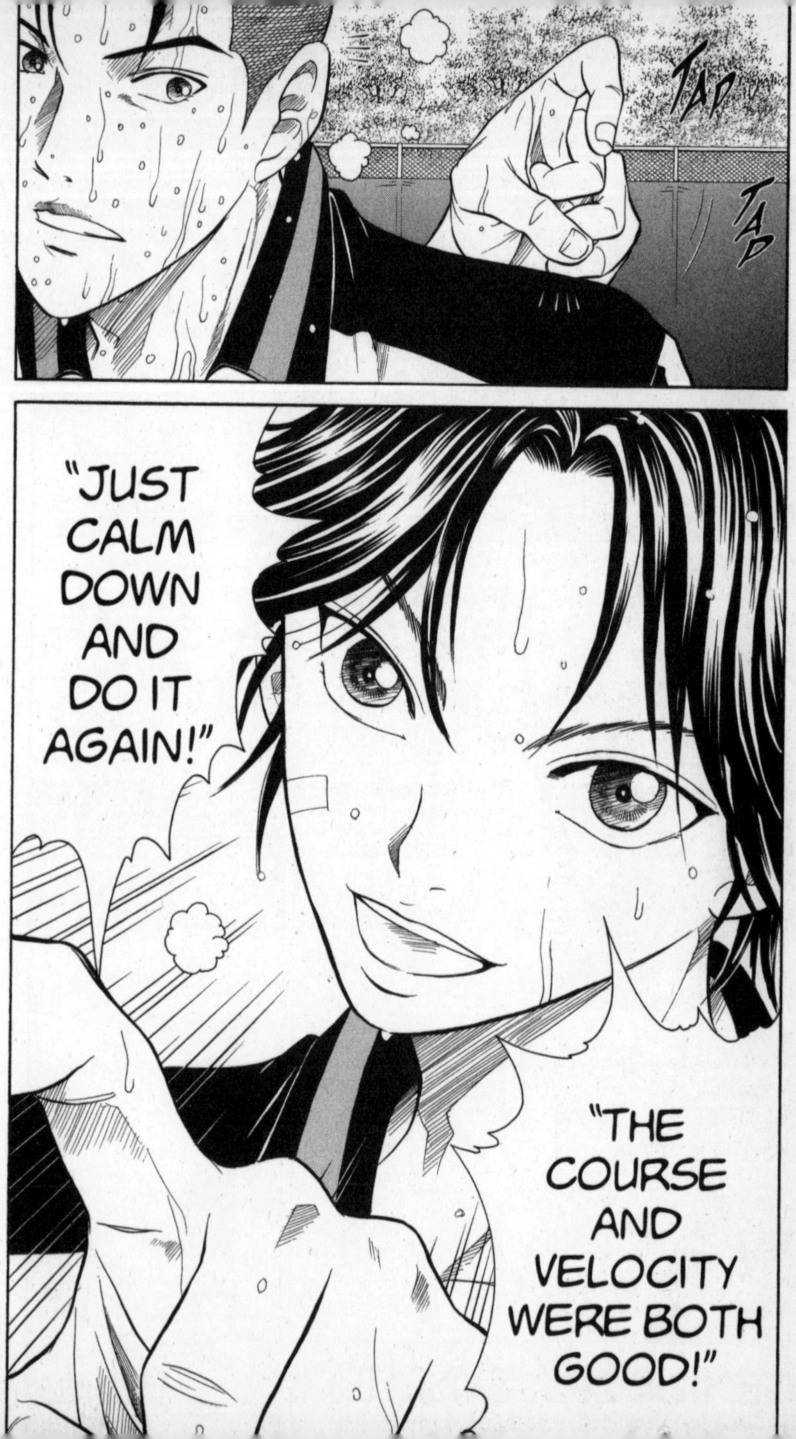
TAP
TAP
"JUST CALM DOWN AND DO IT AGAIN!"
"THE COURSE AND VELOCITY WERE BOTH GOOD!"

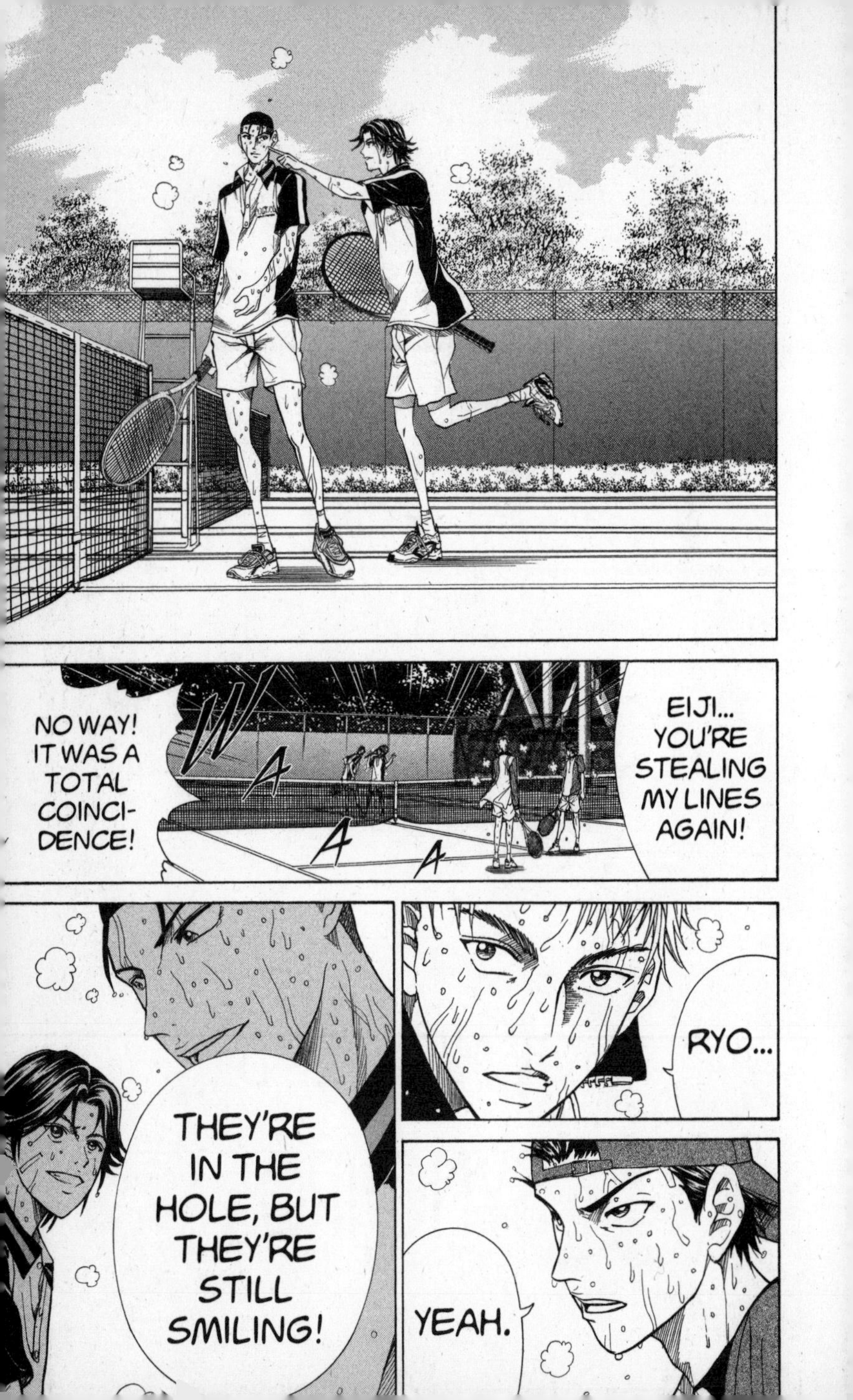
EIJI... YOU'RE STEALING MY LINES AGAIN!
WAAA
NO WAY! IT WAS A TOTAL COINCIDENCE!
RYO...
YEAH.
THEY'RE IN THE HOLE, BUT THEY'RE STILL SMILING!

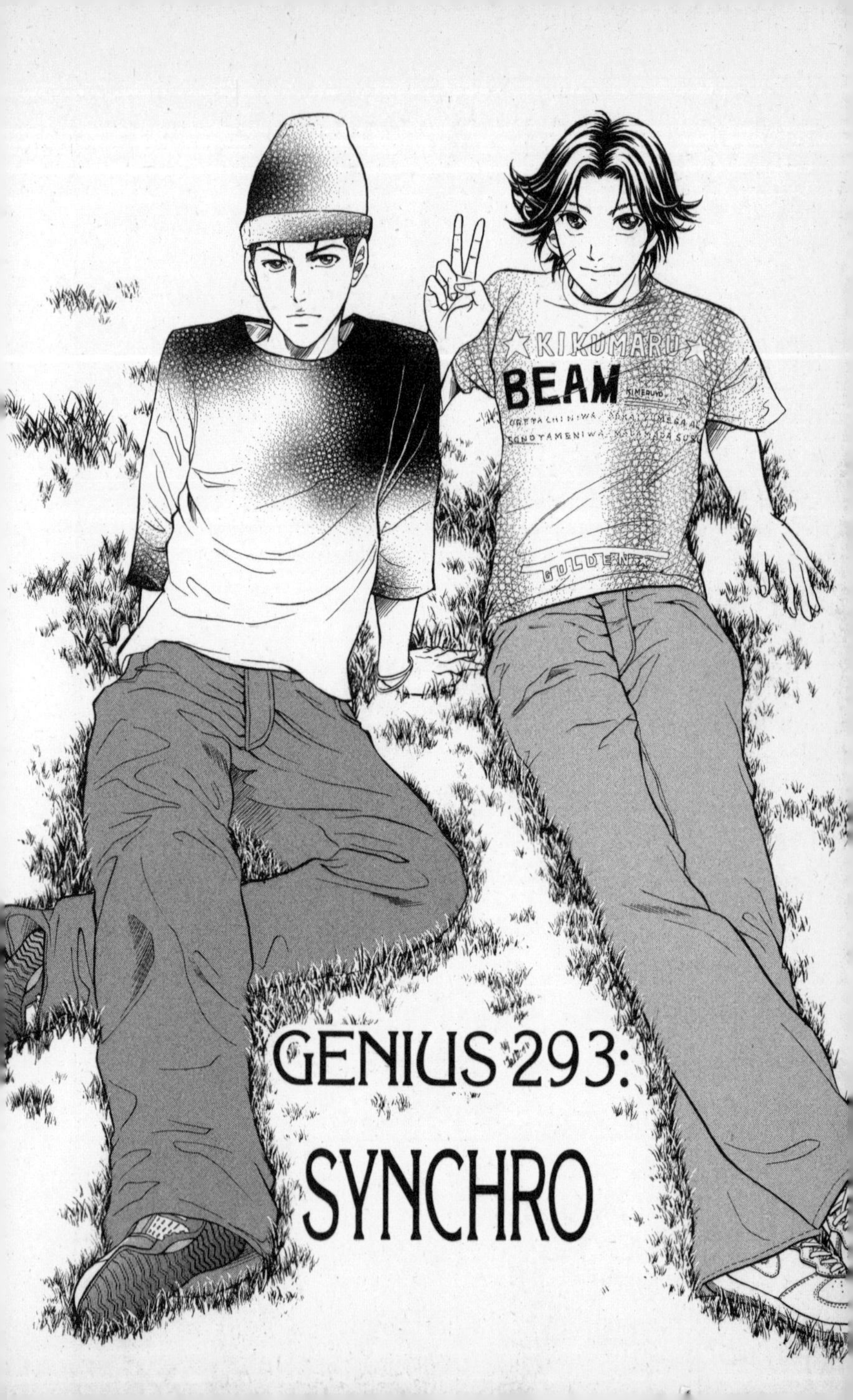
KIKUMARU
BEAM

GENIUS 293: SYNCHRO

READ THIS WAY

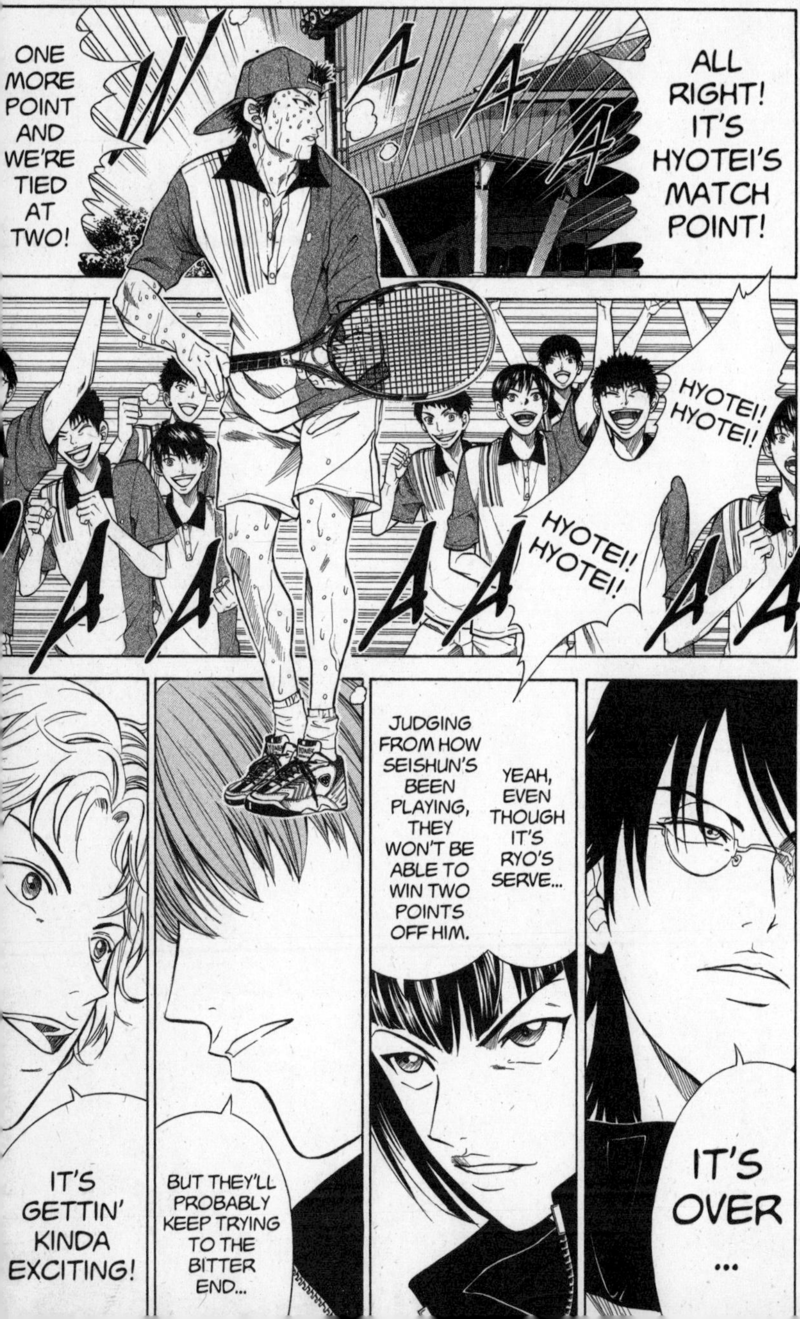
ALL RIGHT! IT'S HYOTEI'S MATCH POINT!
WAAA
ONE MORE POINT AND WE'RE TIED AT TWO!
HYOTEI! HYOTEI!
HYOTEI! HYOTEI!
AA
AA
AA
AA
IT'S OVER...
YEAH, EVEN THOUGH IT'S RYO'S SERVE...
JUDGING FROM HOW SEISHUN'S BEEN PLAYING, THEY WON'T BE ABLE TO WIN TWO POINTS OFF HIM.
BUT THEY'LL PROBABLY KEEP TRYING TO THE BITTER END...
IT'S GETTIN' KINDA EXCITING!

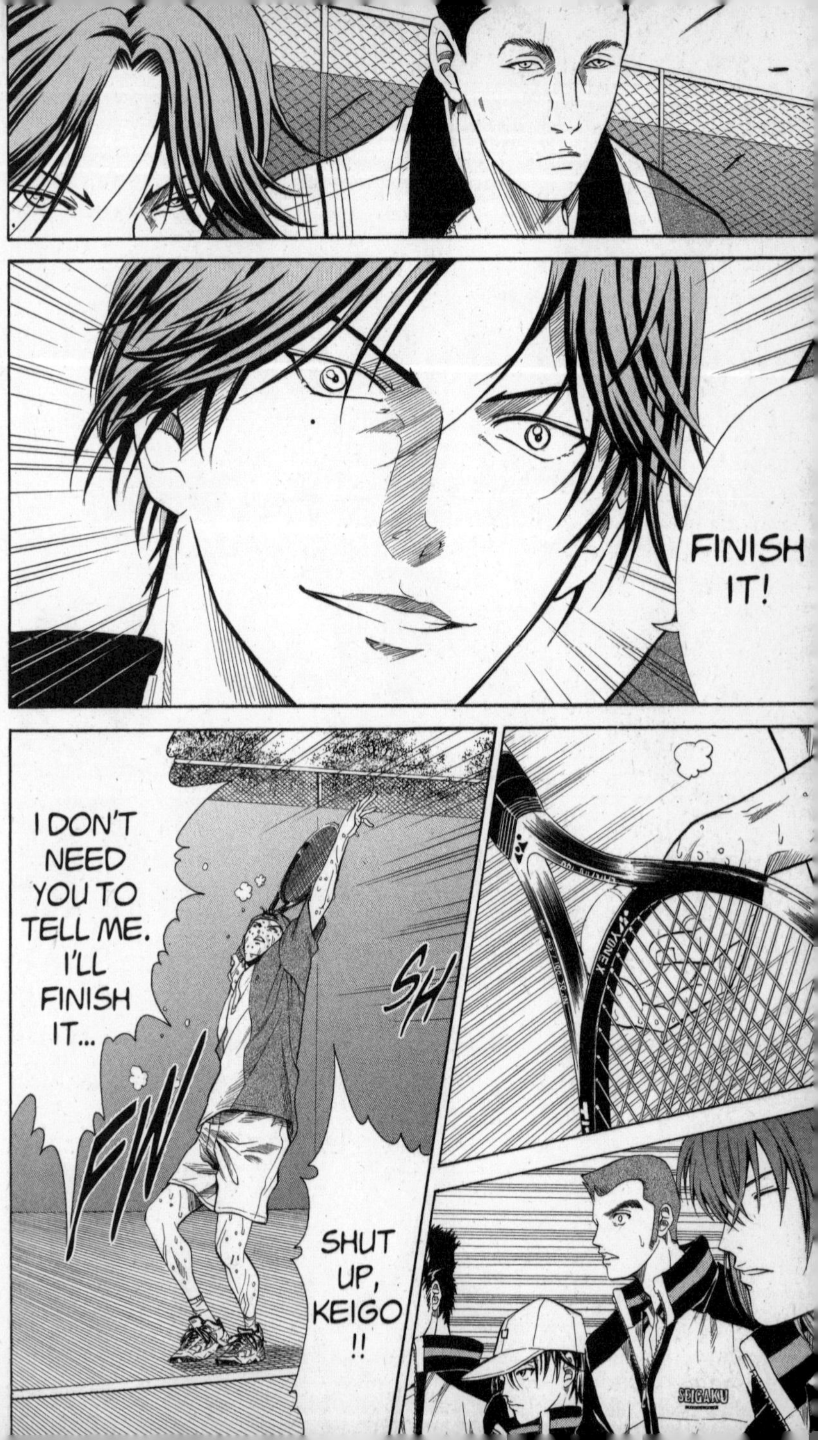
FINISH IT!
SHUT UP, KEIGO !!
SH
I DON'T NEED YOU TO TELL ME. I'LL FINISH IT...
FW
SEIGAKU

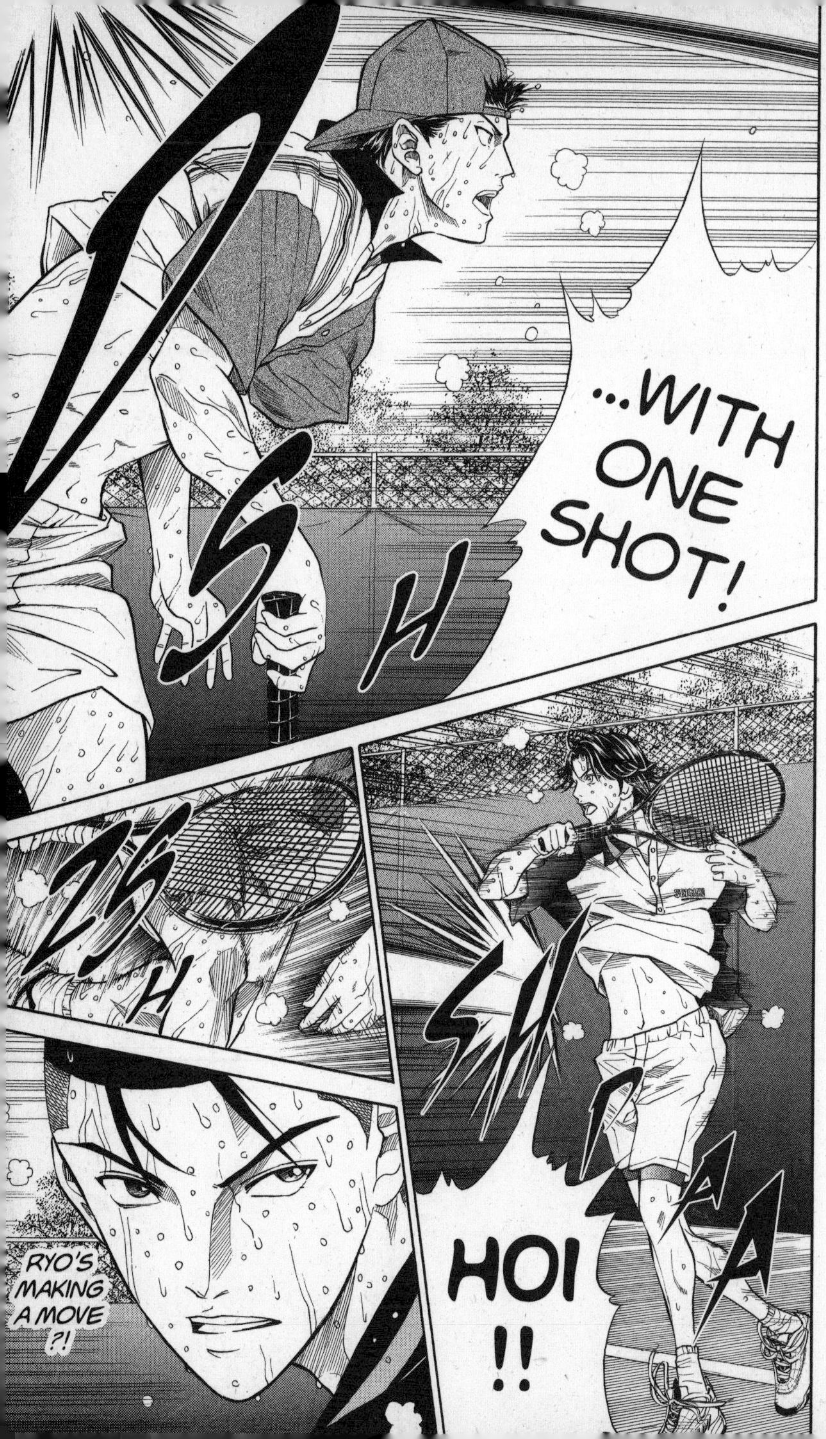

...WITH ONE SHOT!
HOI !!
RYO'S MAKING A MOVE ?!

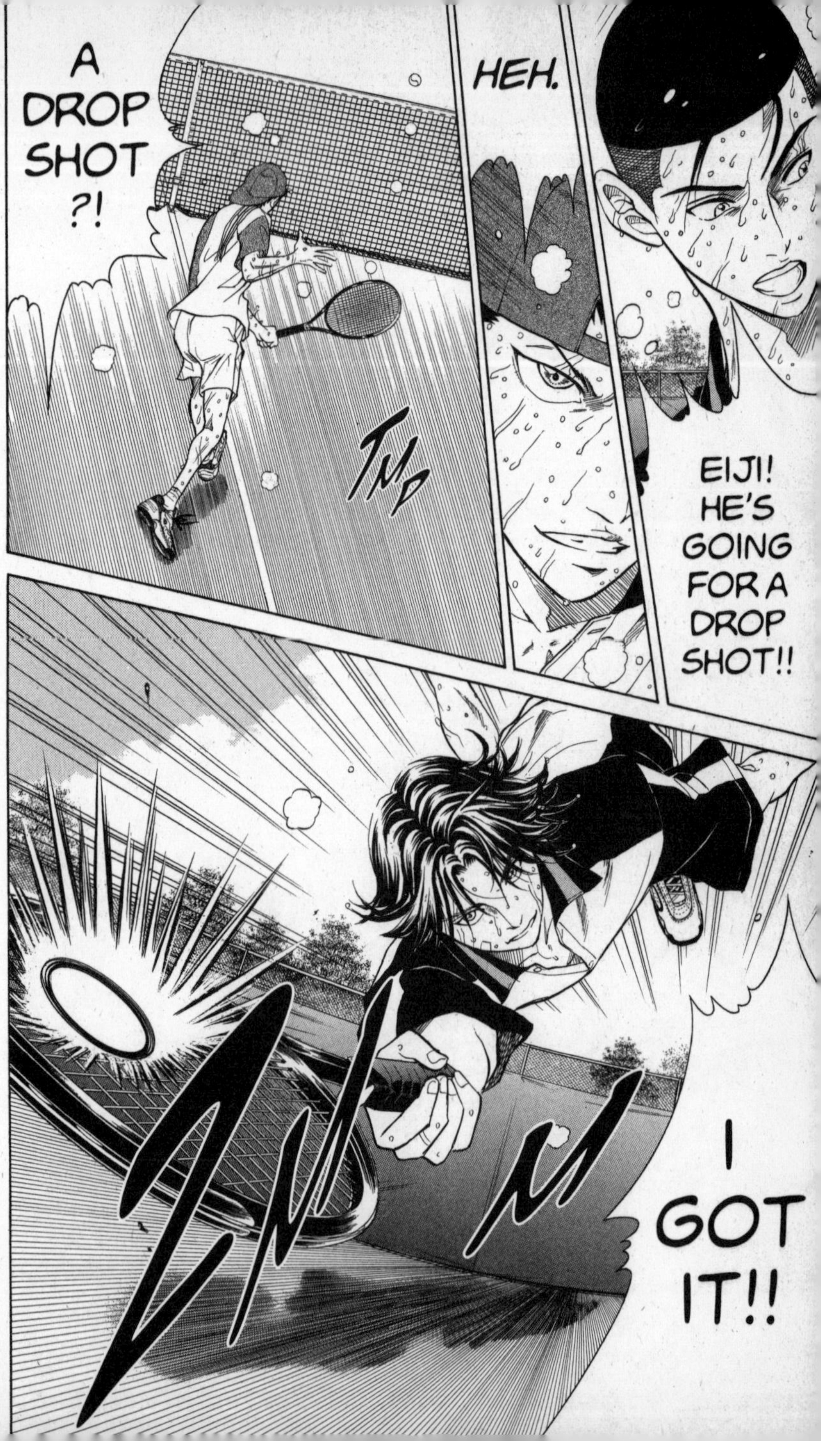
EIJI! HE'S GOING FOR A DROP SHOT!!
HEH.
A DROP SHOT ?!
TMP
I GOT IT!!

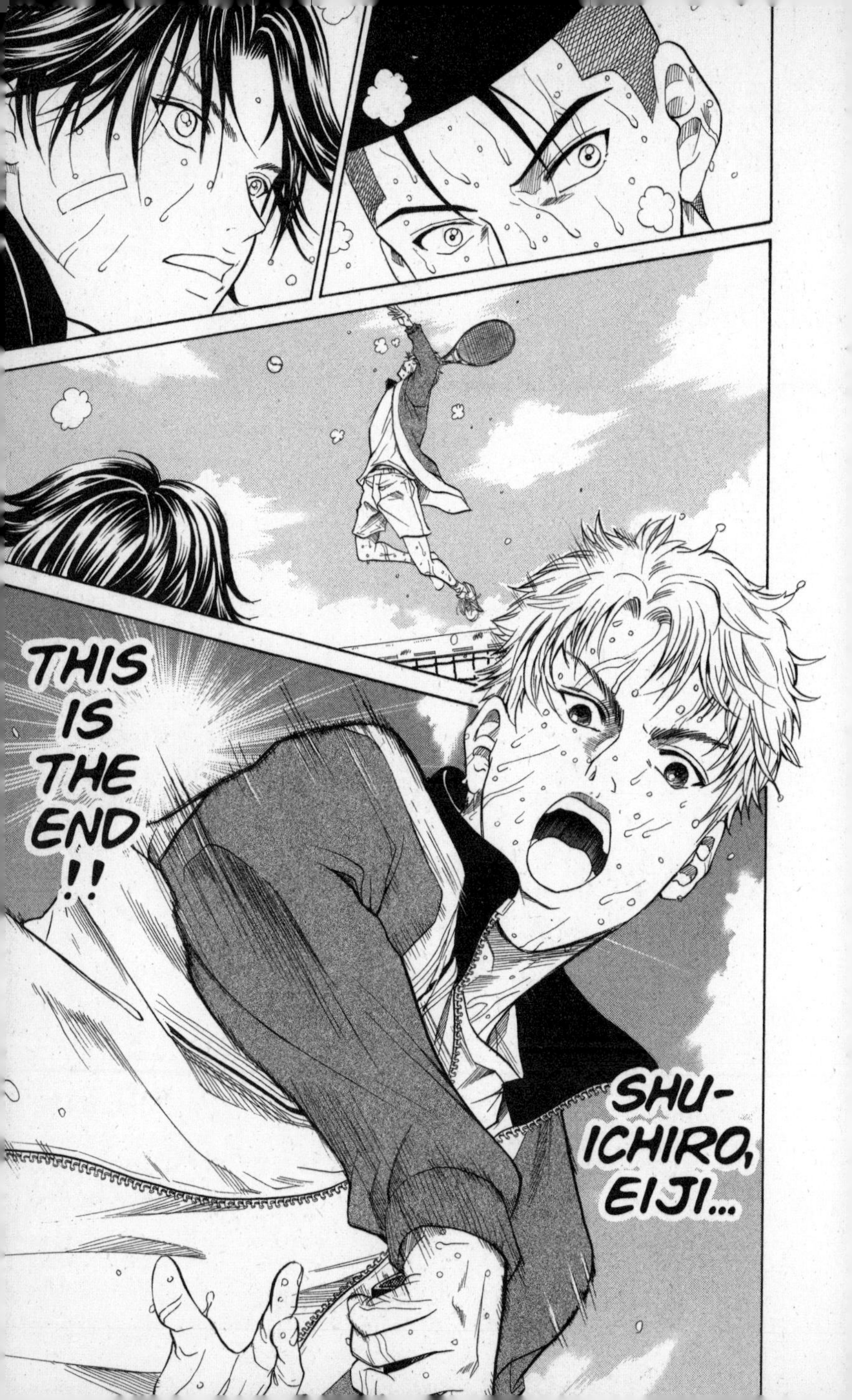
SHU-ICHIRO, EIJI...
THIS IS THE END!!

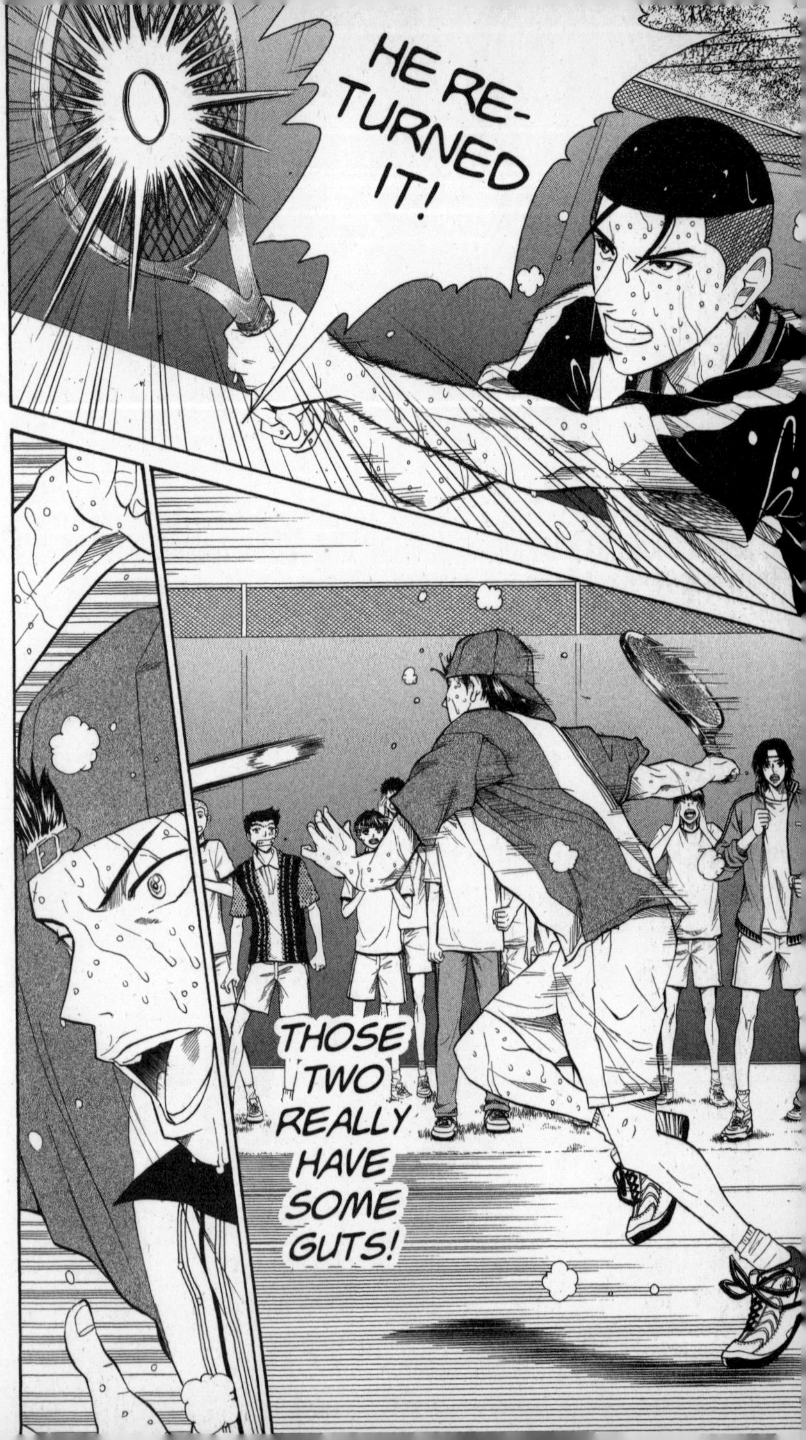
HE RE-TURNED IT!
THOSE TWO REALLY HAVE SOME GUTS!

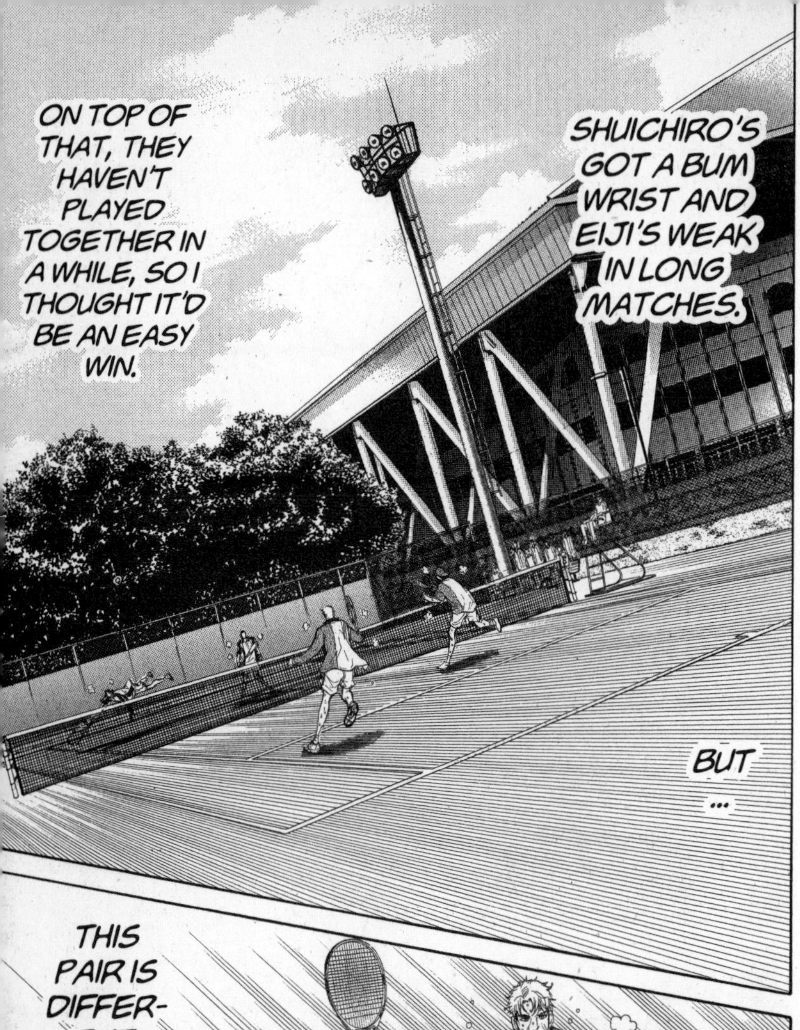
SHUICHIRO'S GOT A BUM WRIST AND EIJI'S WEAK IN LONG MATCHES.
ON TOP OF THAT, THEY HAVEN'T PLAYED TOGETHER IN A WHILE, SO I THOUGHT IT'D BE AN EASY WIN.
BUT ...
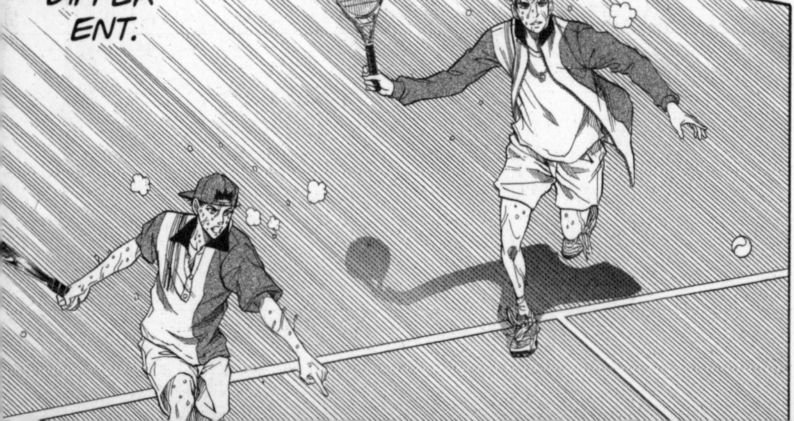
THIS PAIR IS DIFFER-ENT.

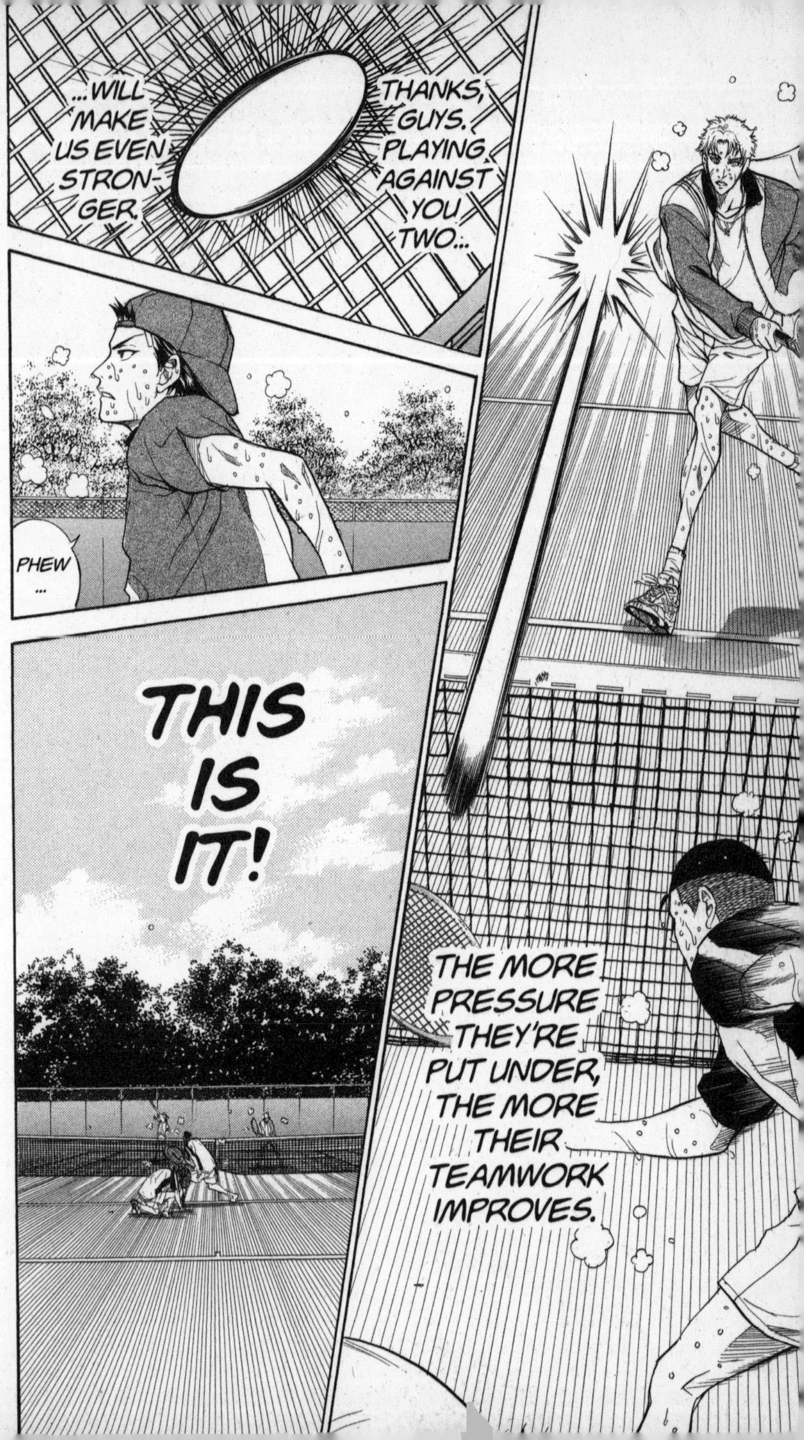

THANKS, GUYS. PLAYING AGAINST YOU TWO...
...WILL MAKE US EVEN STRONGER.
PHEW ...
THIS IS IT!
THE MORE PRESSURE THEY'RE PUT UNDER, THE MORE THEIR TEAMWORK IMPROVES.

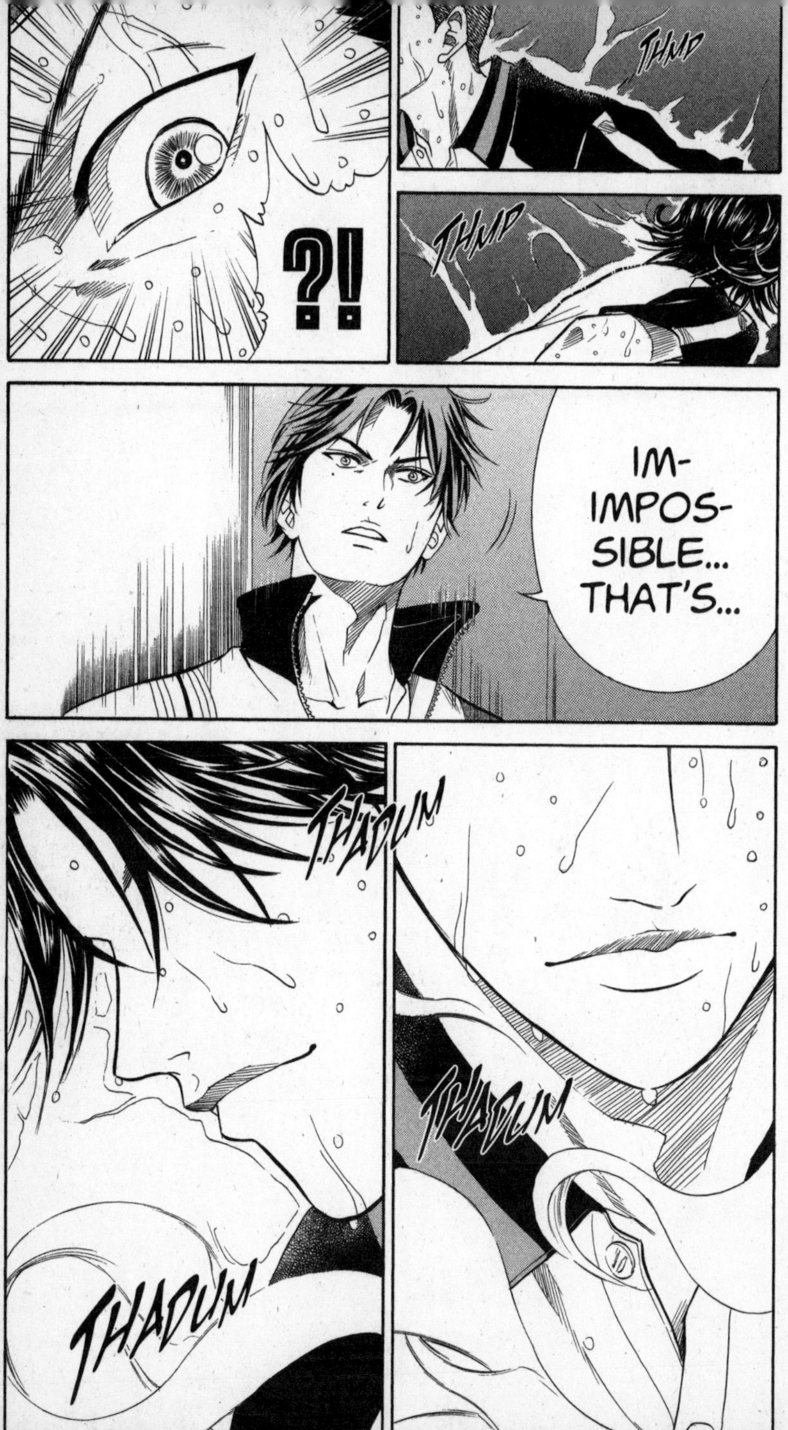
THMP
THMP
?!
IM- IMPOS- SIBLE... THAT'S...
THADUM
THADUM
THADUM

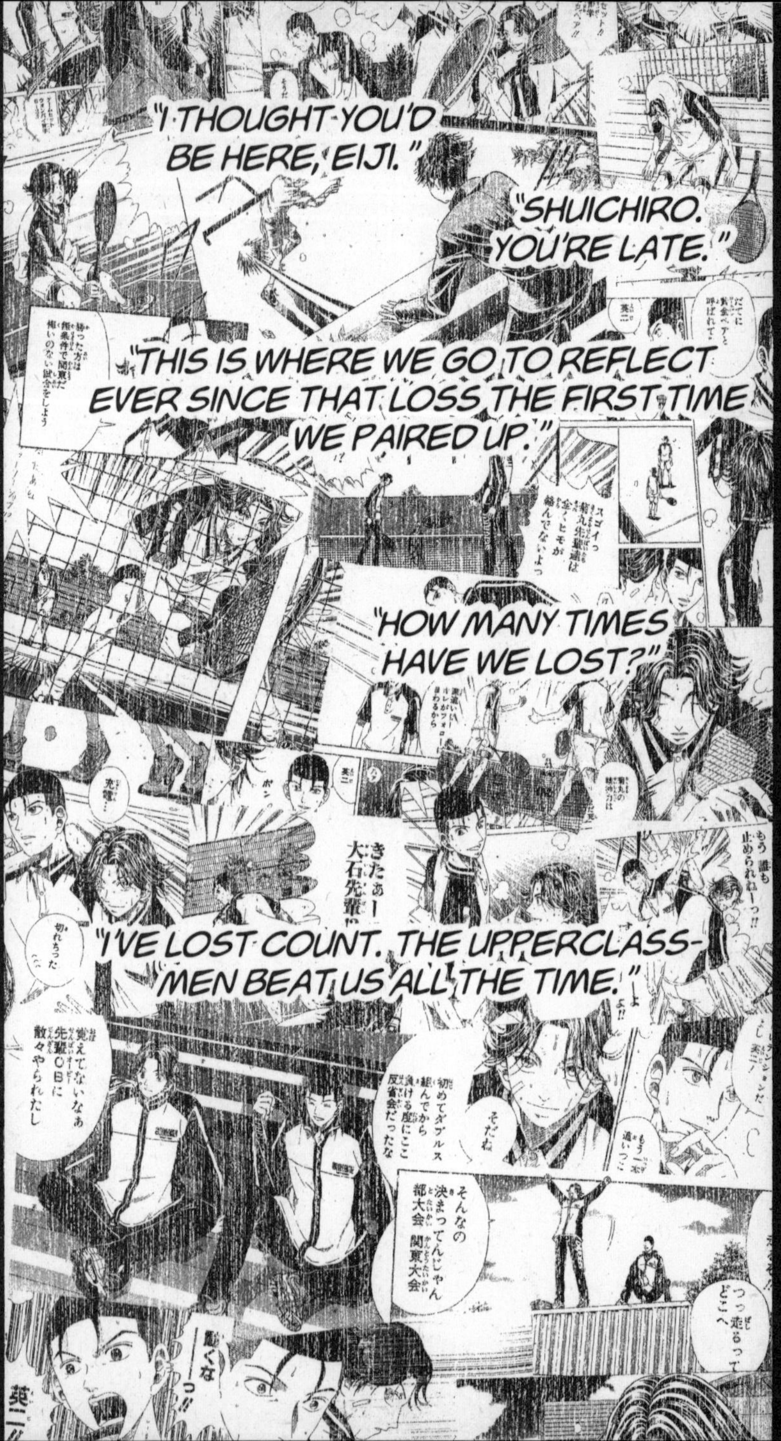
"I THOUGHT YOU'D BE HERE, EIJI."
"SHUICHIRO. YOU'RE LATE."
"THIS IS WHERE WE GO TO REFLECT EVER SINCE THAT LOSS THE FIRST TIME WE PAIRED UP."
"HOW MANY TIMES HAVE WE LOST?"
"I'VE LOST COUNT. THE UPPERCLASS-MEN BEAT US ALL THE TIME."

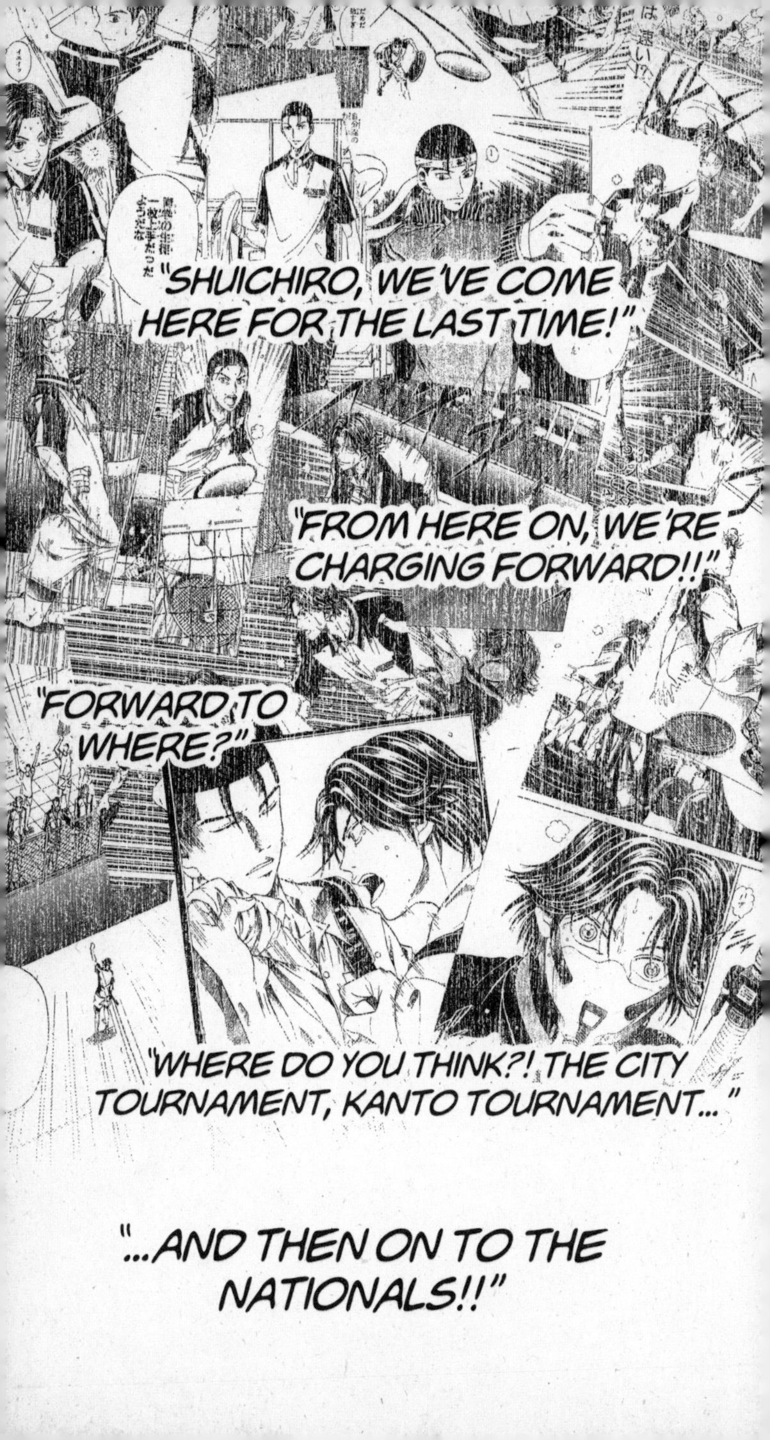
"SHUICHIRO, WE'VE COME HERE FOR THE LAST TIME!"
"FROM HERE ON, WE'RE CHARGING FORWARD!!"
"FORWARD TO WHERE?"
"WHERE DO YOU THINK?! THE CITY TOURNAMENT, KANTO TOURNAMENT..."
"...AND THEN ON TO THE NATIONALS!!"

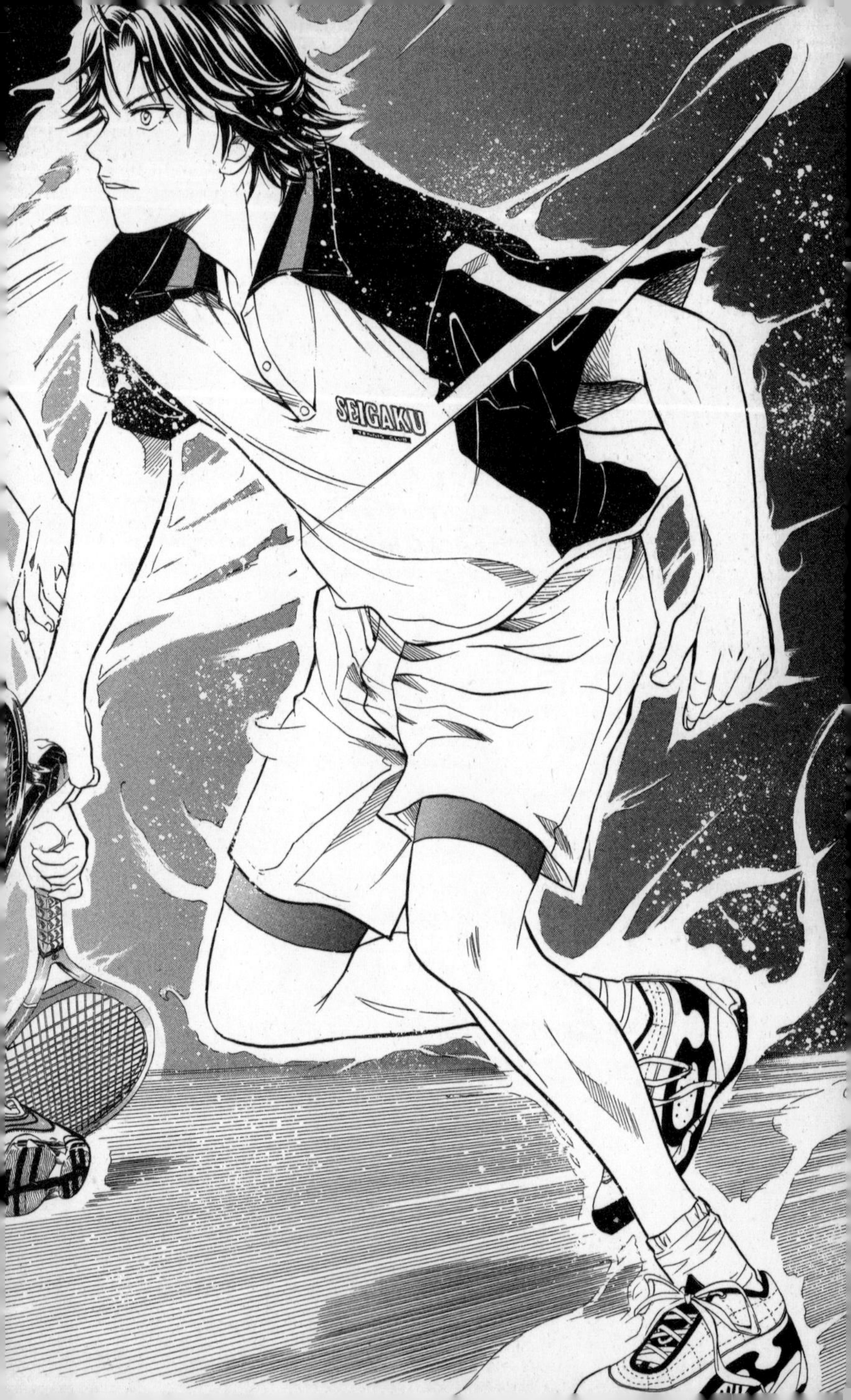
SEIGAKU

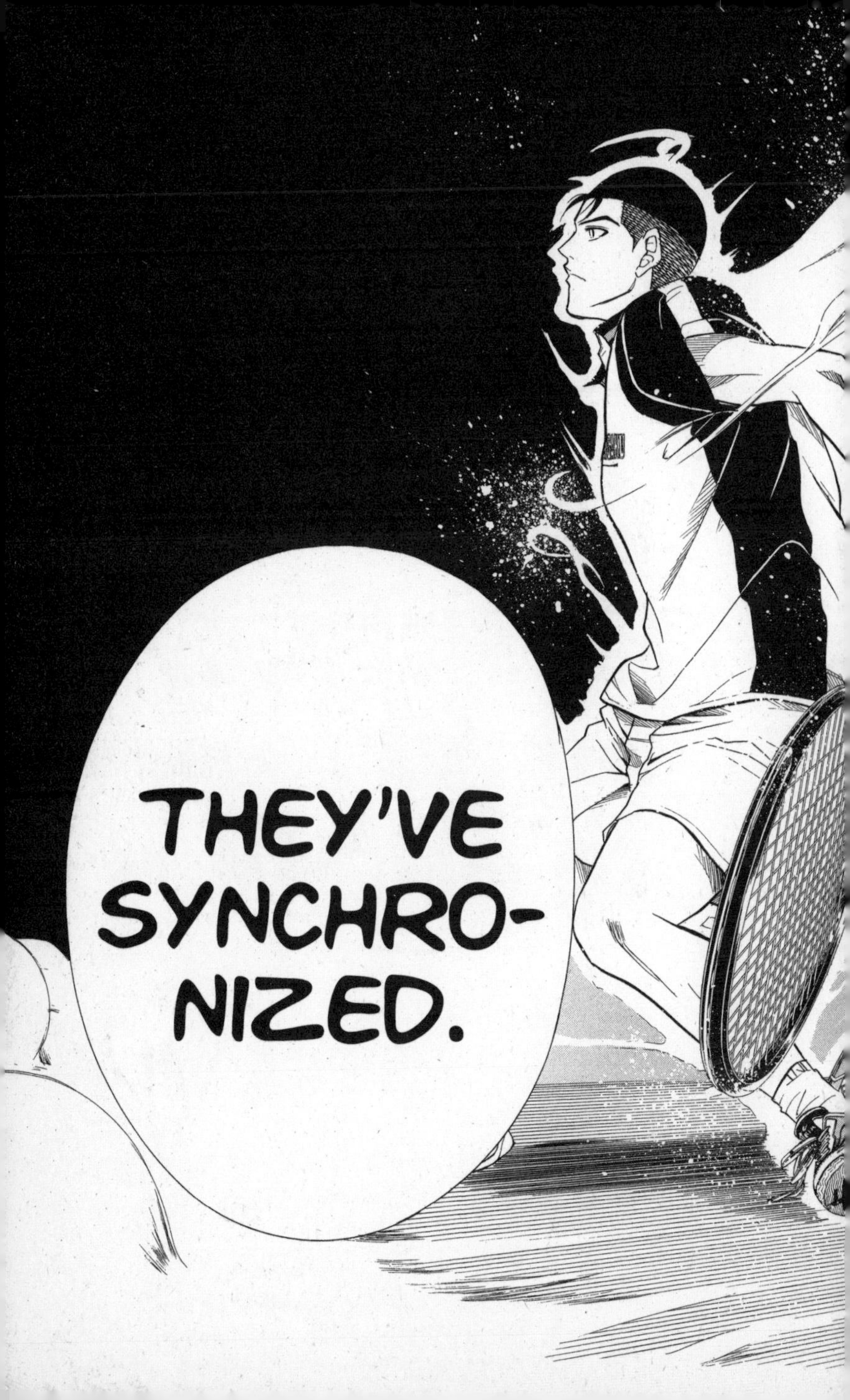
THEY'VE SYNCHRO-NIZED.

テニスの王子様

THE PRINCE OF TENNIS

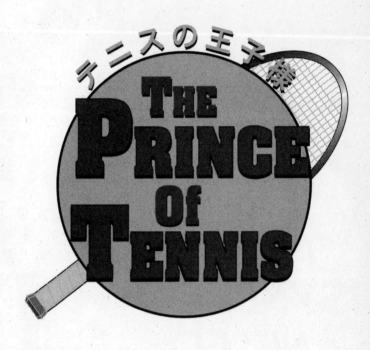

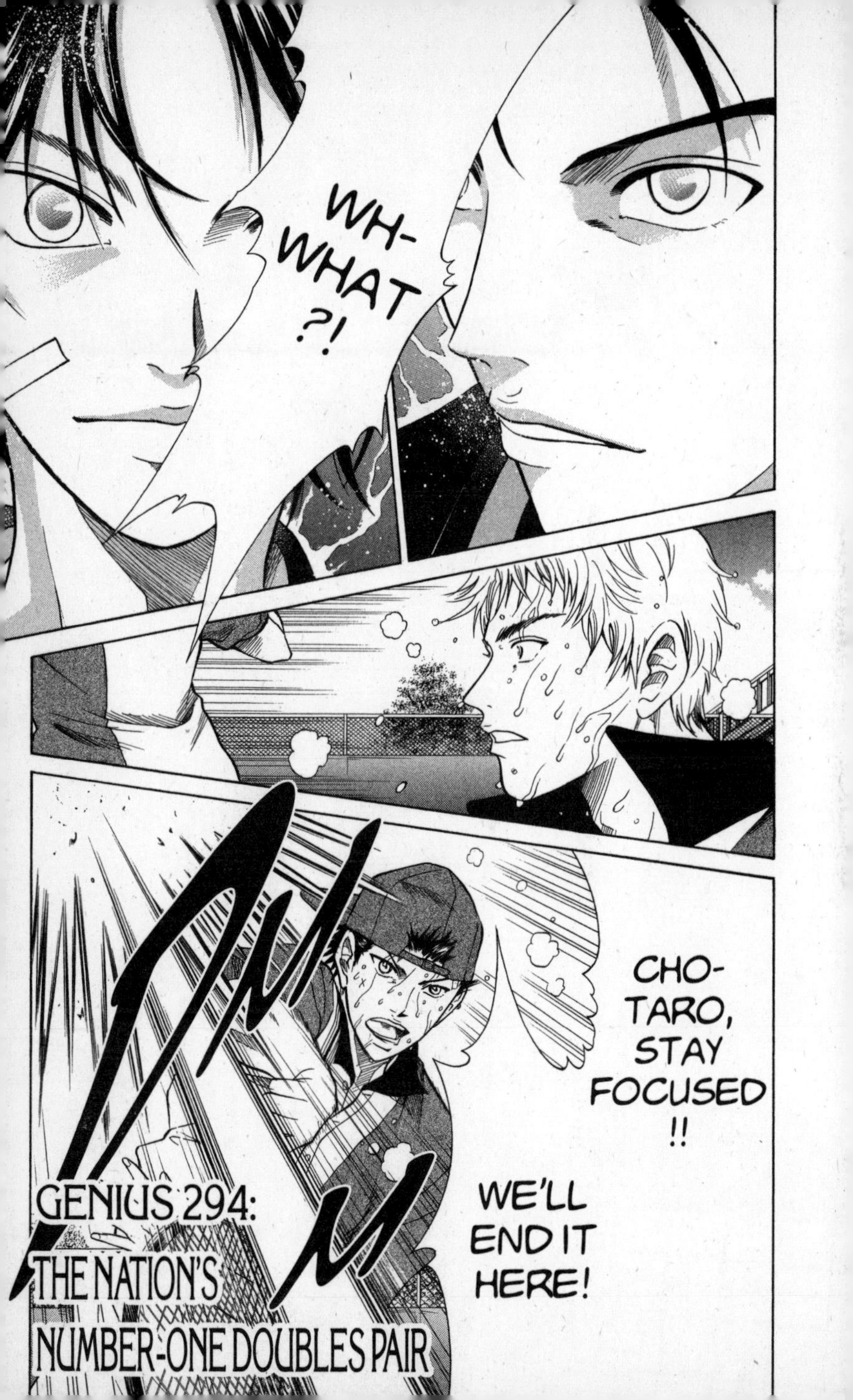
WH-WHAT?!
CHOTARO, STAY FOCUSED!!
WE'LL END IT HERE!
GENIUS 294: THE NATION'S NUMBER-ONE DOUBLES PAIR

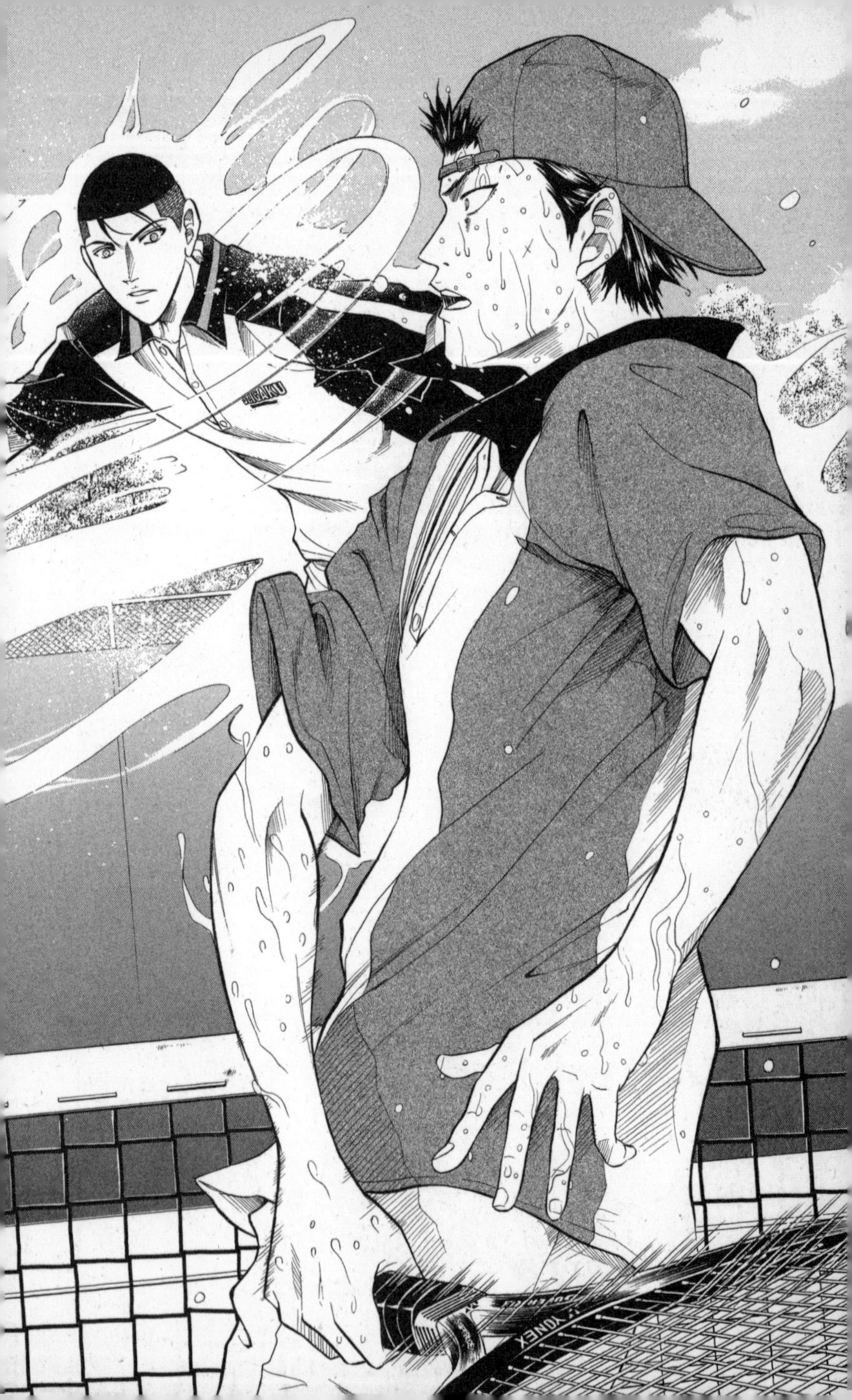

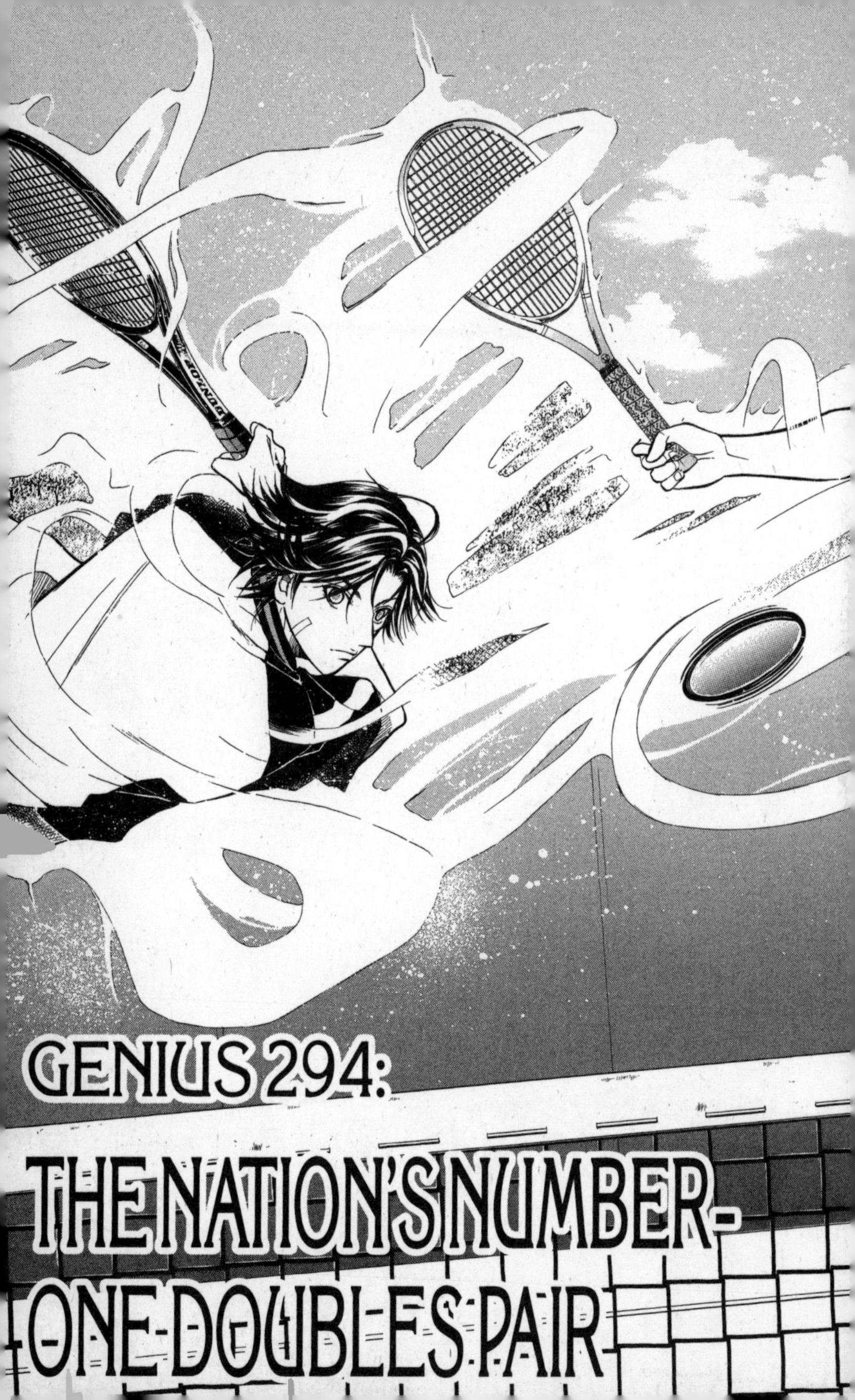
GENIUS 294:
THE NATION'S NUMBER-ONE DOUBLES PAIR

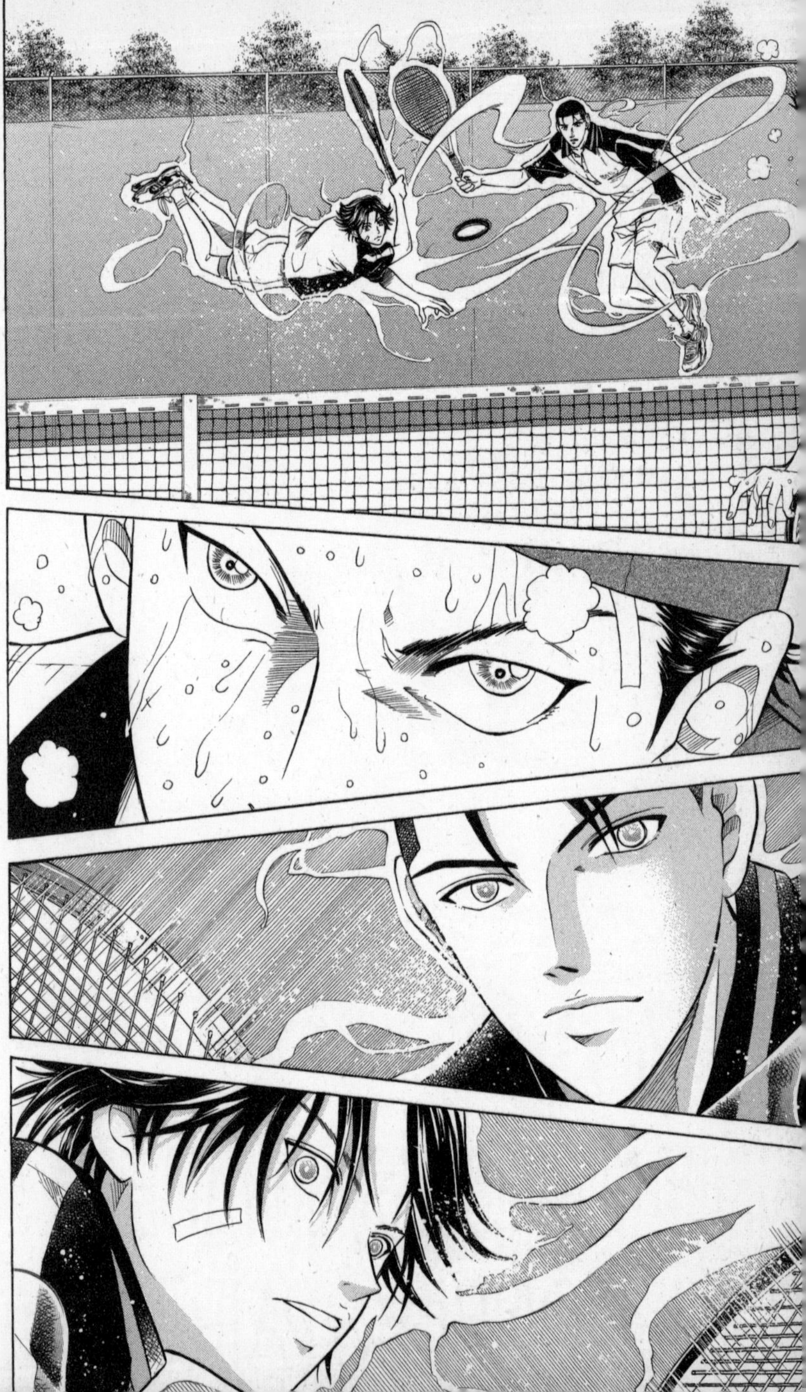

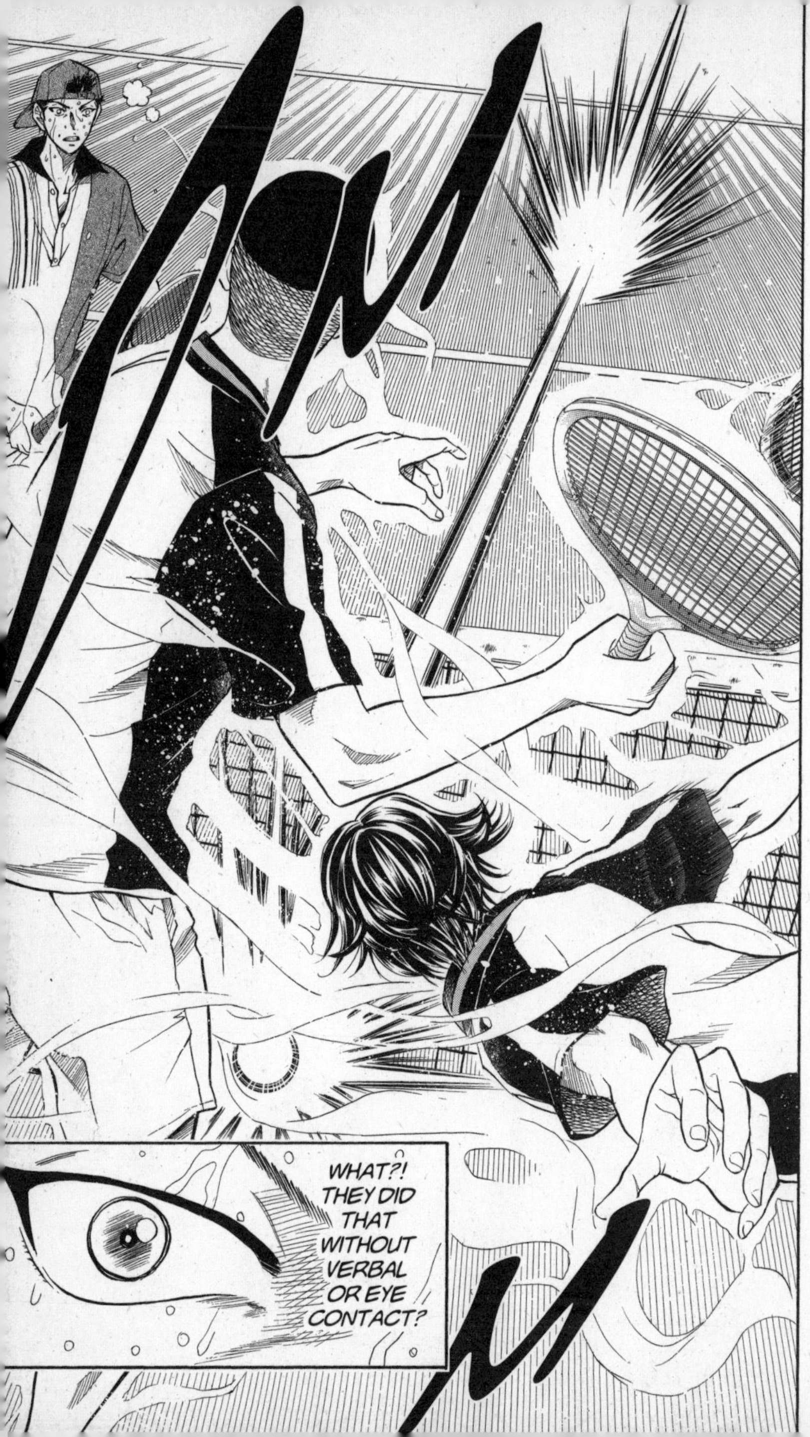
WHAT?! THEY DID THAT WITHOUT VERBAL OR EYE CONTACT?

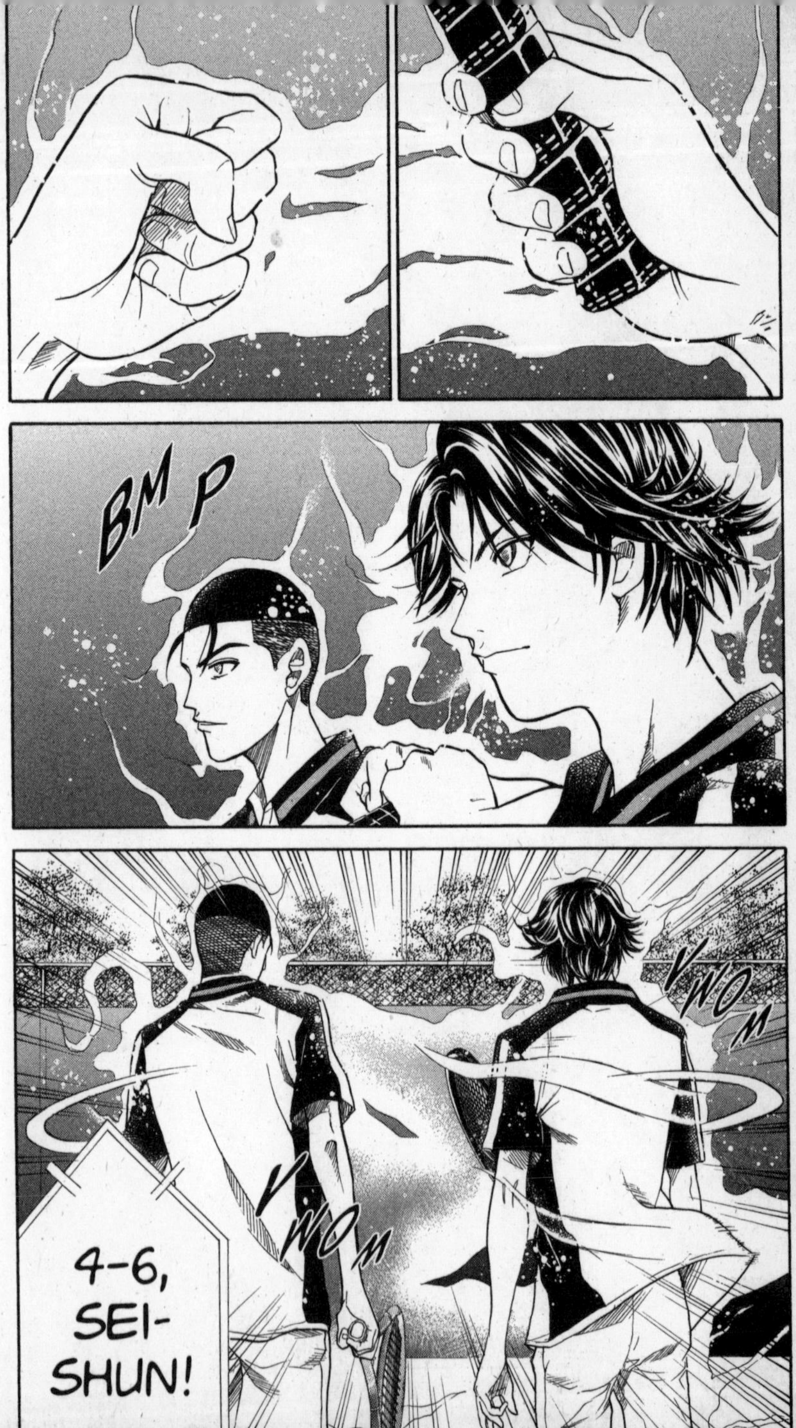
BMP
VWOM
VWOM
4-6, SEI-SHUN!

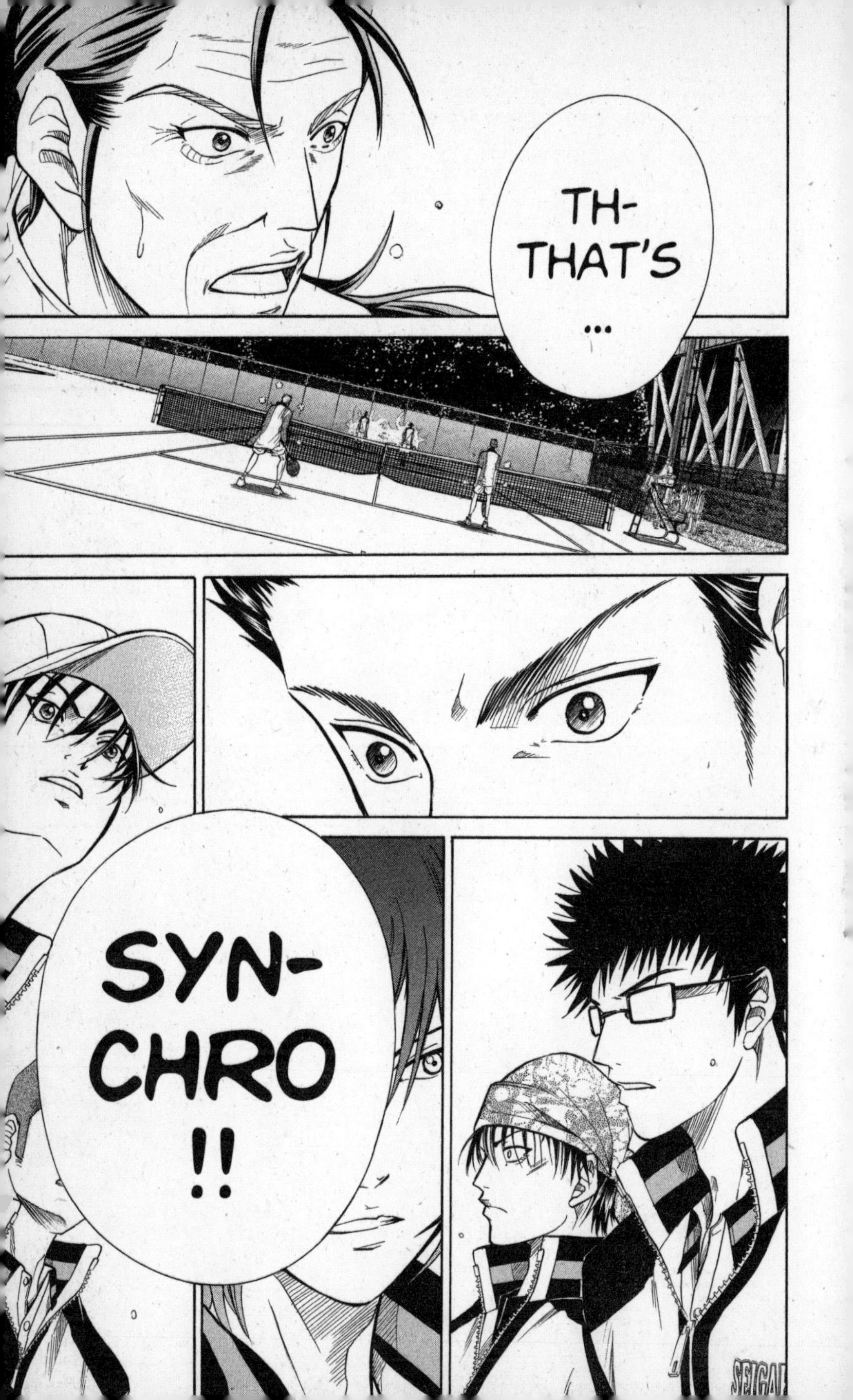
TH- THAT'S ...
SYN- CHRO !!
SEIGAKU

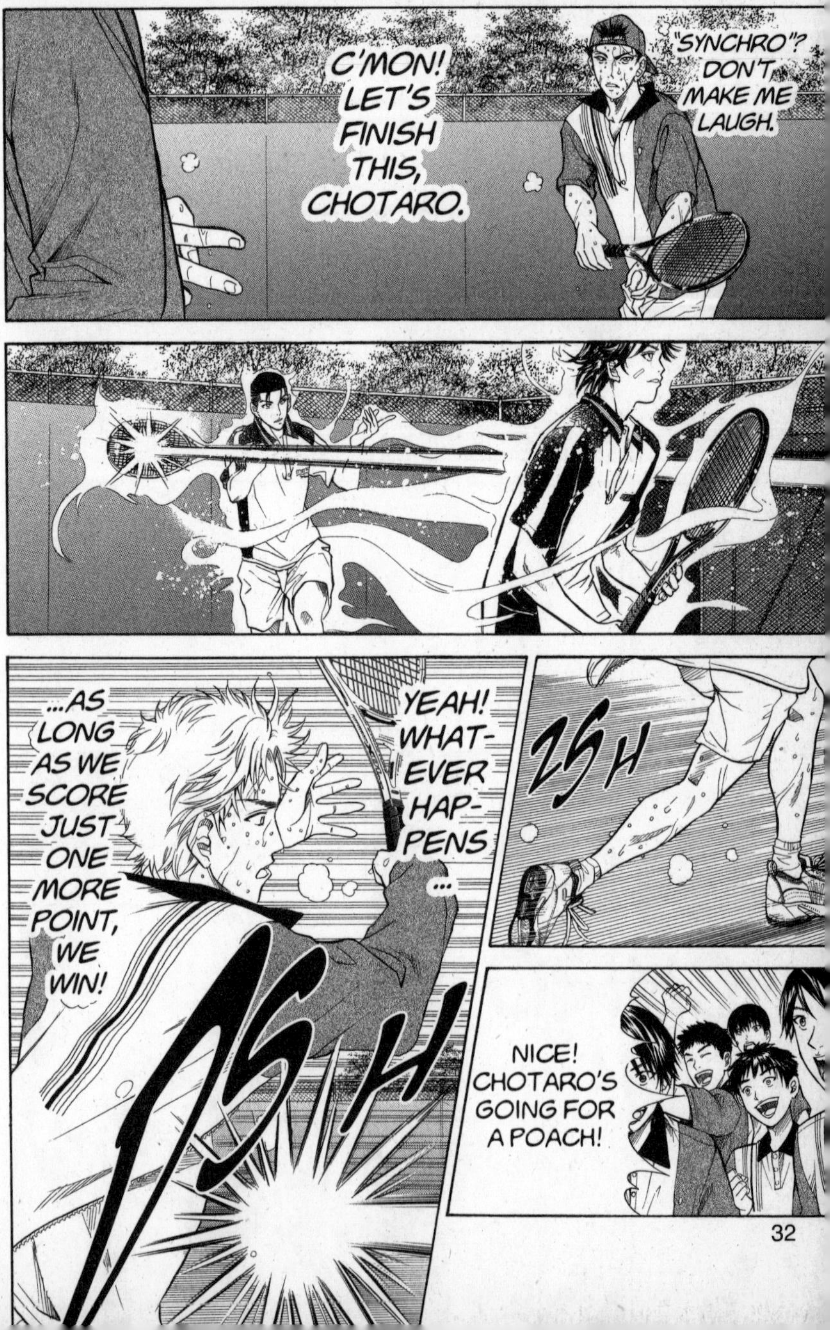
"SYNCHRO"? DON'T MAKE ME LAUGH.
C'MON! LET'S FINISH THIS, CHOTARO.
ZSH
NICE! CHOTARO'S GOING FOR A POACH!
YEAH! WHAT-EVER HAP-PENS...
...AS LONG AS WE SCORE JUST ONE MORE POINT, WE WIN!
ZSH

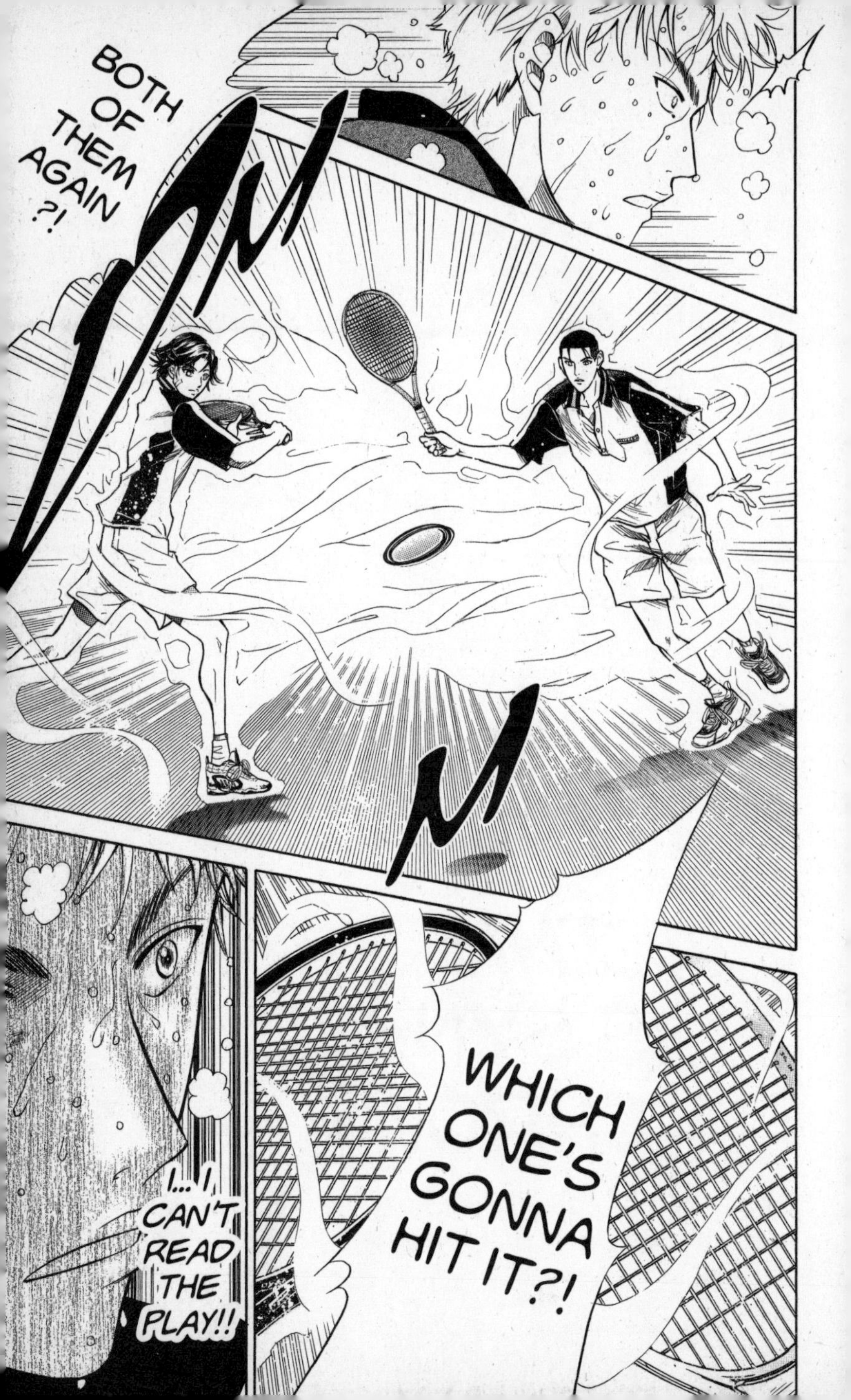
BOTH OF THEM AGAIN ?!
WHICH ONE'S GONNA HIT IT?!
I... I CAN'T READ THE PLAY!!

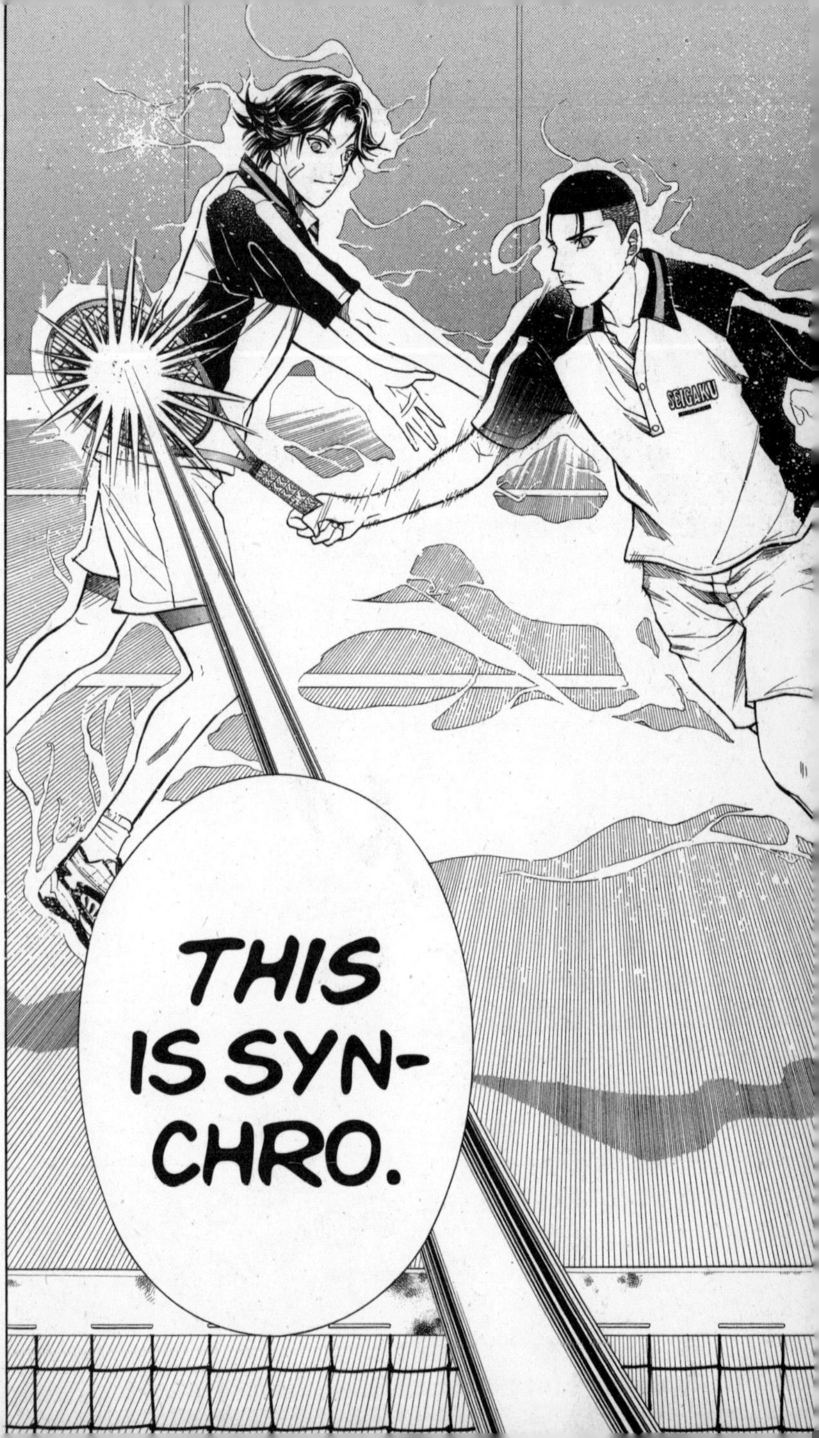
SEIGAKU
THIS IS SYN-CHRO.

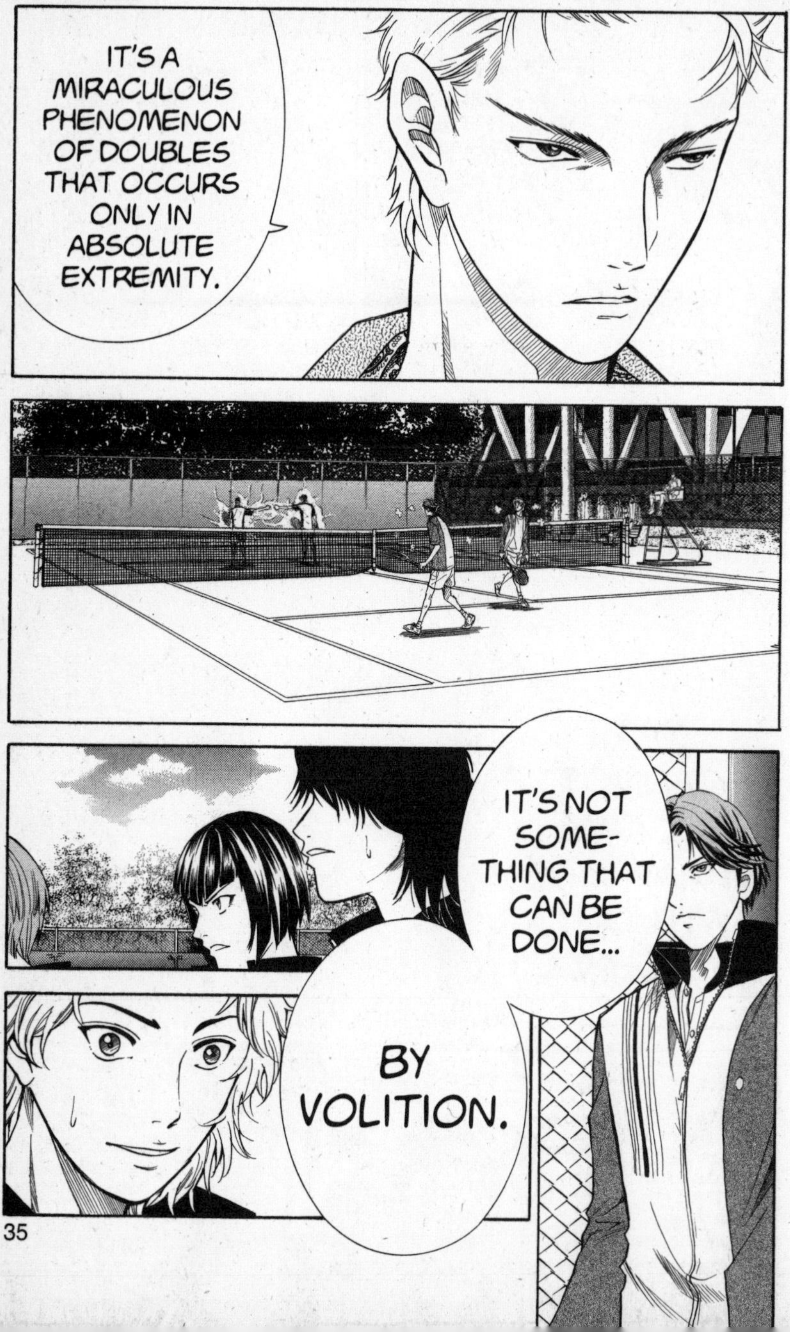
READ THIS WAY
IT'S A MIRACULOUS PHENOMENON OF DOUBLES THAT OCCURS ONLY IN ABSOLUTE EXTREMITY.
IT'S NOT SOME-THING THAT CAN BE DONE...
BY VOLITION.

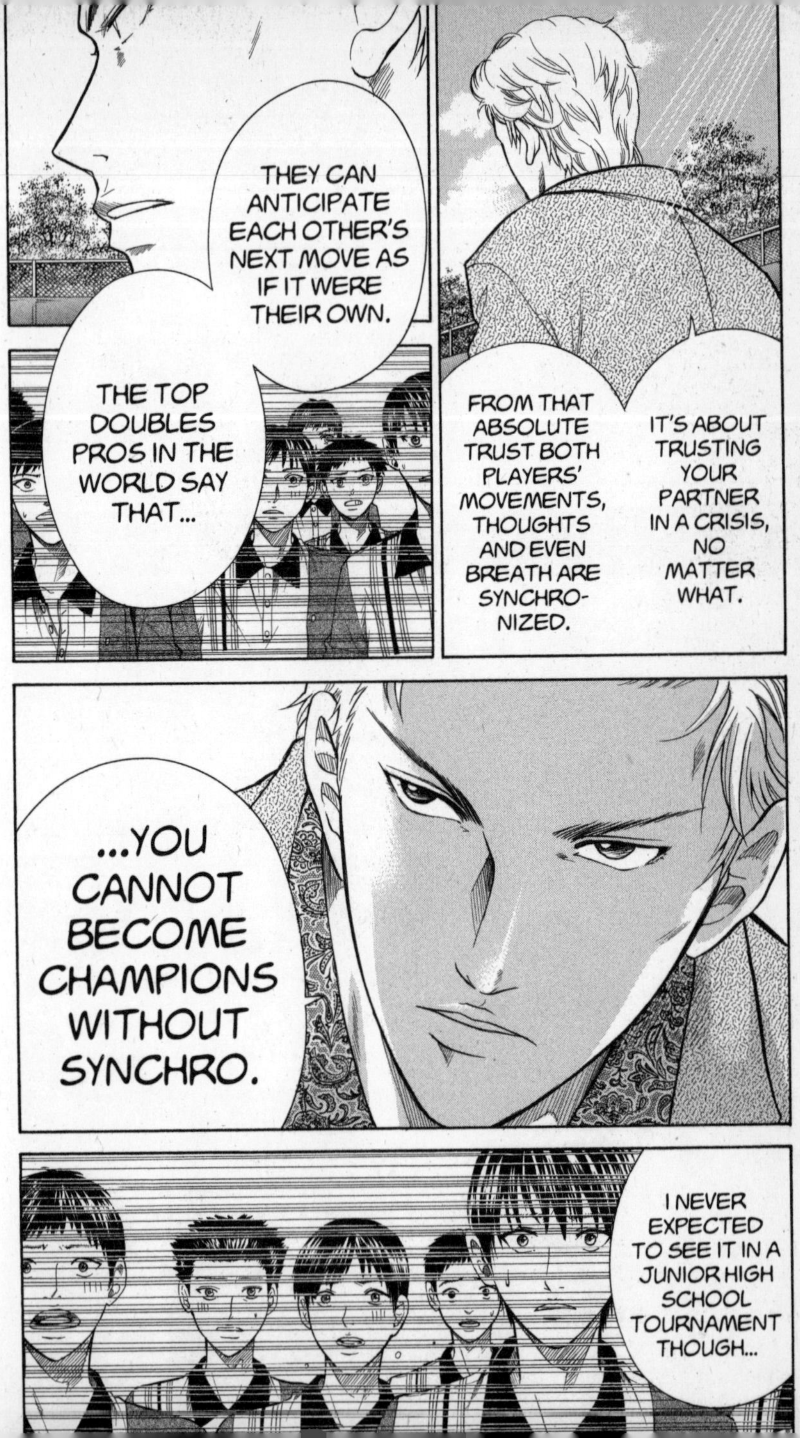
IT'S ABOUT TRUSTING YOUR PARTNER IN A CRISIS, NO MATTER WHAT.
FROM THAT ABSOLUTE TRUST BOTH PLAYERS' MOVEMENTS, THOUGHTS AND EVEN BREATH ARE SYNCHRONIZED.
THEY CAN ANTICIPATE EACH OTHER'S NEXT MOVE AS IF IT WERE THEIR OWN.
THE TOP DOUBLES PROS IN THE WORLD SAY THAT...
...YOU CANNOT BECOME CHAMPIONS WITHOUT SYNCHRO.
I NEVER EXPECTED TO SEE IT IN A JUNIOR HIGH SCHOOL TOURNAMENT THOUGH...

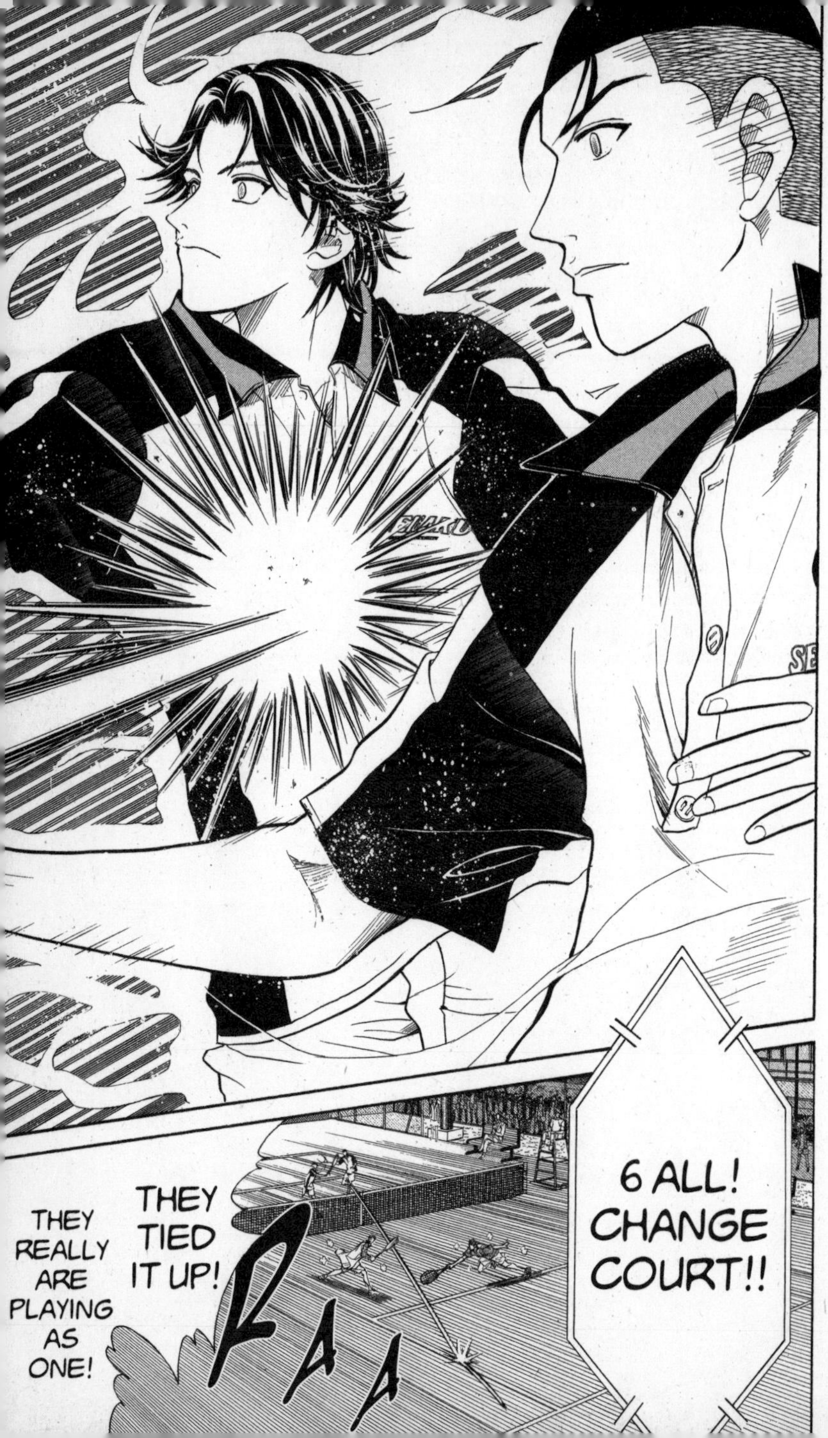
6 ALL! CHANGE COURT!!
THEY TIED IT UP!
RAAA
THEY REALLY ARE PLAYING AS ONE!

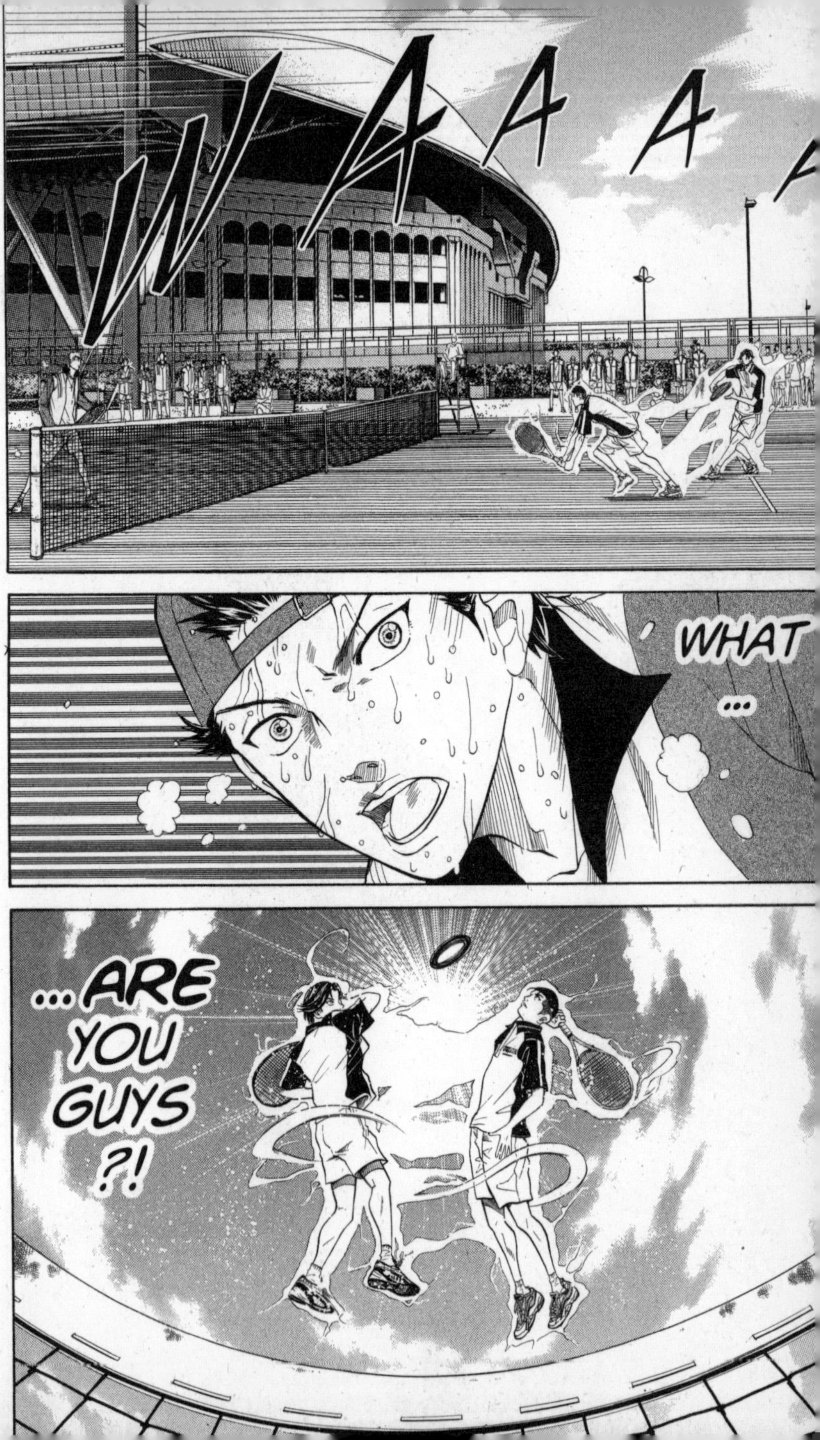
WAAAA
WHAT ...
...ARE YOU GUYS ?!

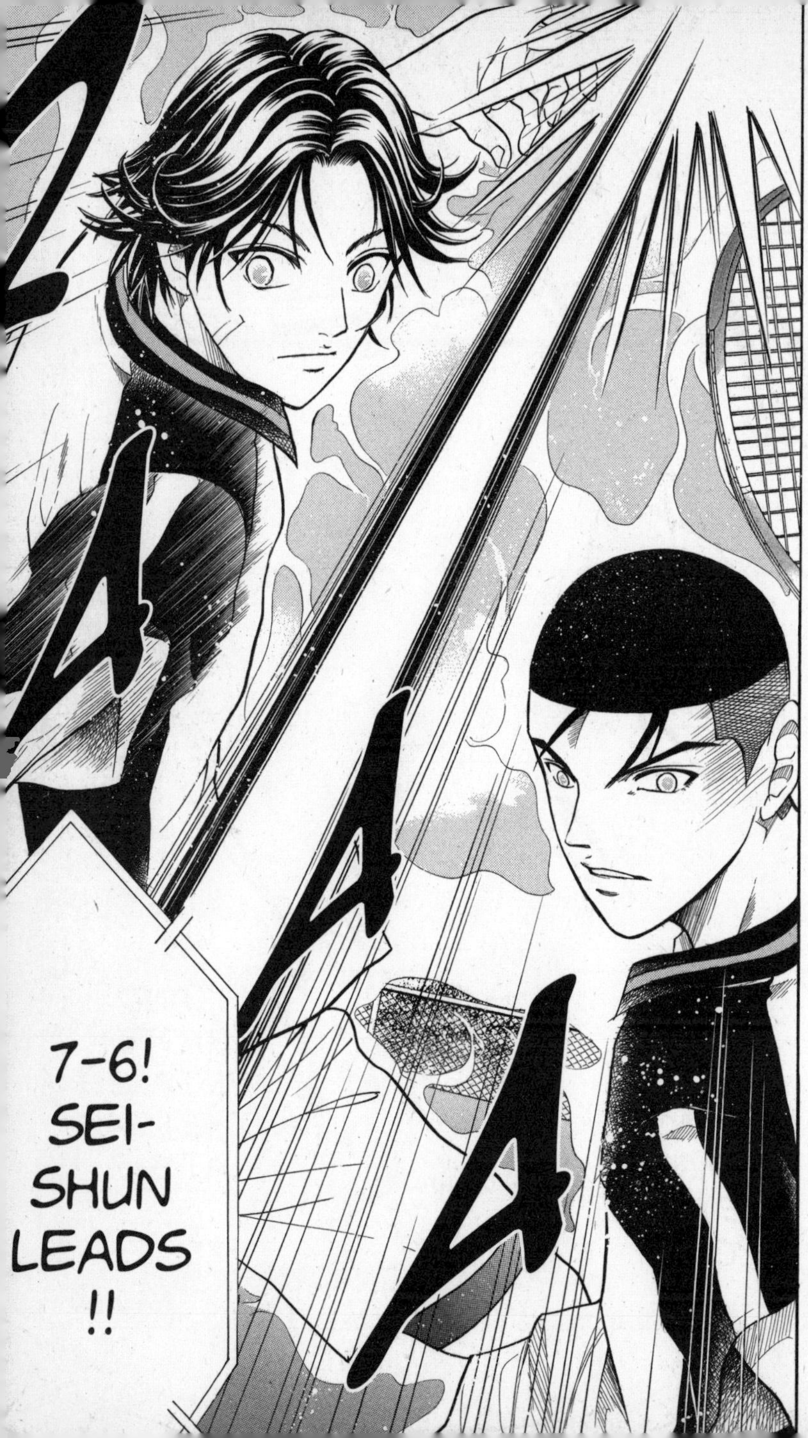
7-6! SEI-SHUN LEADS !!

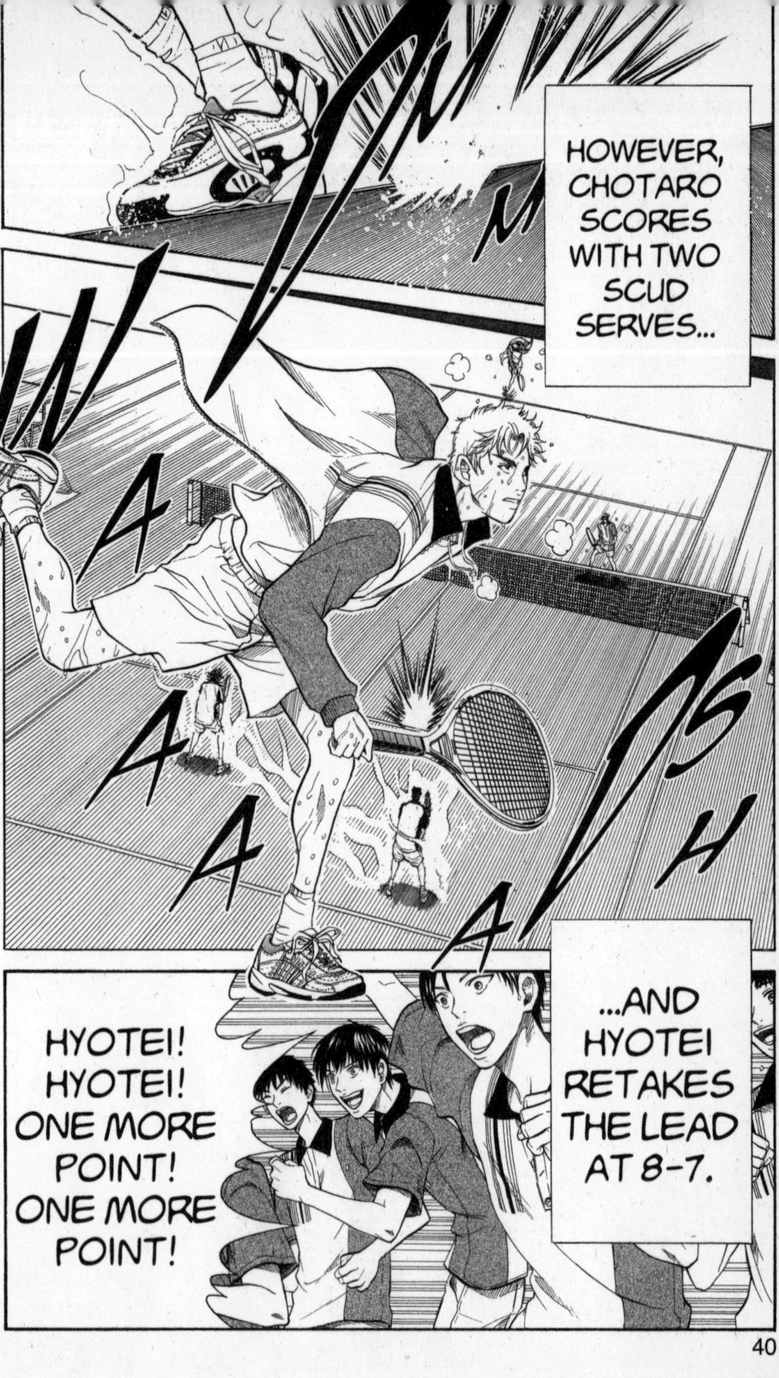
HOWEVER, CHOTARO SCORES WITH TWO SCUD SERVES...
WAAAA
...AND HYOTEI RETAKES THE LEAD AT 8-7.
HYOTEI! HYOTEI! ONE MORE POINT! ONE MORE POINT!

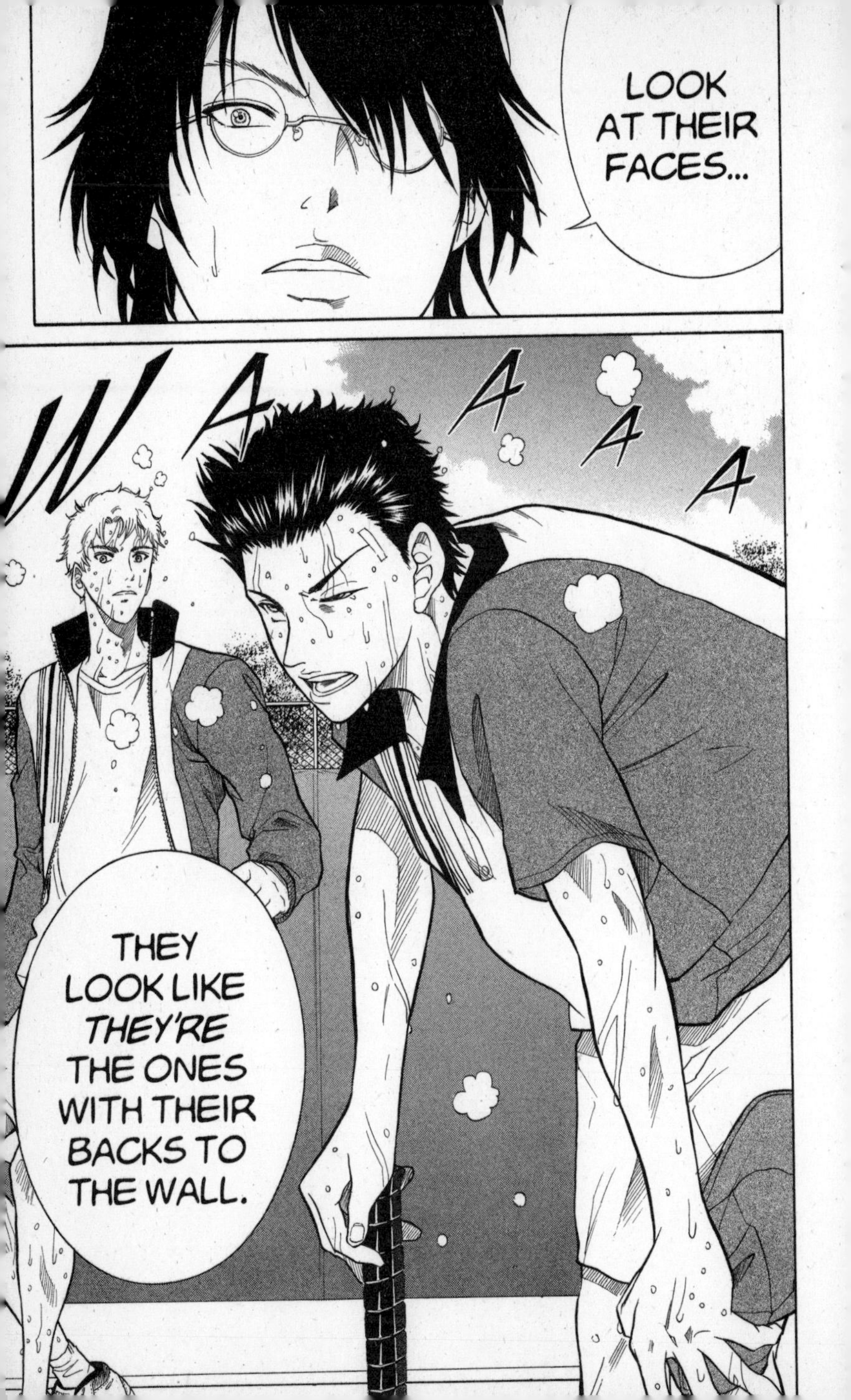
LOOK AT THEIR FACES...
WAAAA
THEY LOOK LIKE *THEY'RE* THE ONES WITH THEIR BACKS TO THE WALL.

テニスの王子様

THE PRINCE OF TENNIS

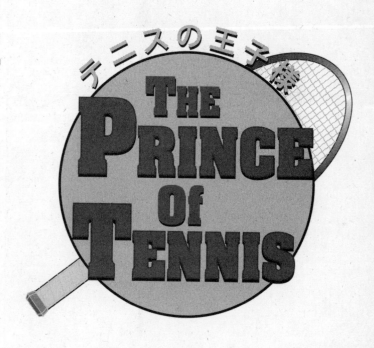

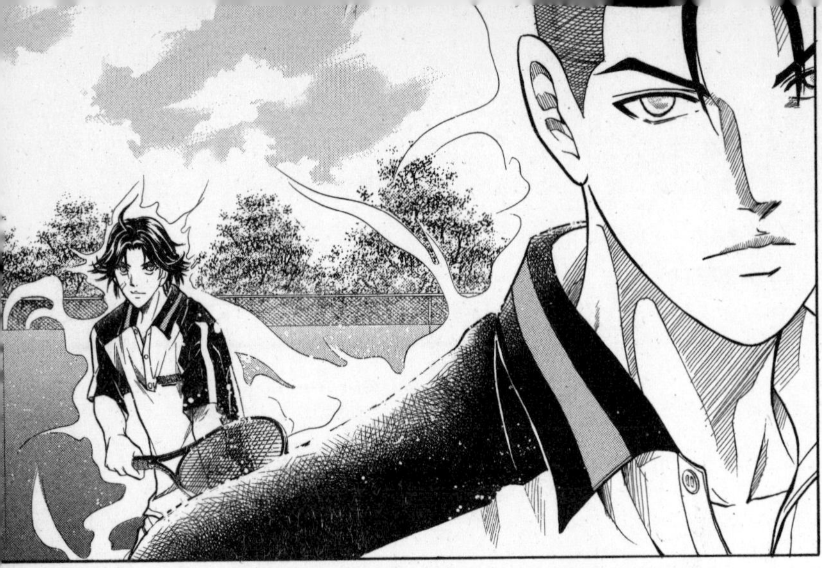

GENIUS 295: WHAT IS A SATISFYING GAME?

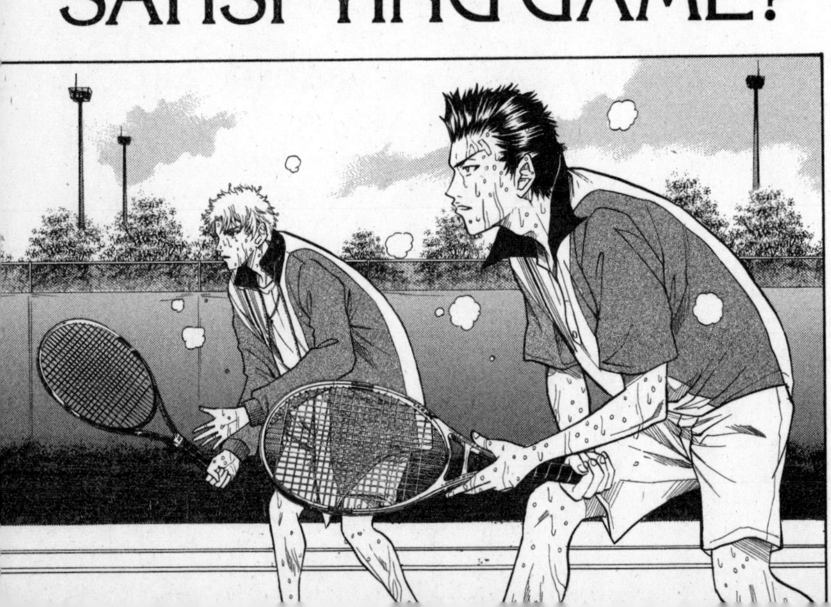

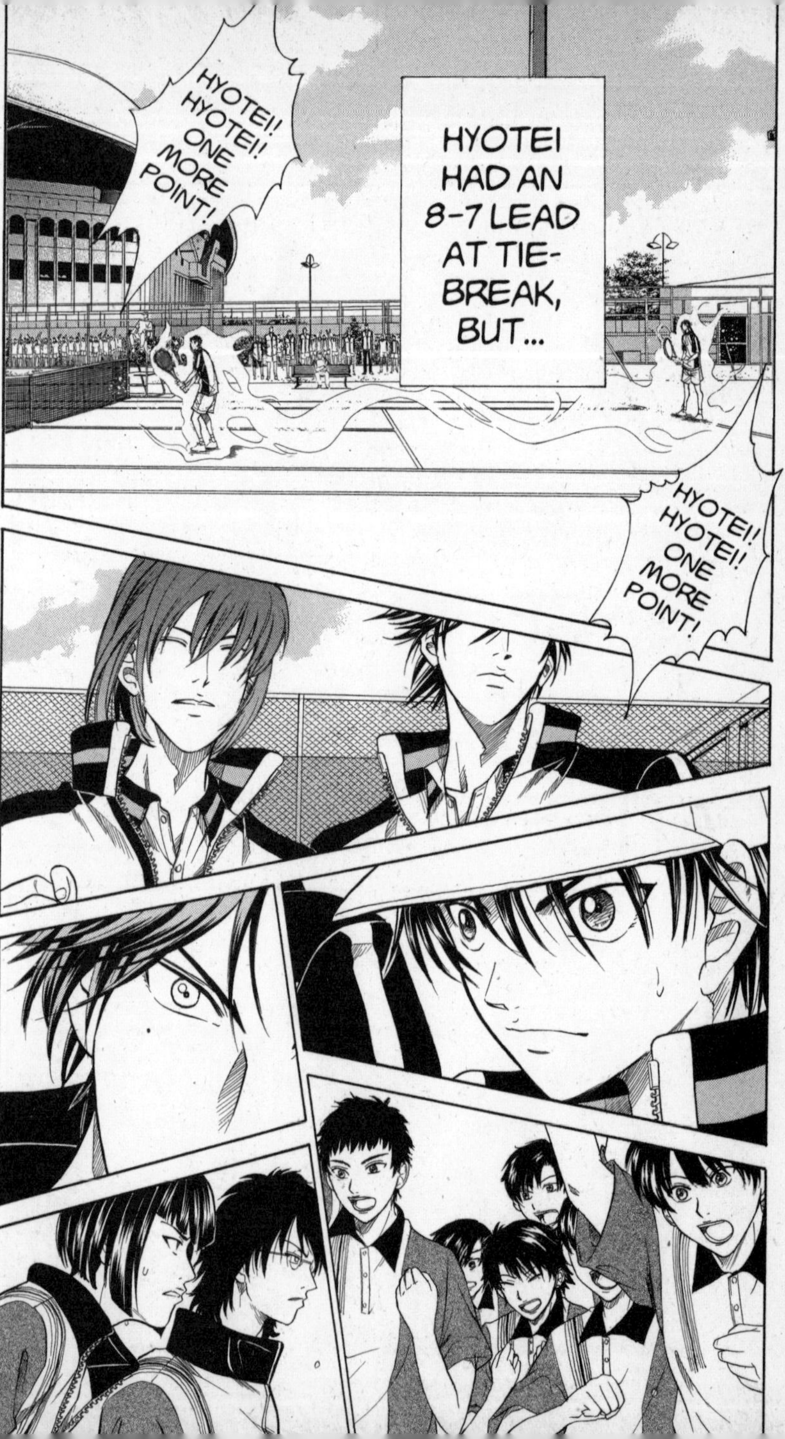
HYOTEI HAD AN 8-7 LEAD AT TIE-BREAK, BUT...
HYOTEI!! HYOTEI!! ONE MORE POINT!
HYOTEI!! HYOTEI!! ONE MORE POINT!

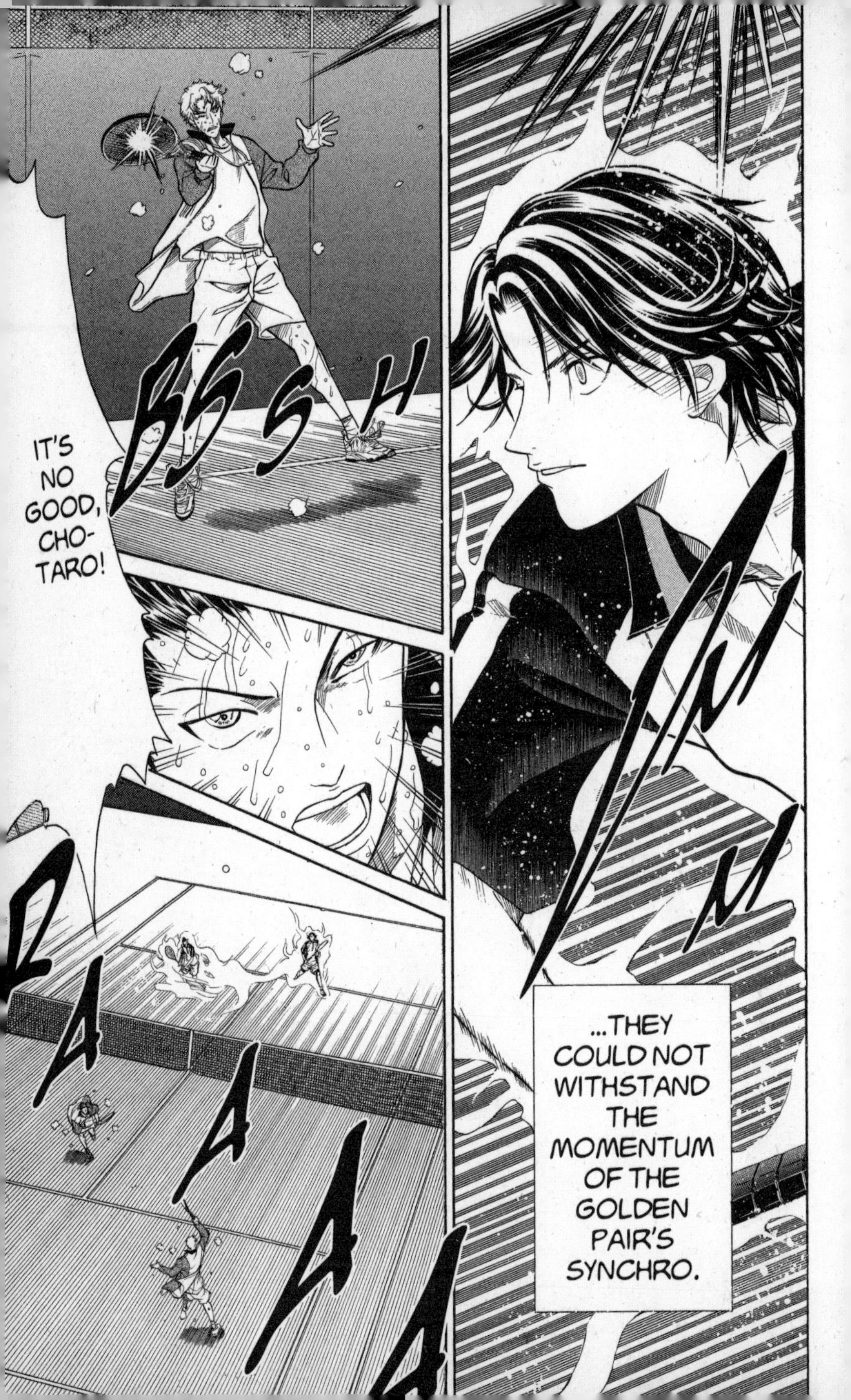
...THEY COULD NOT WITHSTAND THE MOMENTUM OF THE GOLDEN PAIR'S SYNCHRO.
BSSH
IT'S NO GOOD, CHO-TARO!
BAAAA

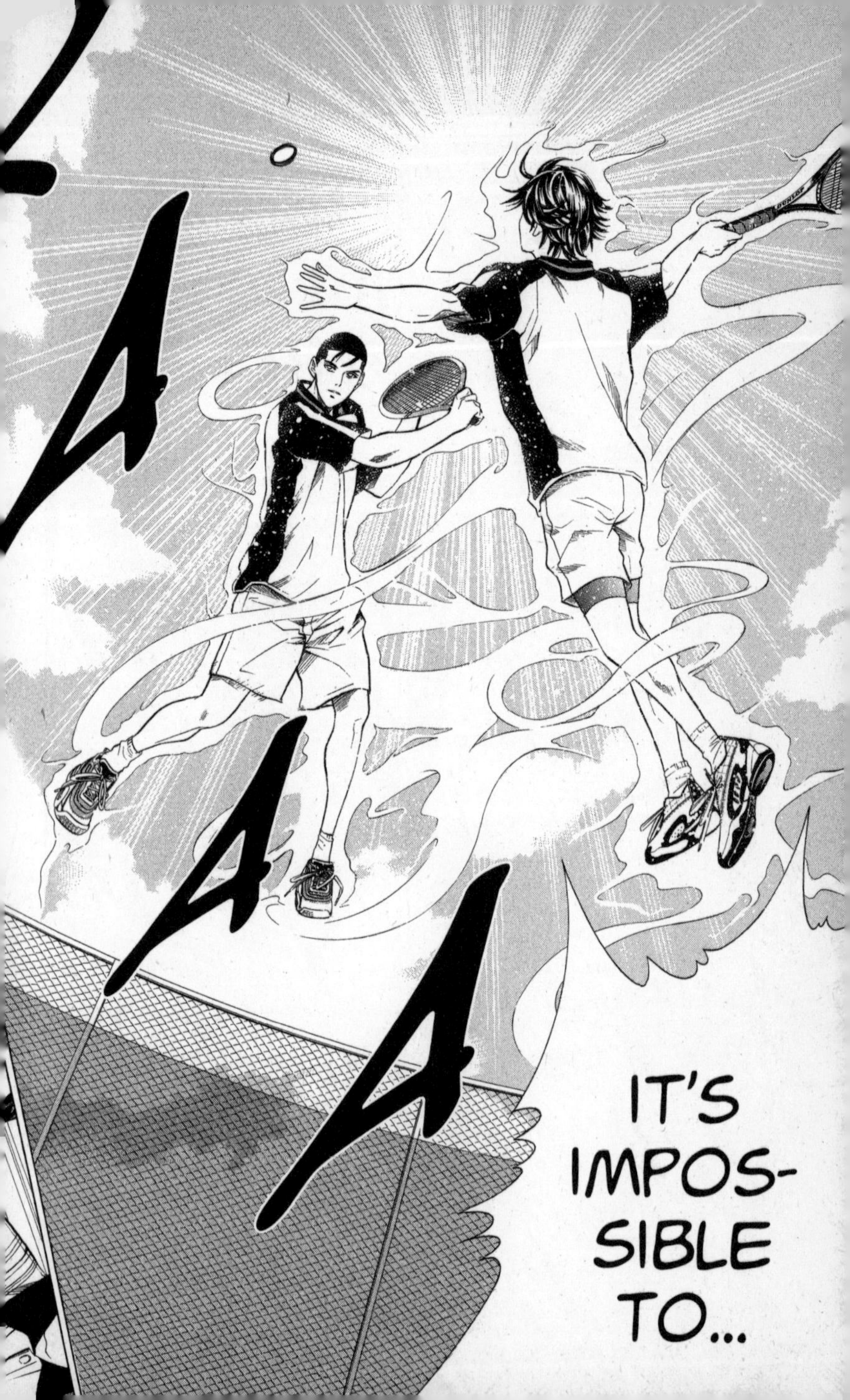
IT'S IMPOSSIBLE TO...

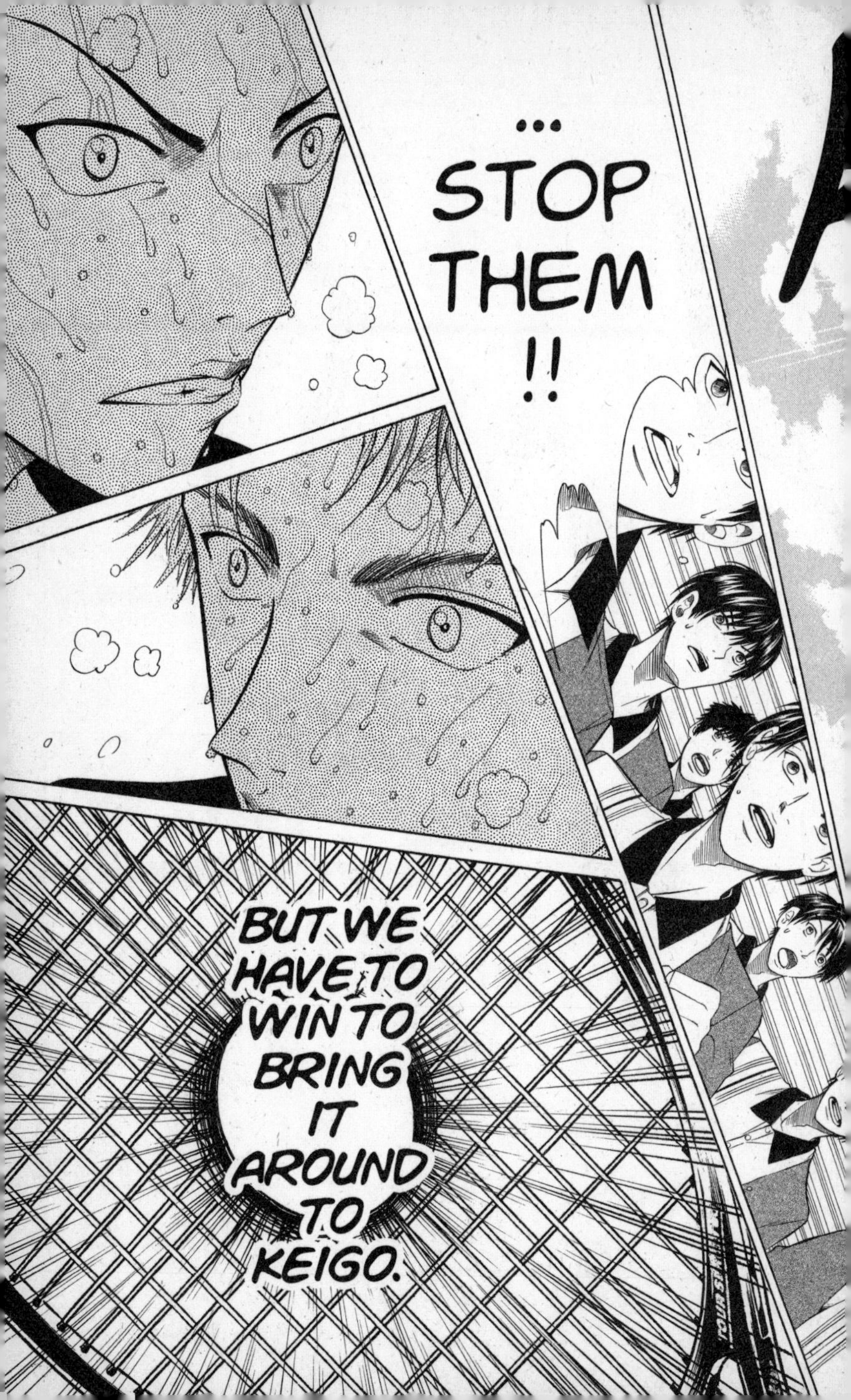
...STOP THEM!!
BUT WE HAVE TO WIN TO BRING IT AROUND TO KEIGO.

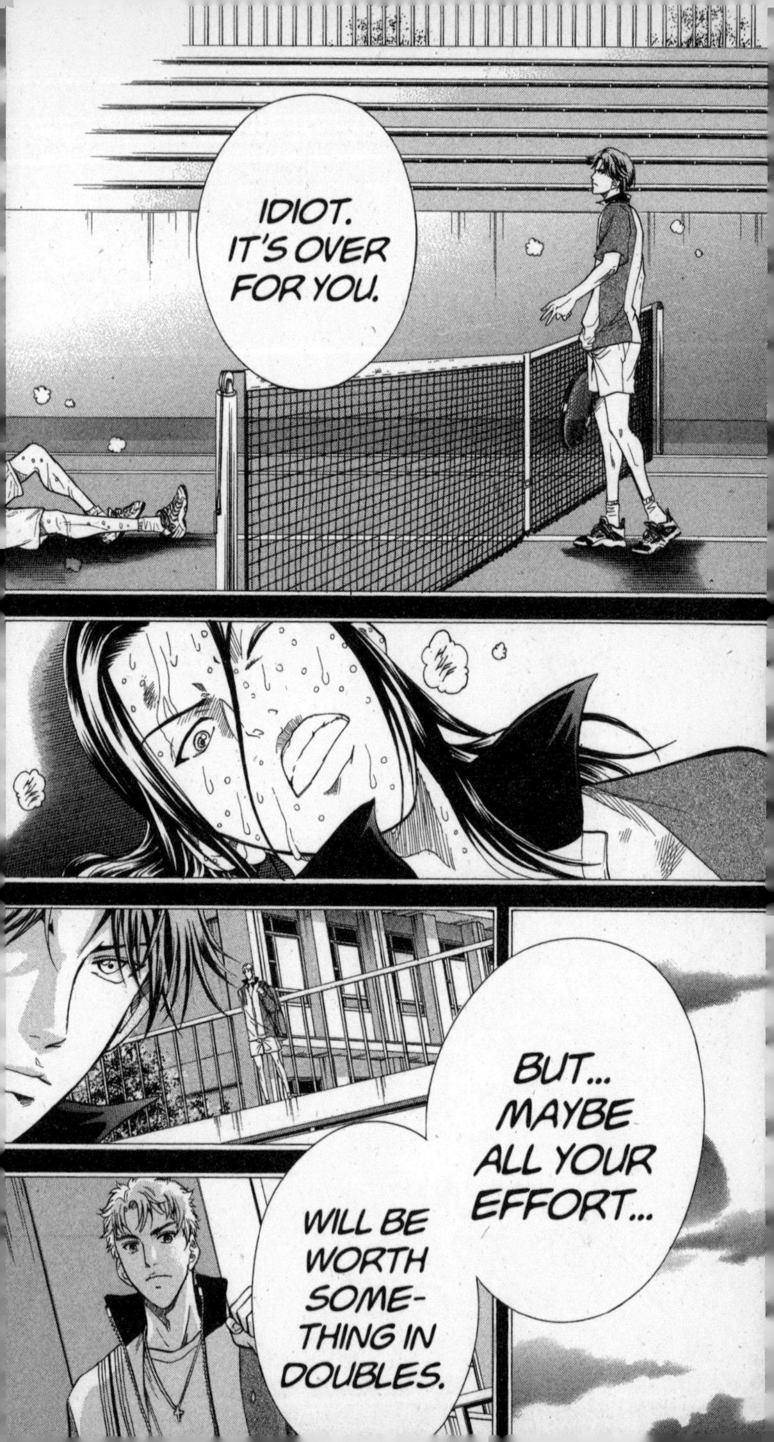
IDIOT. IT'S OVER FOR YOU.
BUT... MAYBE ALL YOUR EFFORT...
WILL BE WORTH SOME-THING IN DOUBLES.

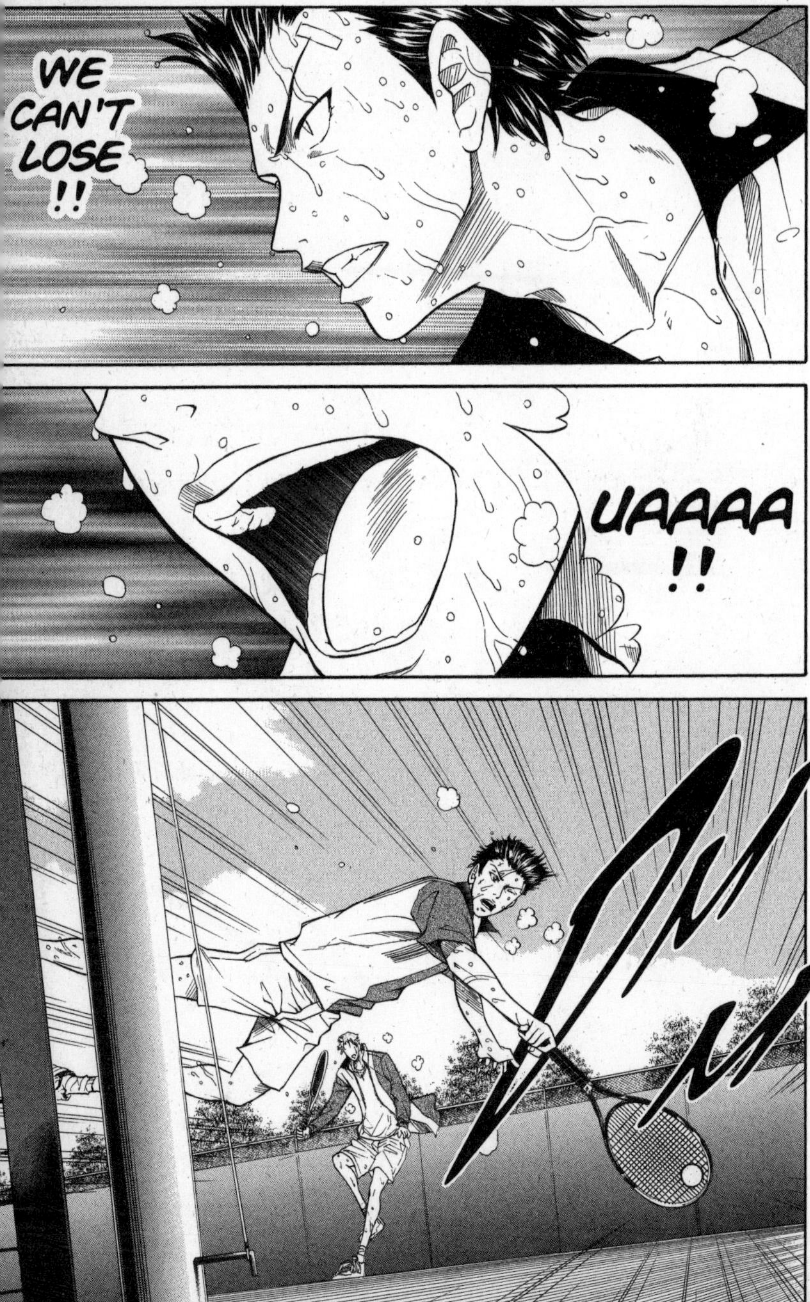
READ THIS WAY
WE CAN'T LOSE !!
UAAAA !!

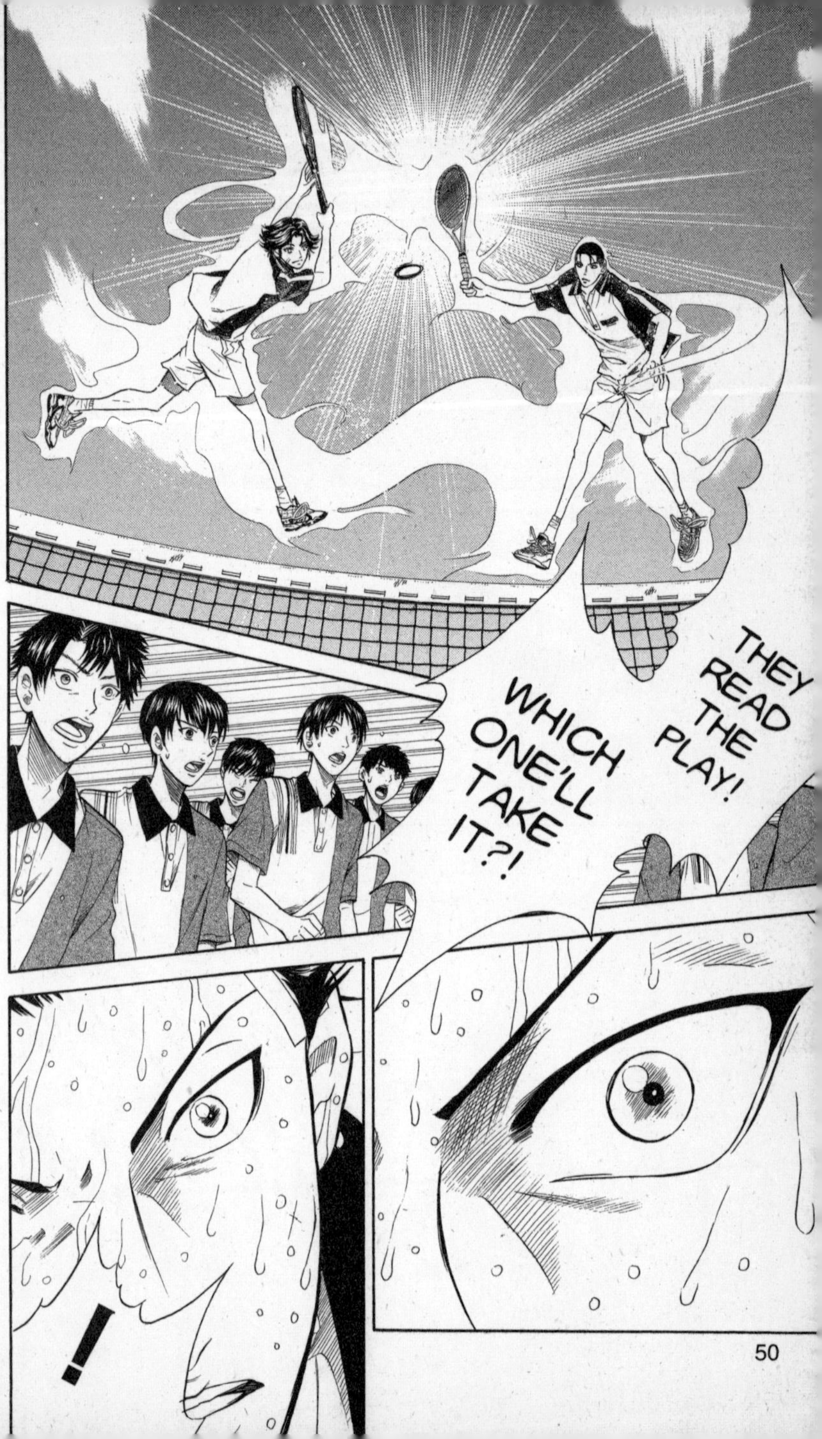
THEY READ THE PLAY!
WHICH ONE'LL TAKE IT?!
!

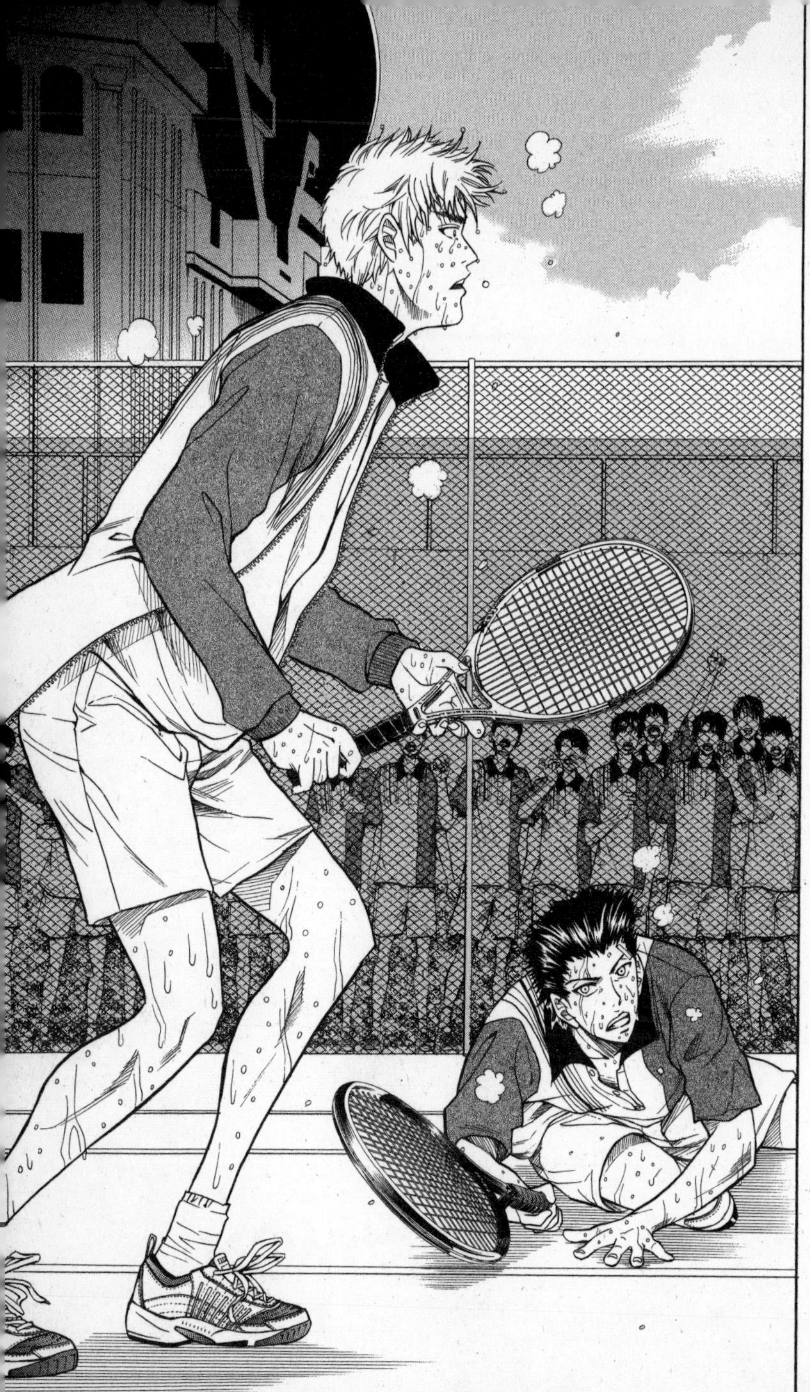

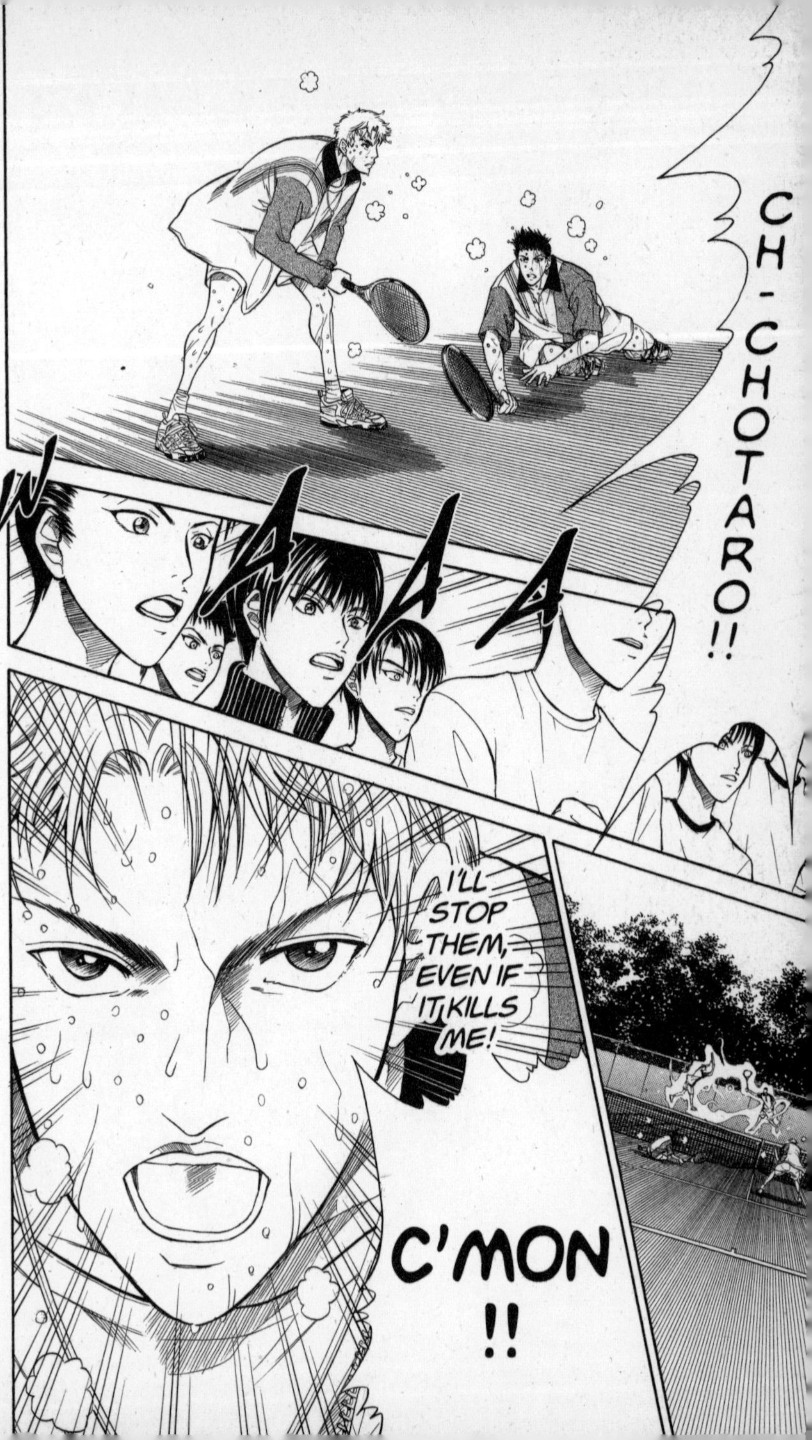
CH-CHOTARO!!
WAAA
I'LL STOP THEM, EVEN IF IT KILLS ME!
C'MON!!

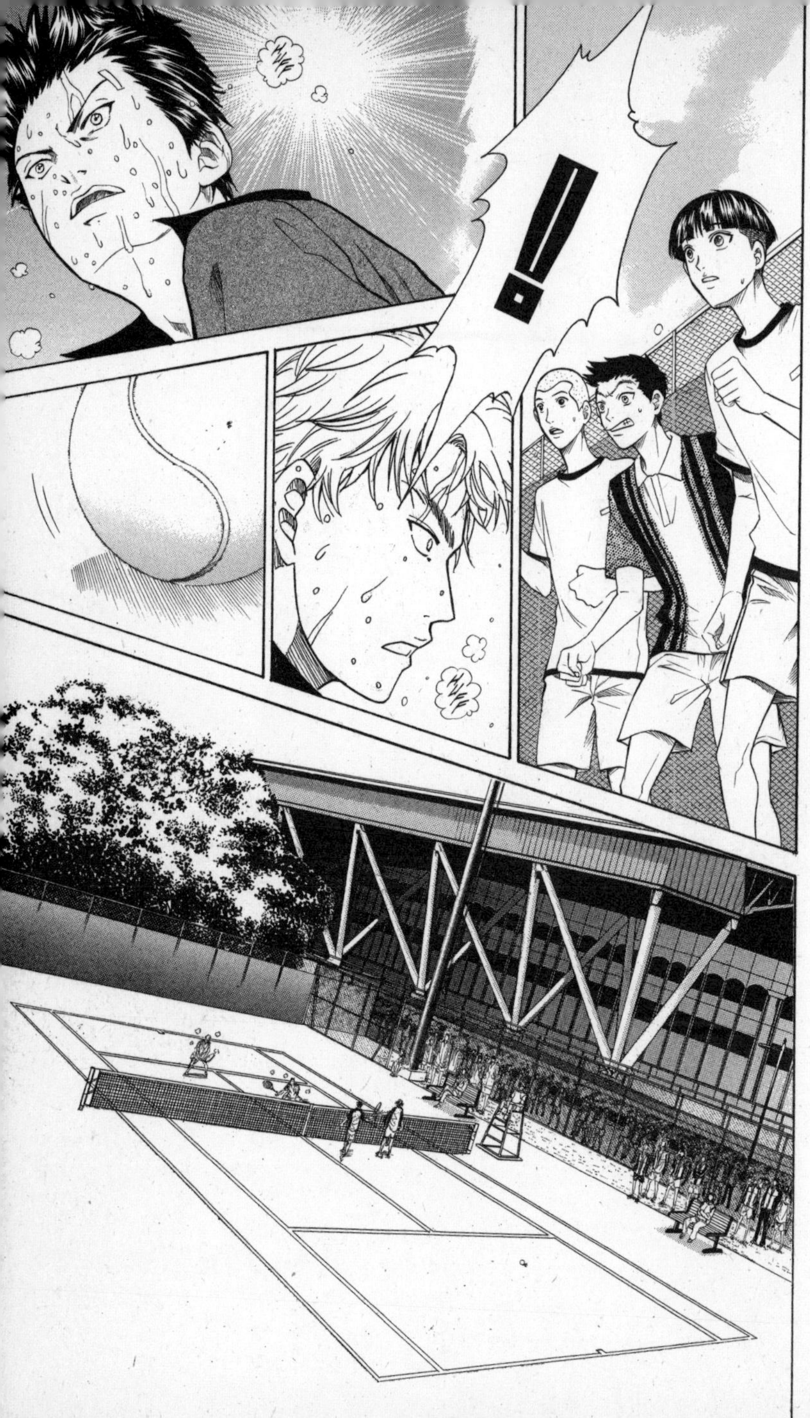
!
HUFF
HUFF

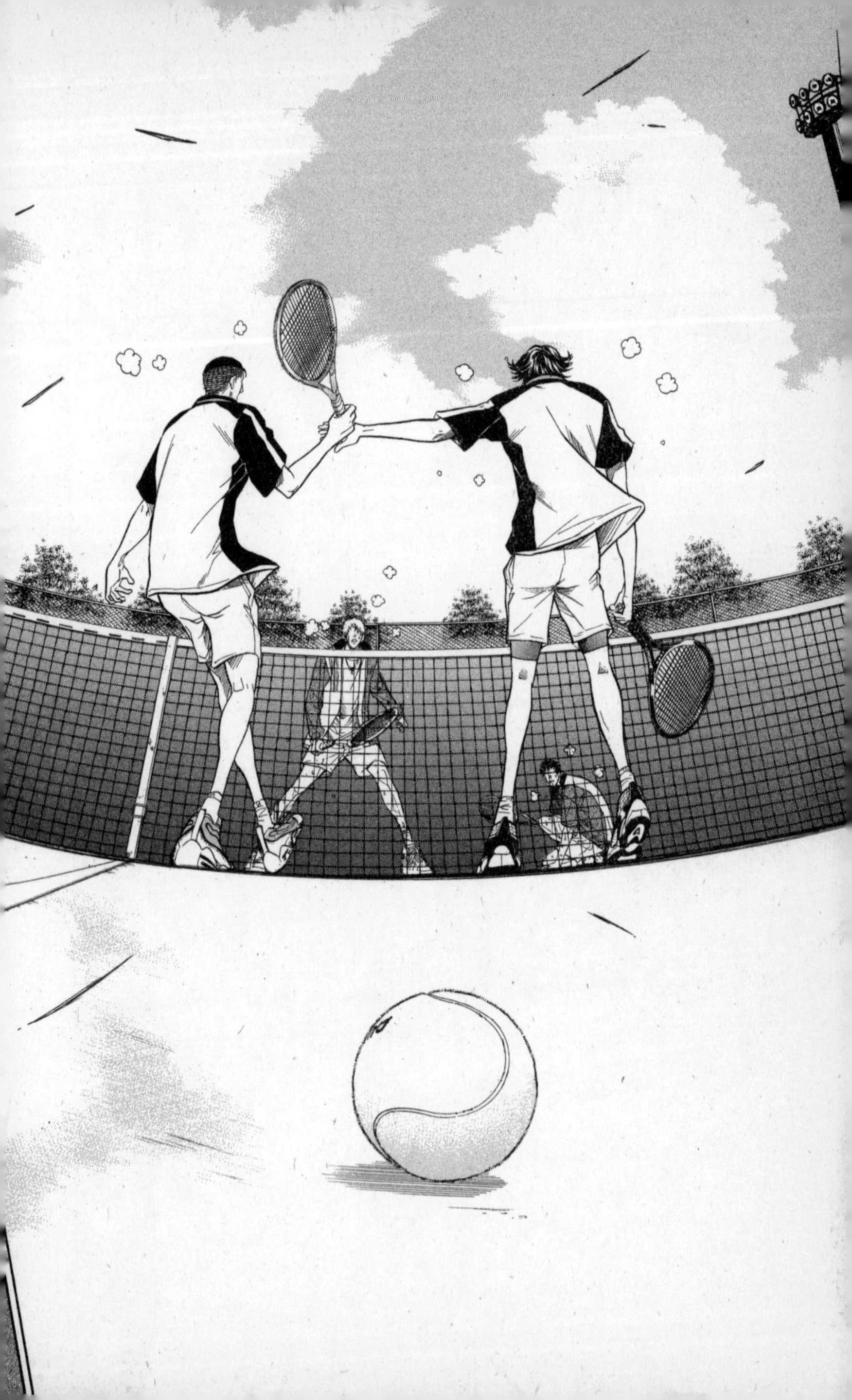

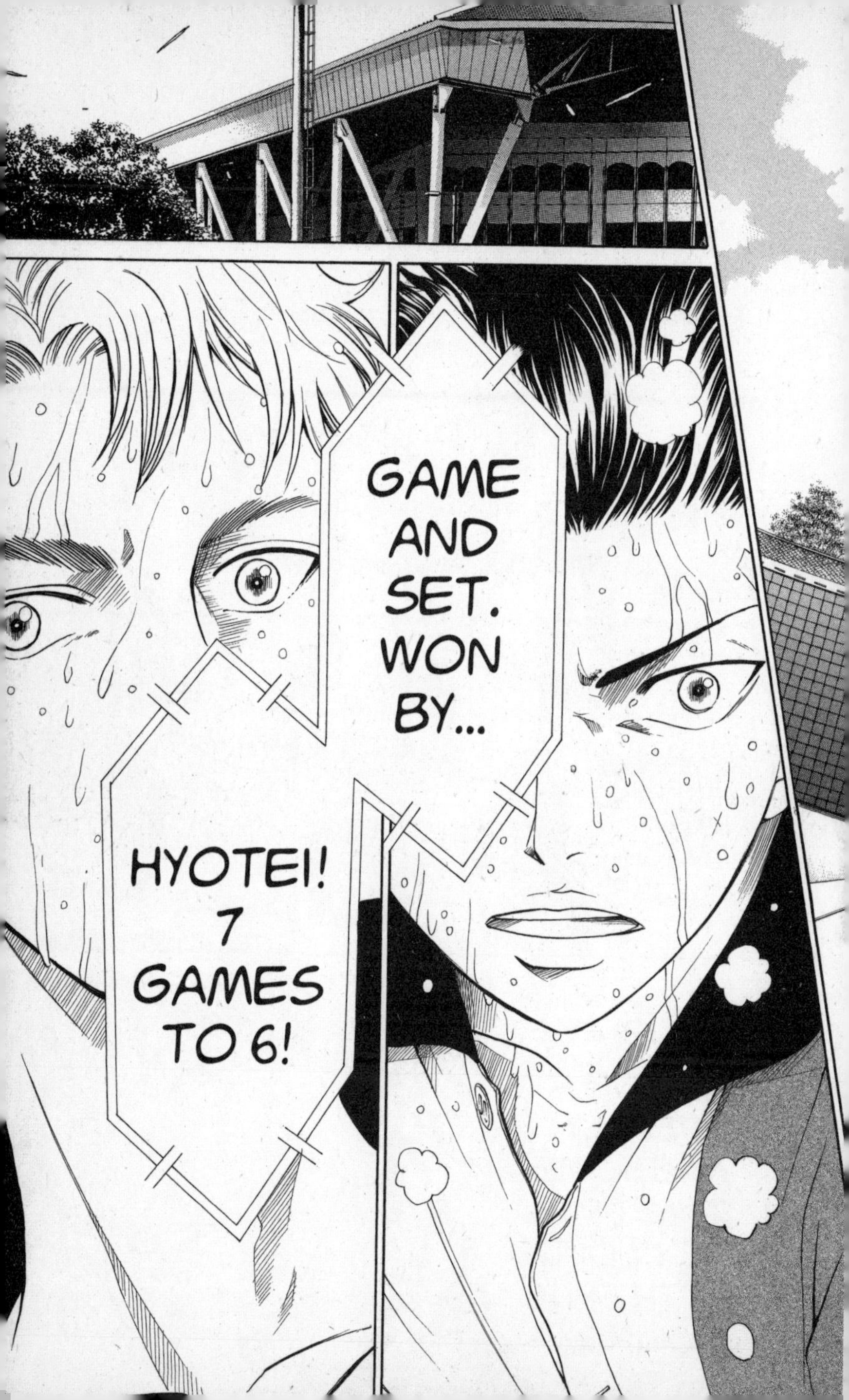
GAME AND SET. WON BY...
HYOTEI! 7 GAMES TO 6!

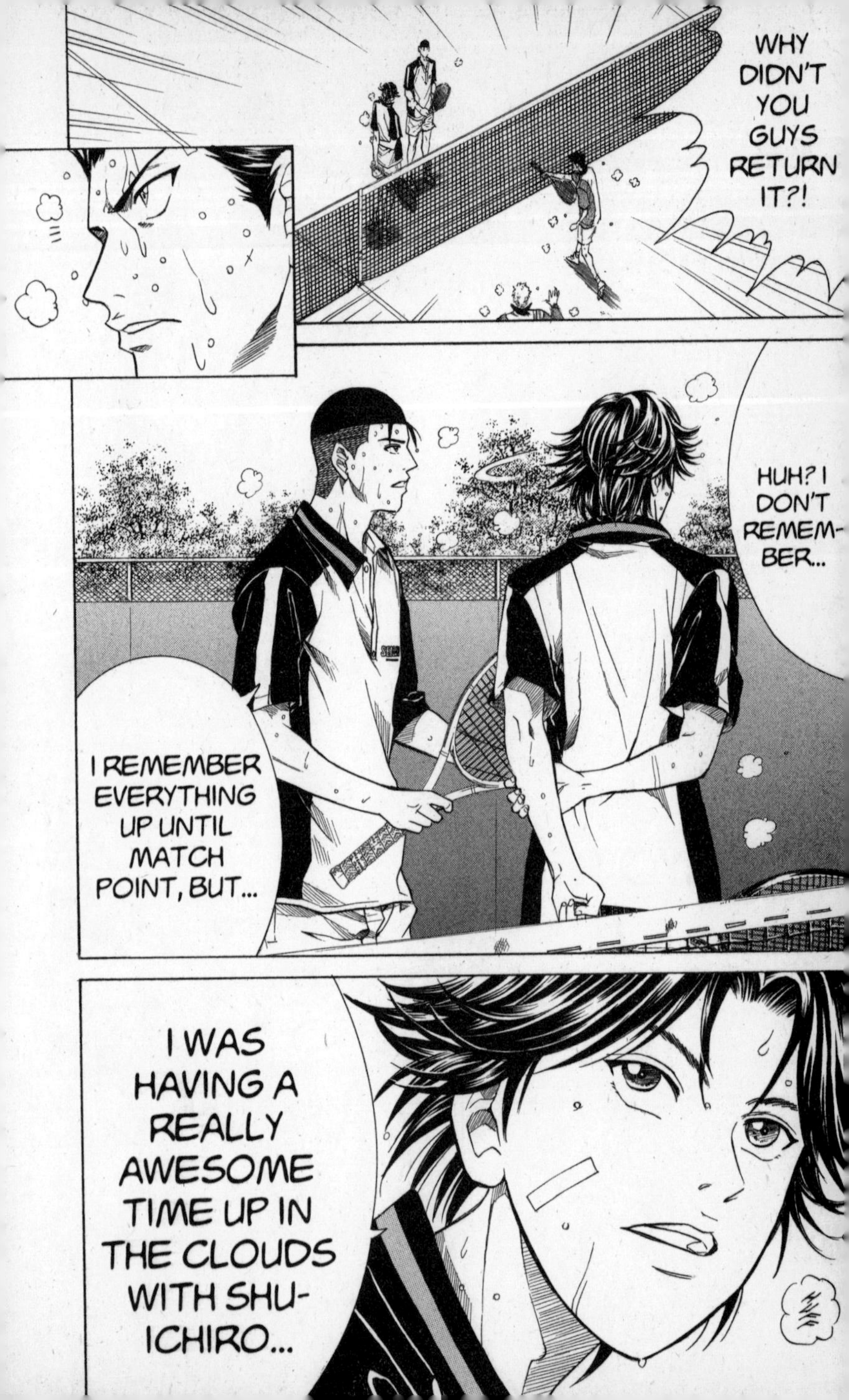
WHY DIDN'T YOU GUYS RETURN IT?!
HUH? I DON'T REMEM-BER...
I REMEMBER EVERYTHING UP UNTIL MATCH POINT, BUT...
I WAS HAVING A REALLY AWESOME TIME UP IN THE CLOUDS WITH SHU-ICHIRO...

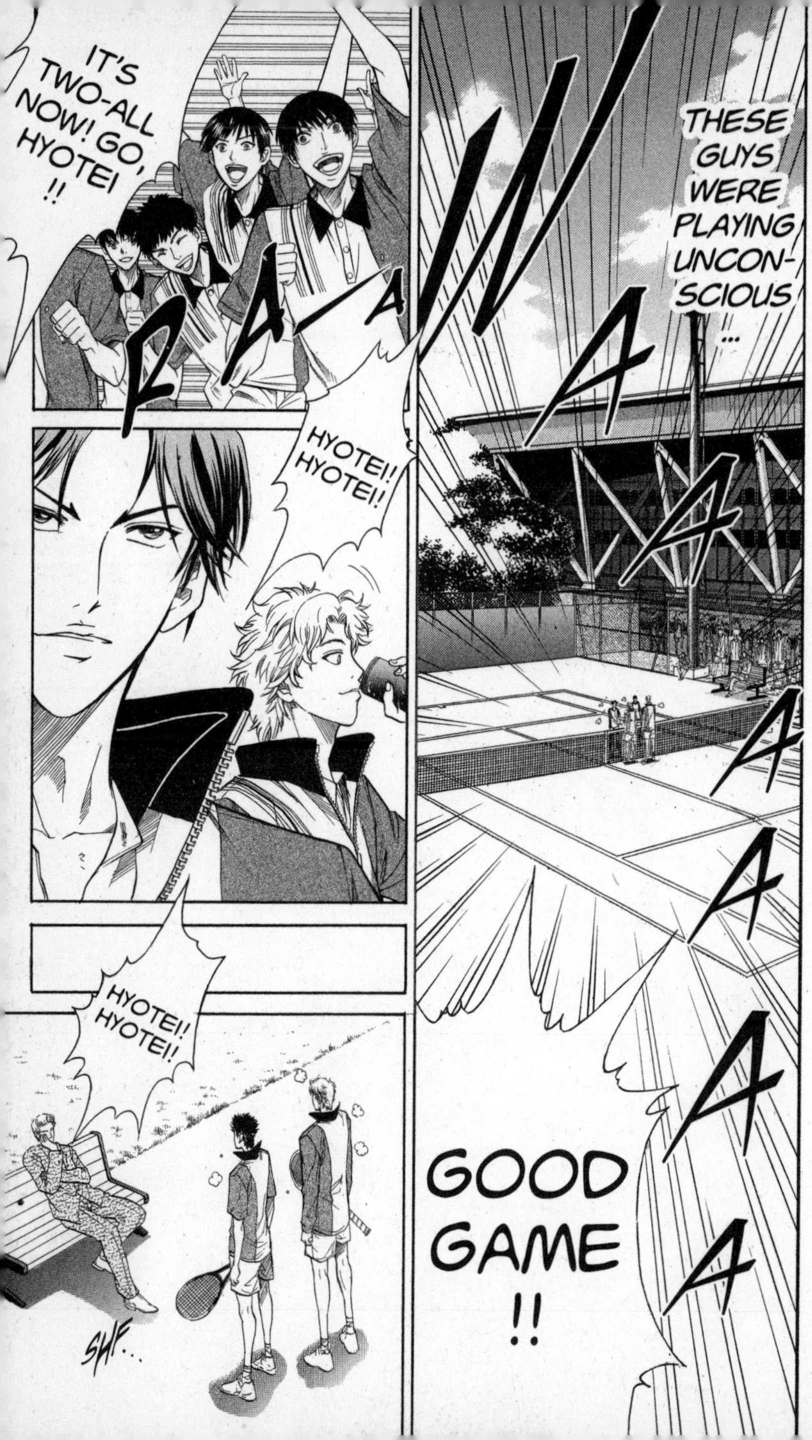
THESE GUYS WERE PLAYING UNCONSCIOUS...
WAAAAAAA
GOOD GAME!!
IT'S TWO-ALL NOW! GO, HYOTEI!!
RA-A
HYOTEI!! HYOTEI!!
HYOTEI!! HYOTEI!!
SHF...

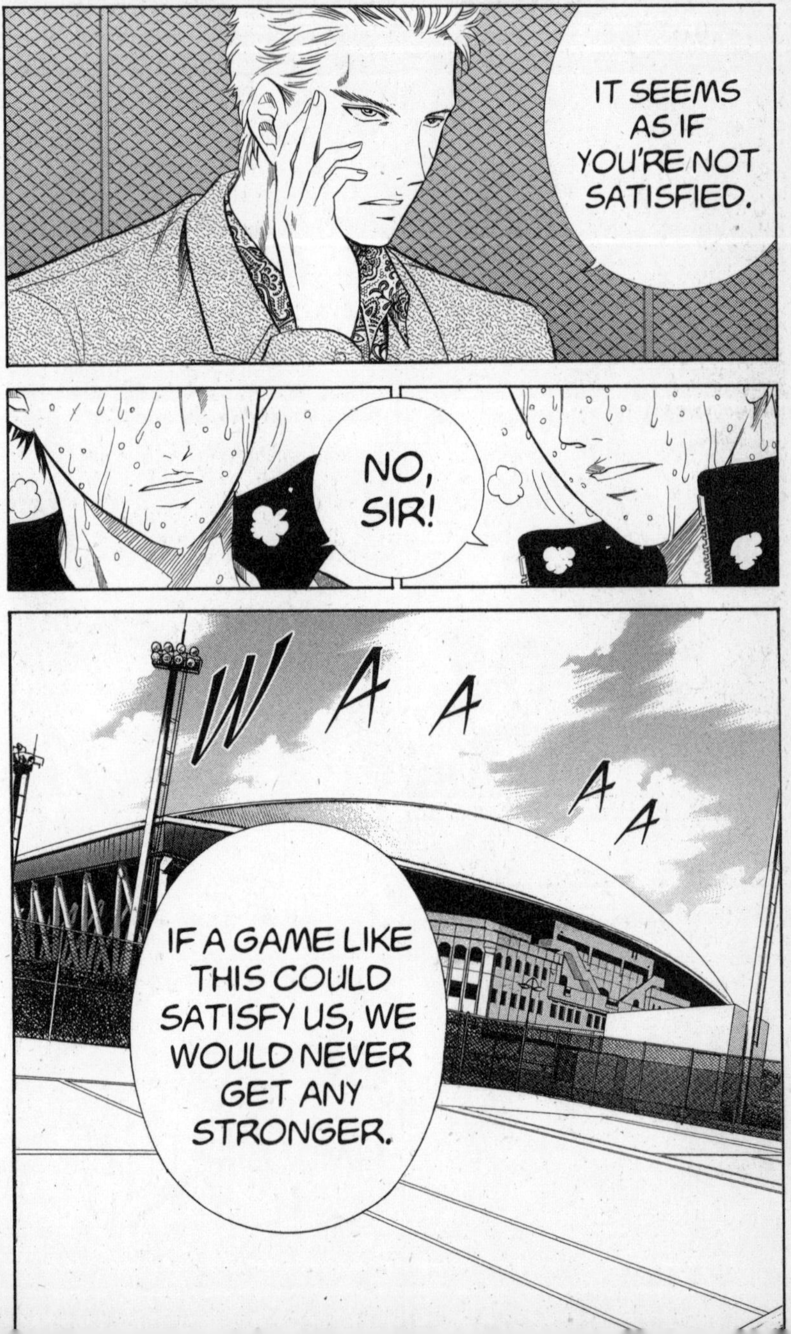
IT SEEMS AS IF YOU'RE NOT SATISFIED.
NO, SIR!
WAAAA
IF A GAME LIKE THIS COULD SATISFY US, WE WOULD NEVER GET ANY STRONGER.

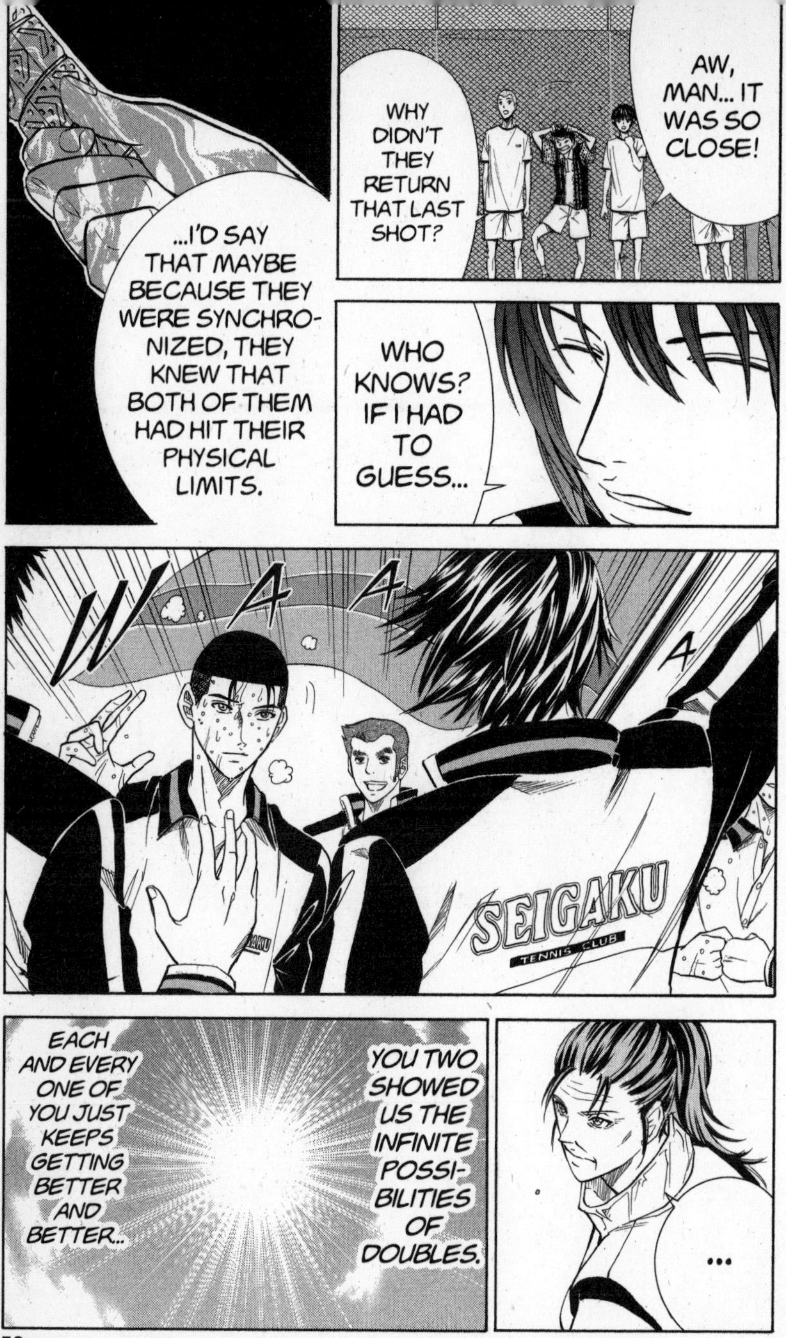
AW, MAN... IT WAS SO CLOSE!
WHY DIDN'T THEY RETURN THAT LAST SHOT?
WHO KNOWS? IF I HAD TO GUESS...
...I'D SAY THAT MAYBE BECAUSE THEY WERE SYNCHRO-NIZED, THEY KNEW THAT BOTH OF THEM HAD HIT THEIR PHYSICAL LIMITS.
W A A A
SEIGAKU
TENNIS CLUB
...
YOU TWO SHOWED US THE INFINITE POSSI-BILITIES OF DOUBLES.
EACH AND EVERY ONE OF YOU JUST KEEPS GETTING BETTER AND BETTER...

テニスの王子様

THE PRINCE OF TENNIS

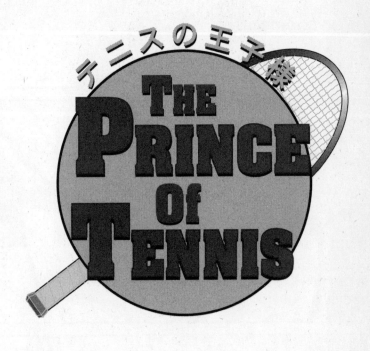

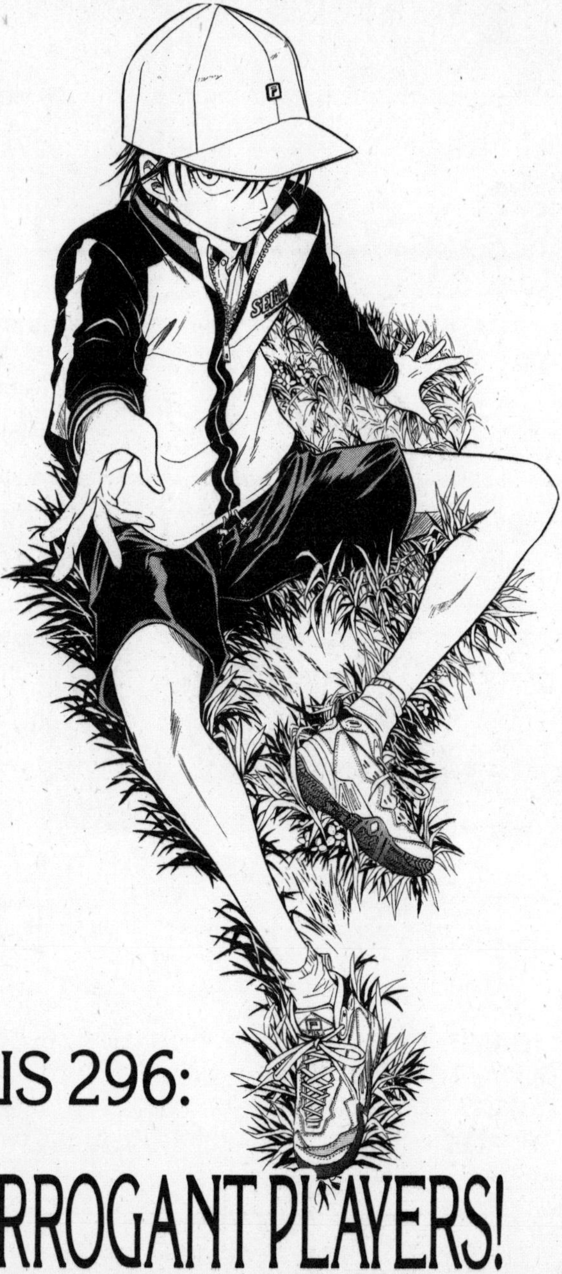

GENIUS 296:

TWO ARROGANT PLAYERS!

THE NATIONAL TOURNAMENT SEMIFINALS— SEISHUN ACADEMY VS. HYOTEI ACADEMY

	S_3	D_2	S_2	D_1	S_1	TOTAL
SEISHUN ACADEMY (TOKYO)	4	7	7	6		2
HYOTEI ACADEMY (TOKYO)	6	5	6	7		2

AFTER TWO SINGLES AND TWO DOUBLES MATCHES, THE SCORE WAS TIED AT TWO.

EVERYTHING NOW CAME DOWN TO NO. 1 SINGLES.

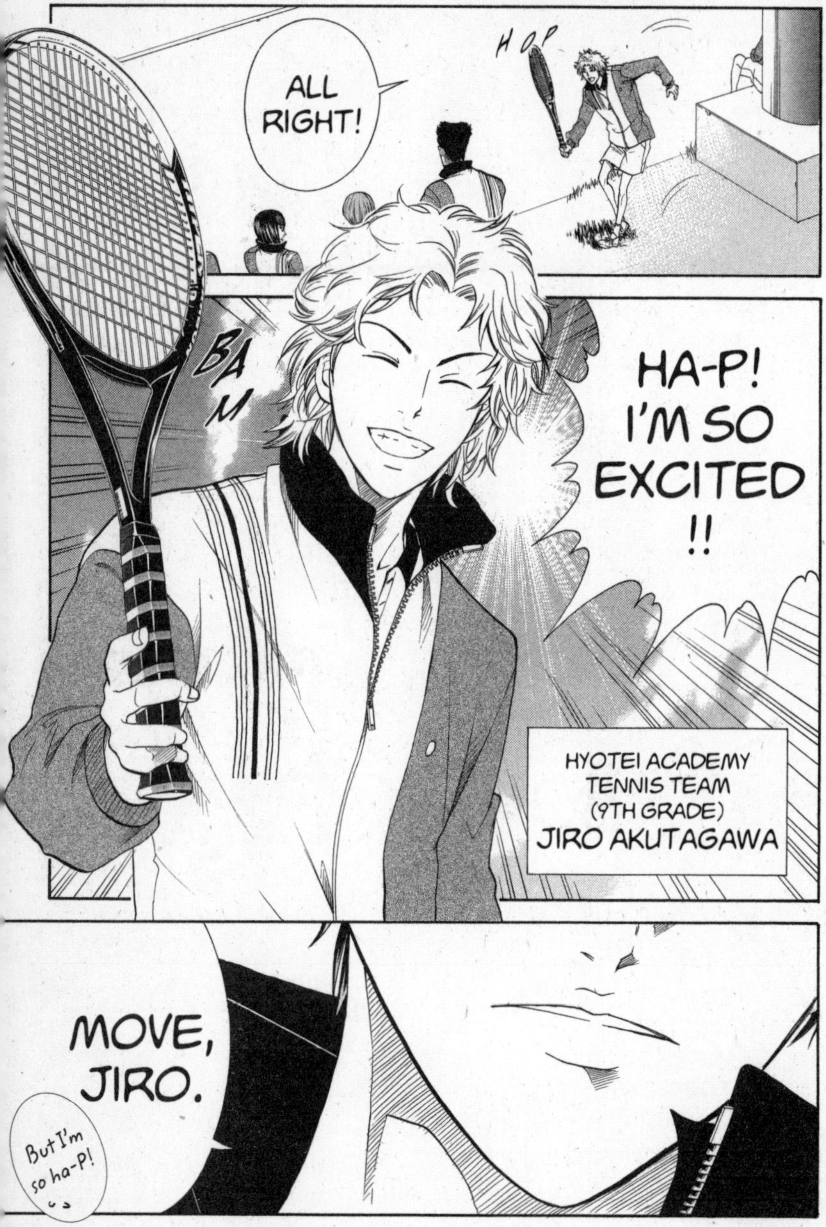
READ THIS WAY
HOP
ALL RIGHT!
BAM
HA-P! I'M SO EXCITED !!
HYOTEI ACADEMY TENNIS TEAM (9TH GRADE) JIRO AKUTAGAWA
MOVE, JIRO.
But I'm so ha-P!

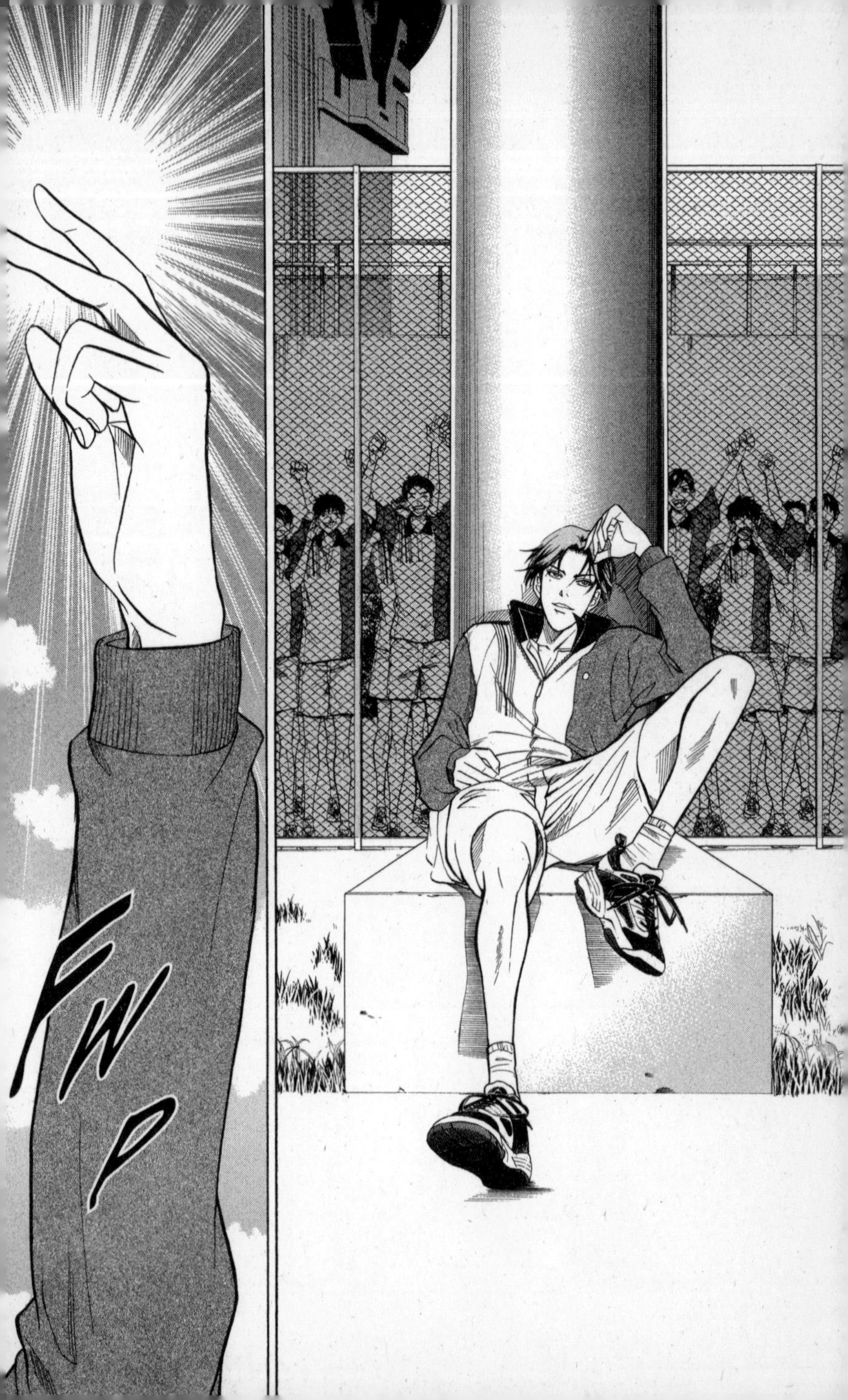
FWP

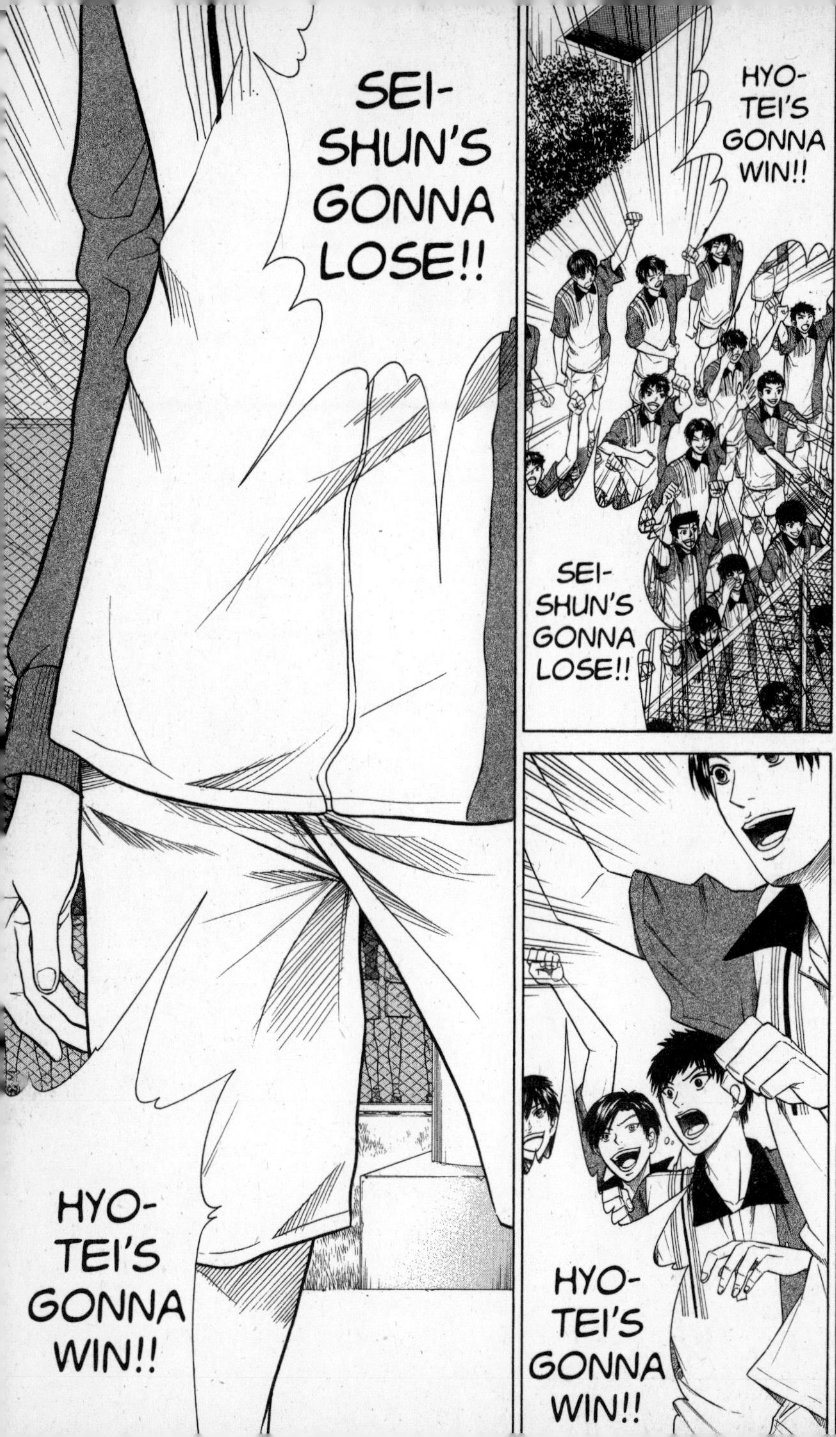
HYO-TEI'S GONNA WIN!!
SEI-SHUN'S GONNA LOSE!!
HYO-TEI'S GONNA WIN!!
SEI-SHUN'S GONNA LOSE!!
HYO-TEI'S GONNA WIN!!

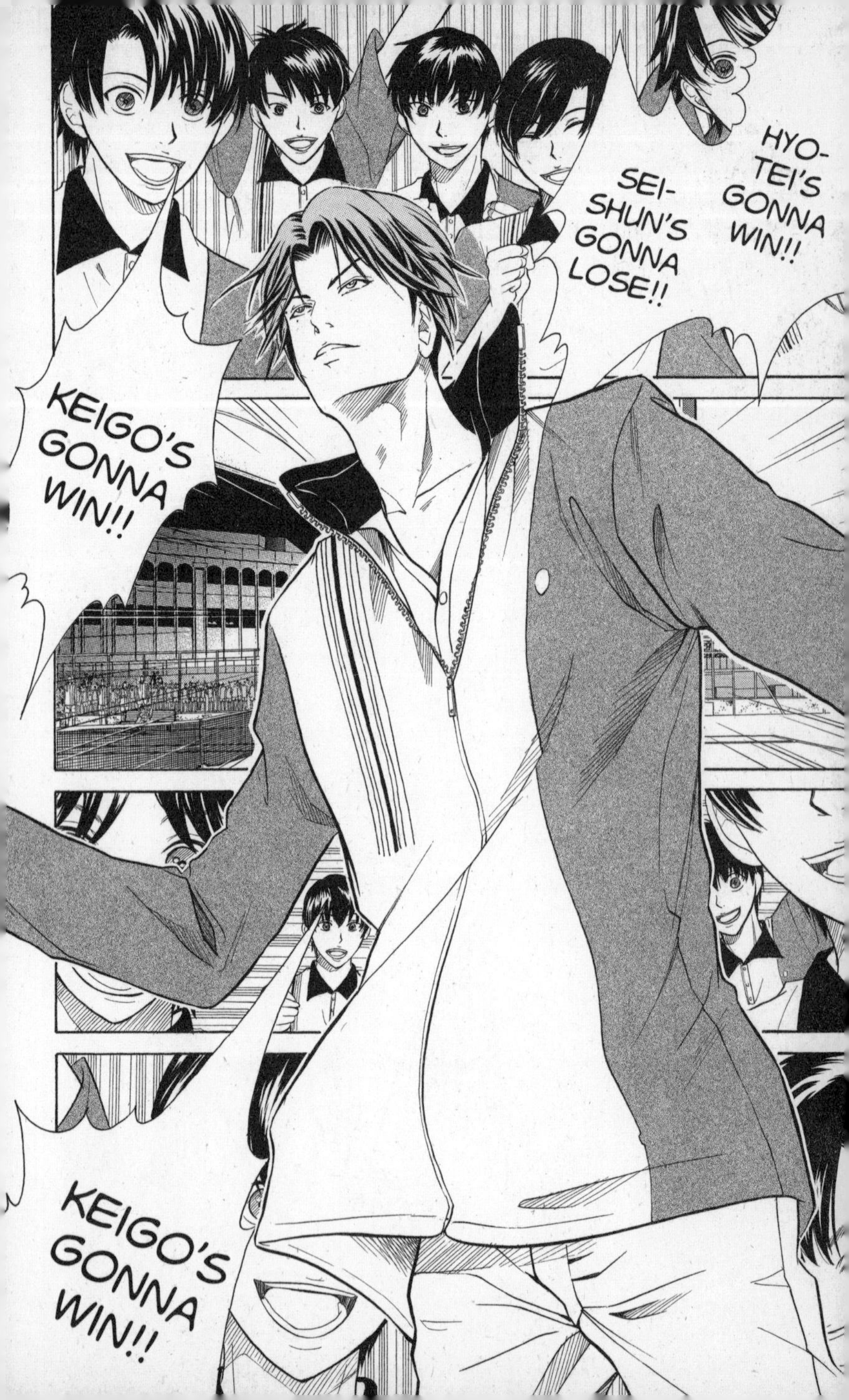
HYO-TEI'S GONNA WIN!!
SEI-SHUN'S GONNA LOSE!!
KEIGO'S GONNA WIN!!
KEIGO'S GONNA WIN!!

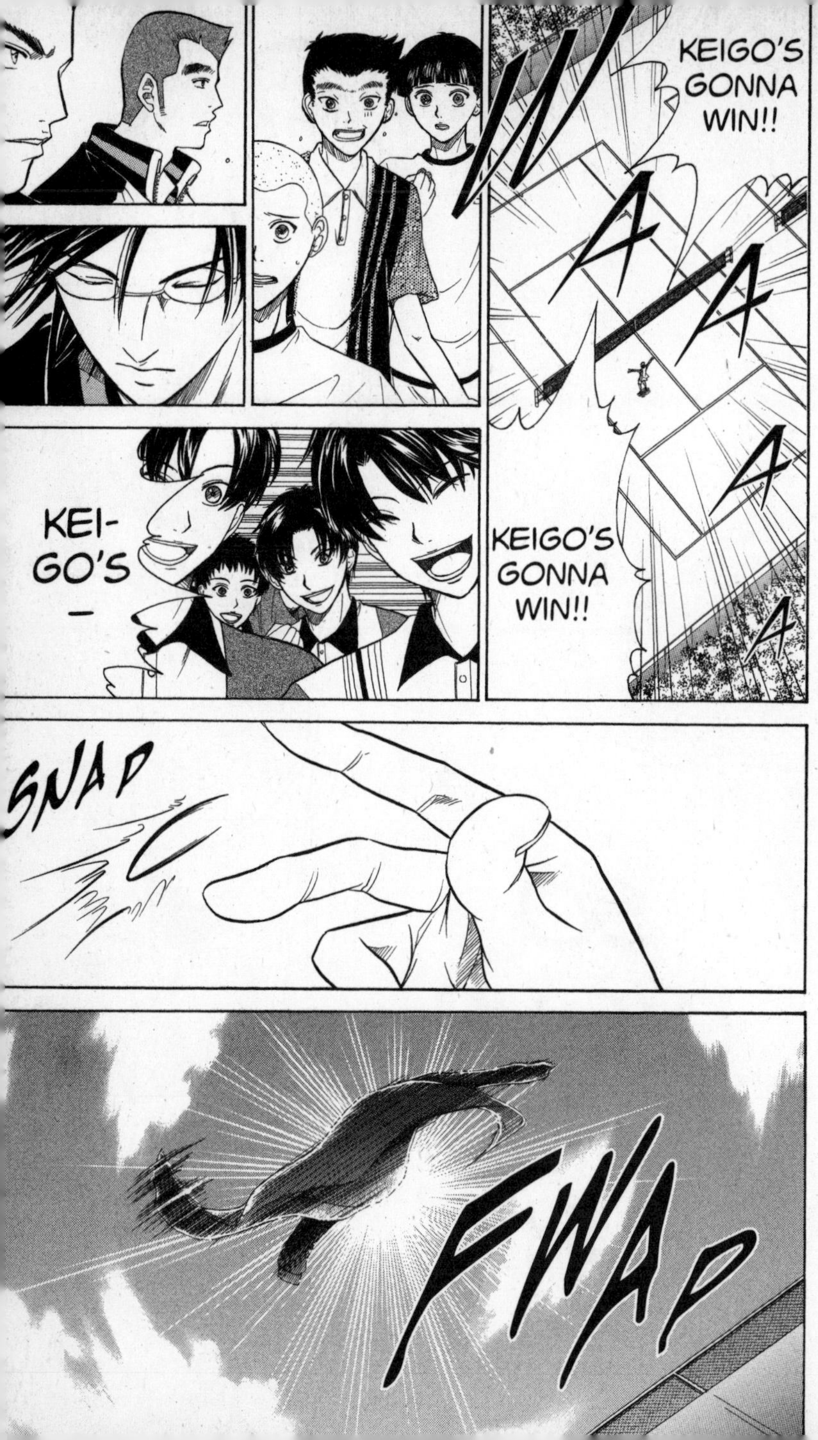
KEIGO'S GONNA WIN!!
WAAAAA
KEIGO'S GONNA WIN!!
KEI-GO'S —
SNAP
FWAP

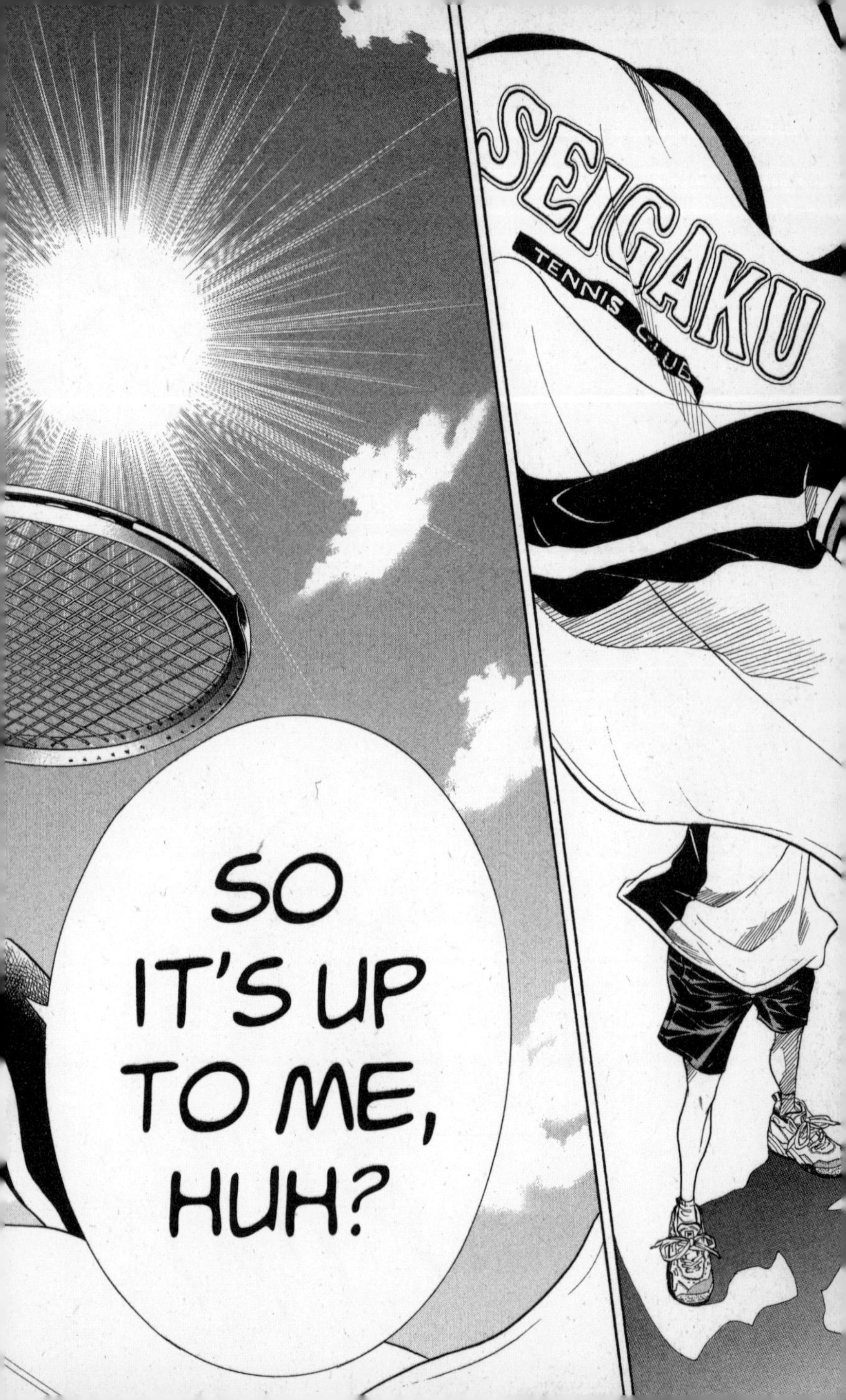
SEIGAKU
TENNIS CLUB
SO IT'S UP TO ME, HUH?

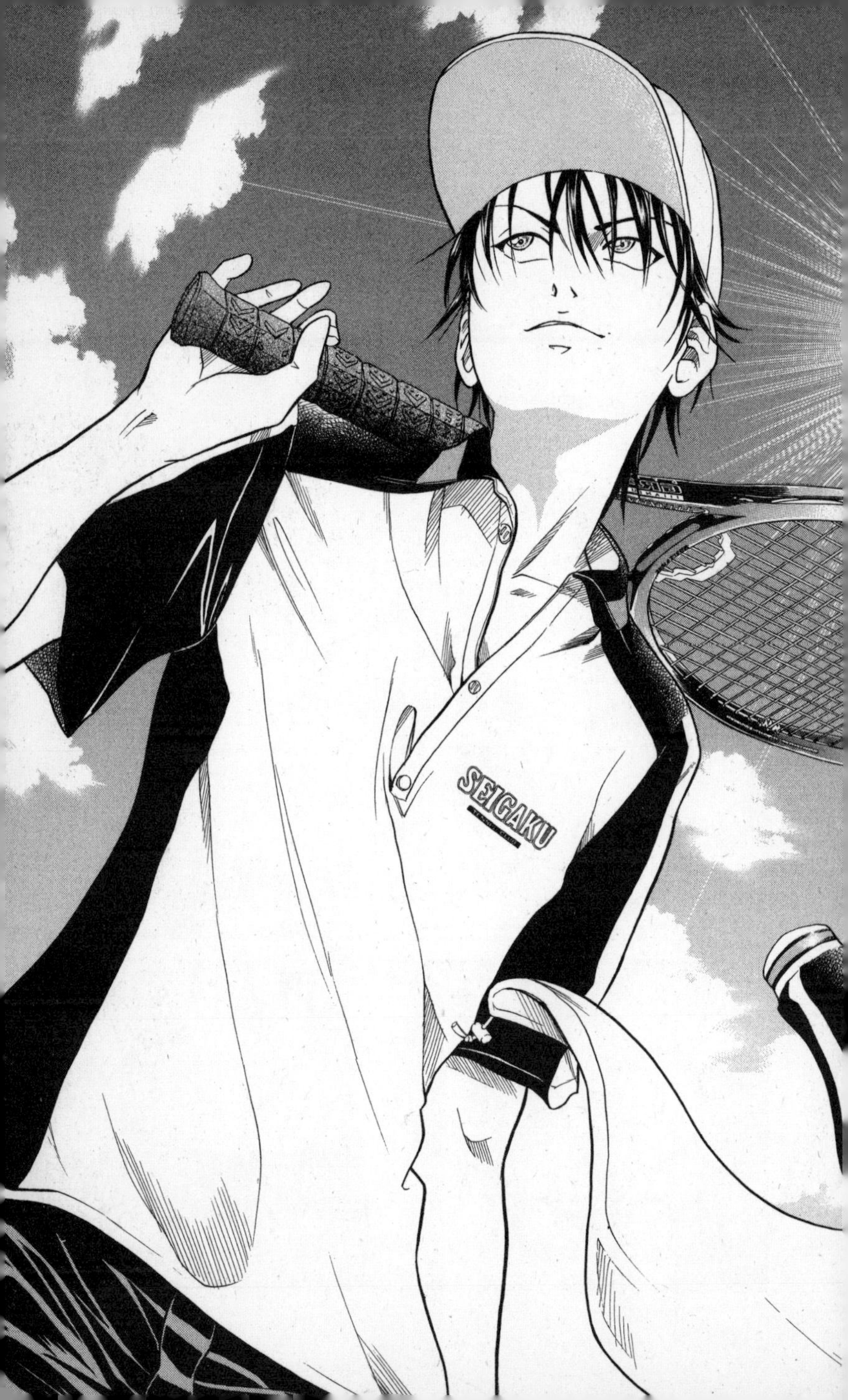
SEIGAKU

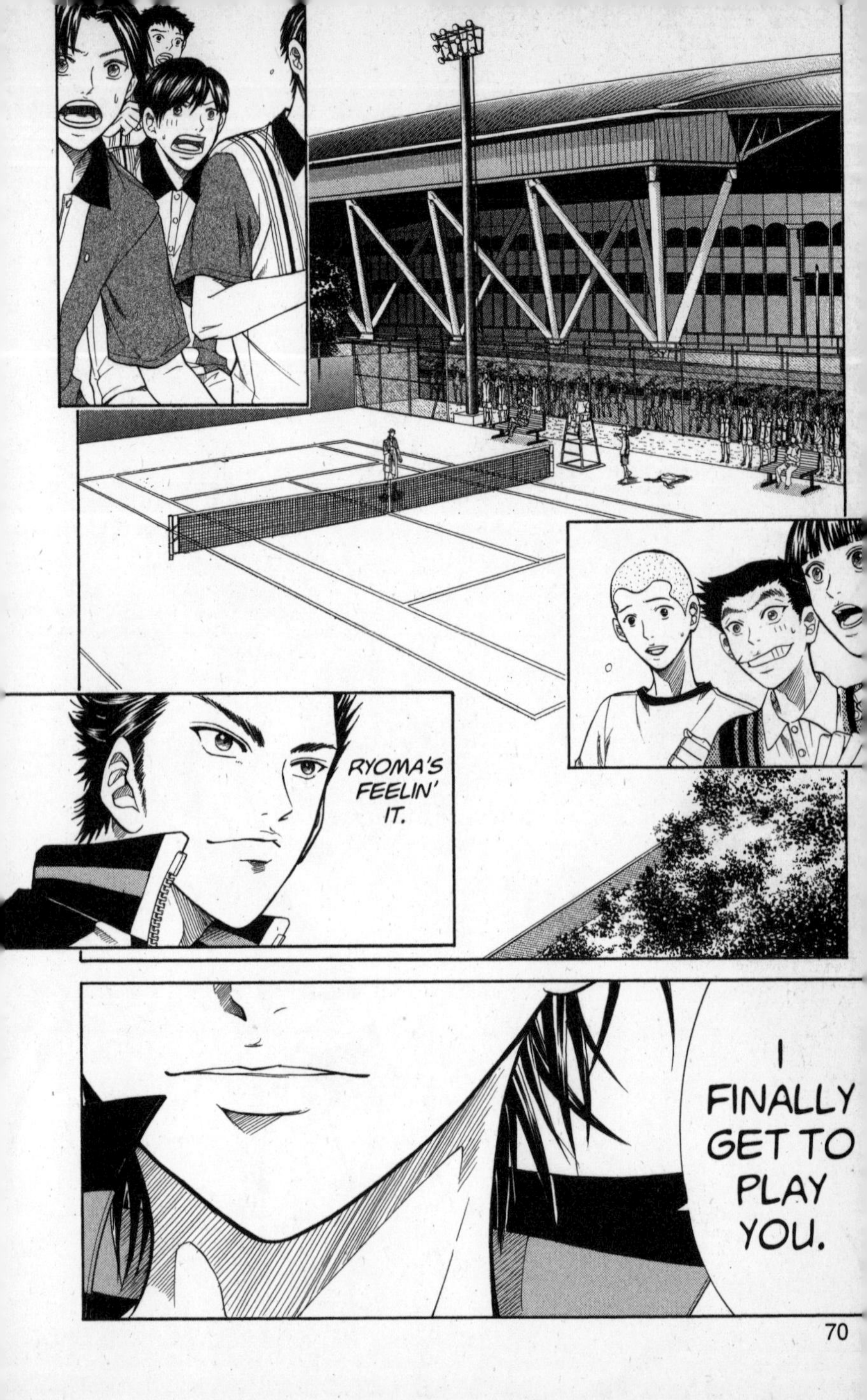
RYOMA'S FEELIN' IT.
I FINALLY GET TO PLAY YOU.

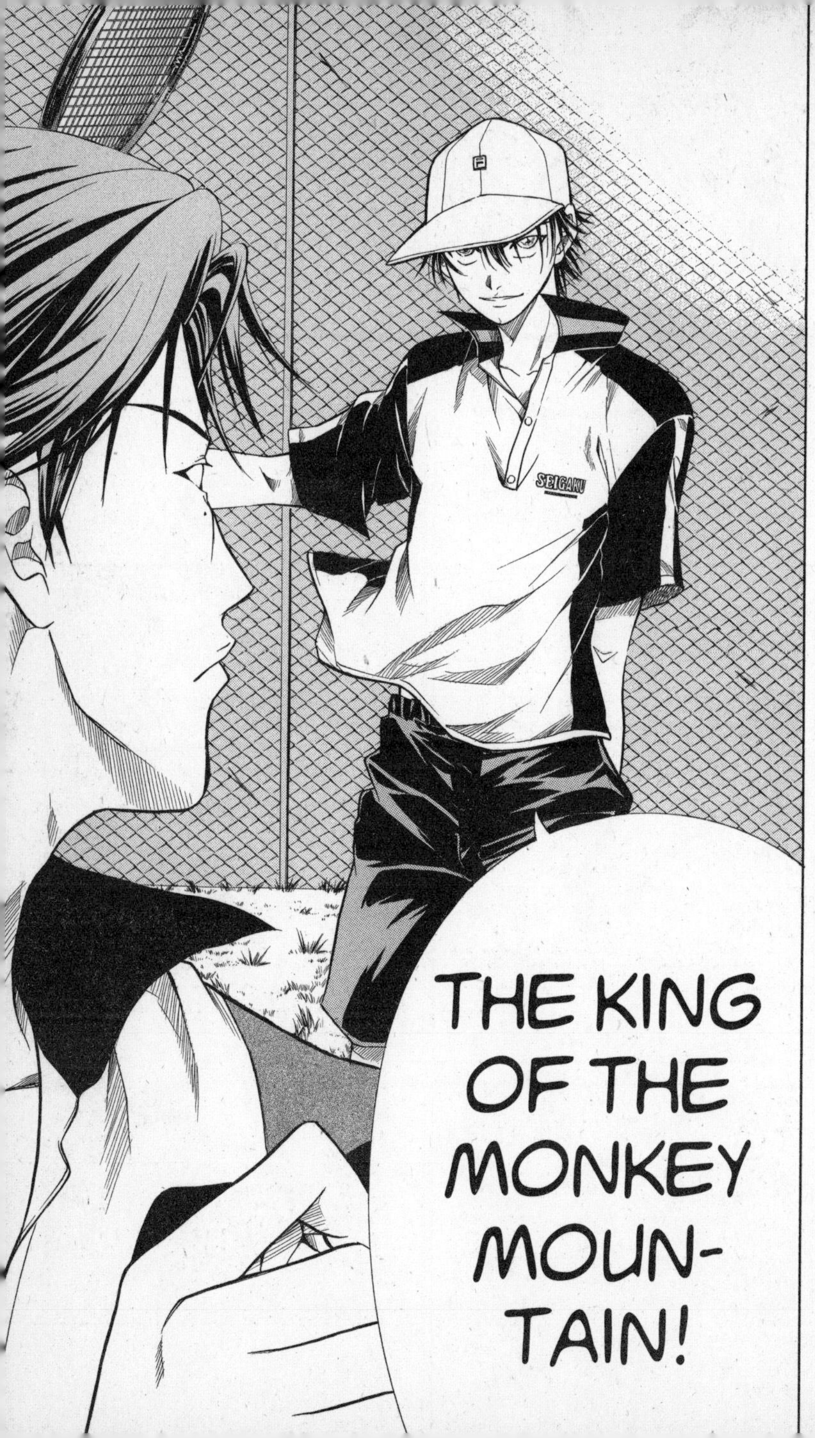
SEIGAKU
THE KING OF THE MONKEY MOUNTAIN!

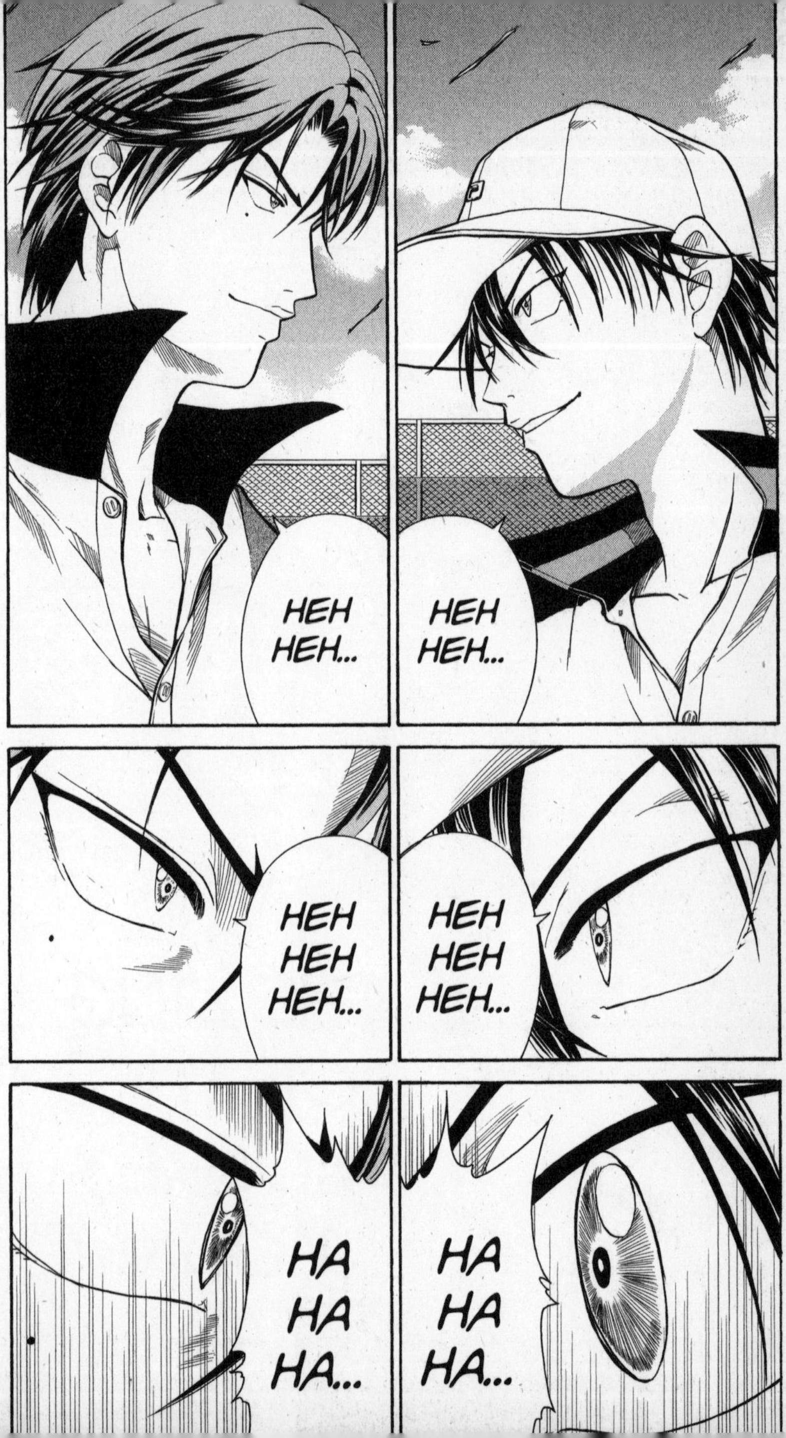
HEH HEH...
HEH HEH...
HEH HEH HEH...
HEH HEH HEH...
HA HA HA...
HA HA HA...

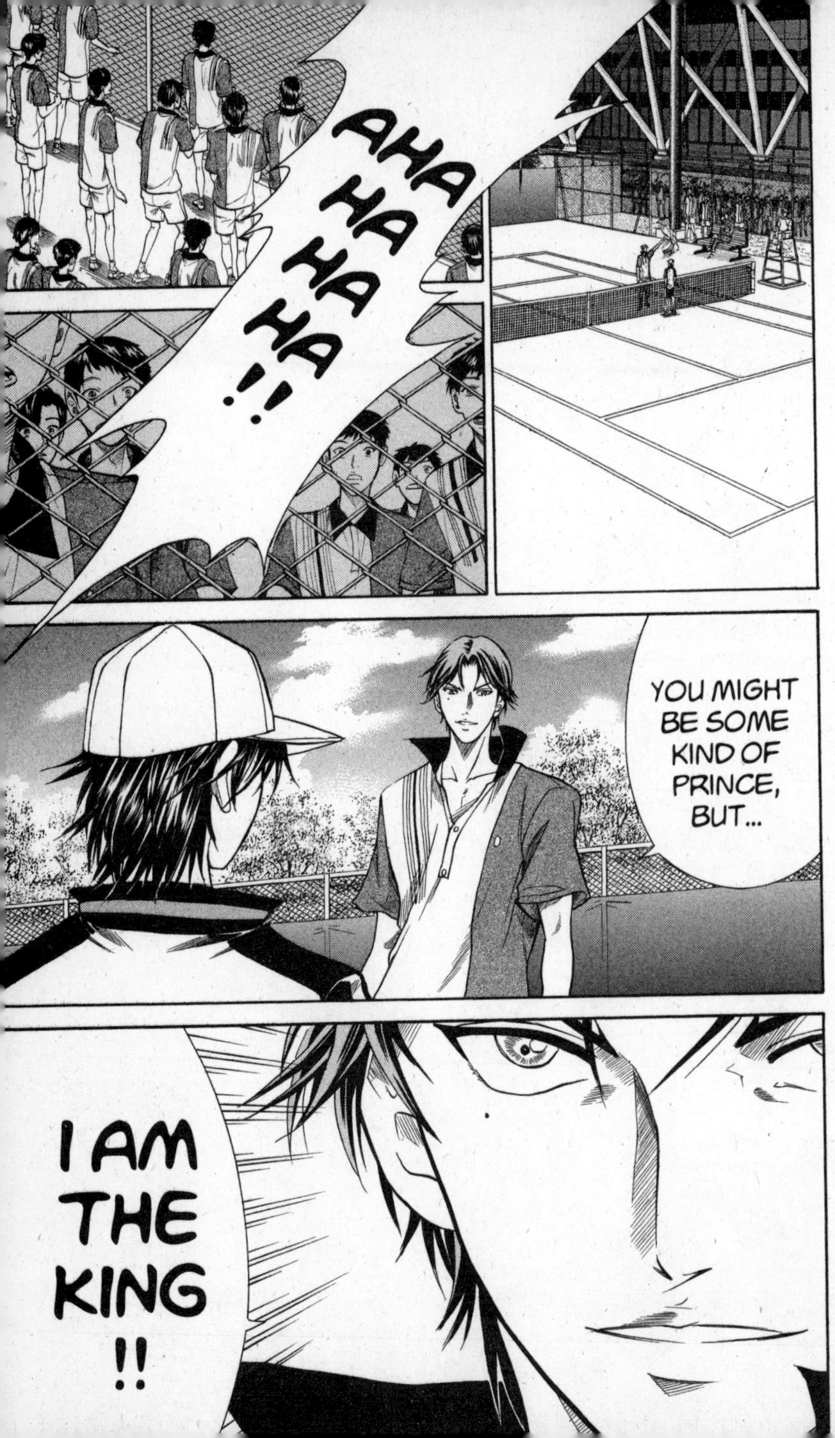
AHA HA HA HA!!
YOU MIGHT BE SOME KIND OF PRINCE, BUT...
I AM THE KING!!

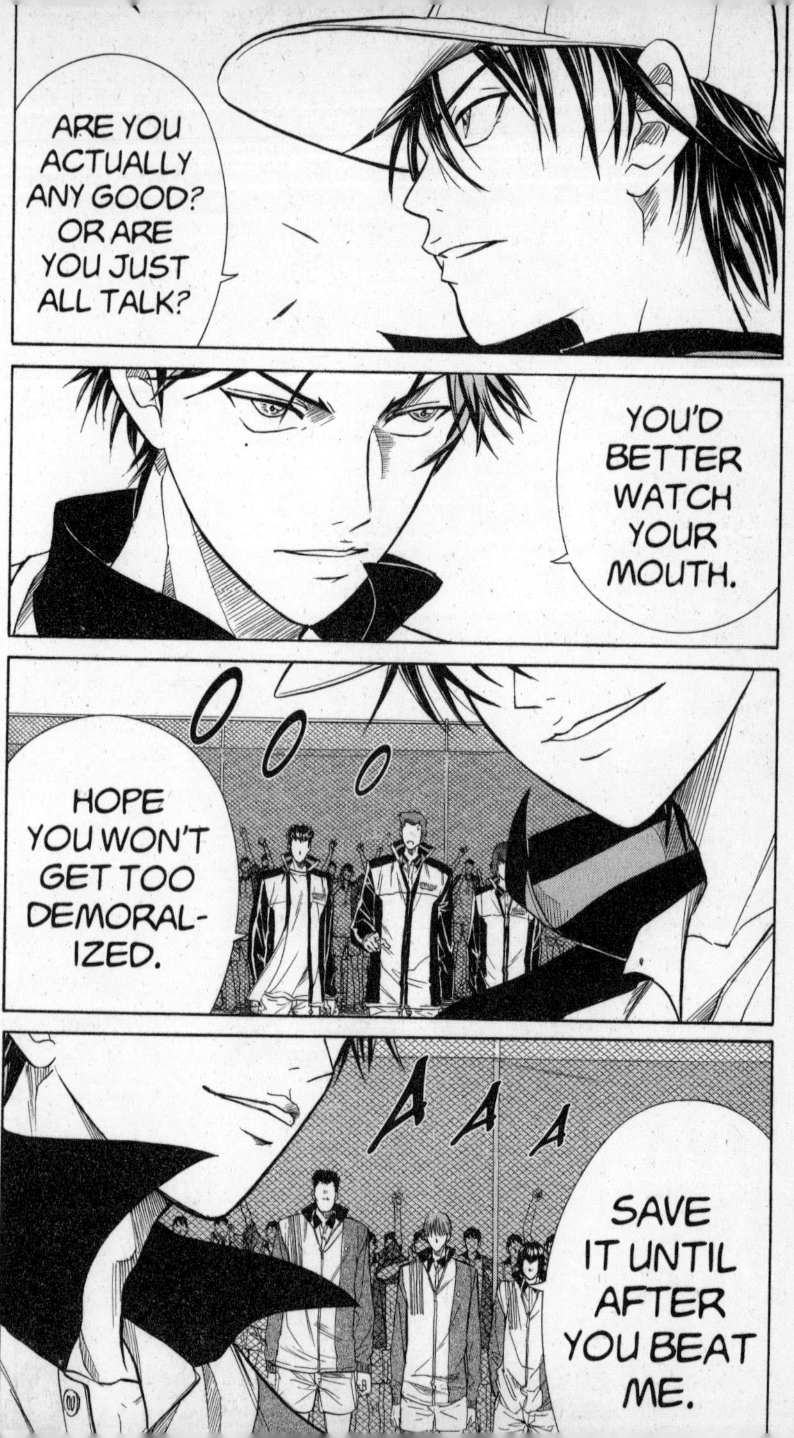
ARE YOU ACTUALLY ANY GOOD? OR ARE YOU JUST ALL TALK?
YOU'D BETTER WATCH YOUR MOUTH.
O O O
HOPE YOU WON'T GET TOO DEMORAL-IZED.
A A A
SAVE IT UNTIL AFTER YOU BEAT ME.

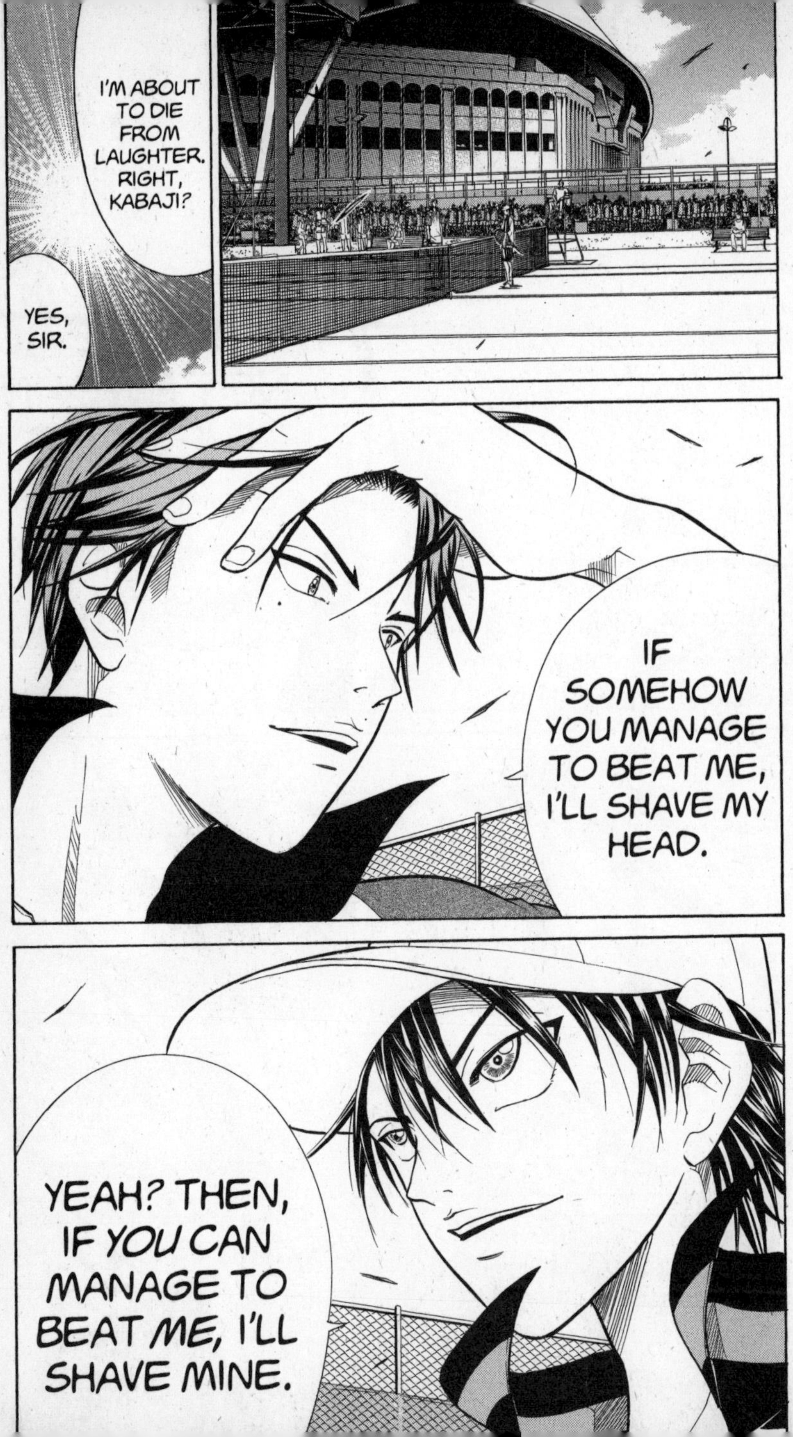
I'M ABOUT TO DIE FROM LAUGHTER. RIGHT, KABAJI?
YES, SIR.
IF SOMEHOW YOU MANAGE TO BEAT ME, I'LL SHAVE MY HEAD.
YEAH? THEN, IF *YOU* CAN MANAGE TO BEAT *ME*, I'LL SHAVE MINE.

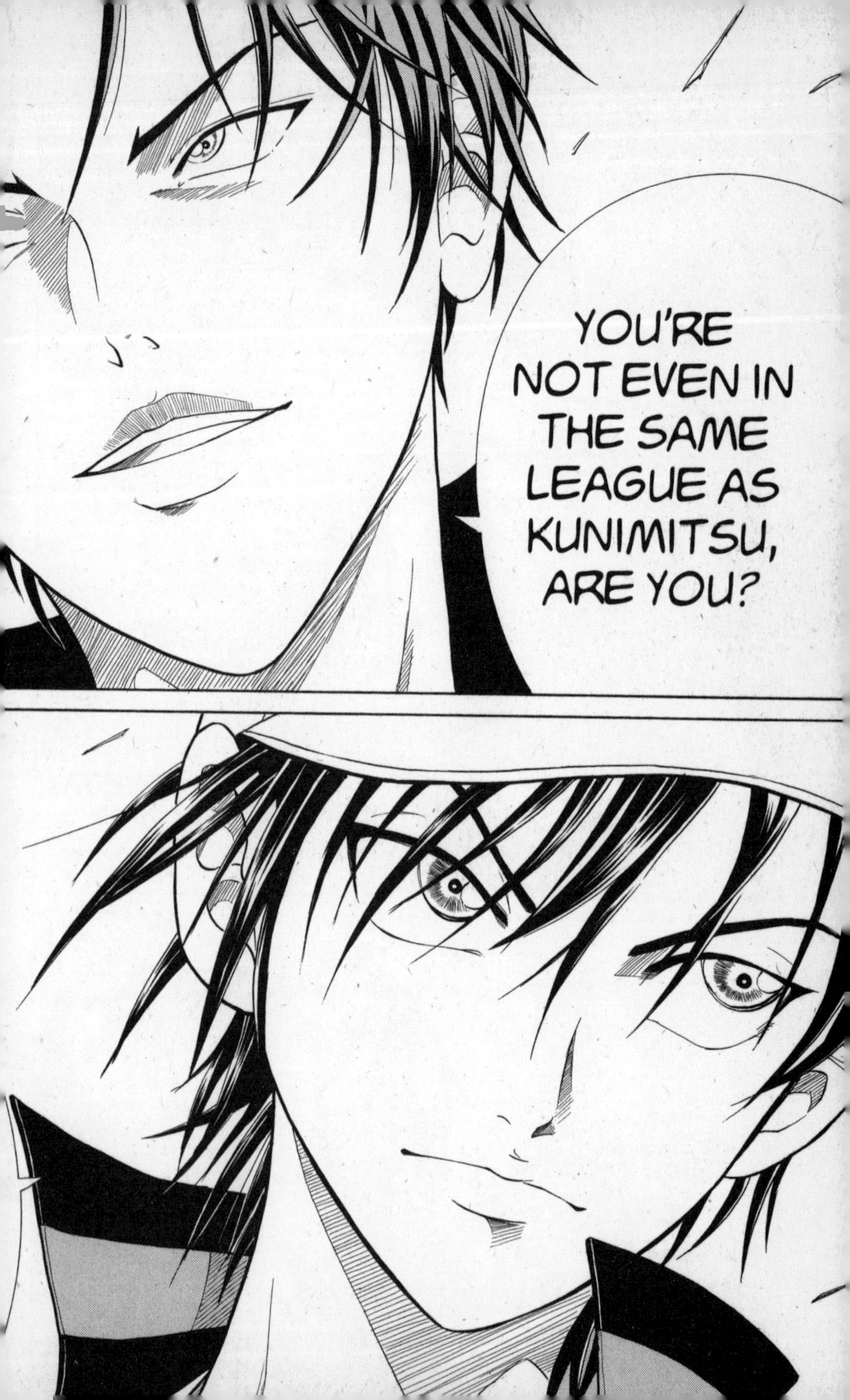
YOU'RE NOT EVEN IN THE SAME LEAGUE AS KUNIMITSU, ARE YOU?

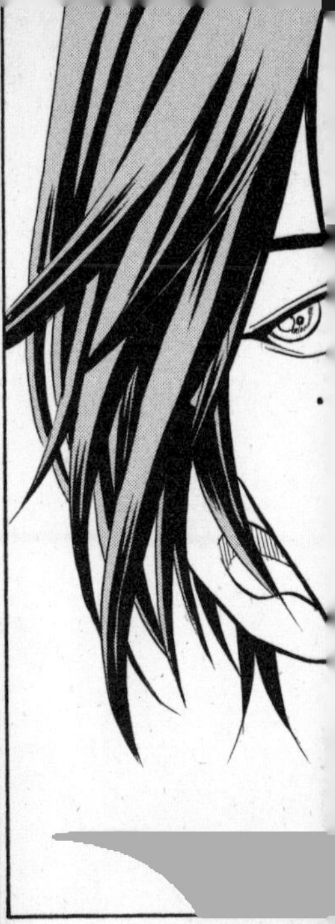
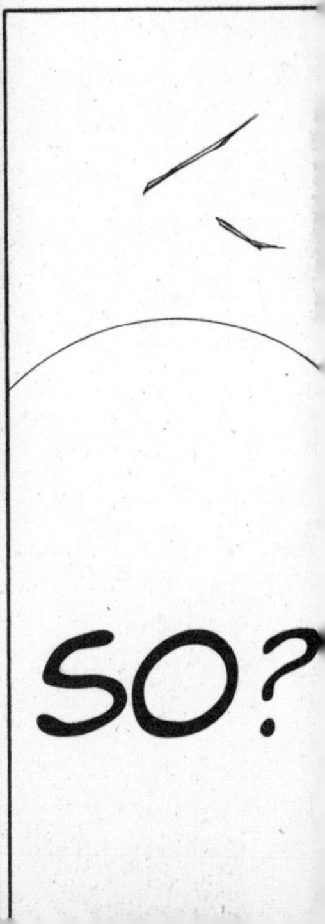
SO?
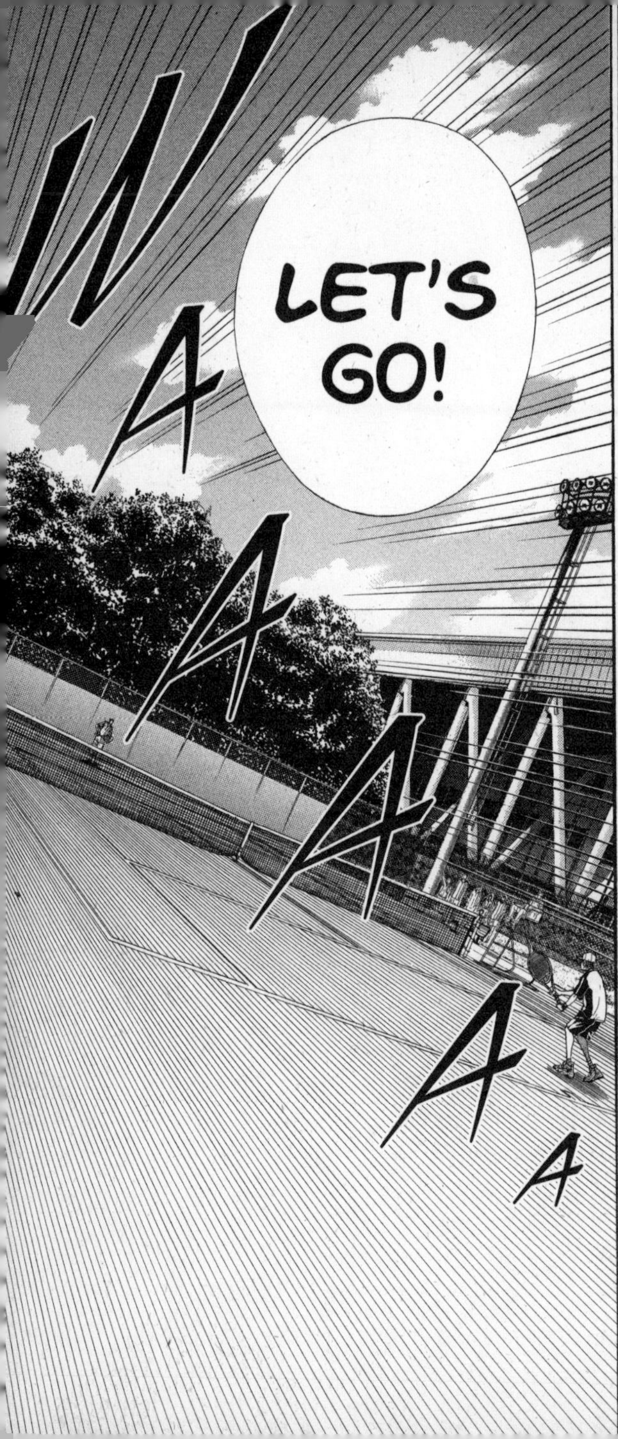
LET'S GO!
WAAAAA

テニスの王子様

THE PRINCE OF TENNIS

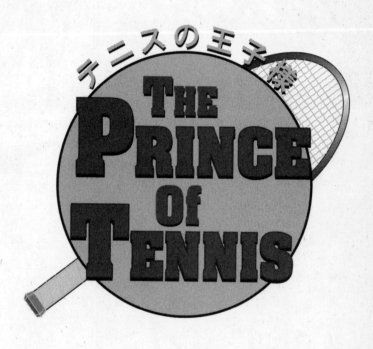

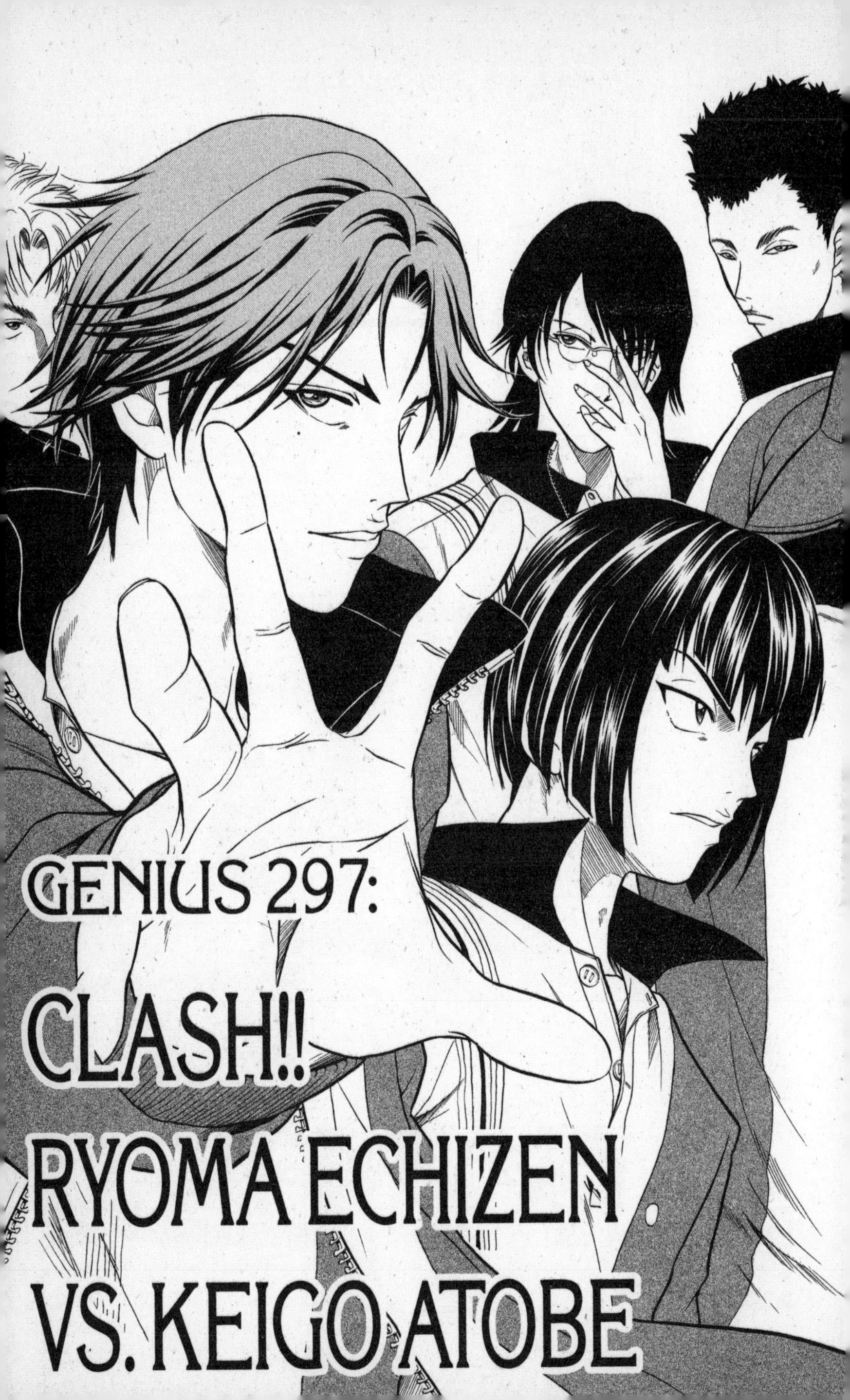
GENIUS 297:
CLASH!! RYOMA ECHIZEN VS. KEIGO ATOBE

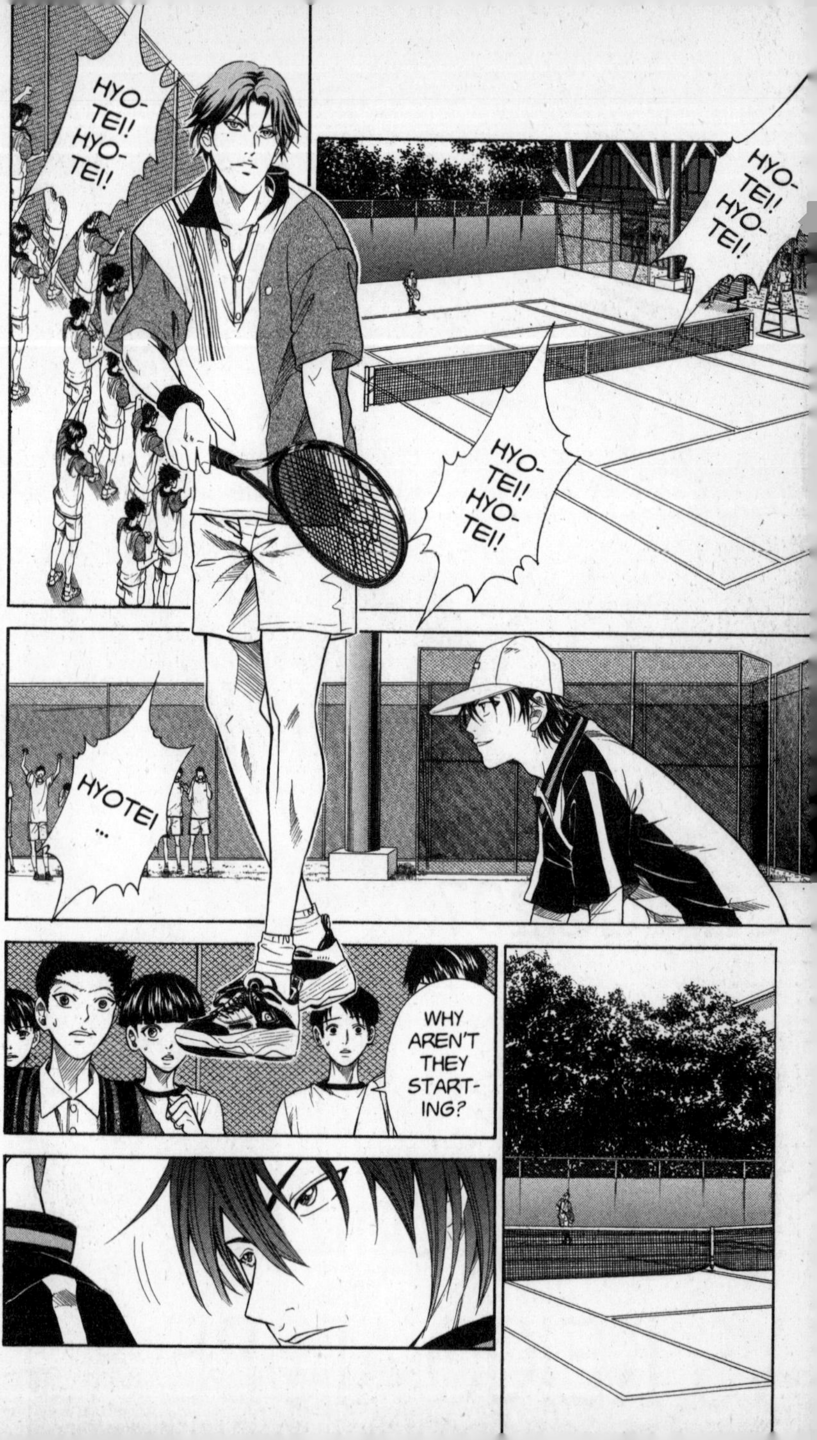
HYO-TEI! HYO-TEI!
HYO-TEI! HYO-TEI!
HYO-TEI! HYO-TEI!
HYOTEI ...
WHY AREN'T THEY START-ING?

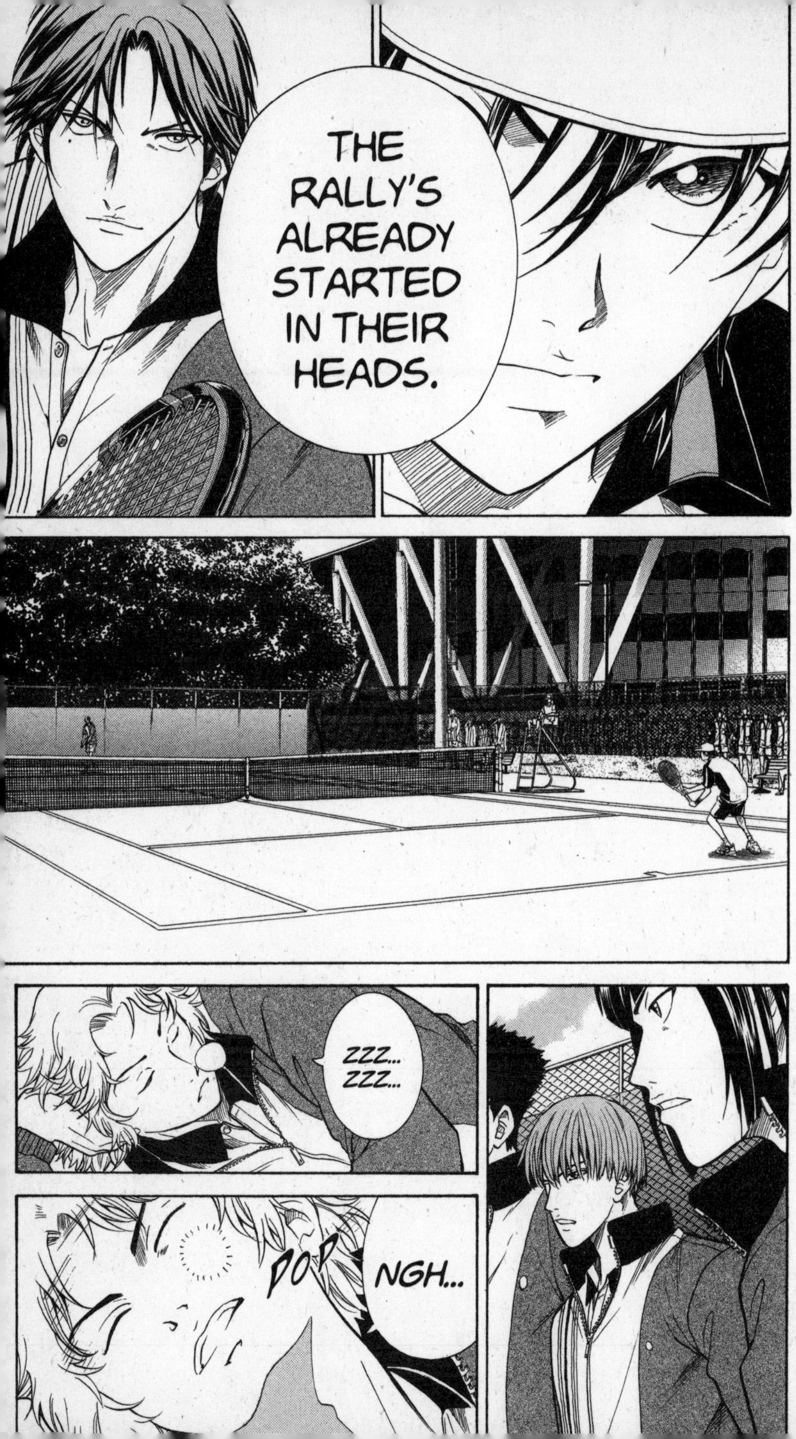
THE RALLY'S ALREADY STARTED IN THEIR HEADS.
ZZZ... ZZZ...
POP
NGH...

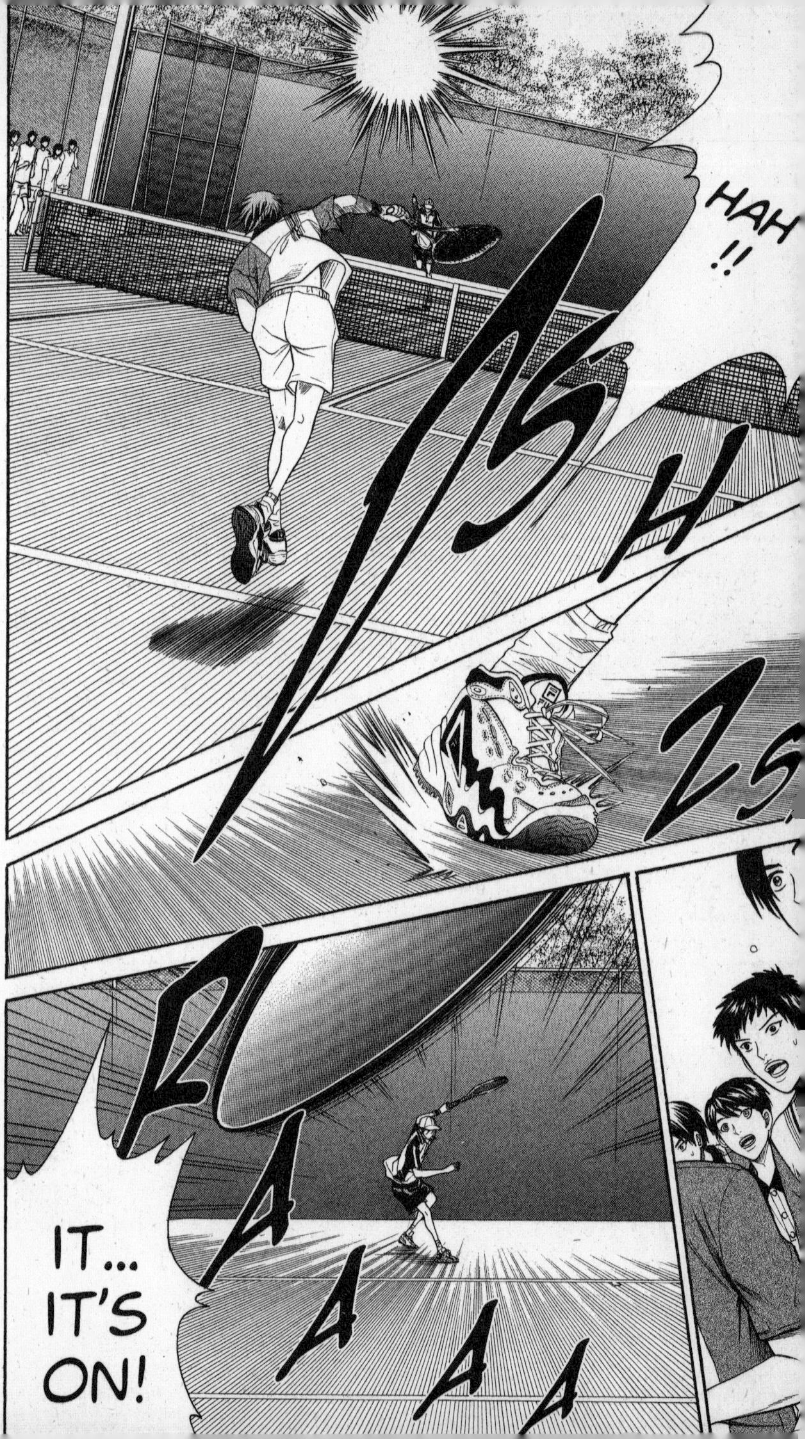
HAH !!
WHSH
ZS...
IT... IT'S ON!
BWAAAAA

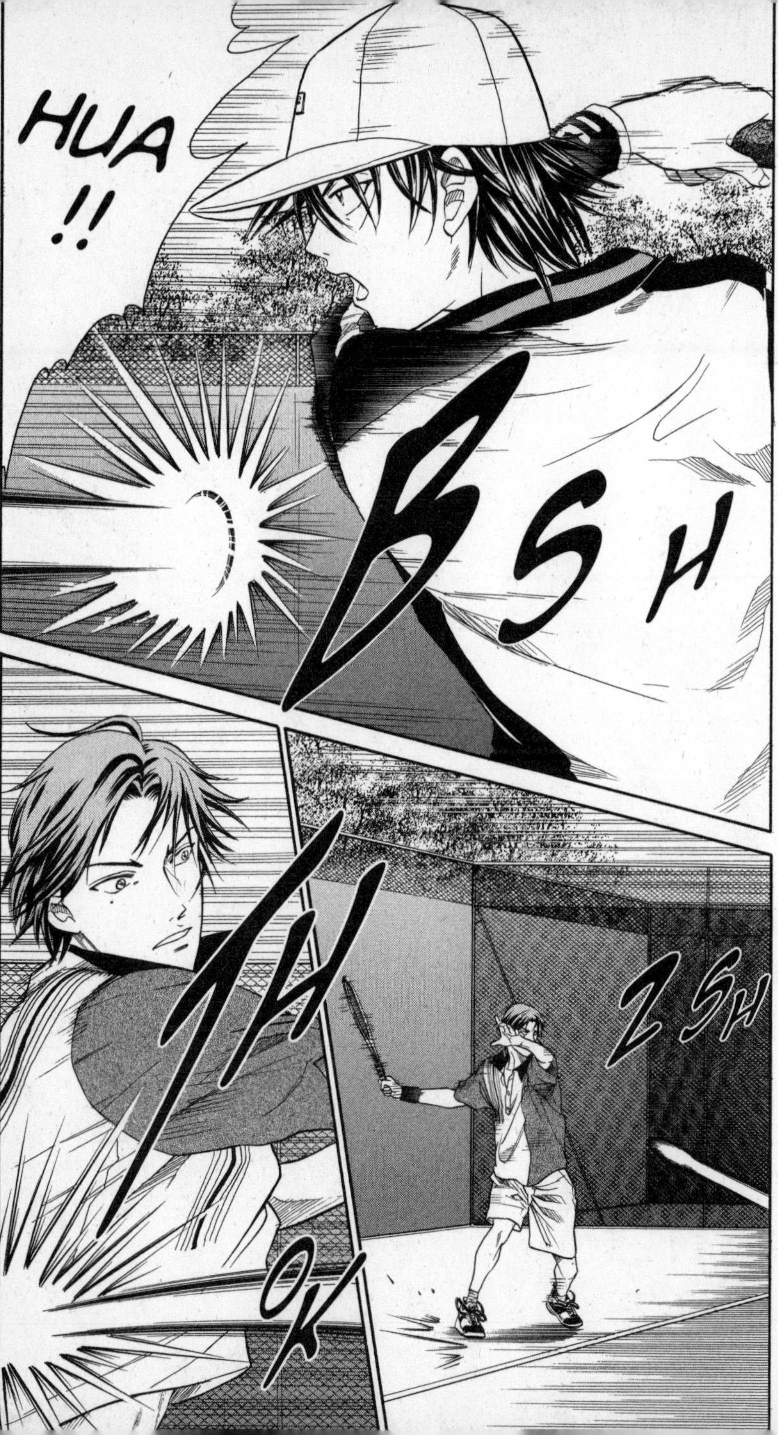
HUA!!
BSH
ZSH

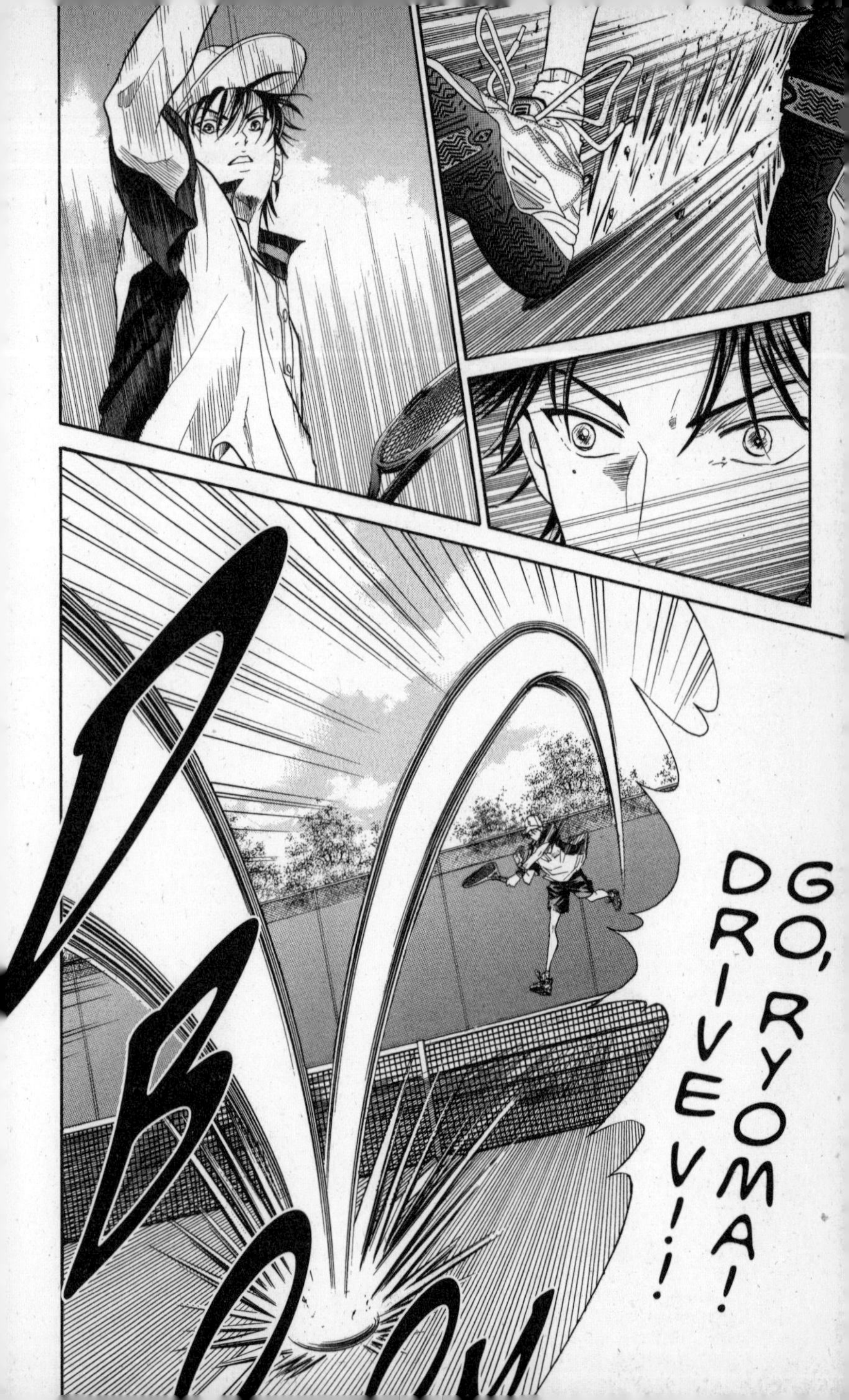
GO, RYOMA!
DRIVE V!!

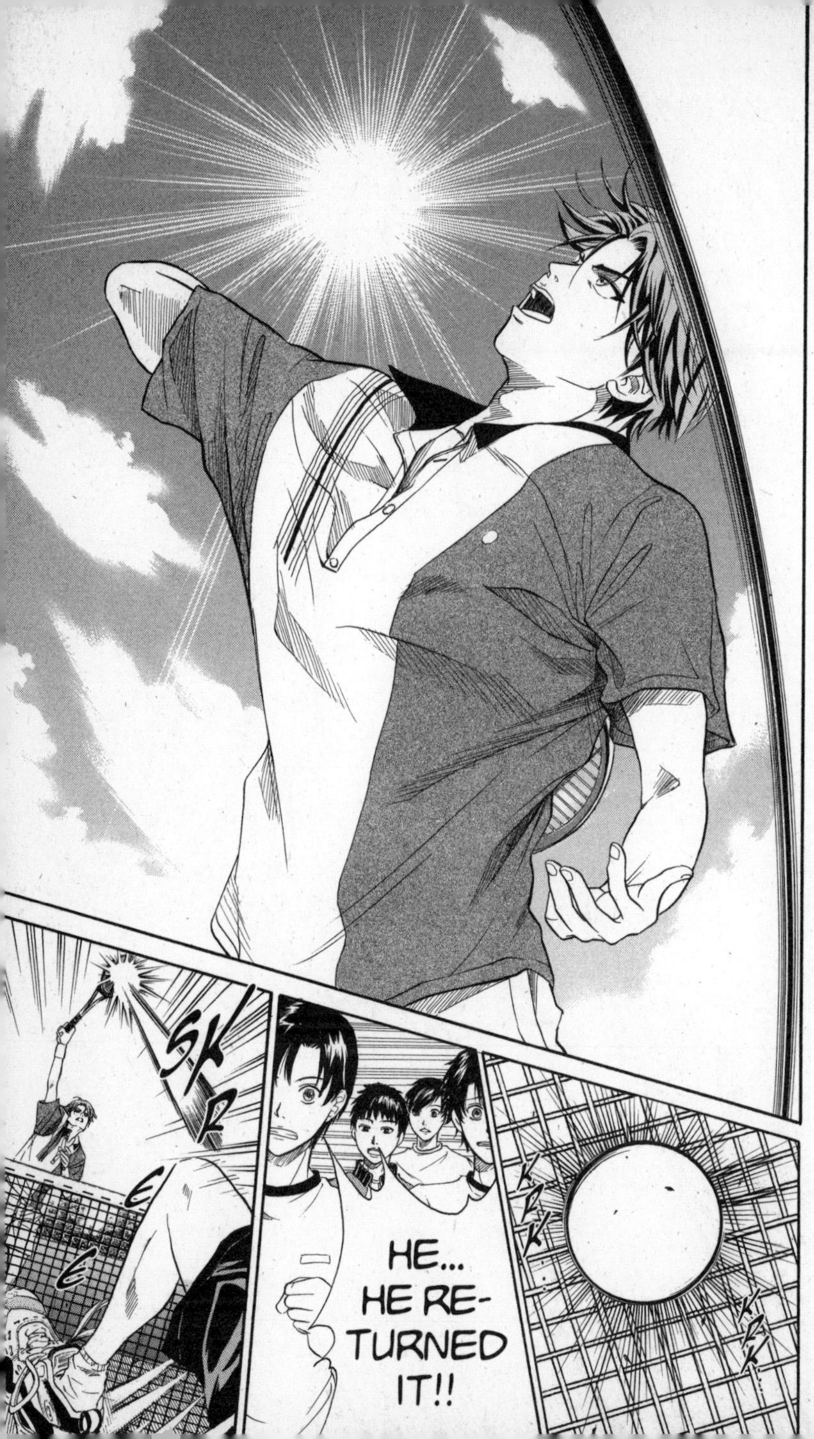
KRK
KRK...
HE... HE RE-TURNED IT!!
SKREE

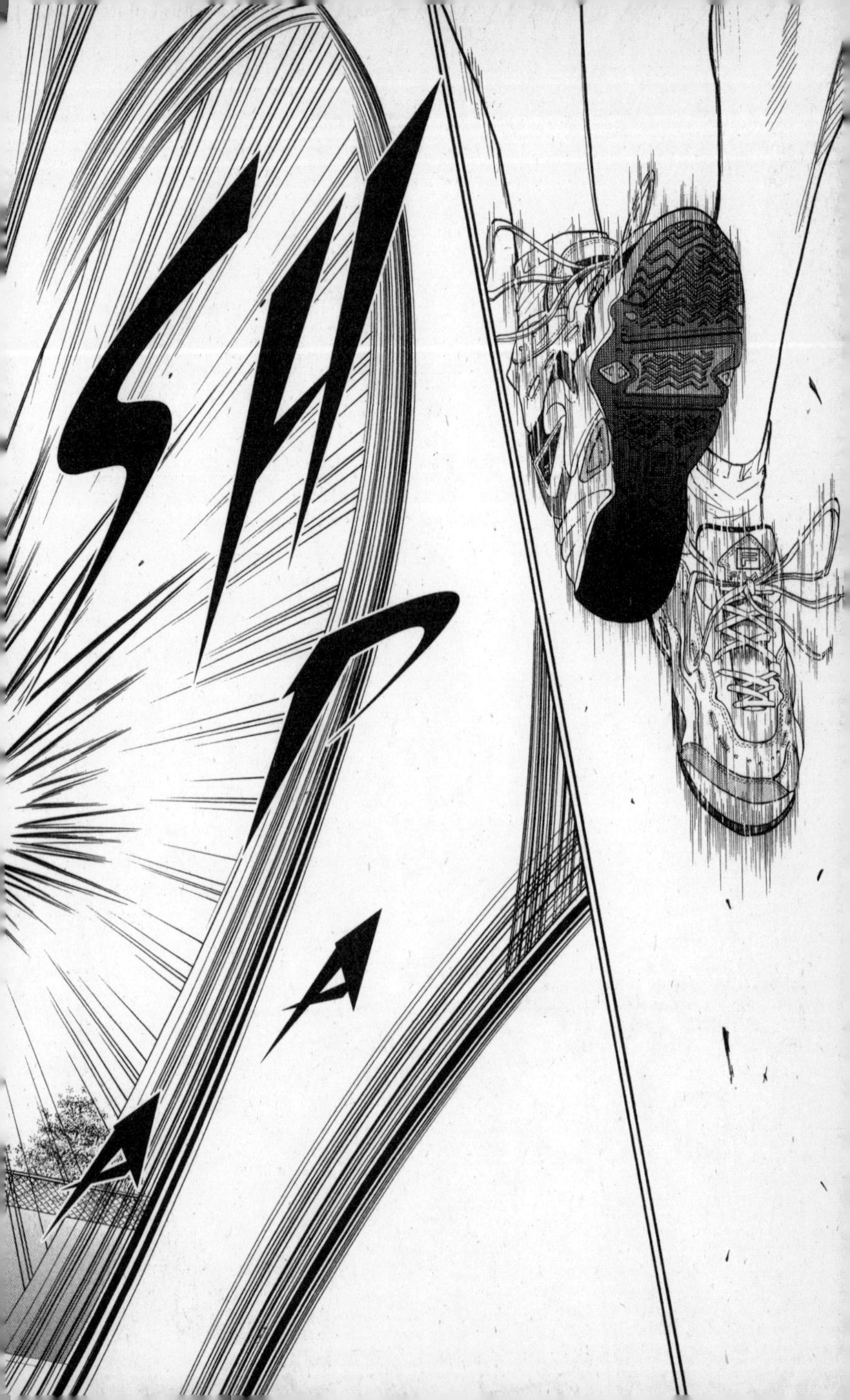

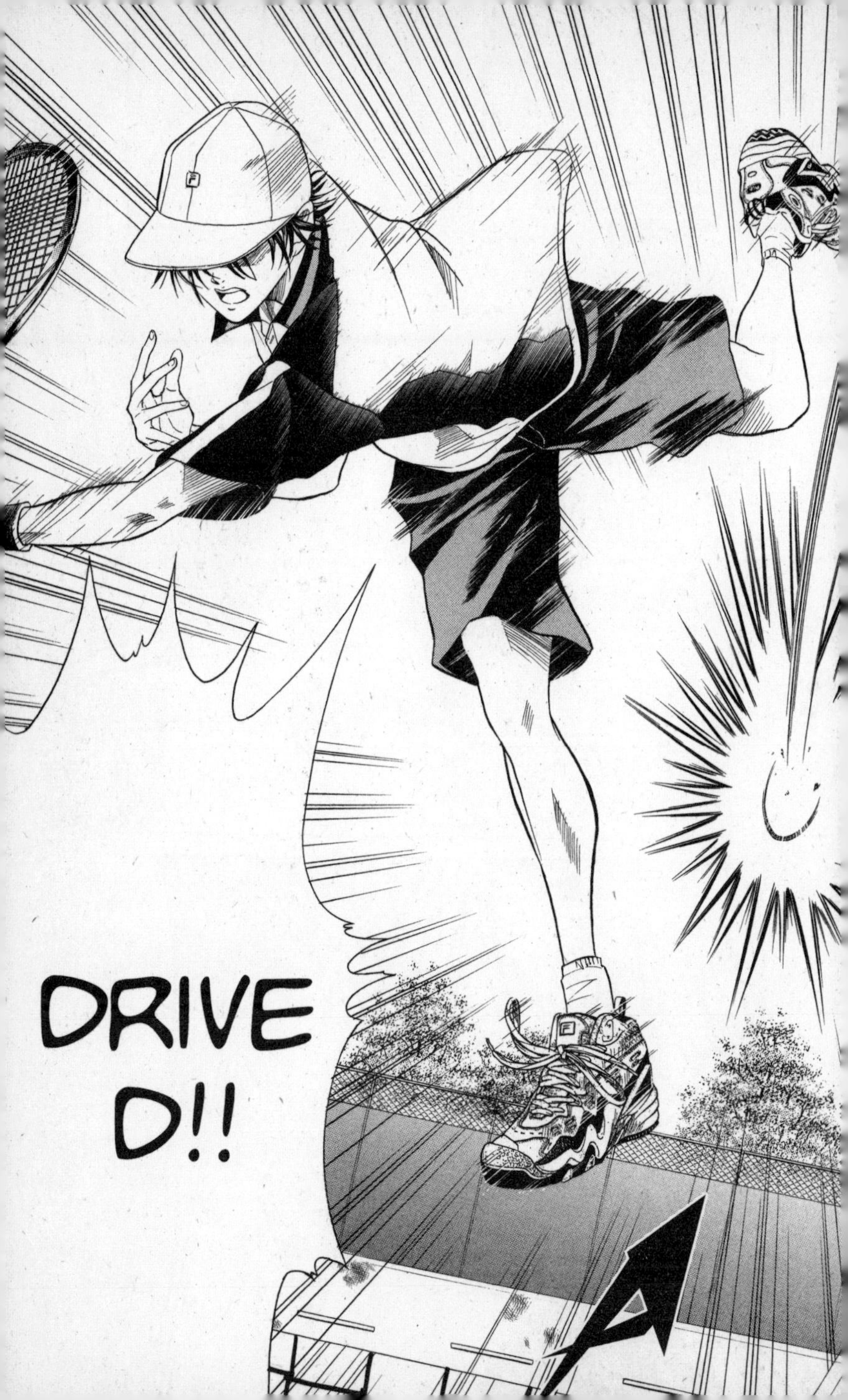
DRIVE D!!

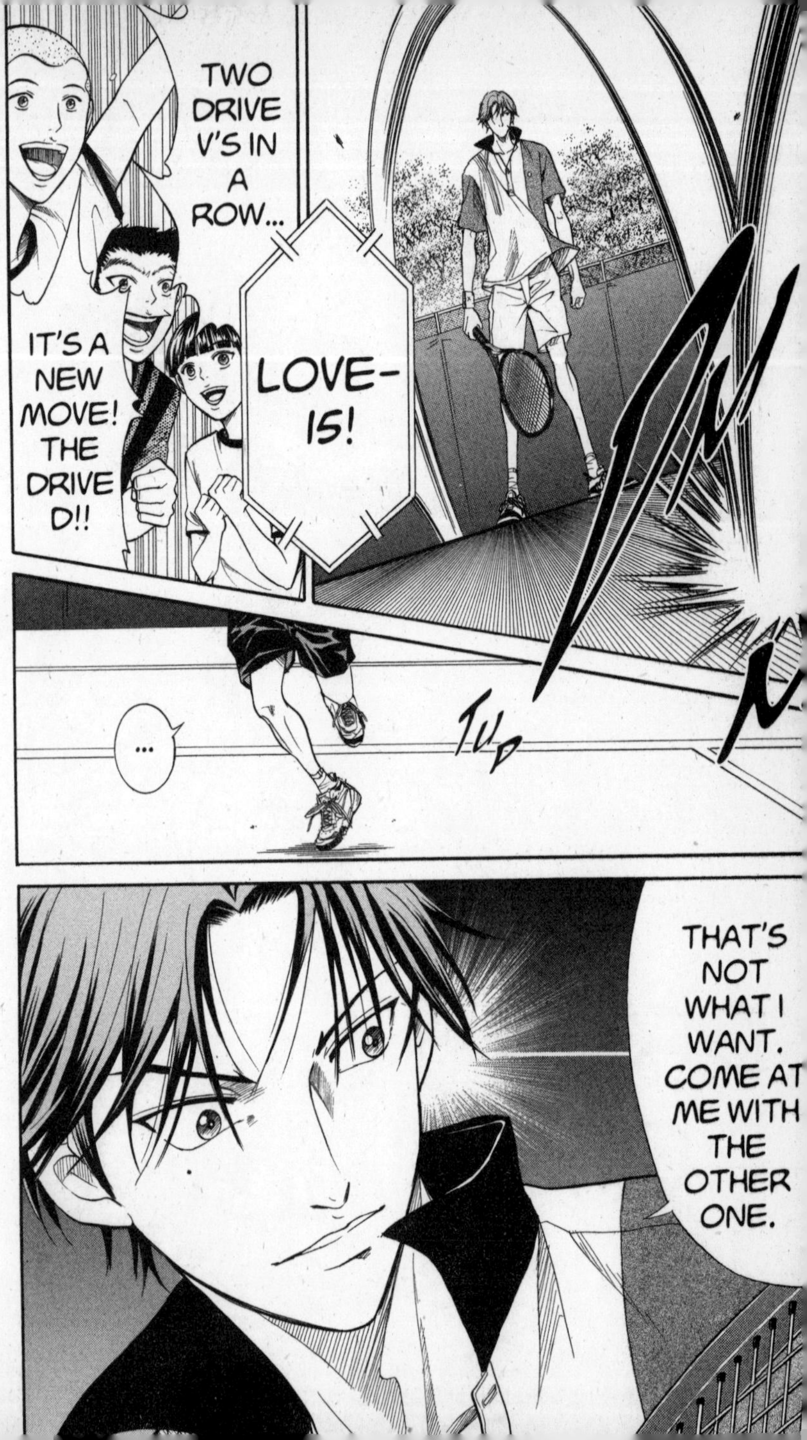
LOVE-15!
TWO DRIVE V'S IN A ROW...
IT'S A NEW MOVE! THE DRIVE D!!
TUD
...
THAT'S NOT WHAT I WANT. COME AT ME WITH THE OTHER ONE.

READ THIS WAY

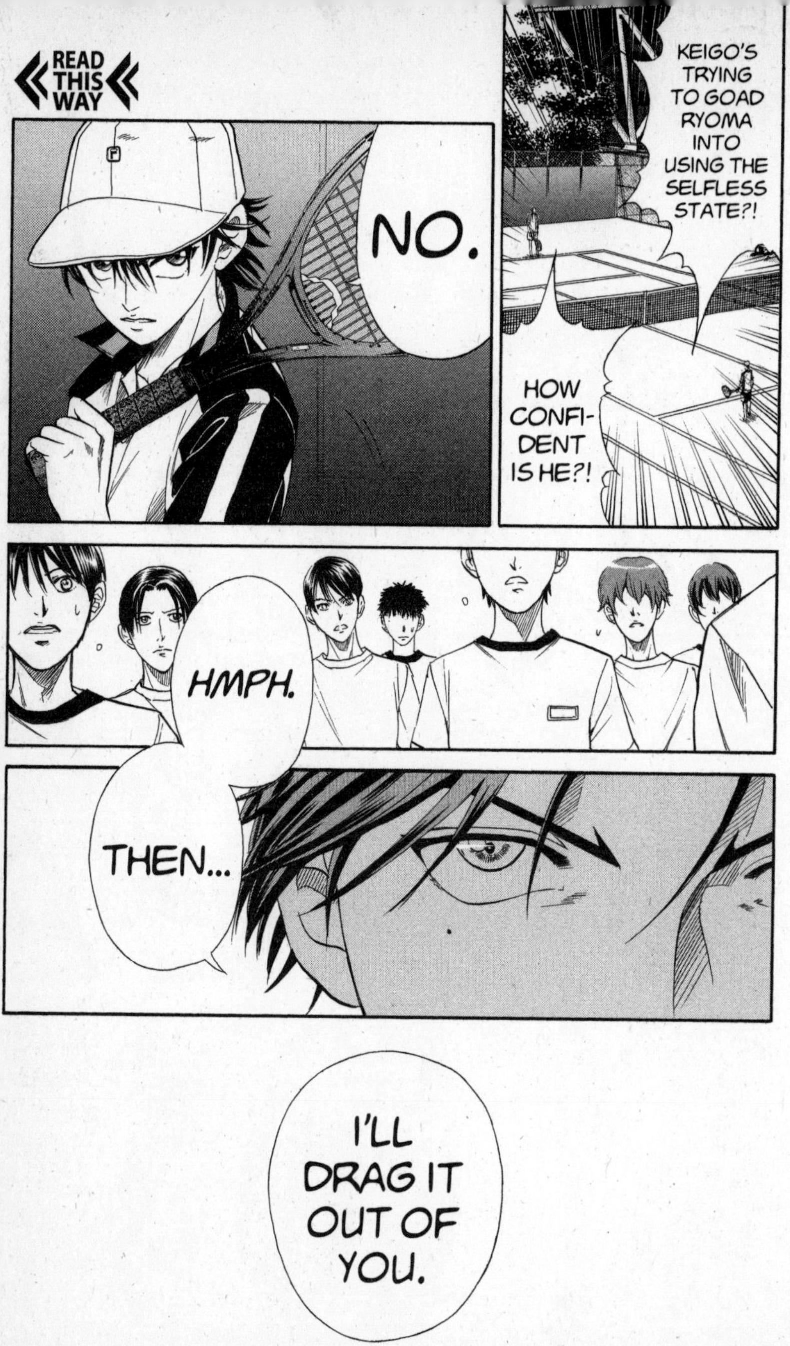
KEIGO'S TRYING TO GOAD RYOMA INTO USING THE SELFLESS STATE?!
HOW CONFI-DENT IS HE?!
NO.
HMPH.
THEN...
I'LL DRAG IT OUT OF YOU.

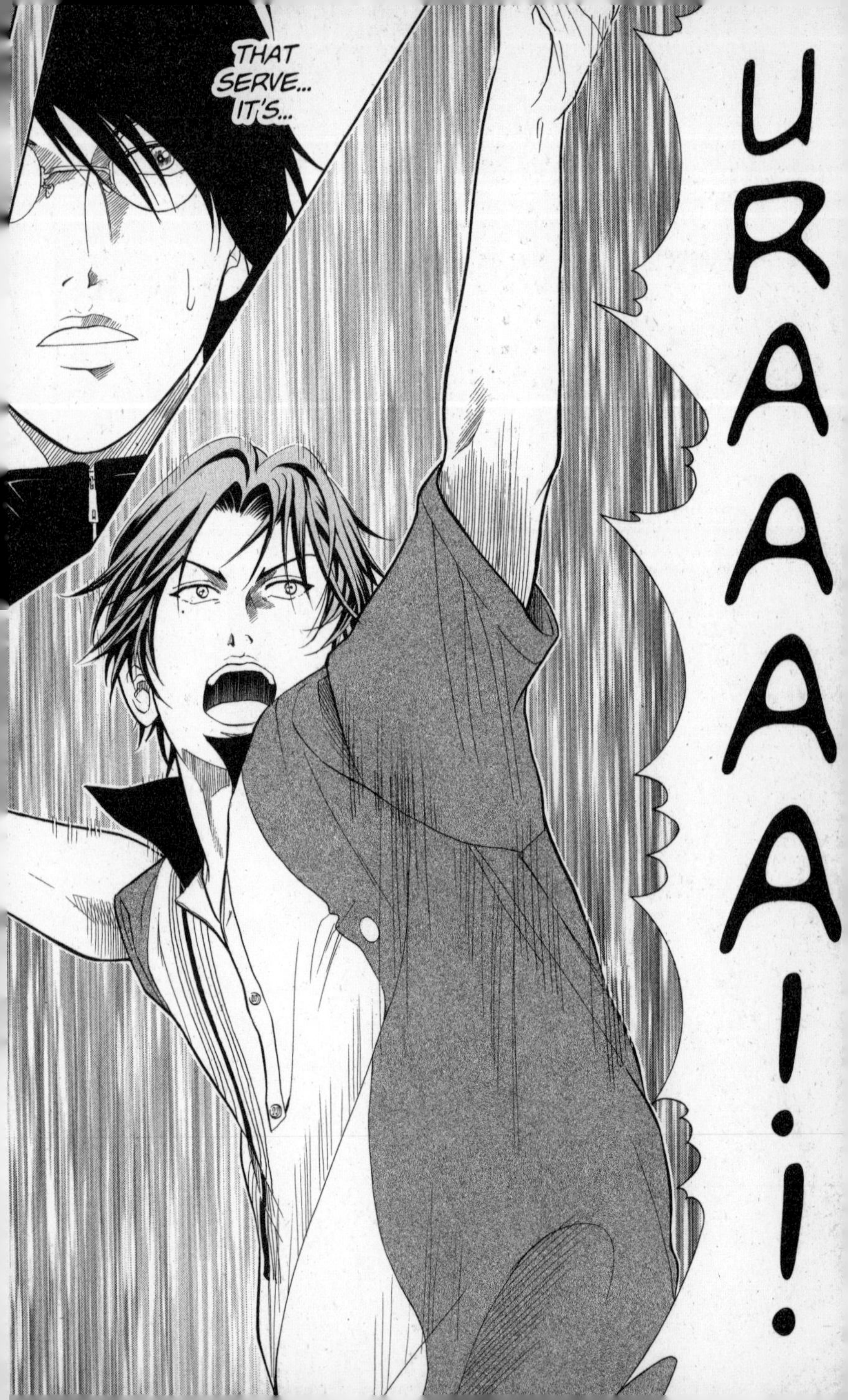
THAT SERVE... IT'S...
URAAAAI!

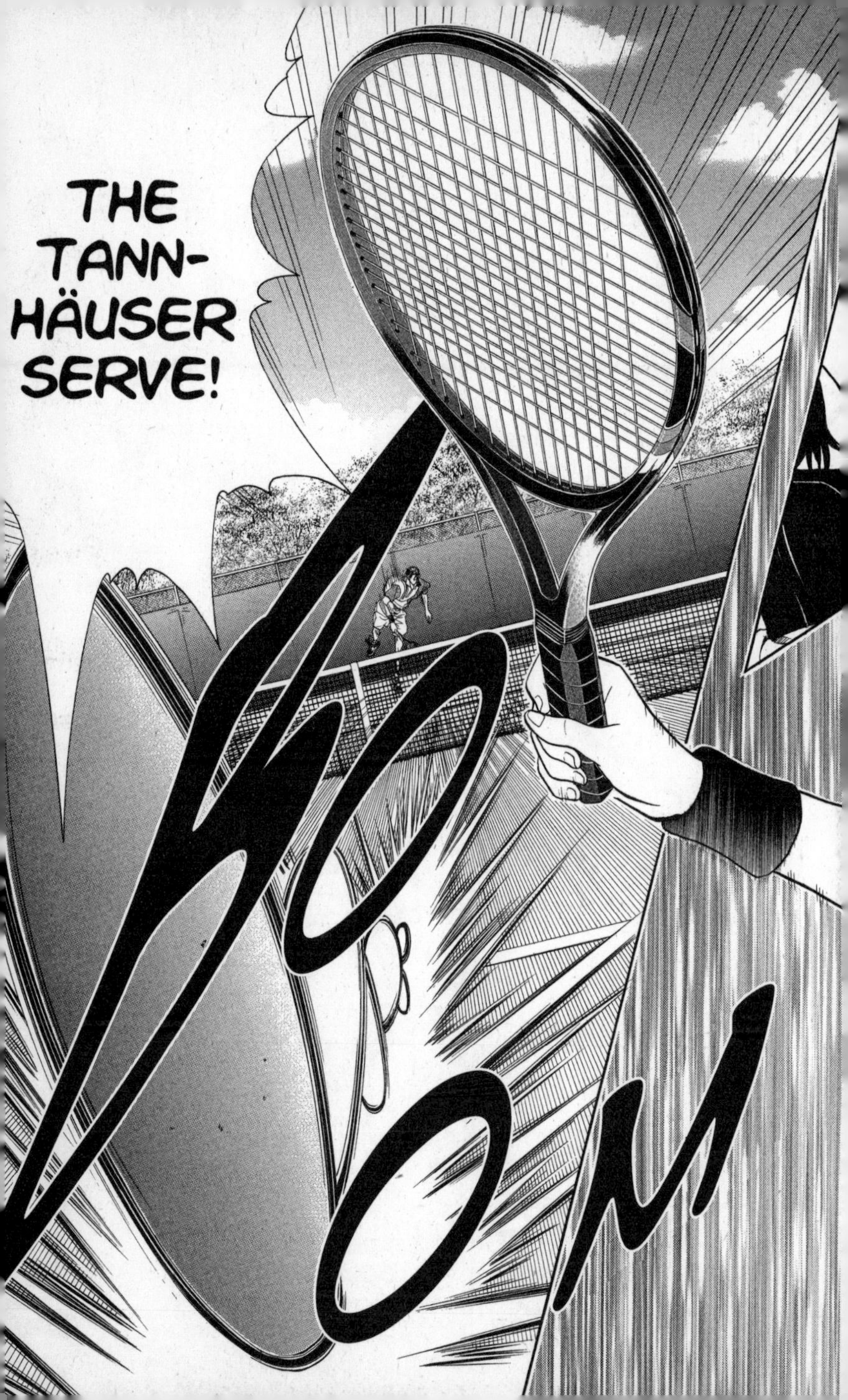
THE TANN-HÄUSER SERVE!
BOOM

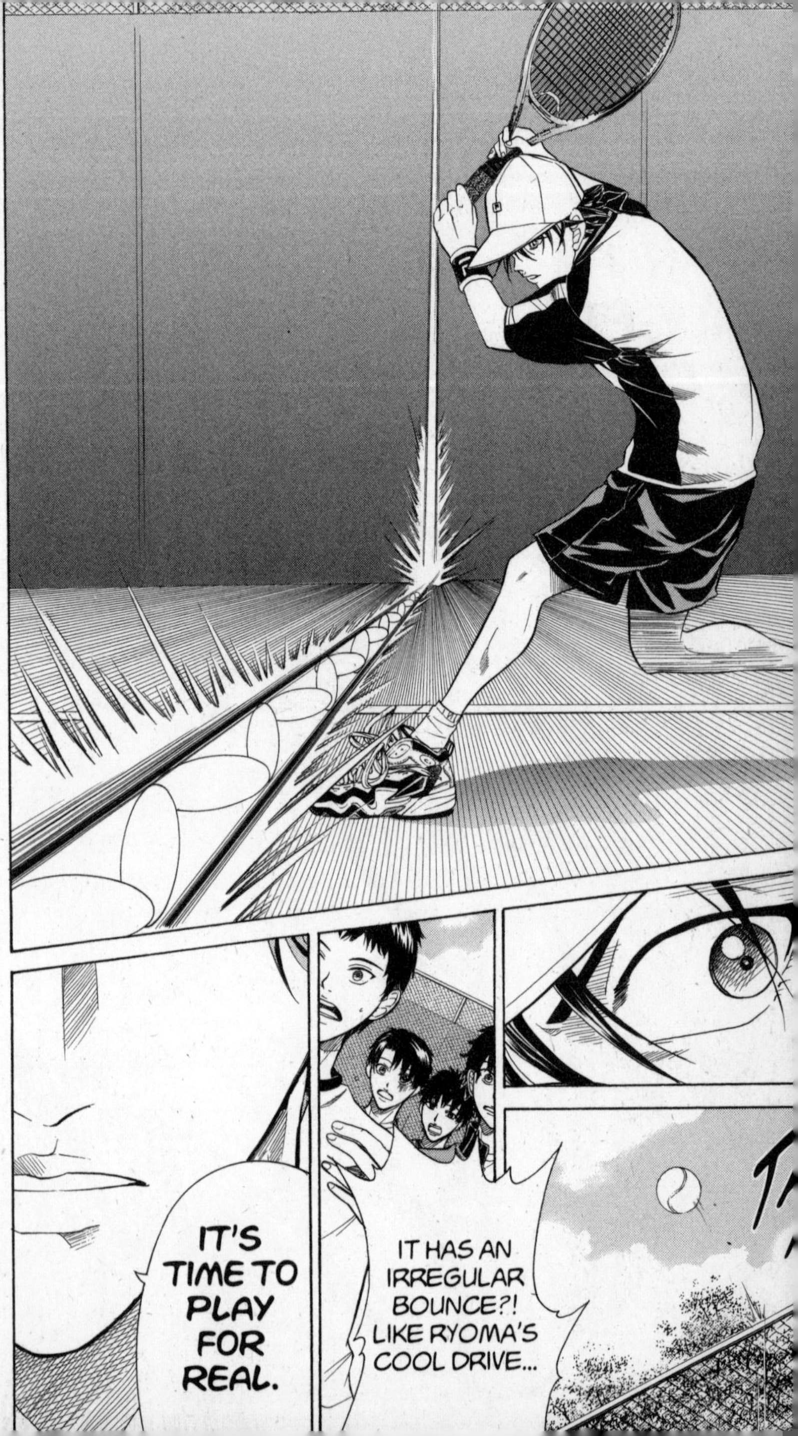
IT HAS AN IRREGULAR BOUNCE?! LIKE RYOMA'S COOL DRIVE...
IT'S TIME TO PLAY FOR REAL.

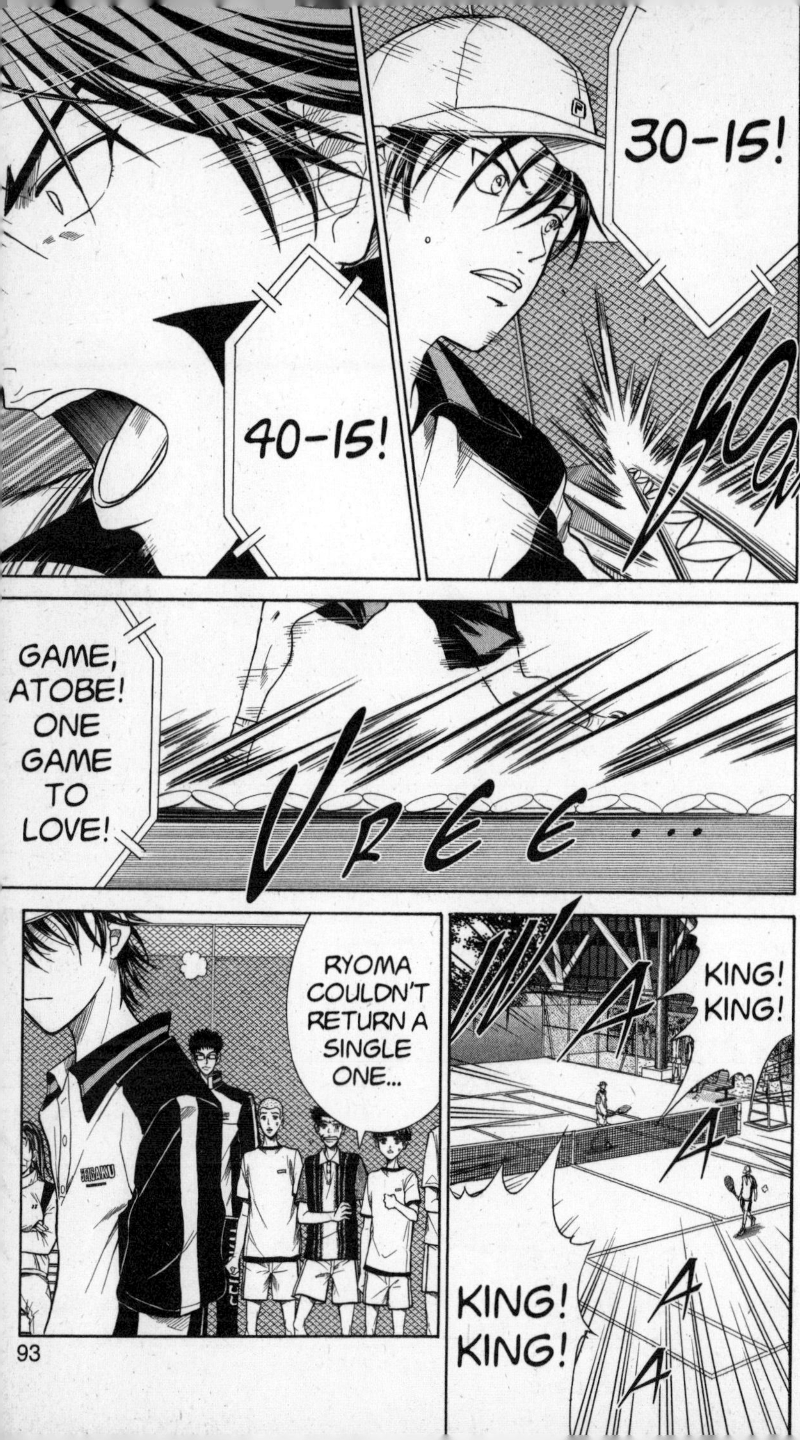
30-15!
40-15!
GAME, ATOBE! ONE GAME TO LOVE!
VREE...
KING! KING!
KING! KING!
RYOMA COULDN'T RETURN A SINGLE ONE...

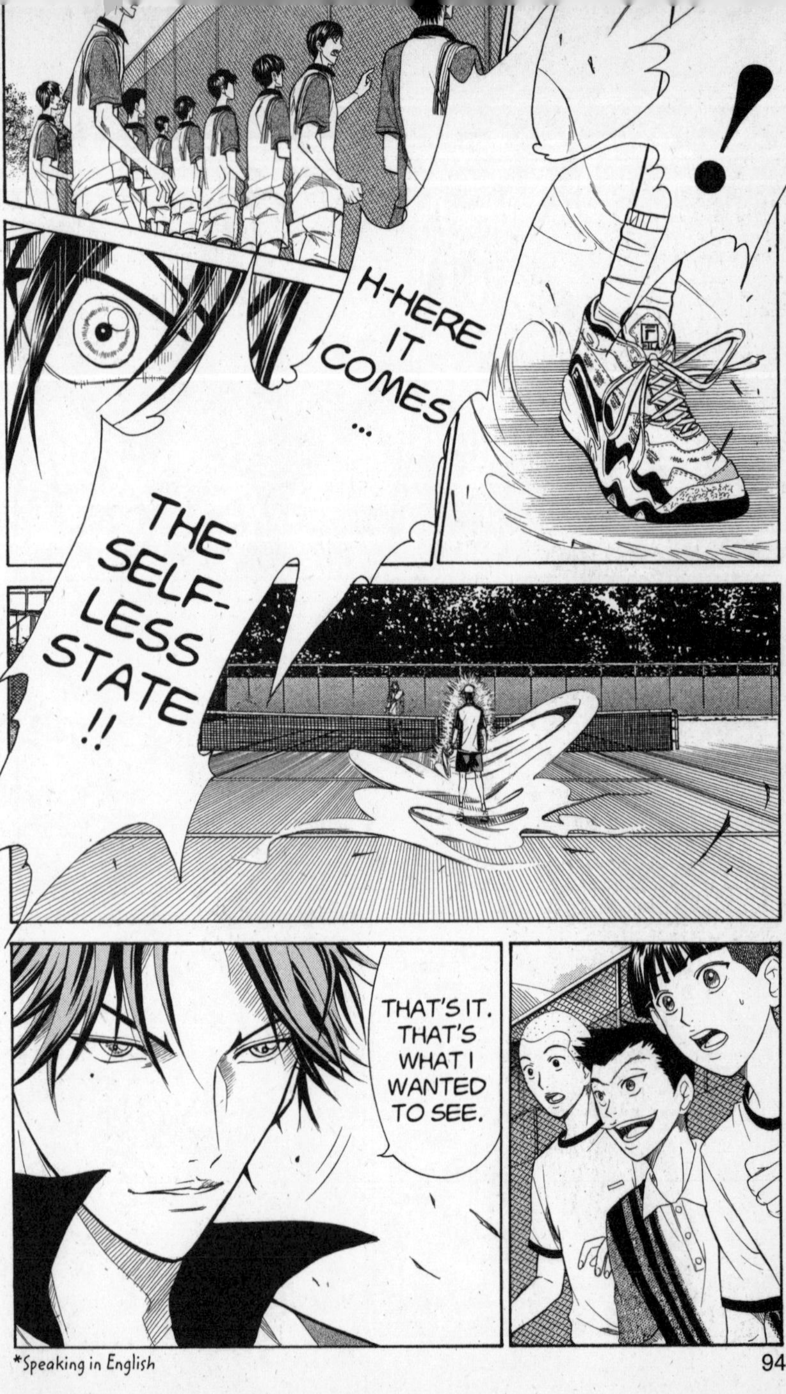
!
H-HERE IT COMES...
THE SELF-LESS STATE!!
THAT'S IT. THAT'S WHAT I WANTED TO SEE.
*Speaking in English

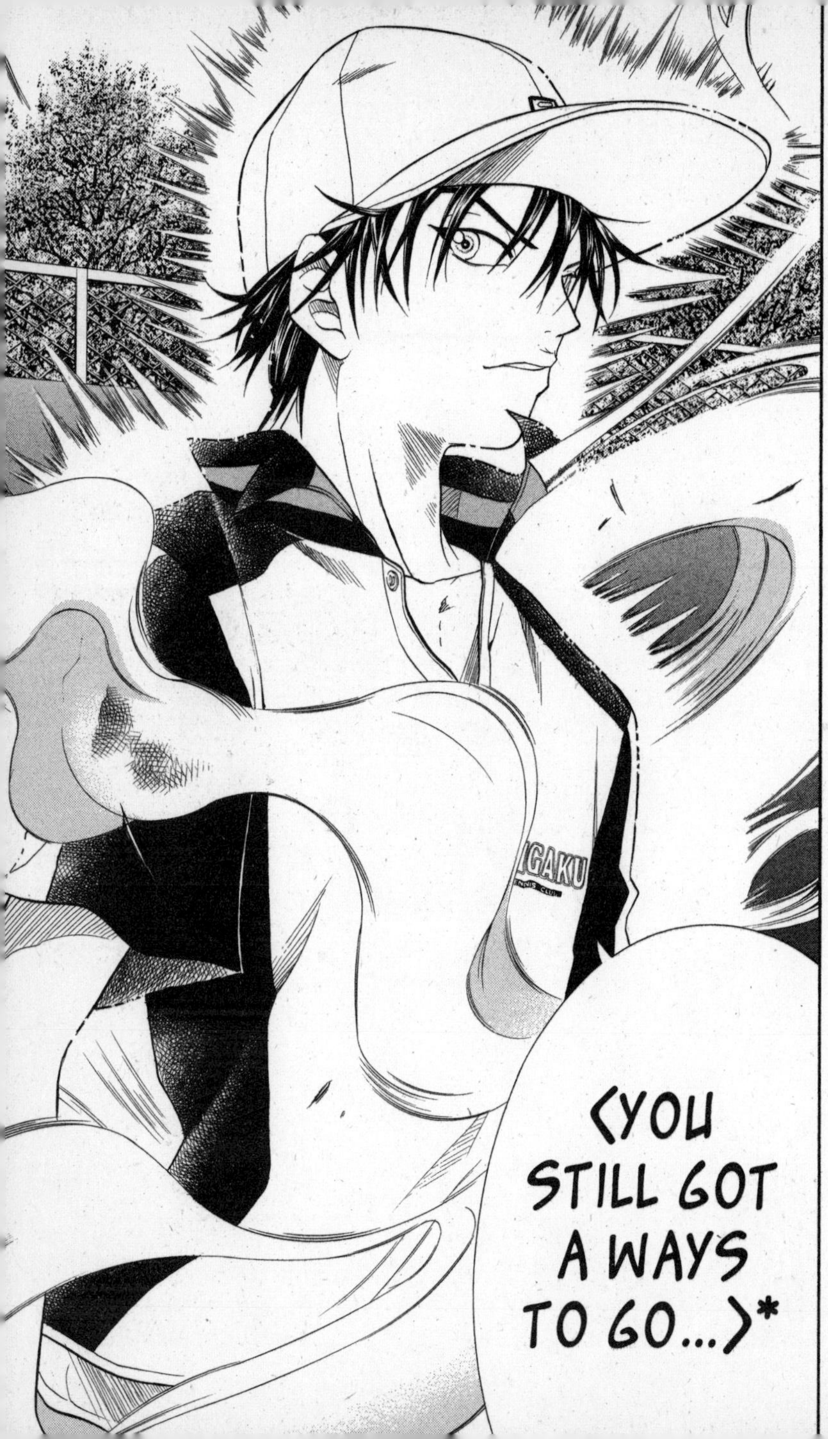
<YOU STILL GOT A WAYS TO GO...>*
SEIGAKU TENNIS CLUB

テニスの王子様

THE PRINCE OF TENNIS

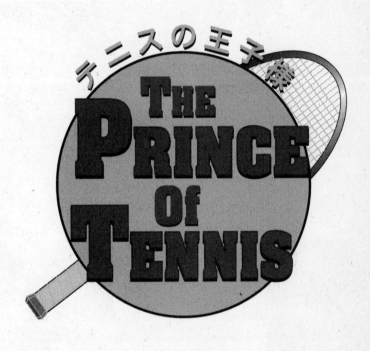

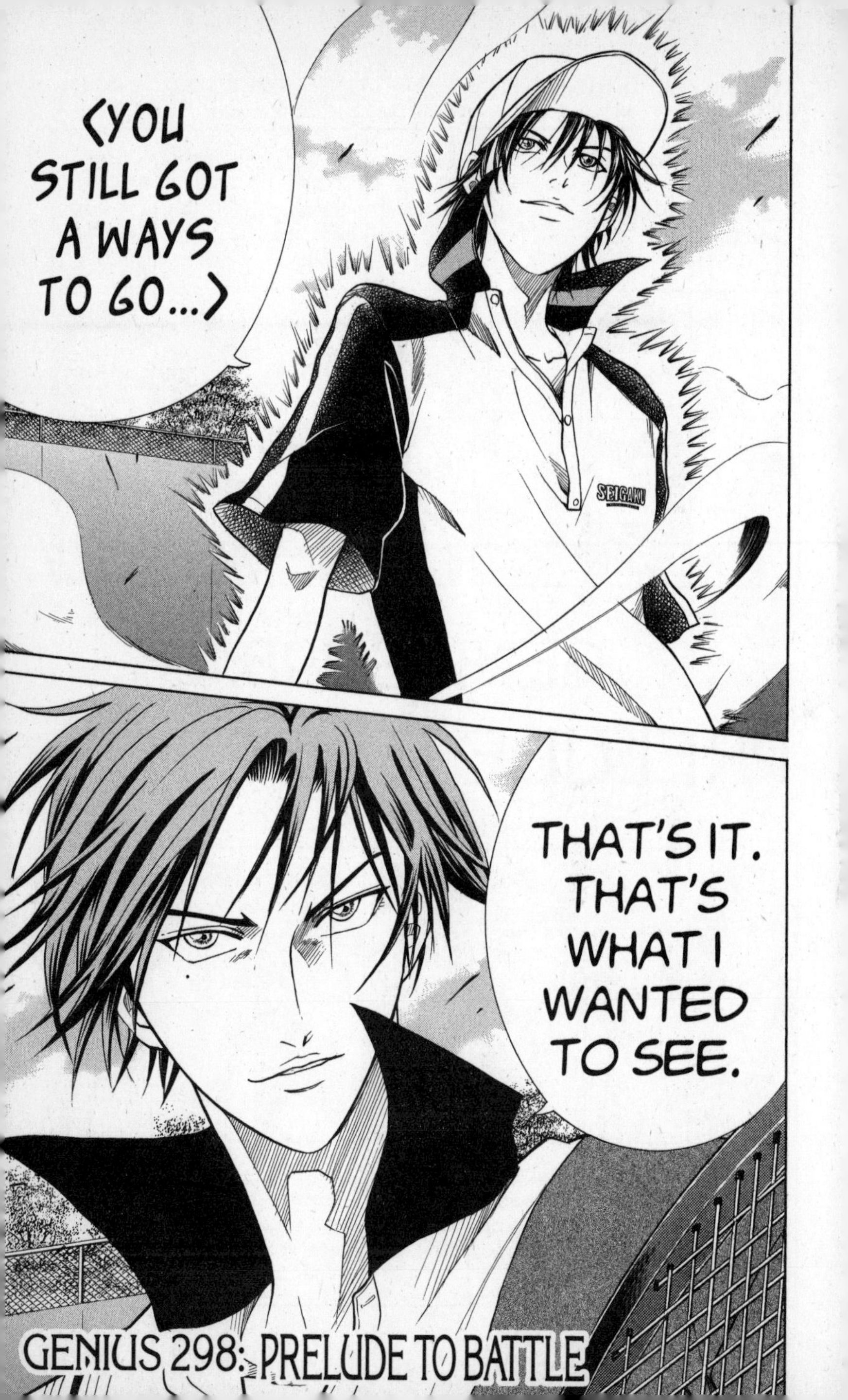
<YOU STILL GOT A WAYS TO GO...>
THAT'S IT. THAT'S WHAT I WANTED TO SEE.
SEIGAKU
GENIUS 298: PRELUDE TO BATTLE

5th Match No. 1 Singles	4th Match No. 1 Doubles		3rd Match No. 2 Singles	2nd Match No. 2 Doubles		1st Match No. 3 Singles
Ryoma Echizen (7th Grade) Blood Type: O	Shuichiro Oishi (9th Grade) Blood Type: O	Eiji Kikumaru (9th Grade) Blood Type: A	Kunimitsu Tezuka (9th Grade) Blood Type: O	Kaoru Kaido (8th Grade) Blood Type: B	Sadaharu Inui (9th Grade) Blood Type: AB	Takeshi Momoshiro (8th Grade) Blood Type: O

SEIGAKU
SEIGAKU
SEIGAKU
SEIGAKU

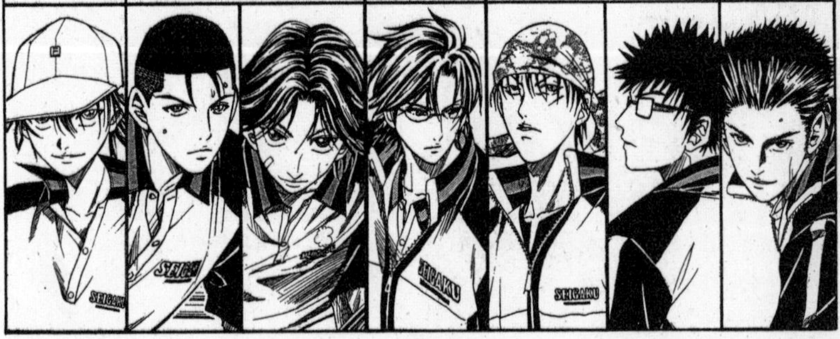

GENIUS 298: PRELUDE TO BATTLE

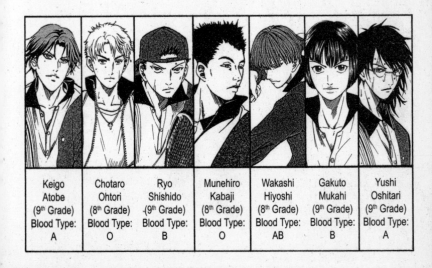

Keigo Atobe (9th Grade) Blood Type: A	Chotaro Ohtori (8th Grade) Blood Type: O	Ryo Shishido (9th Grade) Blood Type: B	Munehiro Kabaji (8th Grade) Blood Type: O	Wakashi Hiyoshi (8th Grade) Blood Type: AB	Gakuto Mukahi (9th Grade) Blood Type: B	Yushi Oshitari (9th Grade) Blood Type: A

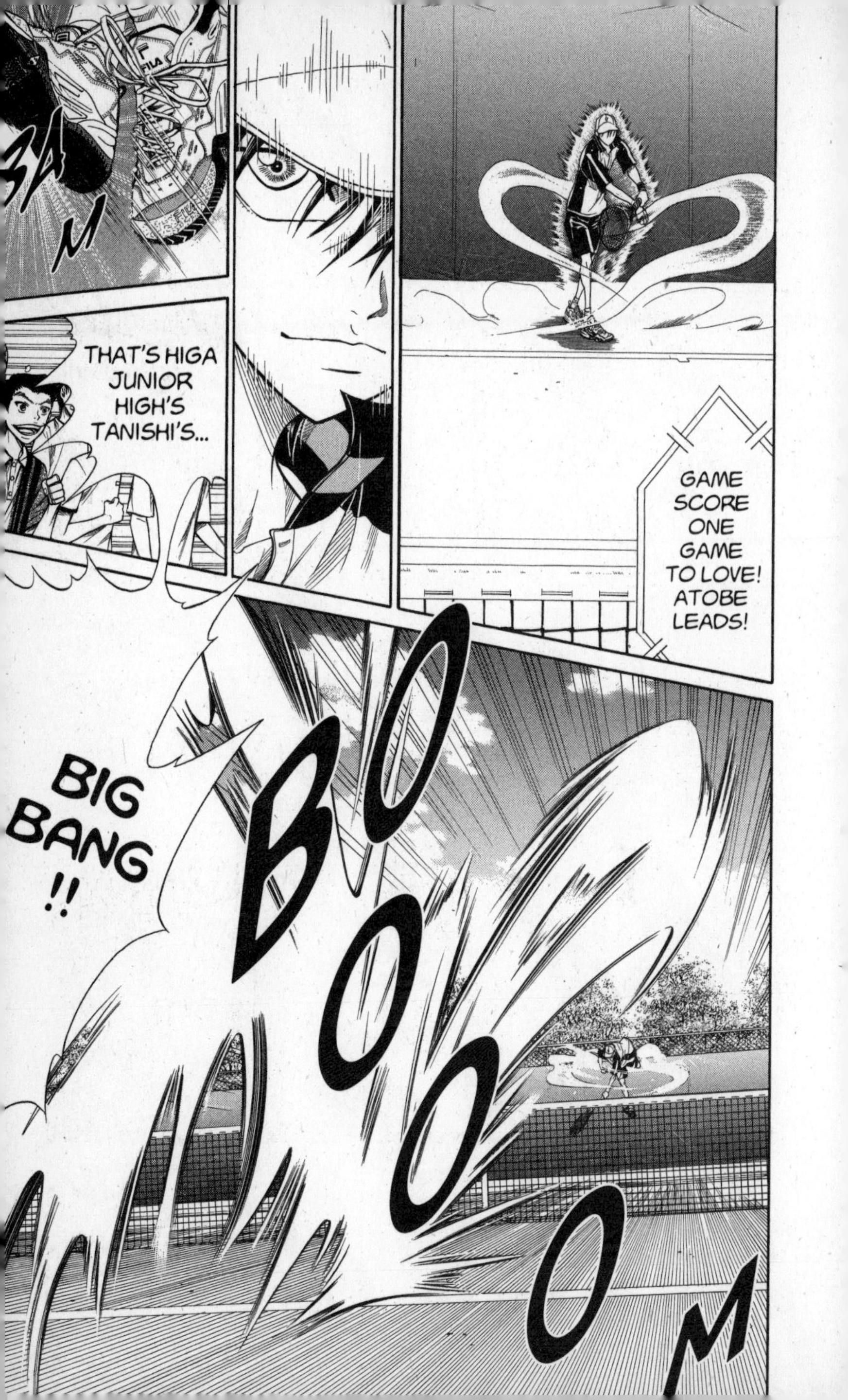

GAME SCORE ONE GAME TO LOVE! ATOBE LEADS!
THAT'S HIGA JUNIOR HIGH'S TANISHI'S...
BIG BANG !!
BOOOOOM

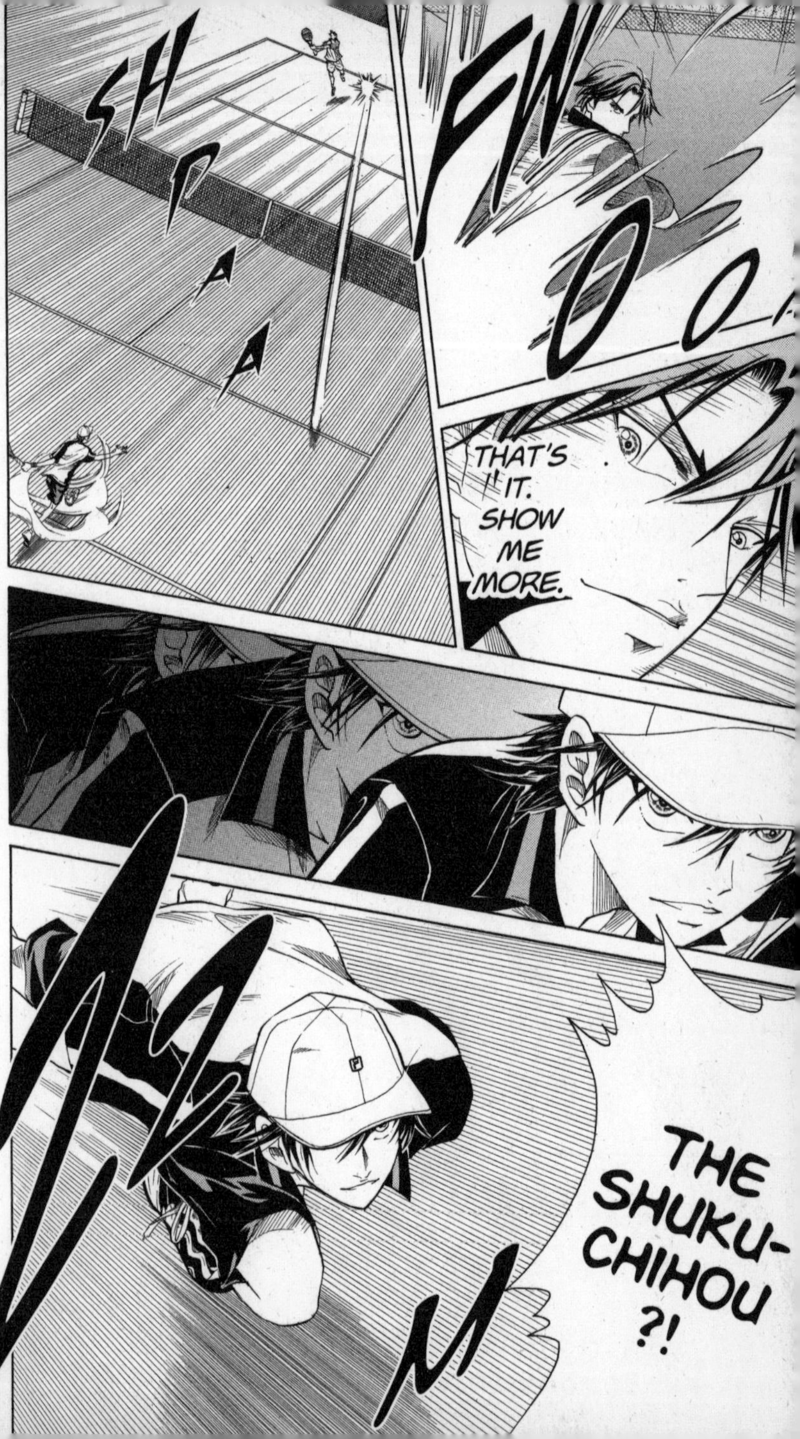
FWOOO
THAT'S IT. SHOW ME MORE.
SHPAA
THE SHUKU-CHIHOU?!

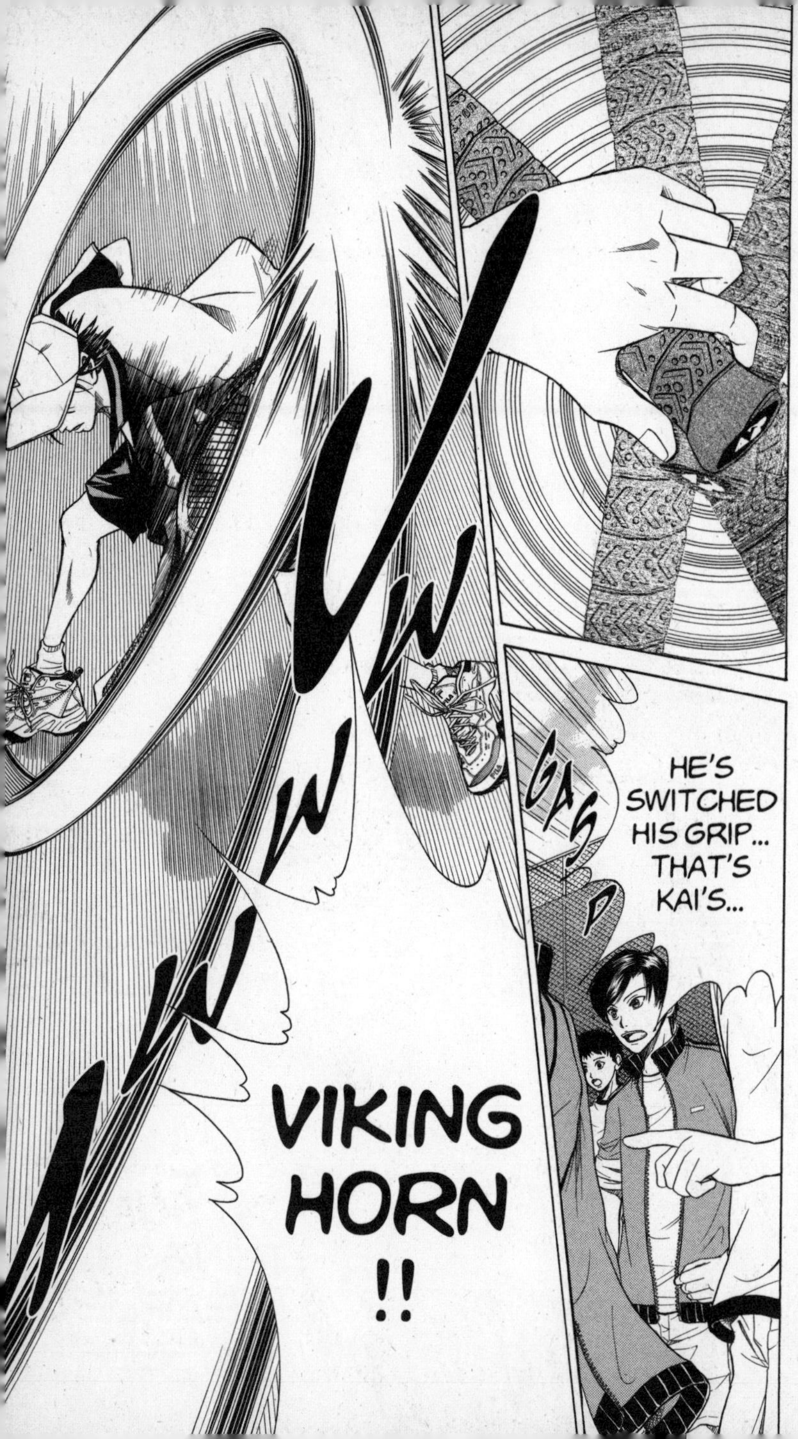
VWWWWM
GASP
HE'S SWITCHED HIS GRIP... THAT'S KAI'S...
VIKING HORN !!

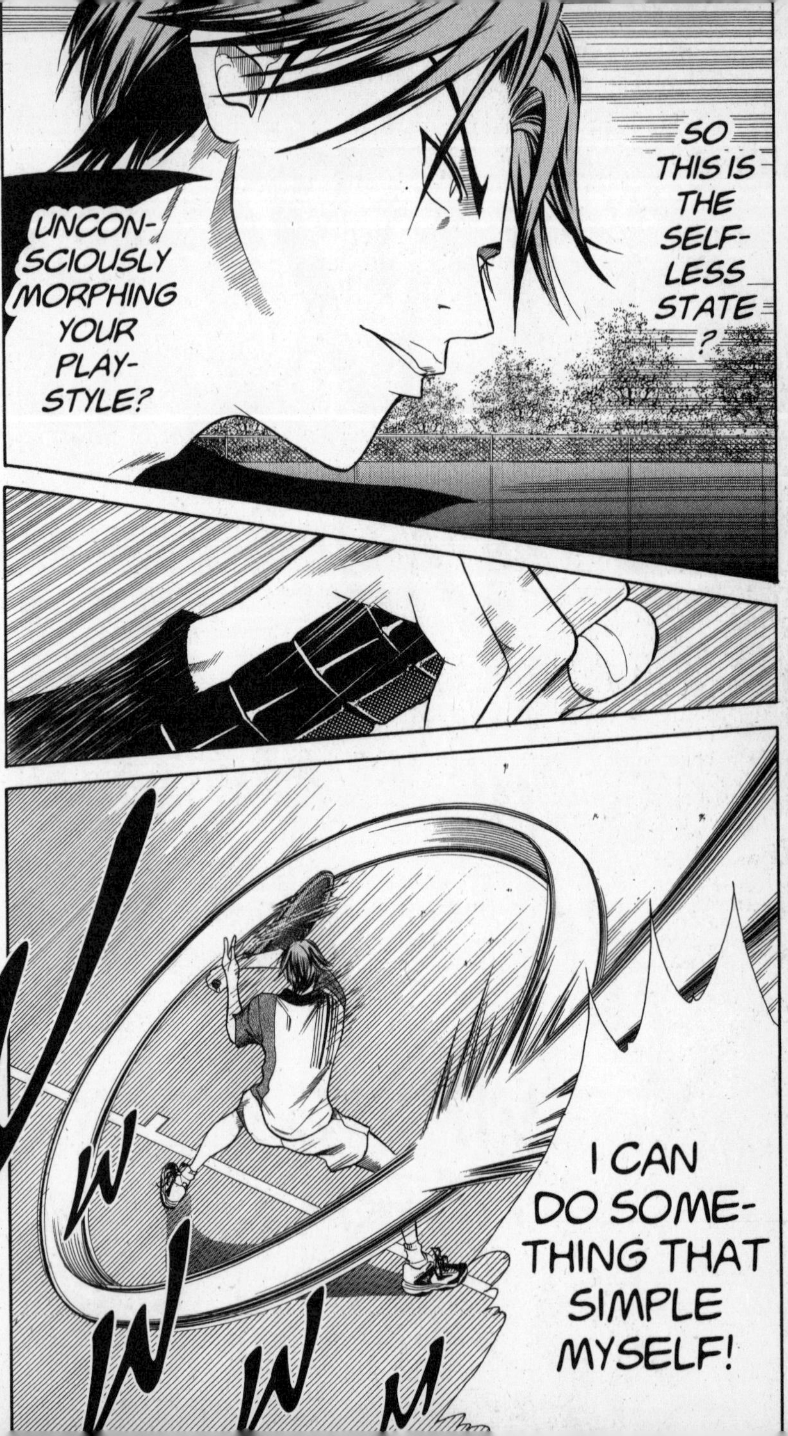
SO THIS IS THE SELF-LESS STATE?
UNCONSCIOUSLY MORPHING YOUR PLAY-STYLE?
I CAN DO SOMETHING THAT SIMPLE MYSELF!

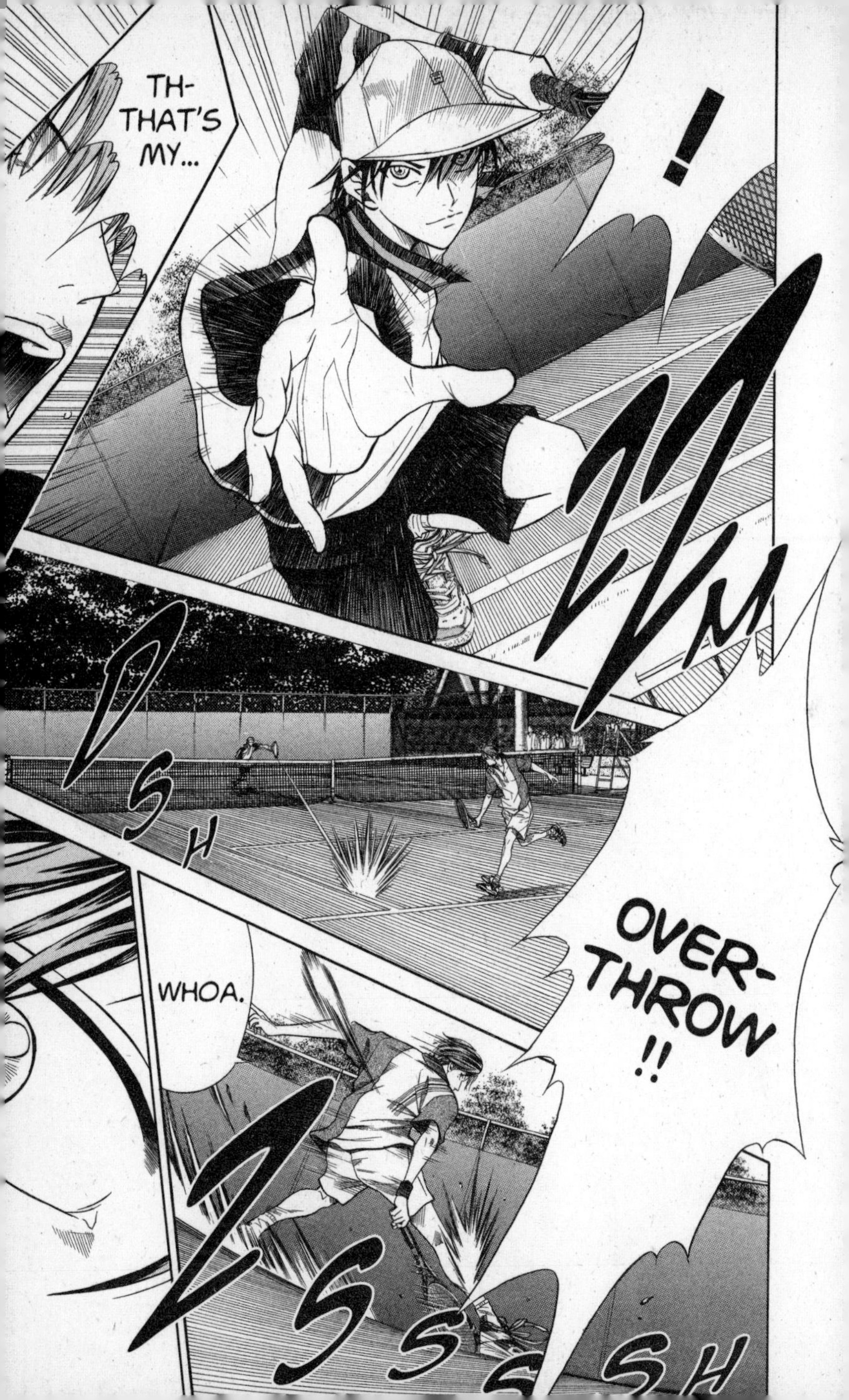
!
TH- THAT'S MY...
DSH
OVER-THROW !!
WHOA.

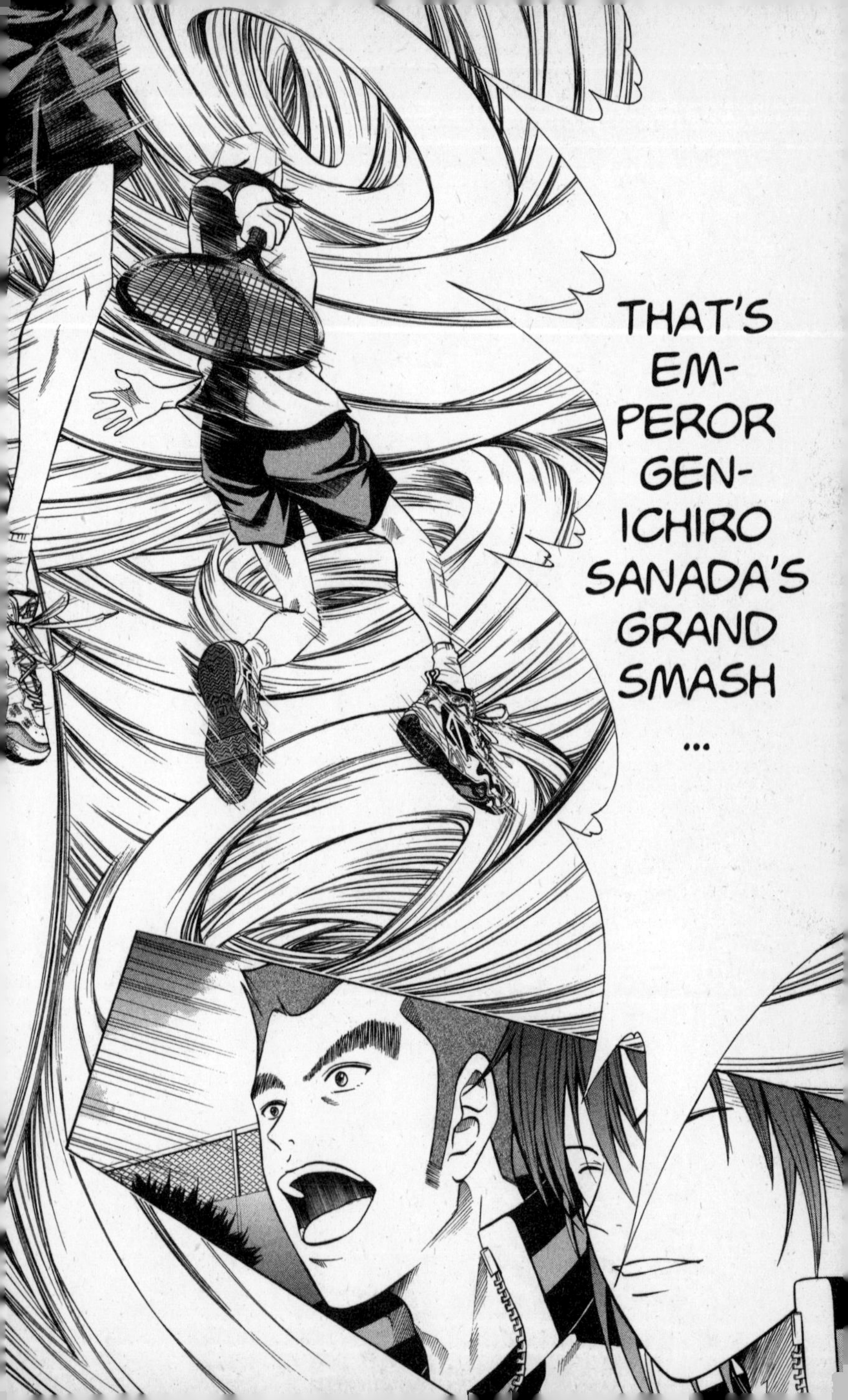
THAT'S EMPEROR GENICHIRO SANADA'S GRAND SMASH...

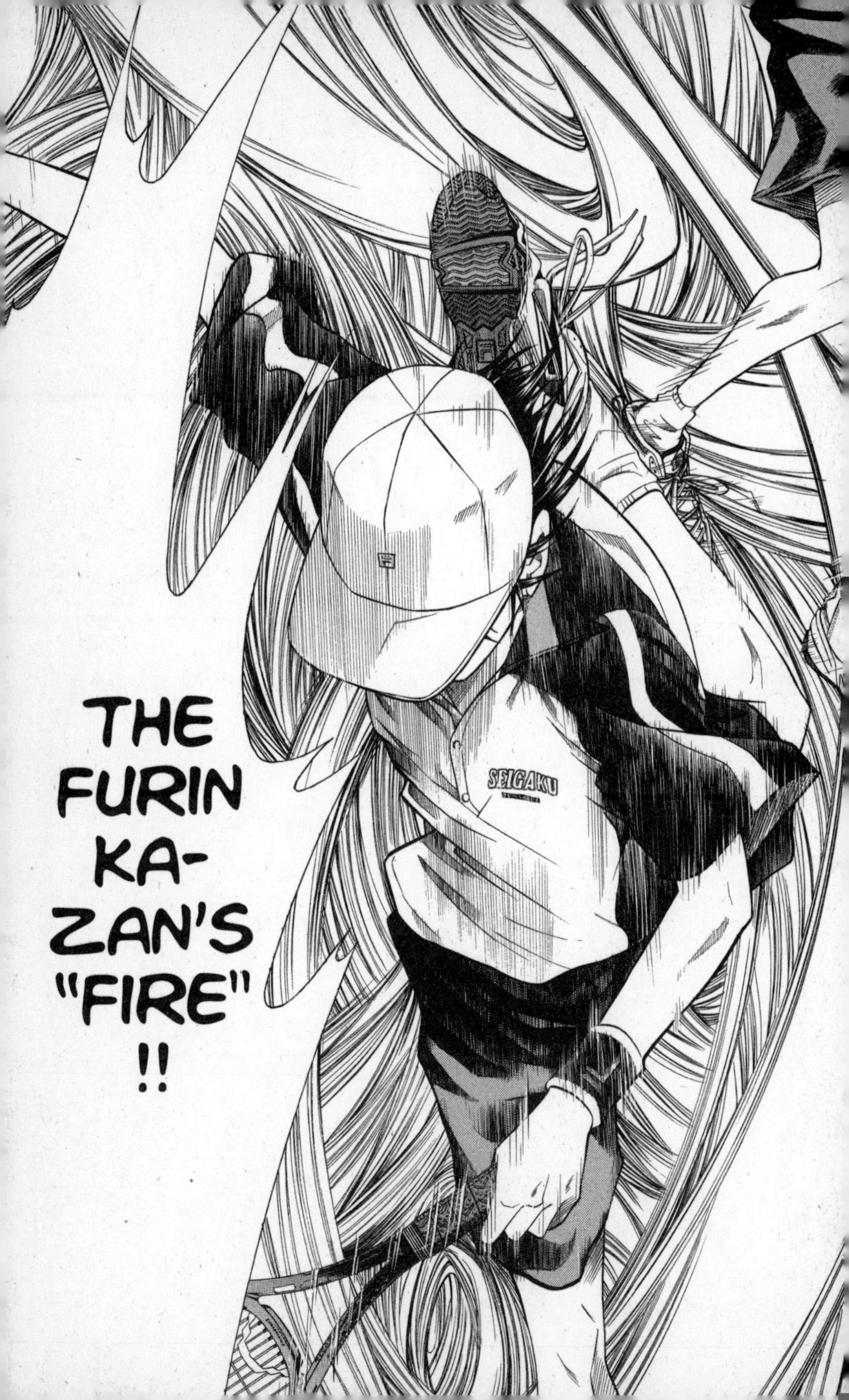
THE FURIN KA-ZAN'S "FIRE" !!
SEIGAKU

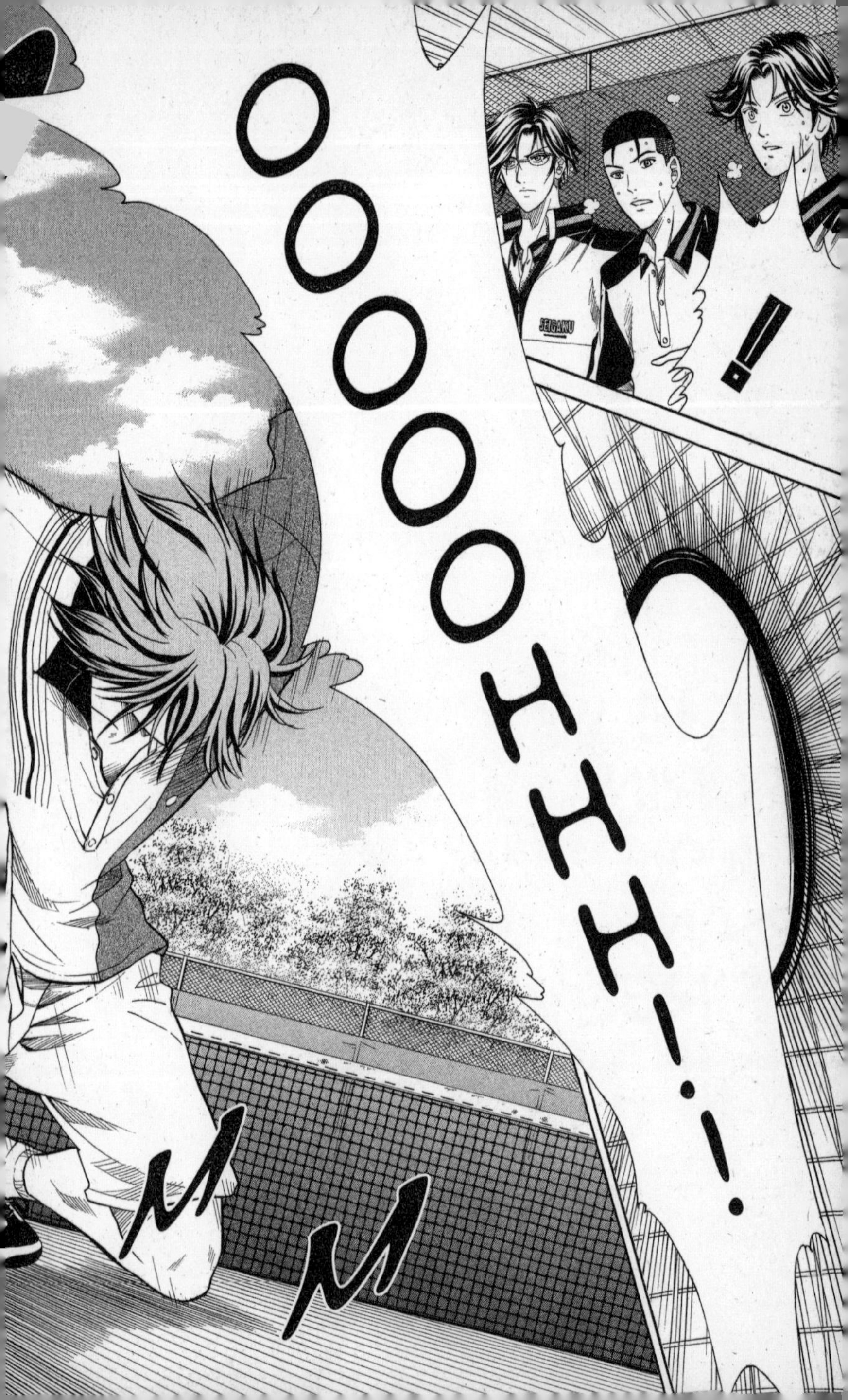
OOOOOHHH!!
!
MM
SEIGAKU

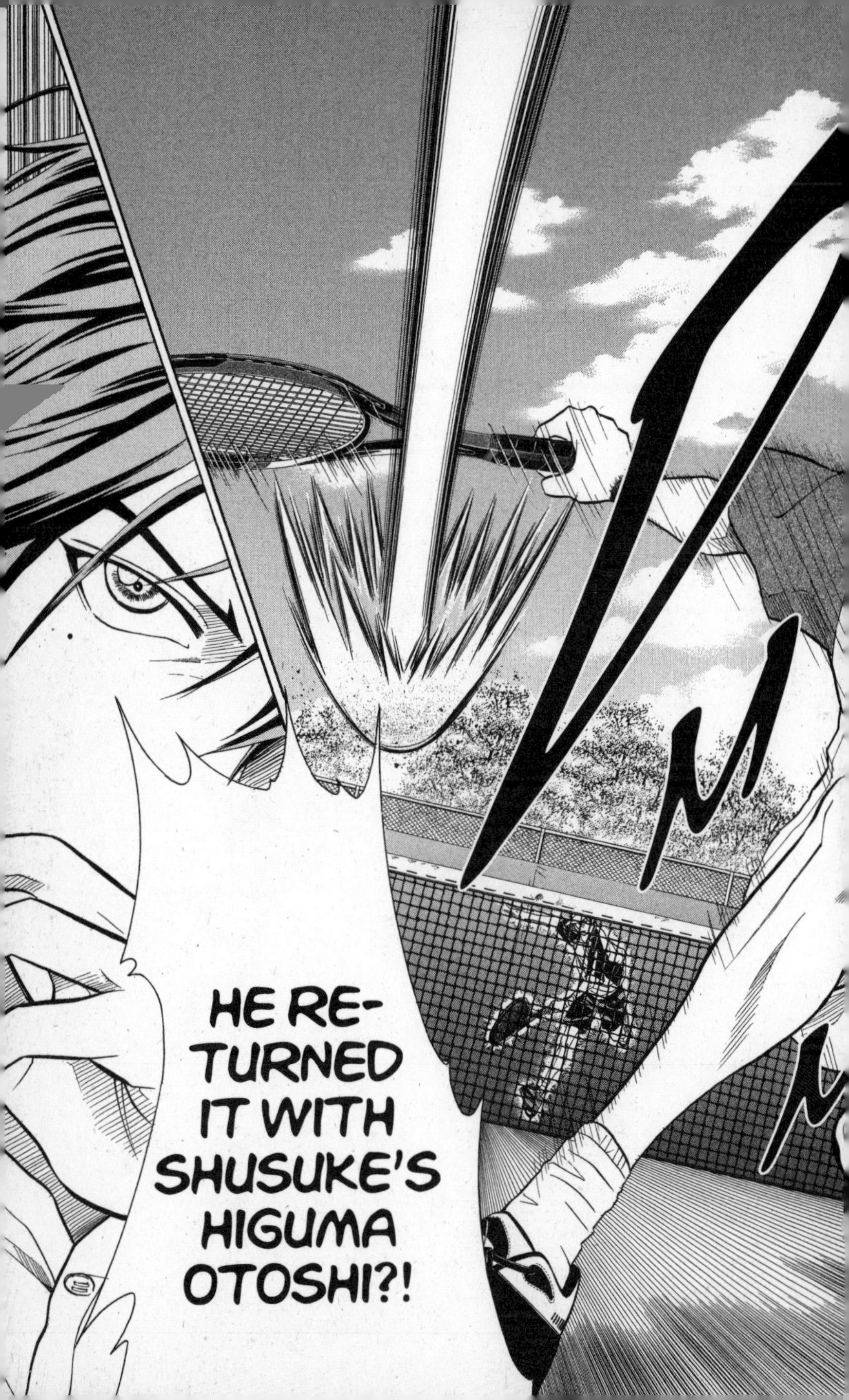
HE RE-TURNED IT WITH SHUSUKE'S HIGUMA OTOSHI?!

テニスの王子様

THE PRINCE OF TENNIS

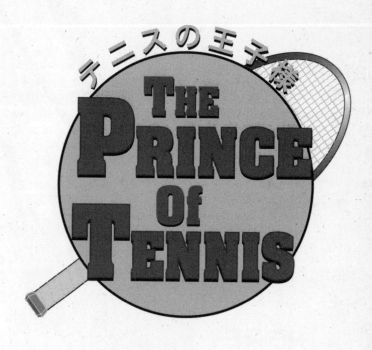

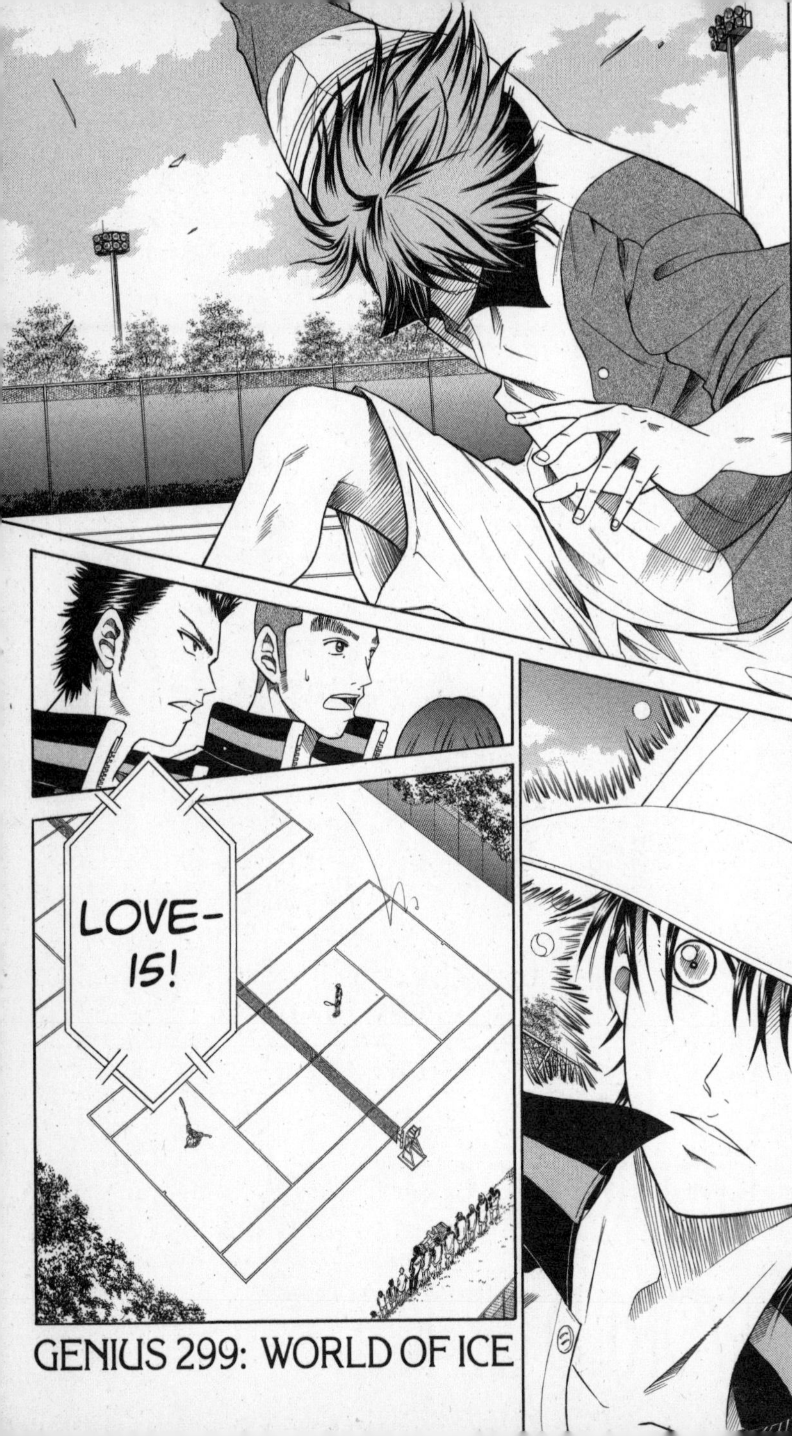
LOVE-15!

GENIUS 299: WORLD OF ICE

GENIUS 299: WORLD OF ICE

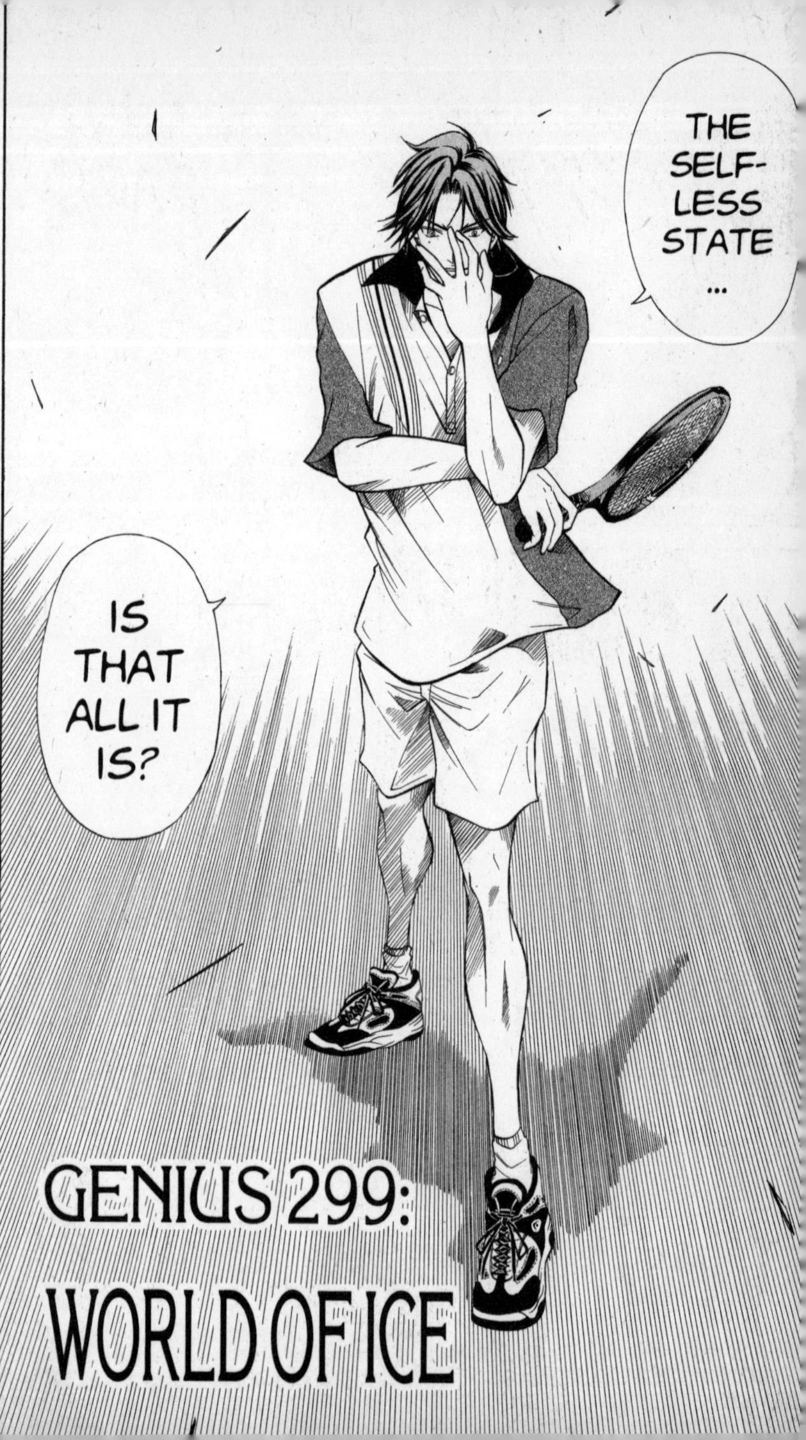
THE SELF-LESS STATE ...
IS THAT ALL IT IS?

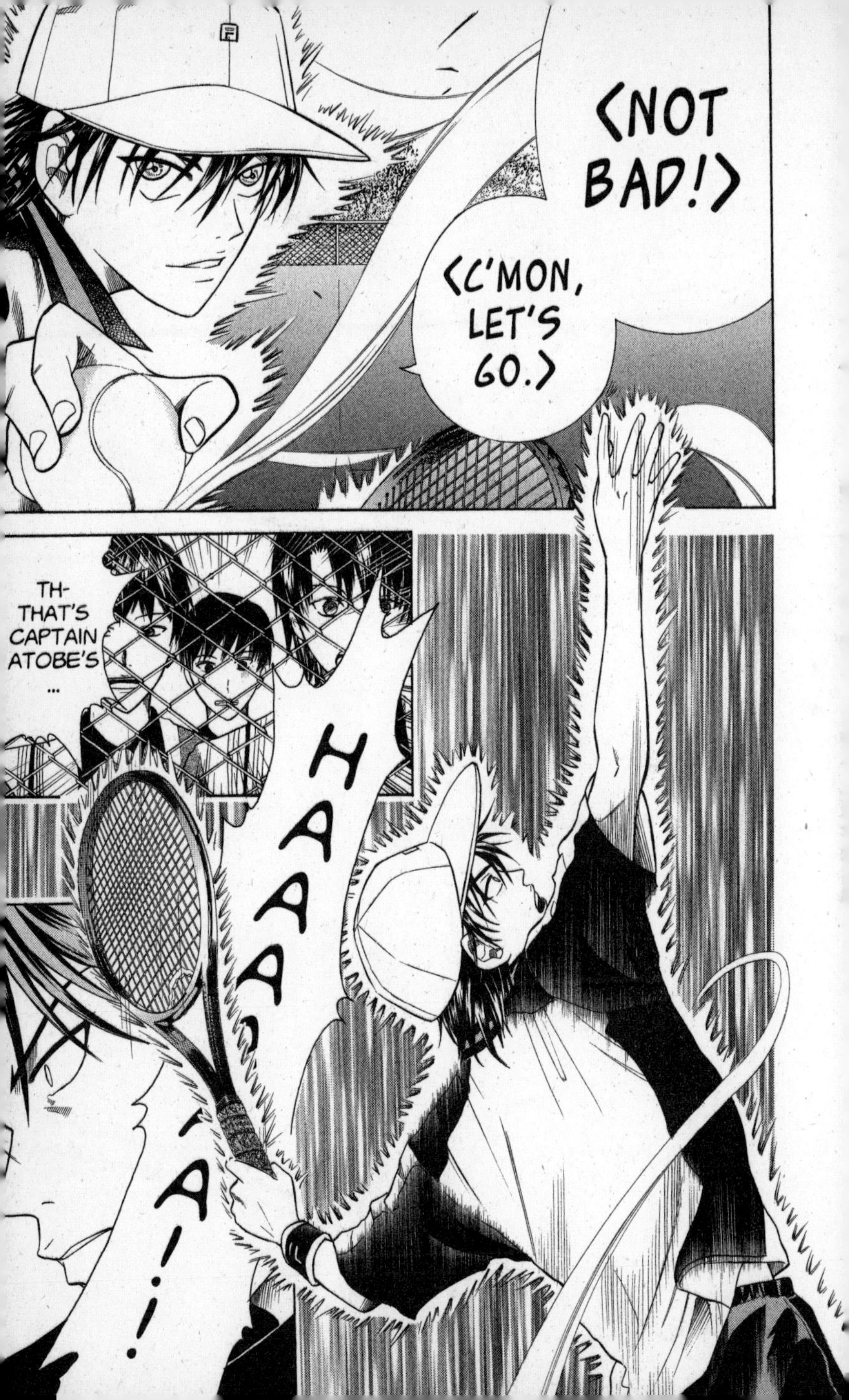
<NOT BAD!>
<C'MON, LET'S GO.>
TH- THAT'S CAPTAIN ATOBE'S ...
HAAAA!!

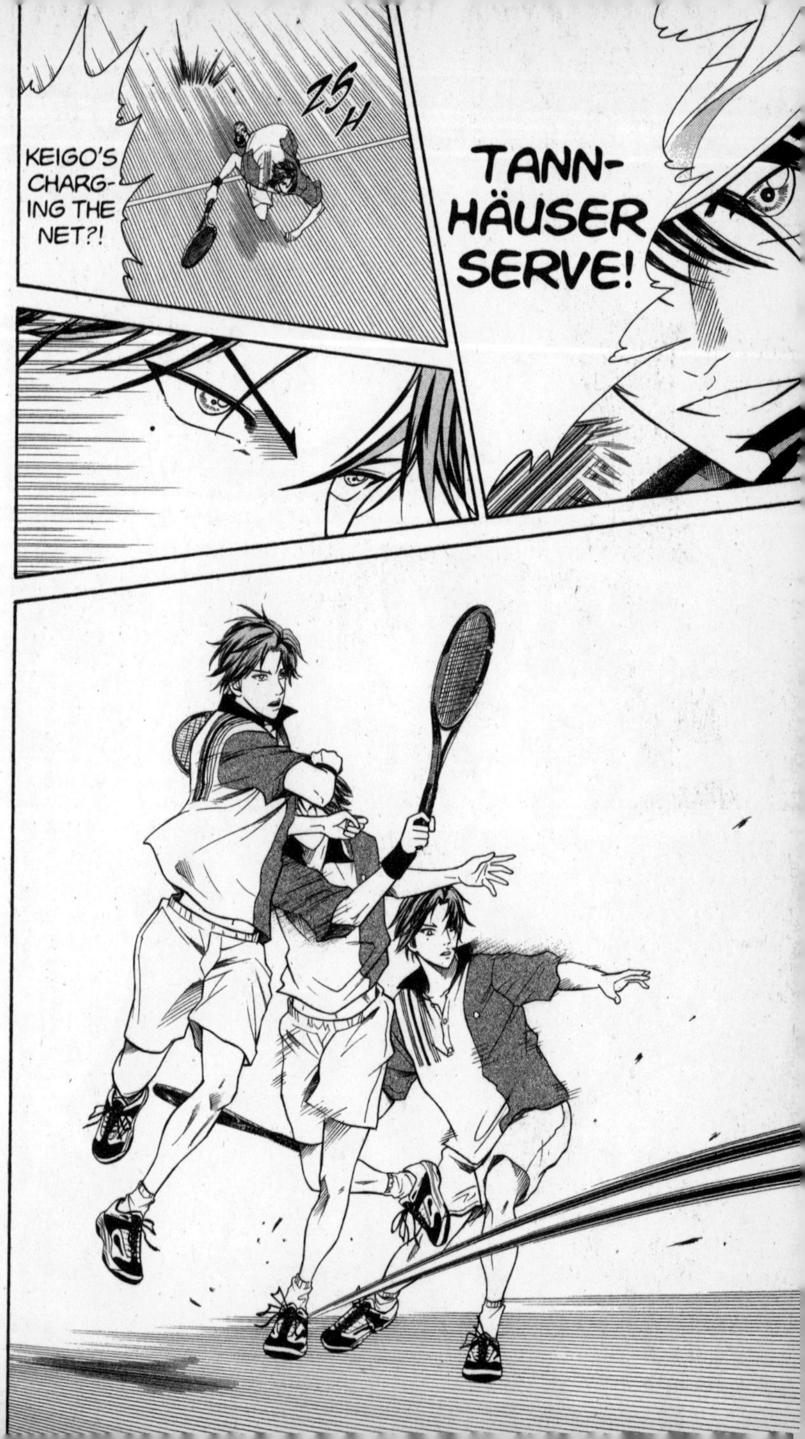
TANN-HÄUSER SERVE!
ZSH
KEIGO'S CHARG-ING THE NET?!

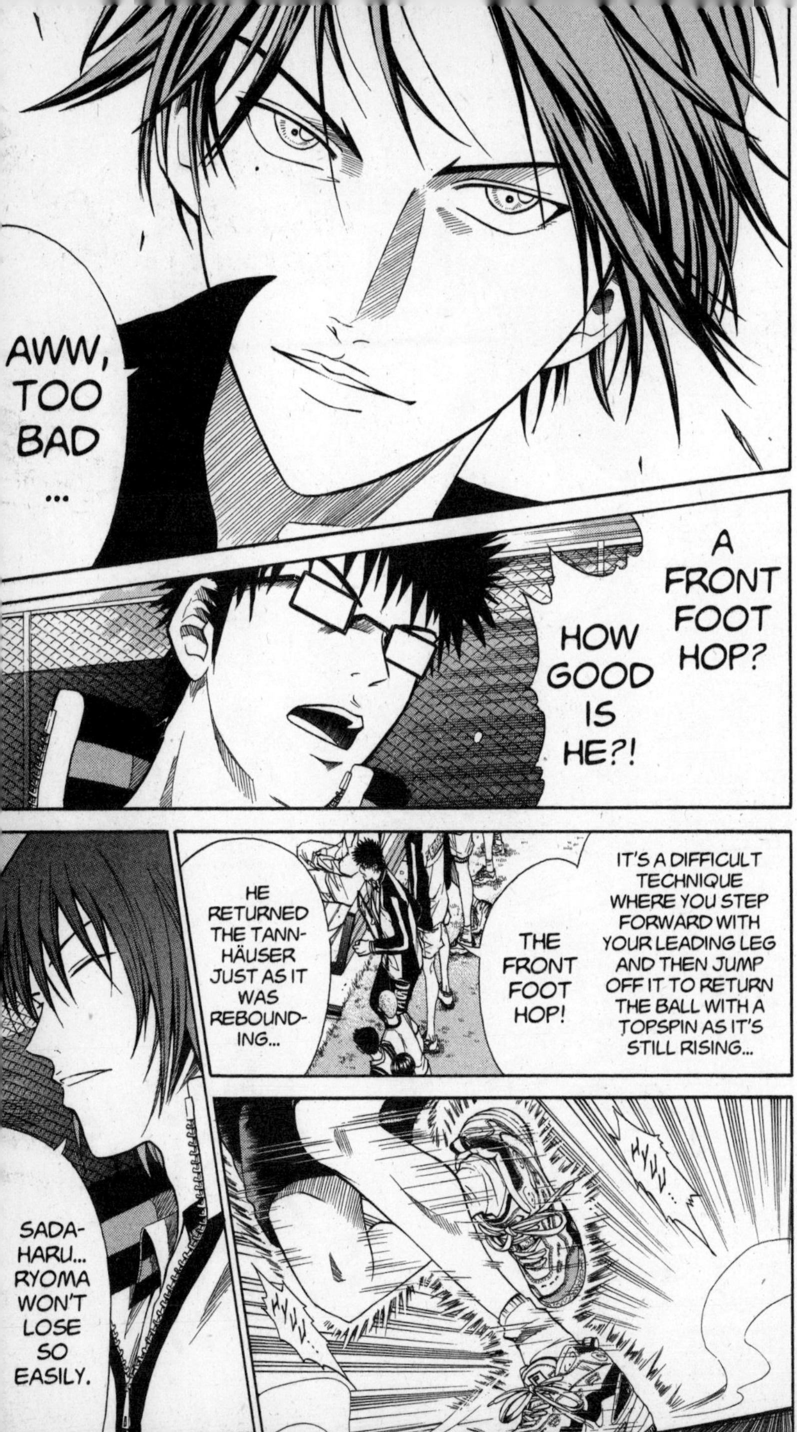
AWW, TOO BAD ...
A FRONT FOOT HOP?
HOW GOOD IS HE?!
IT'S A DIFFICULT TECHNIQUE WHERE YOU STEP FORWARD WITH YOUR LEADING LEG AND THEN JUMP OFF IT TO RETURN THE BALL WITH A TOPSPIN AS IT'S STILL RISING...
THE FRONT FOOT HOP!
HE RETURNED THE TANN-HÄUSER JUST AS IT WAS REBOUND-ING...
SADA-HARU... RYOMA WON'T LOSE SO EASILY.

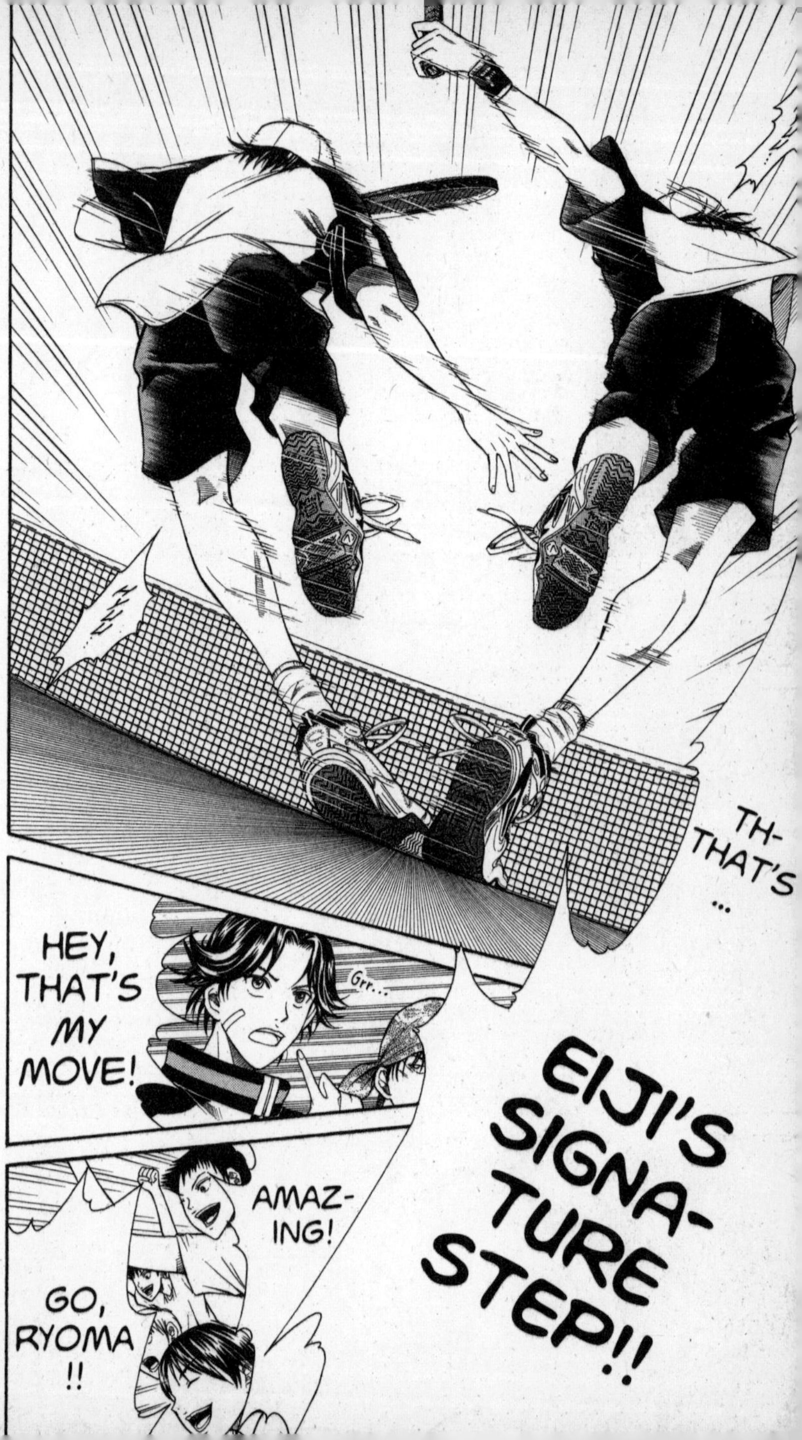
TH-THAT'S...
EIJI'S SIGNATURE STEP!!
HEY, THAT'S MY MOVE!
Grr...
AMAZING!
GO, RYOMA!!

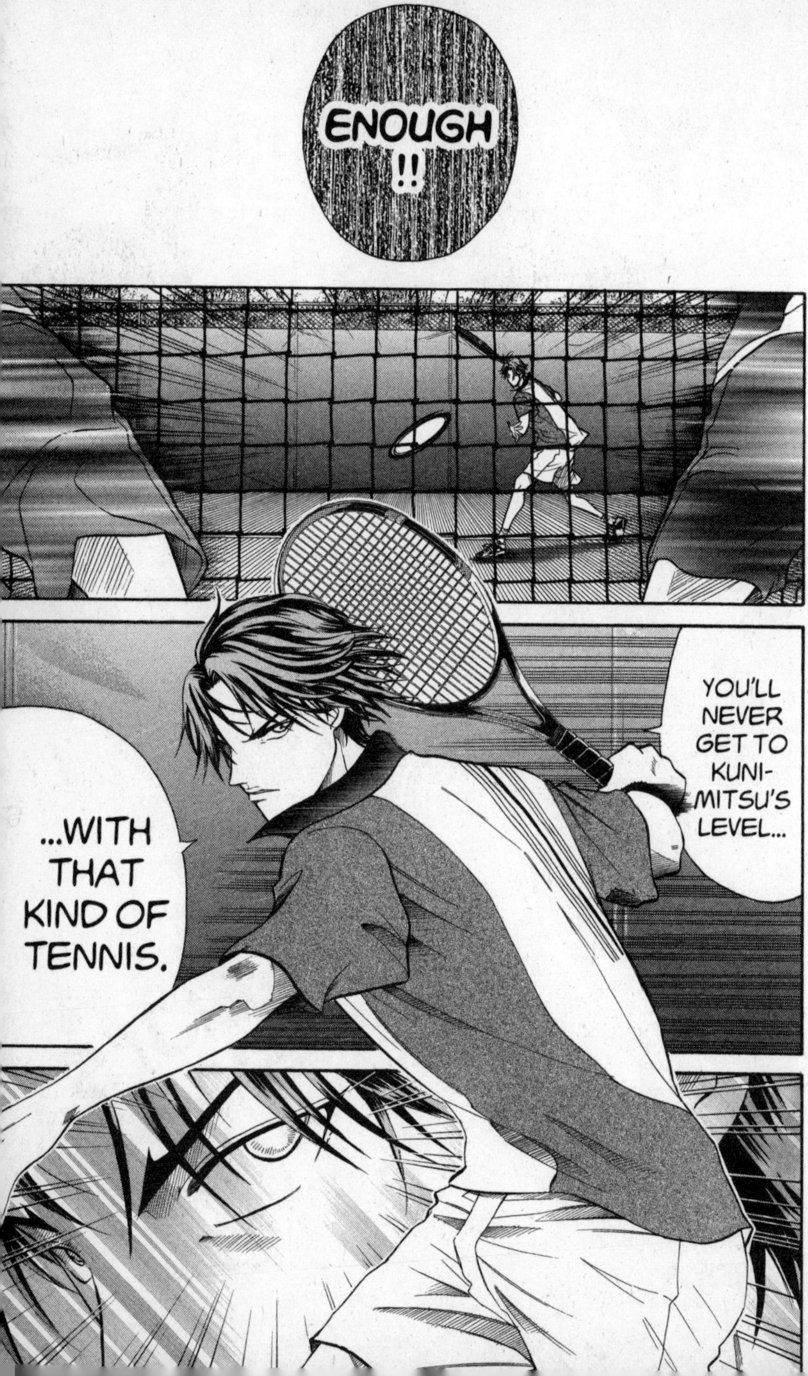
ENOUGH !!
YOU'LL NEVER GET TO KUNI-MITSU'S LEVEL...
...WITH THAT KIND OF TENNIS.

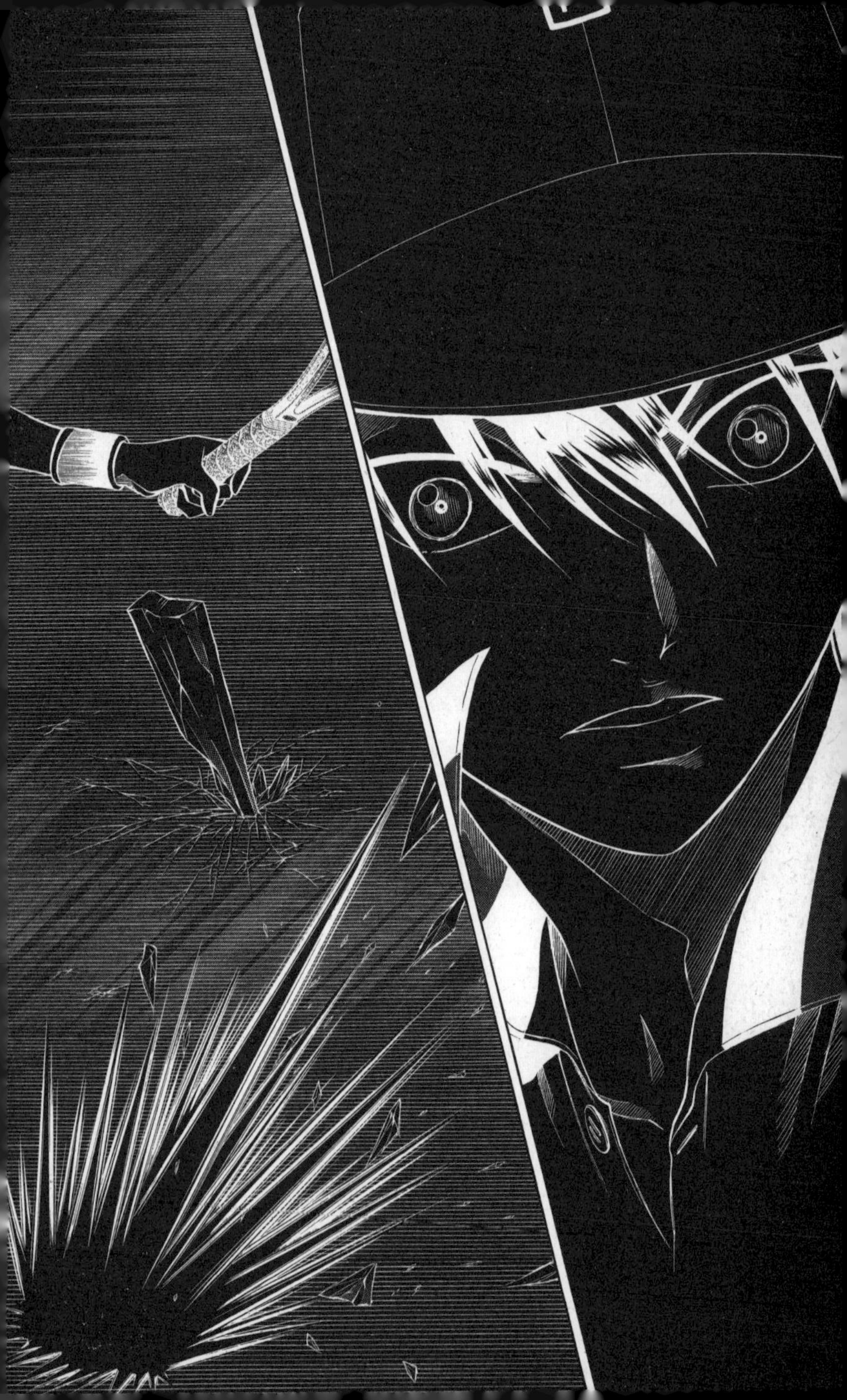

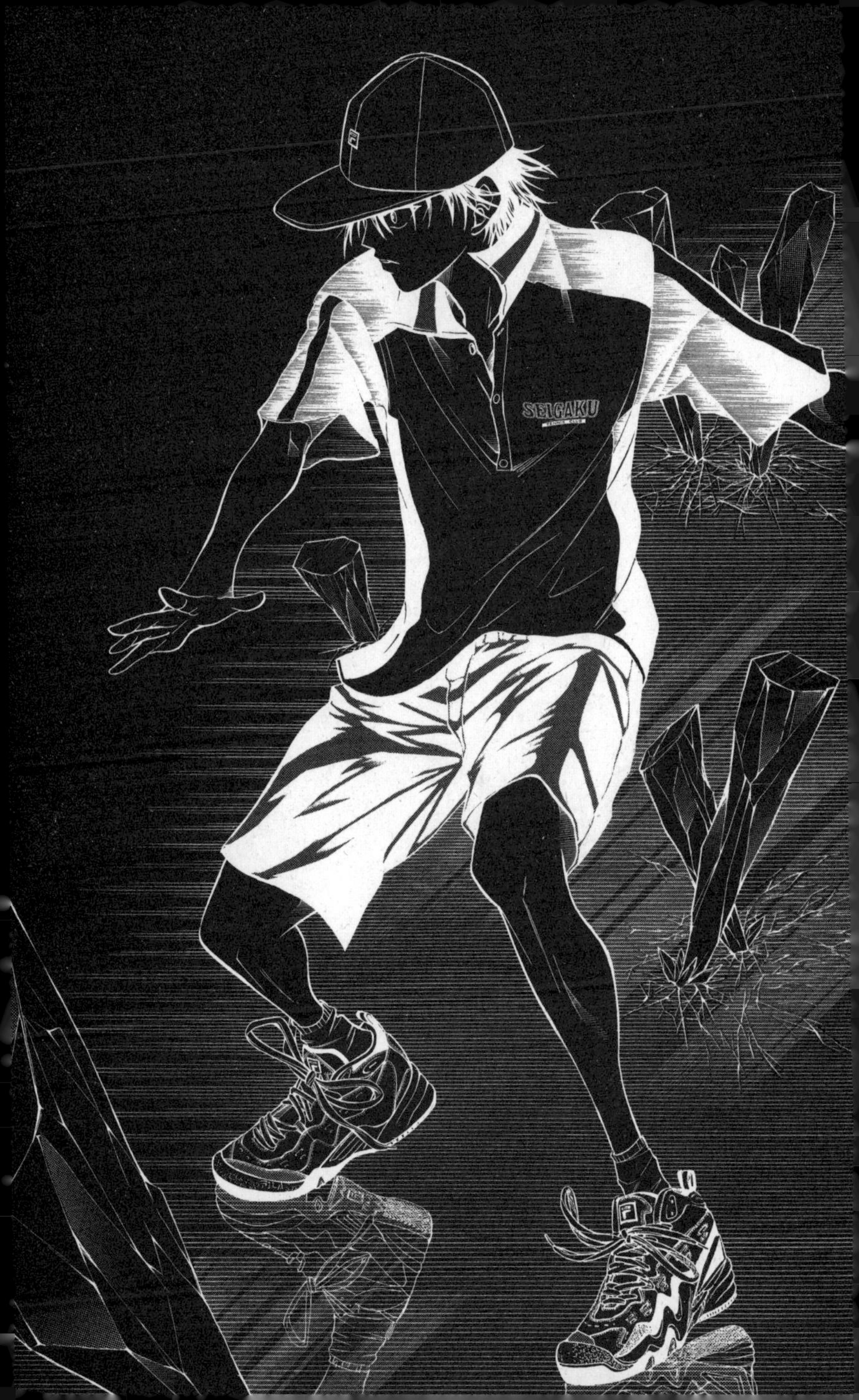
SEIGAKU

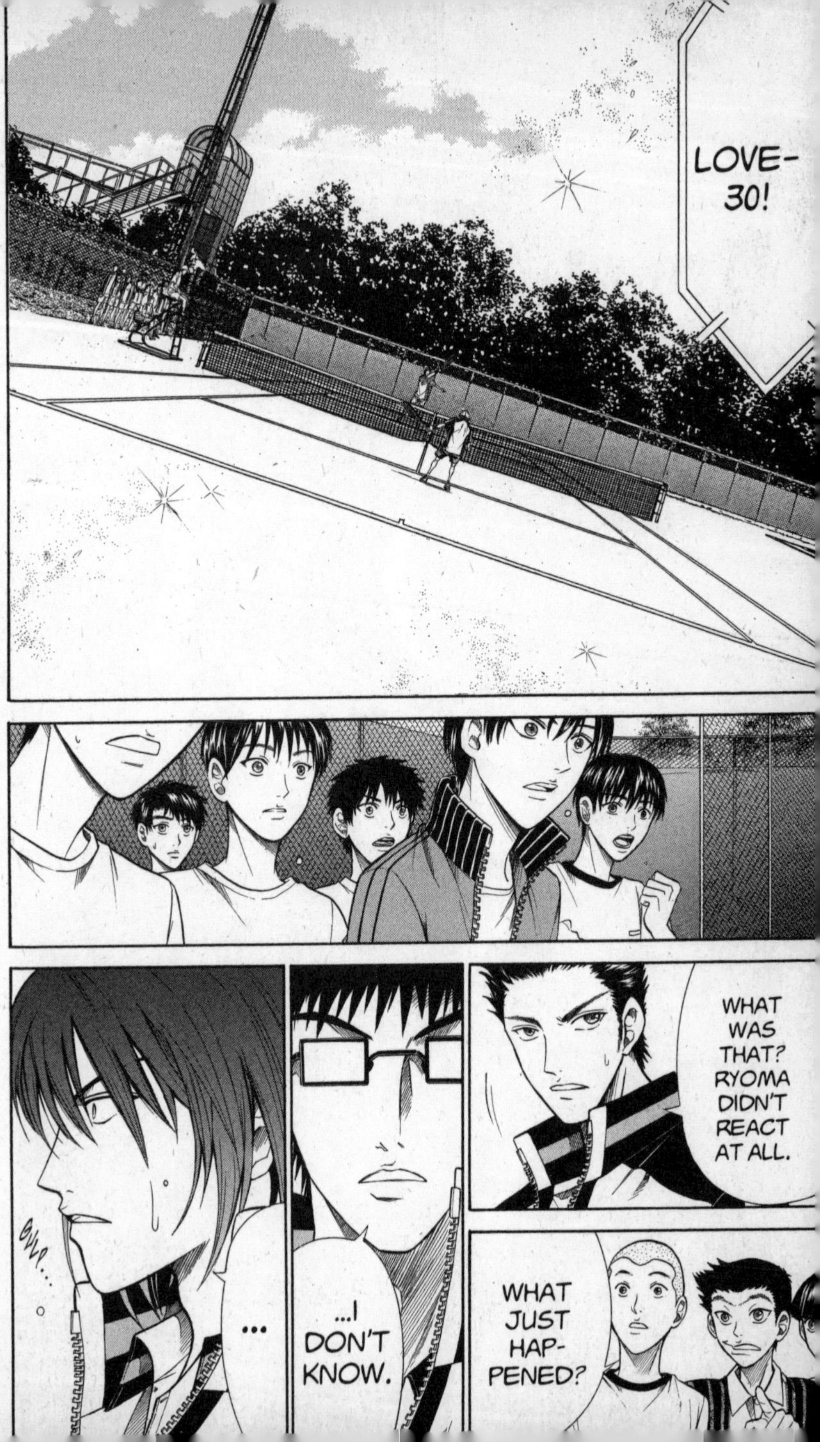
LOVE-30!
WHAT WAS THAT? RYOMA DIDN'T REACT AT ALL.
WHAT JUST HAP-PENED?
...I DON'T KNOW.
...
GULP...

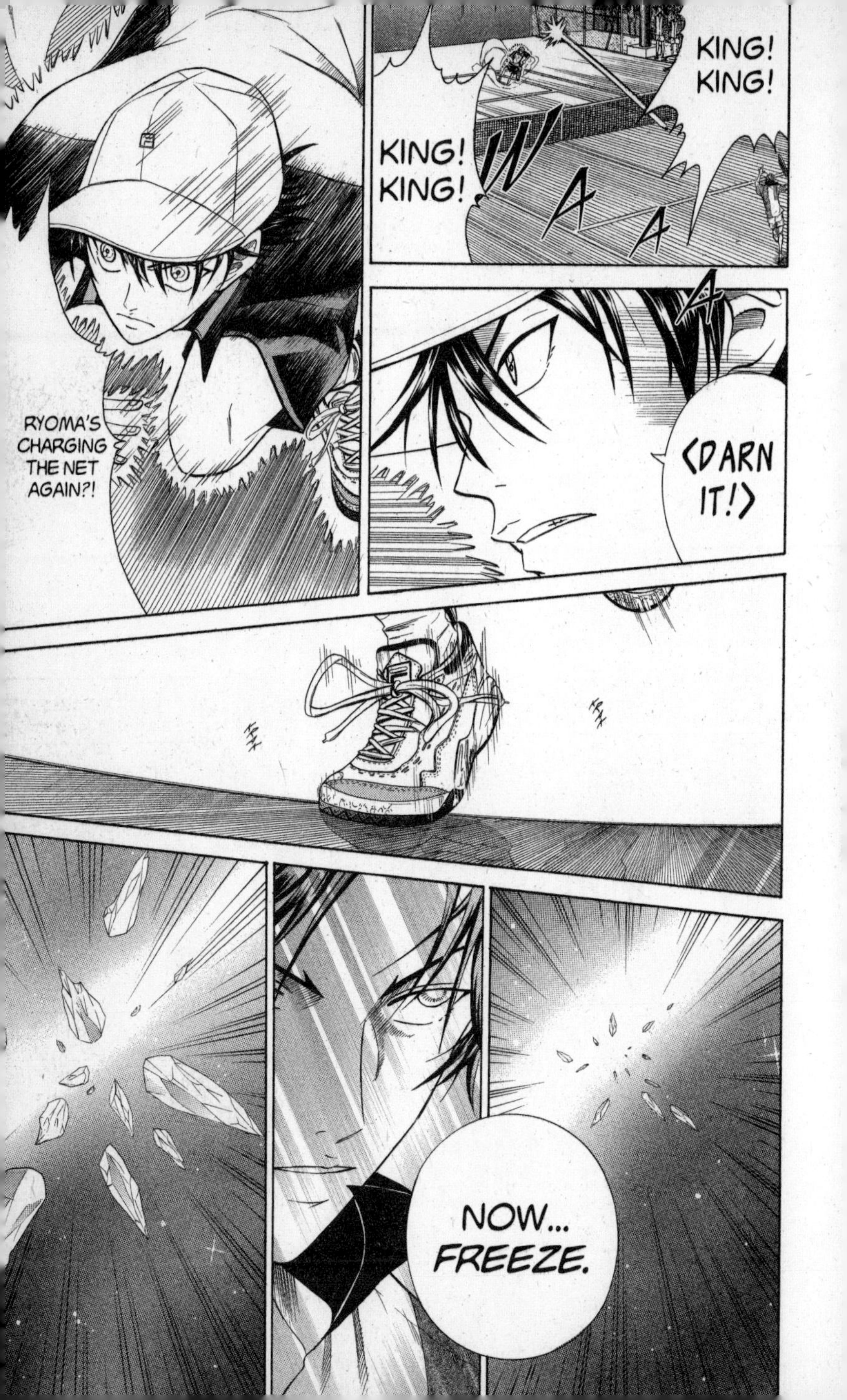
KING! KING!
KING! KING!
WAAAA
<DARN IT!>
RYOMA'S CHARGING THE NET AGAIN?!
NOW... FREEZE.

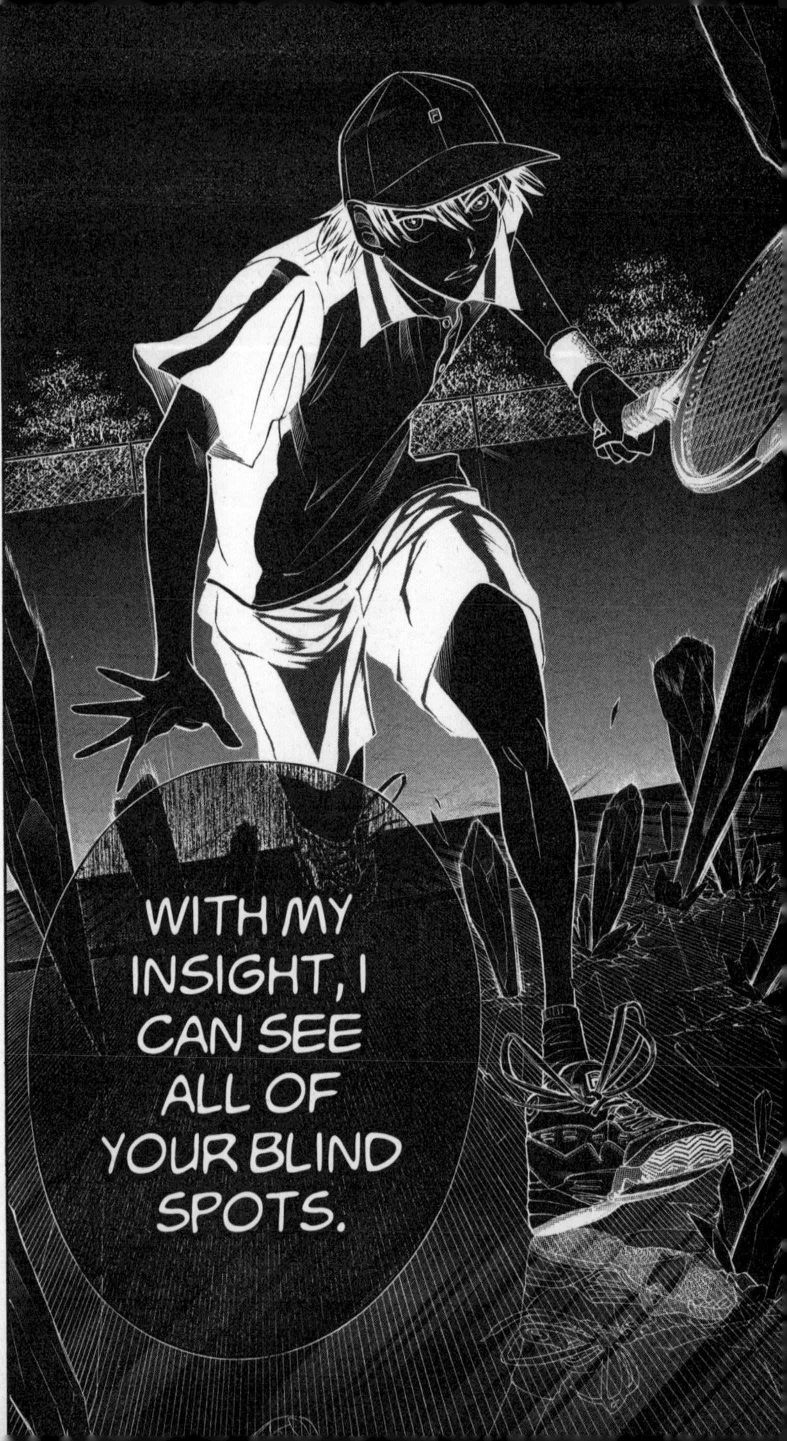
WITH MY INSIGHT, I CAN SEE ALL OF YOUR BLIND SPOTS.

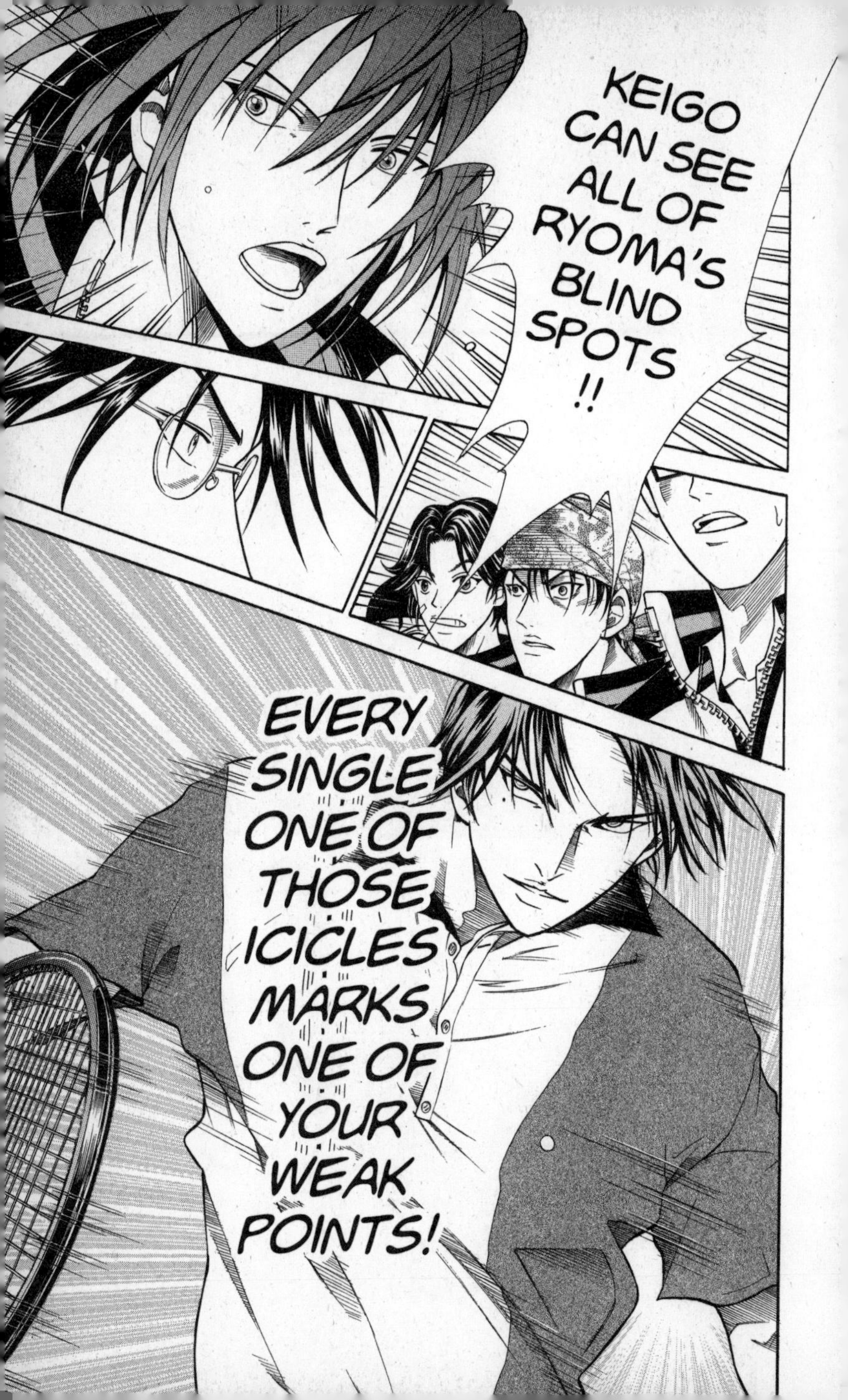
KEIGO CAN SEE ALL OF RYOMA'S BLIND SPOTS !!
EVERY SINGLE ONE OF THOSE ICICLES MARKS ONE OF YOUR WEAK POINTS!

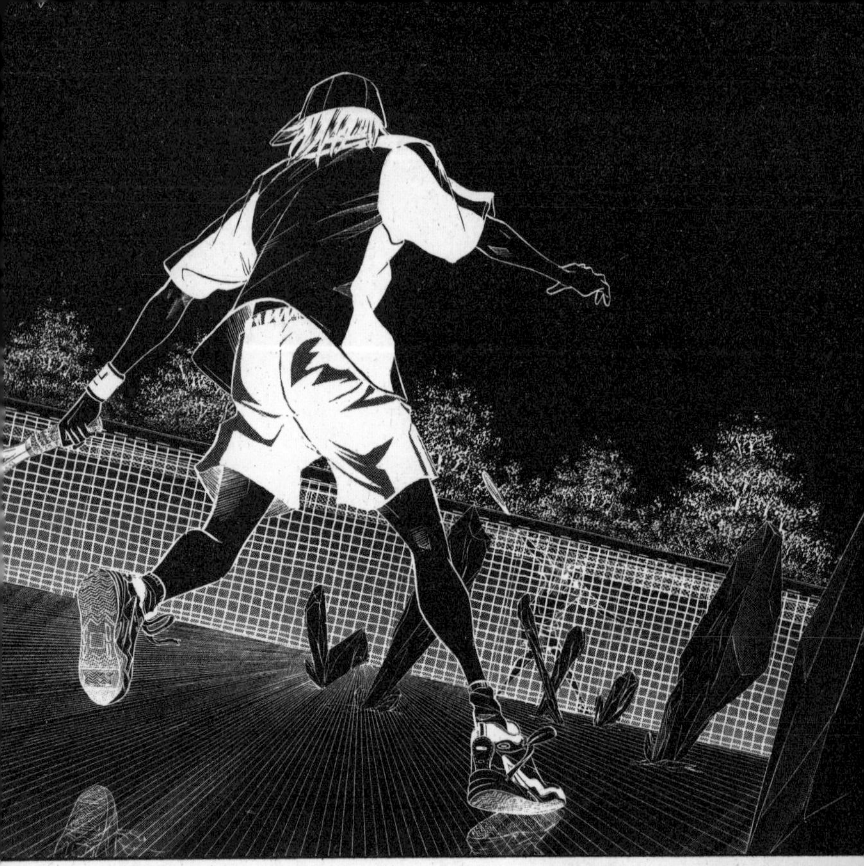

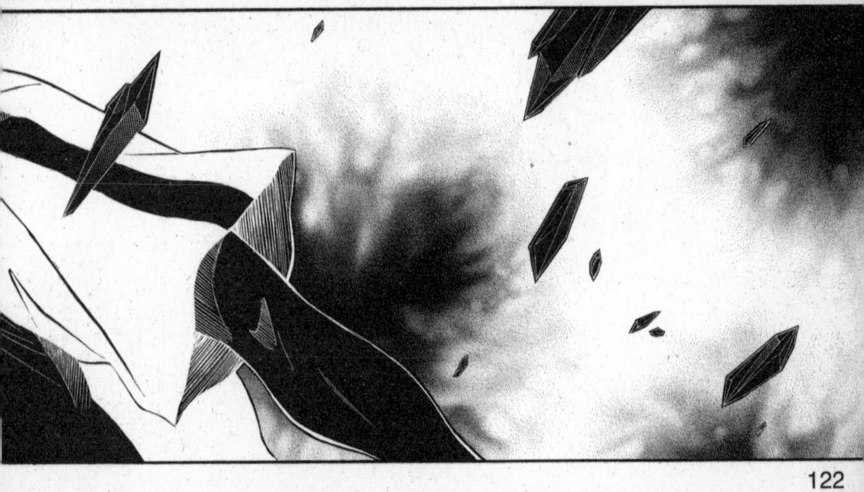

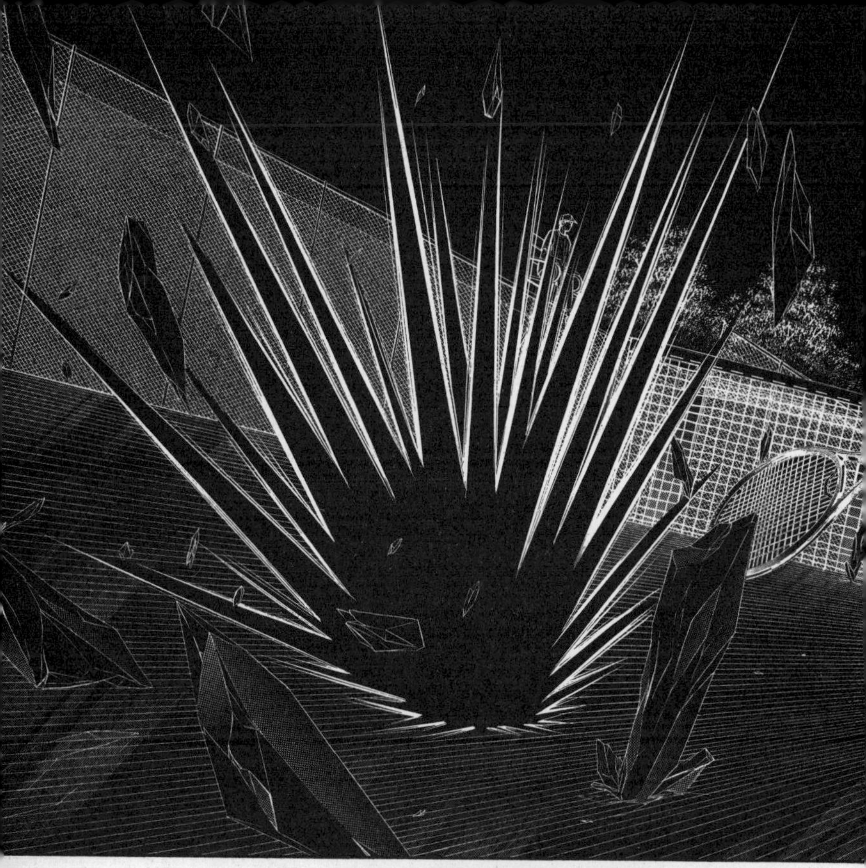
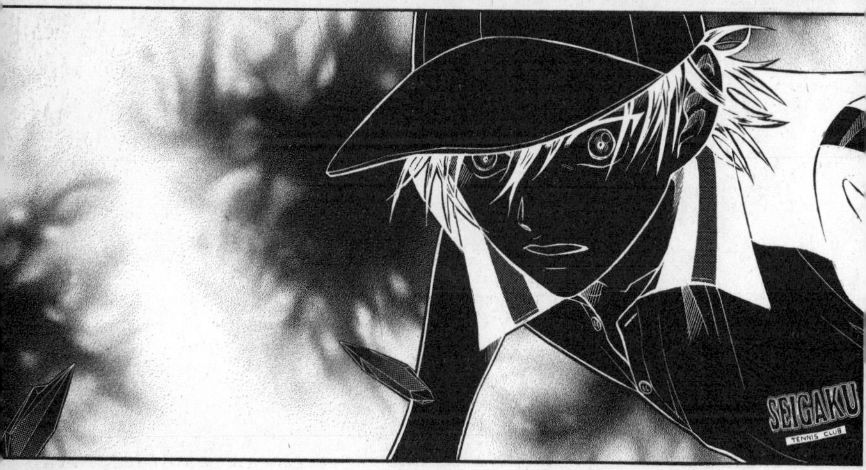
SEIGAKU
TENNIS CLUB

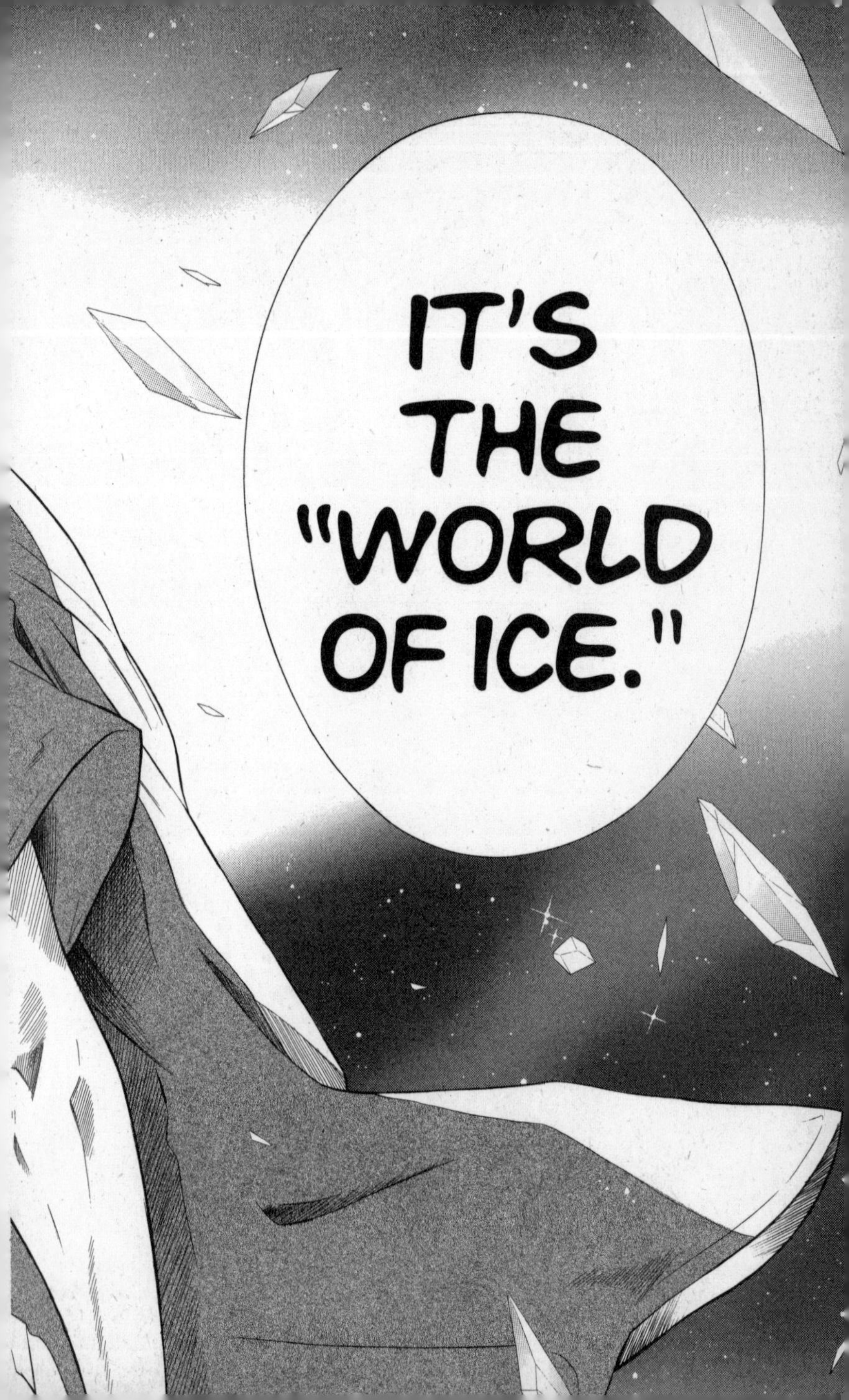
IT'S THE "WORLD OF ICE."

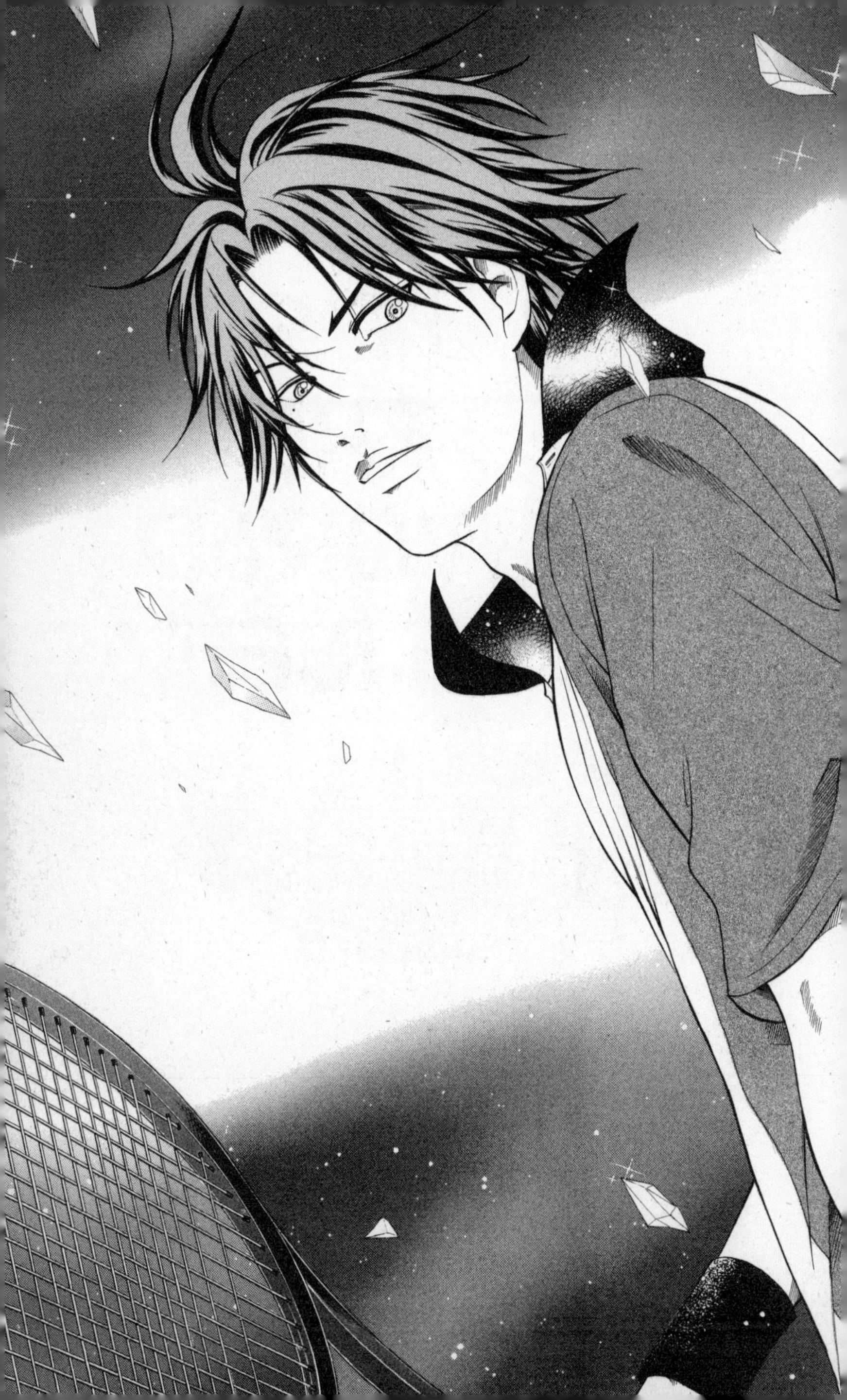

テニスの王子様

THE PRINCE OF TENNIS

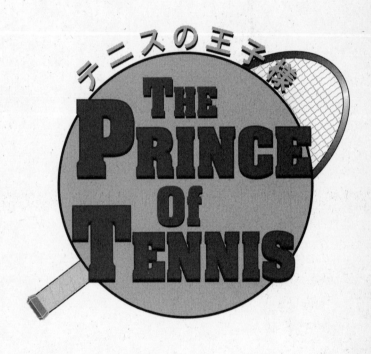

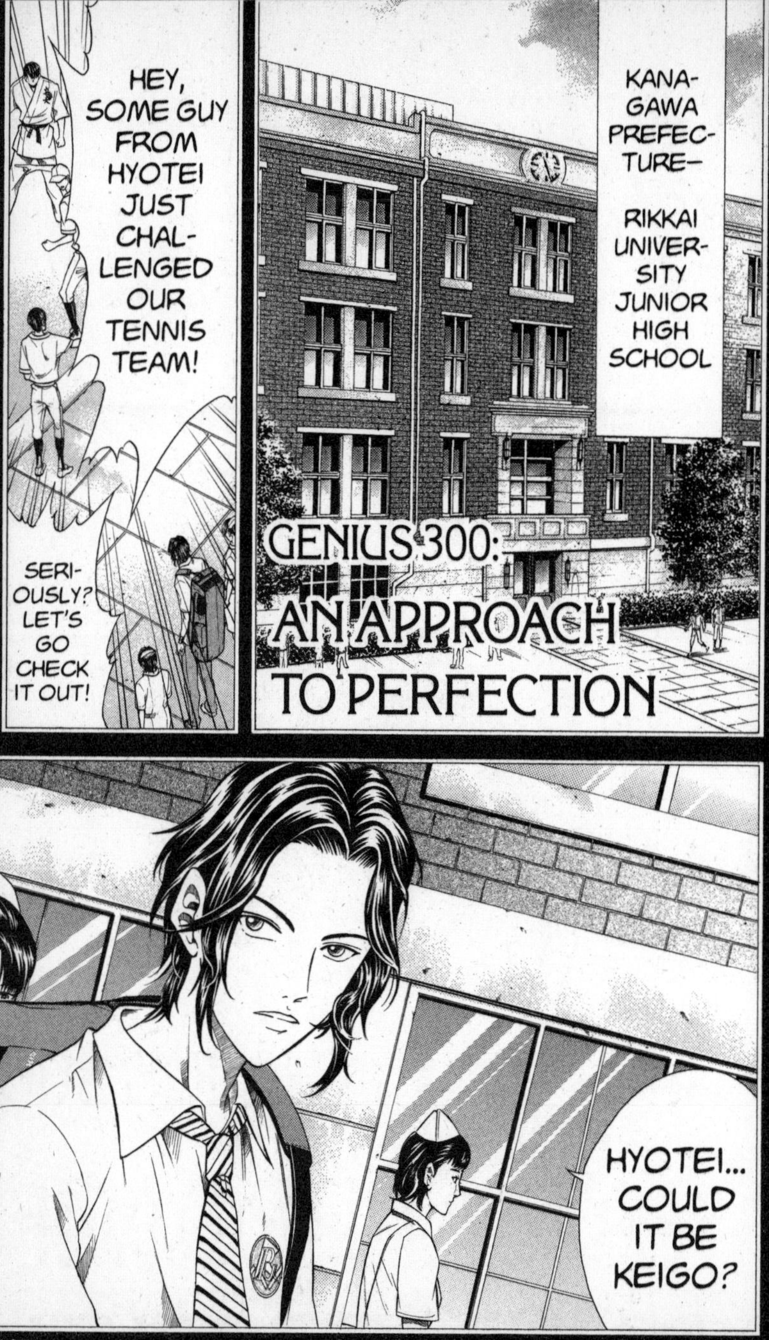
KANAGAWA PREFECTURE—
RIKKAI UNIVERSITY JUNIOR HIGH SCHOOL
GENIUS 300:
AN APPROACH TO PERFECTION
HEY, SOME GUY FROM HYOTEI JUST CHALLENGED OUR TENNIS TEAM!
SERIOUSLY? LET'S GO CHECK IT OUT!
HYOTEI... COULD IT BE KEIGO?

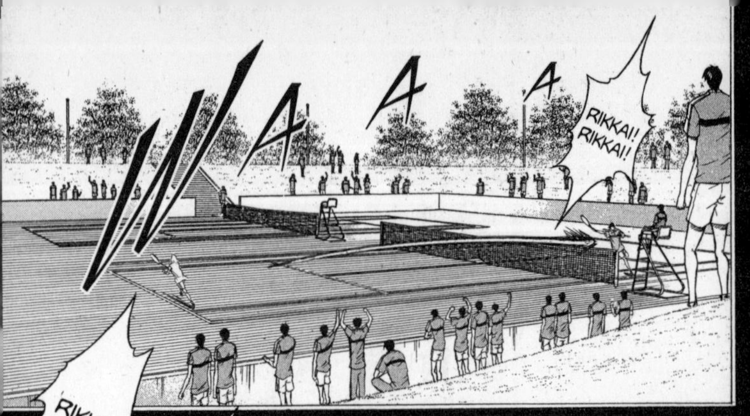
WAAA
RIKKAI! RIKKAI!
RIKKAI! RIKKAI!

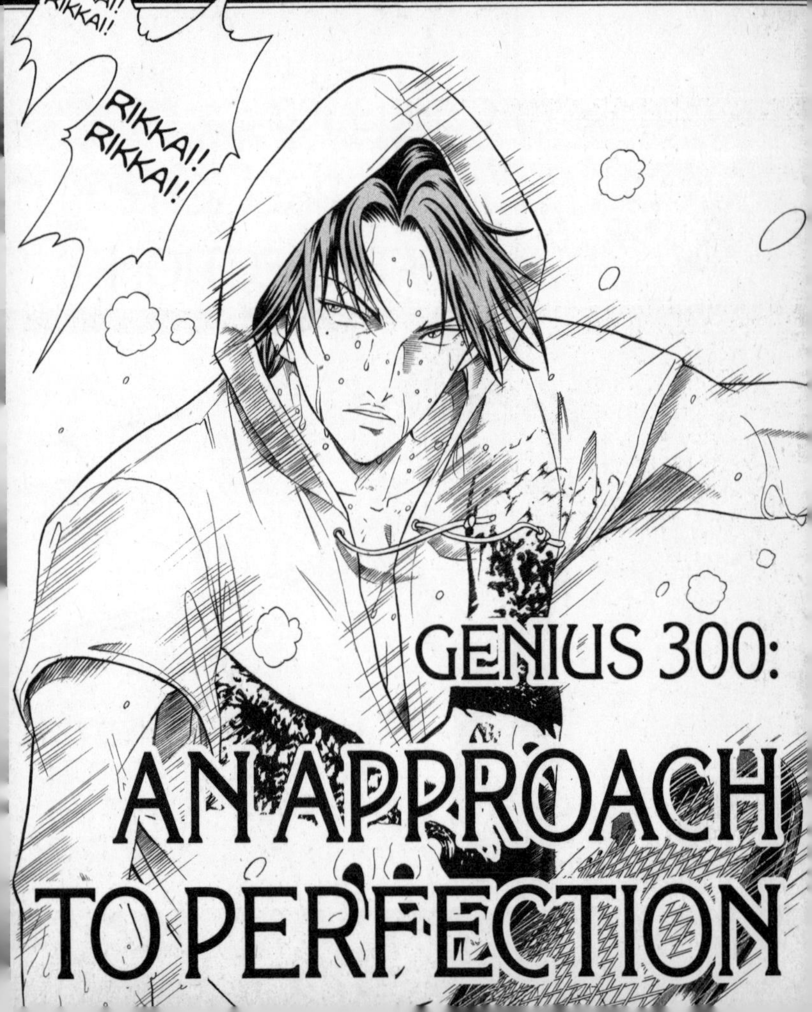
RIKKAI!! RIKKAI!!

GENIUS 300: AN APPROACH TO PERFECTION

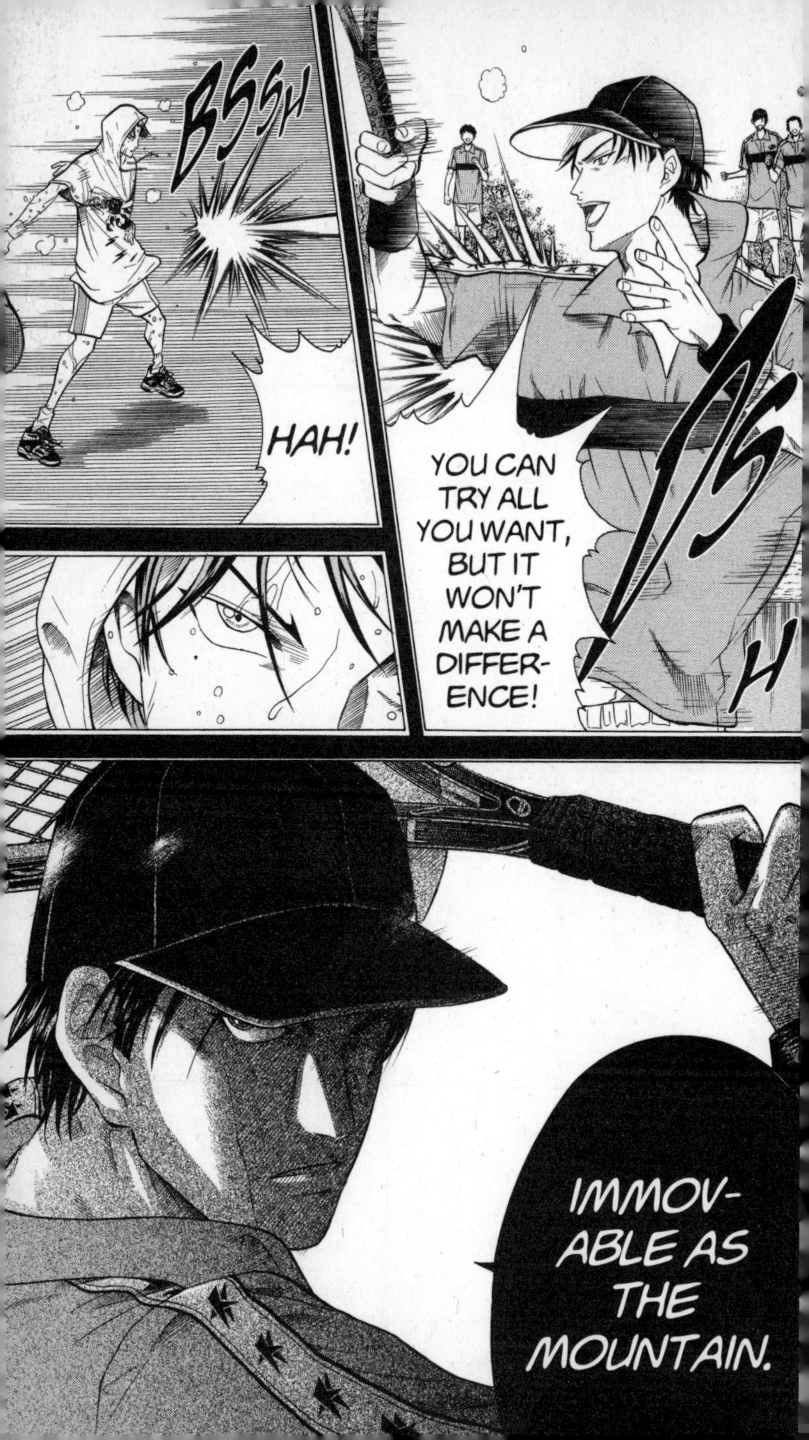
YOU CAN TRY ALL YOU WANT, BUT IT WON'T MAKE A DIFFERENCE!
BSSH
HAH!
IMMOVABLE AS THE MOUNTAIN.

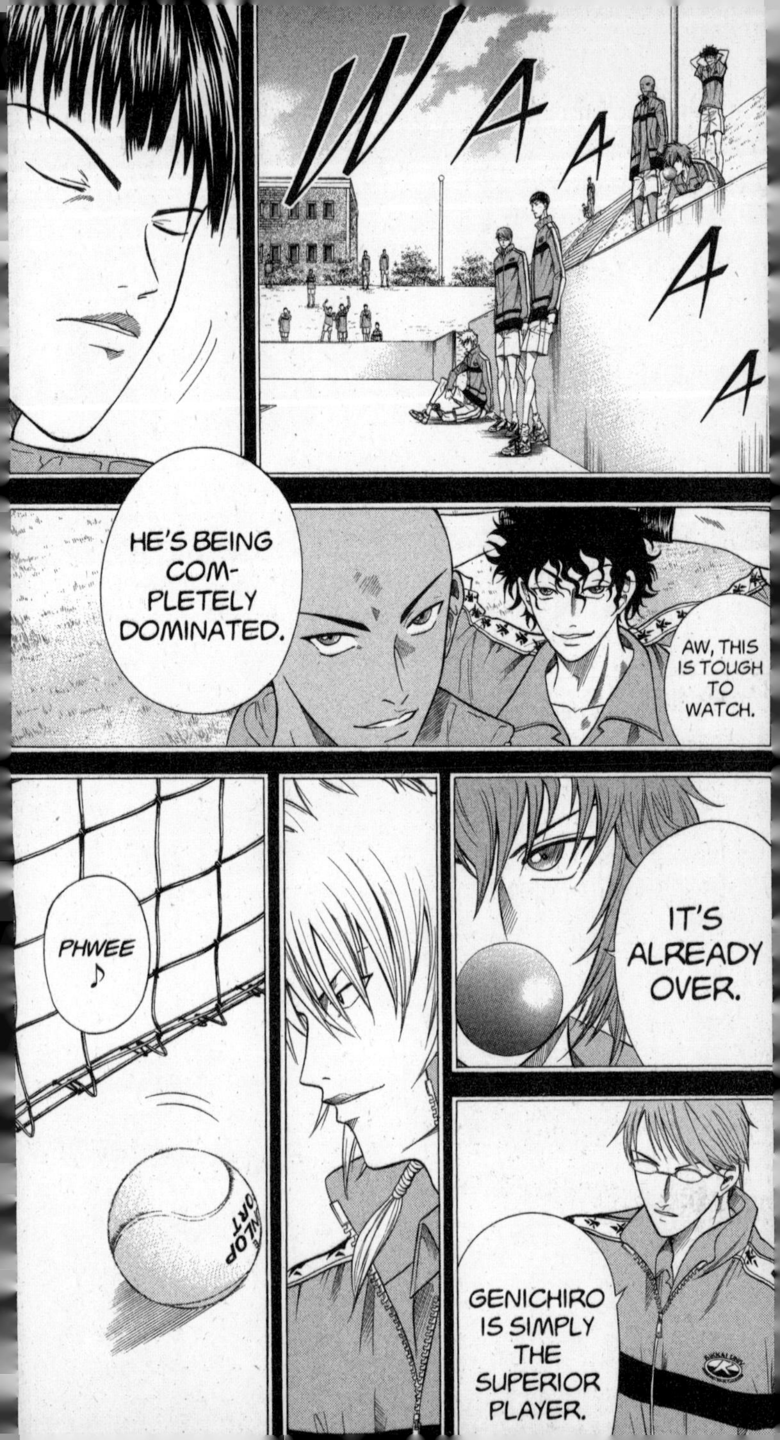
WAAAA
AW, THIS IS TOUGH TO WATCH.
HE'S BEING COM-PLETELY DOMINATED.
IT'S ALREADY OVER.
GENICHIRO IS SIMPLY THE SUPERIOR PLAYER.
PHWEE ♪

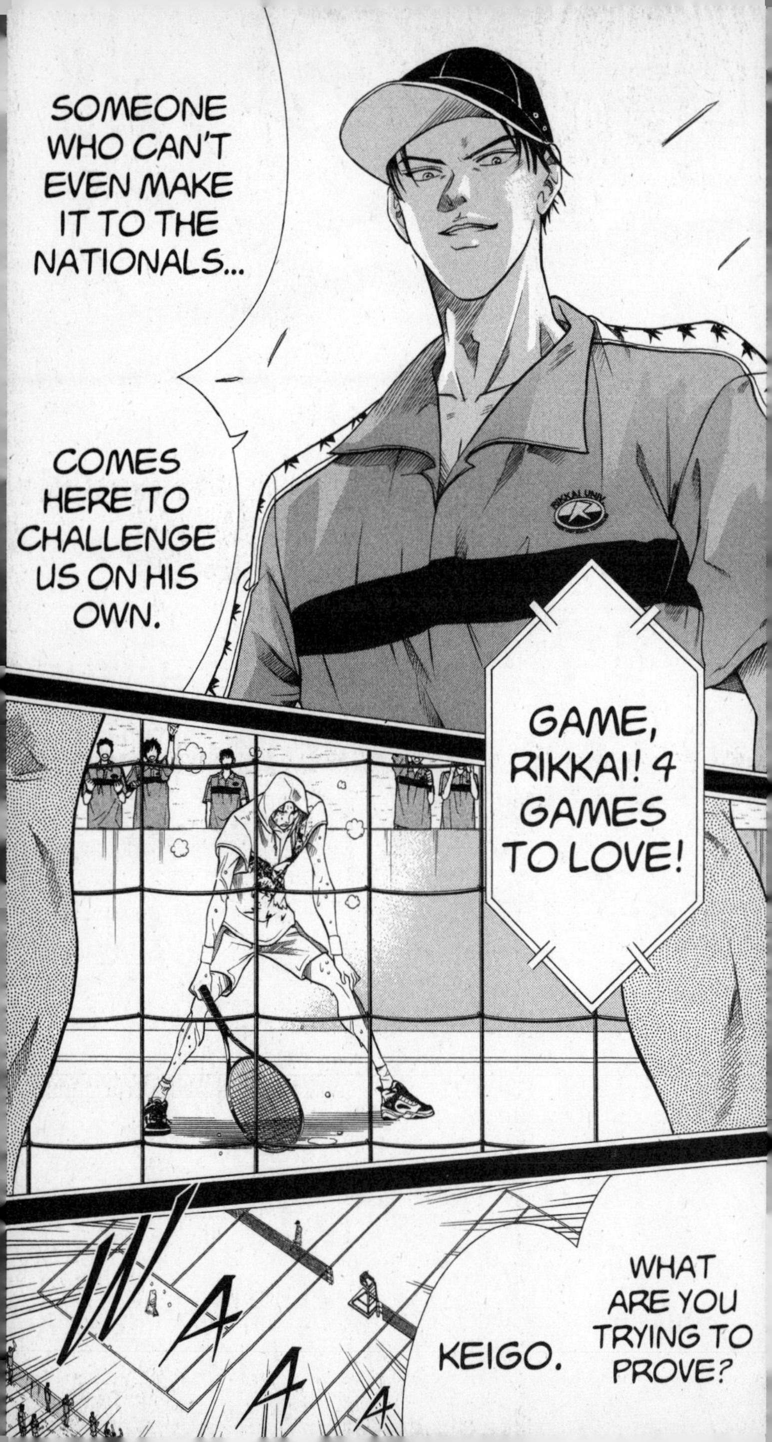
SOMEONE WHO CAN'T EVEN MAKE IT TO THE NATIONALS...
COMES HERE TO CHALLENGE US ON HIS OWN.
GAME, RIKKAI! 4 GAMES TO LOVE!
WHAT ARE YOU TRYING TO PROVE?
KEIGO.
WAAAA

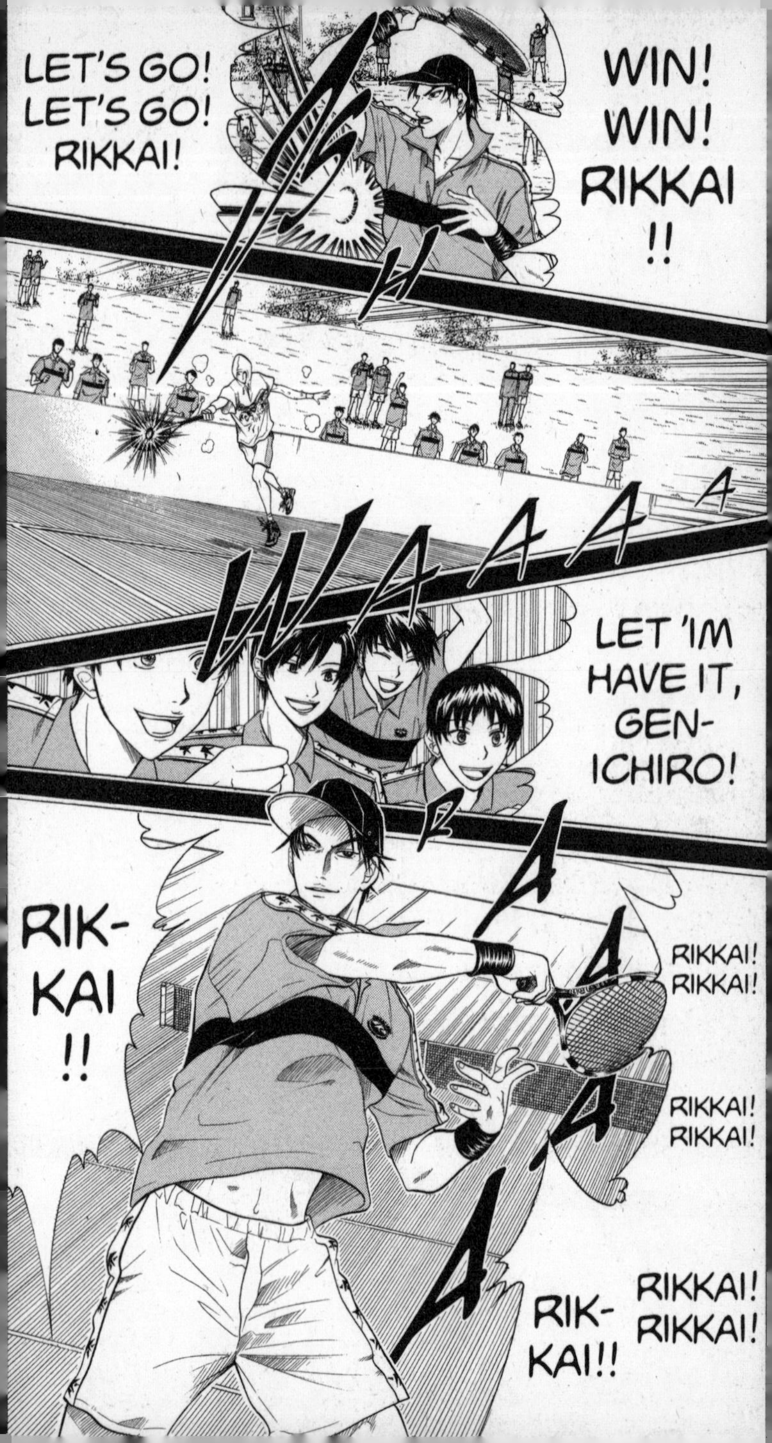

WIN! WIN! RIKKAI!!
LET'S GO! LET'S GO! RIKKAI!
LET 'IM HAVE IT, GEN-ICHIRO!
RIKKAI! RIKKAI!
RIKKAI! RIKKAI!
RIK-KAI!!
RIKKAI! RIKKAI!
RIK-KAI!!

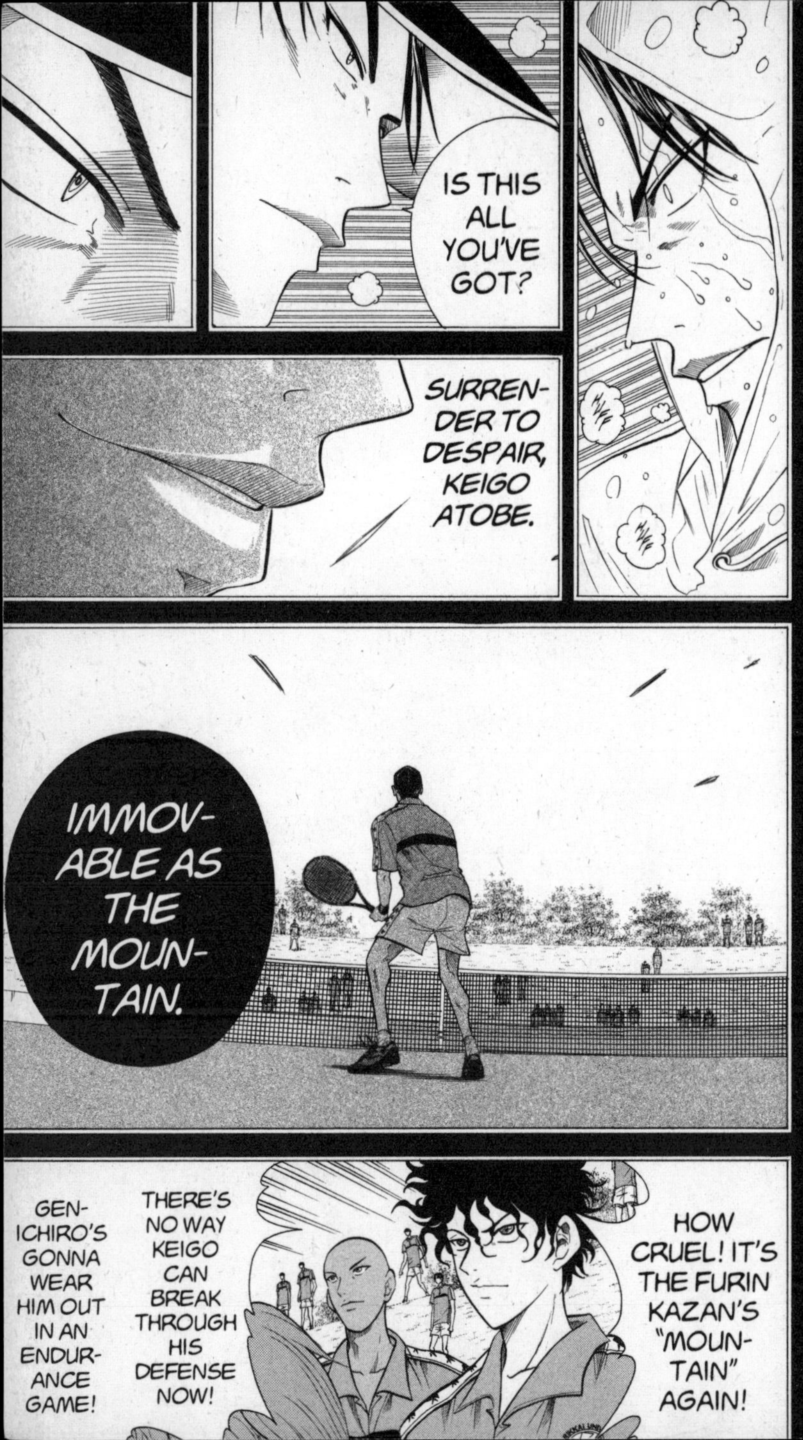
IS THIS ALL YOU'VE GOT?
SURREN-DER TO DESPAIR, KEIGO ATOBE.
IMMOV-ABLE AS THE MOUN-TAIN.
HOW CRUEL! IT'S THE FURIN KAZAN'S "MOUN-TAIN" AGAIN!
THERE'S NO WAY KEIGO CAN BREAK THROUGH HIS DEFENSE NOW!
GEN-ICHIRO'S GONNA WEAR HIM OUT IN AN ENDUR-ANCE GAME!

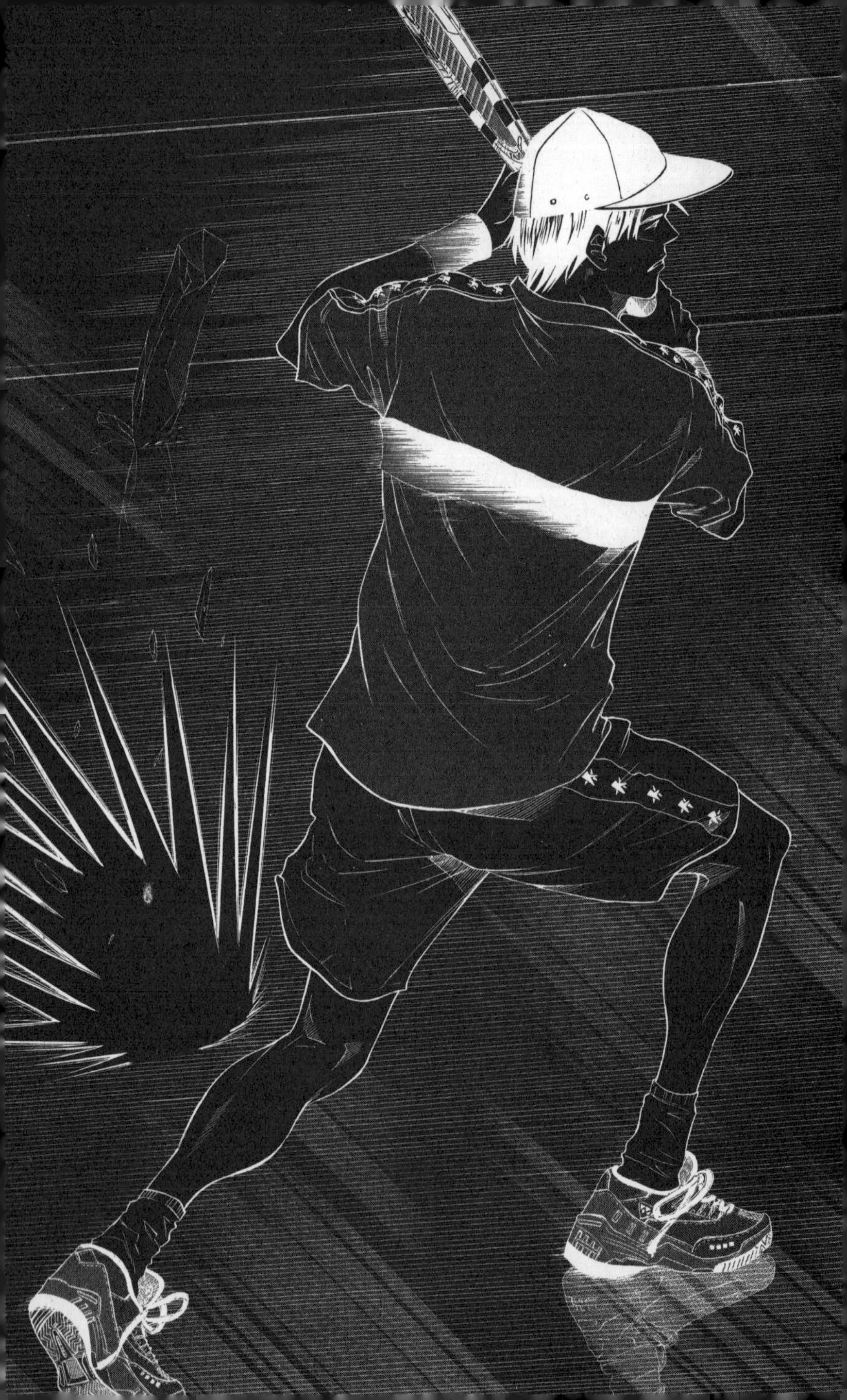

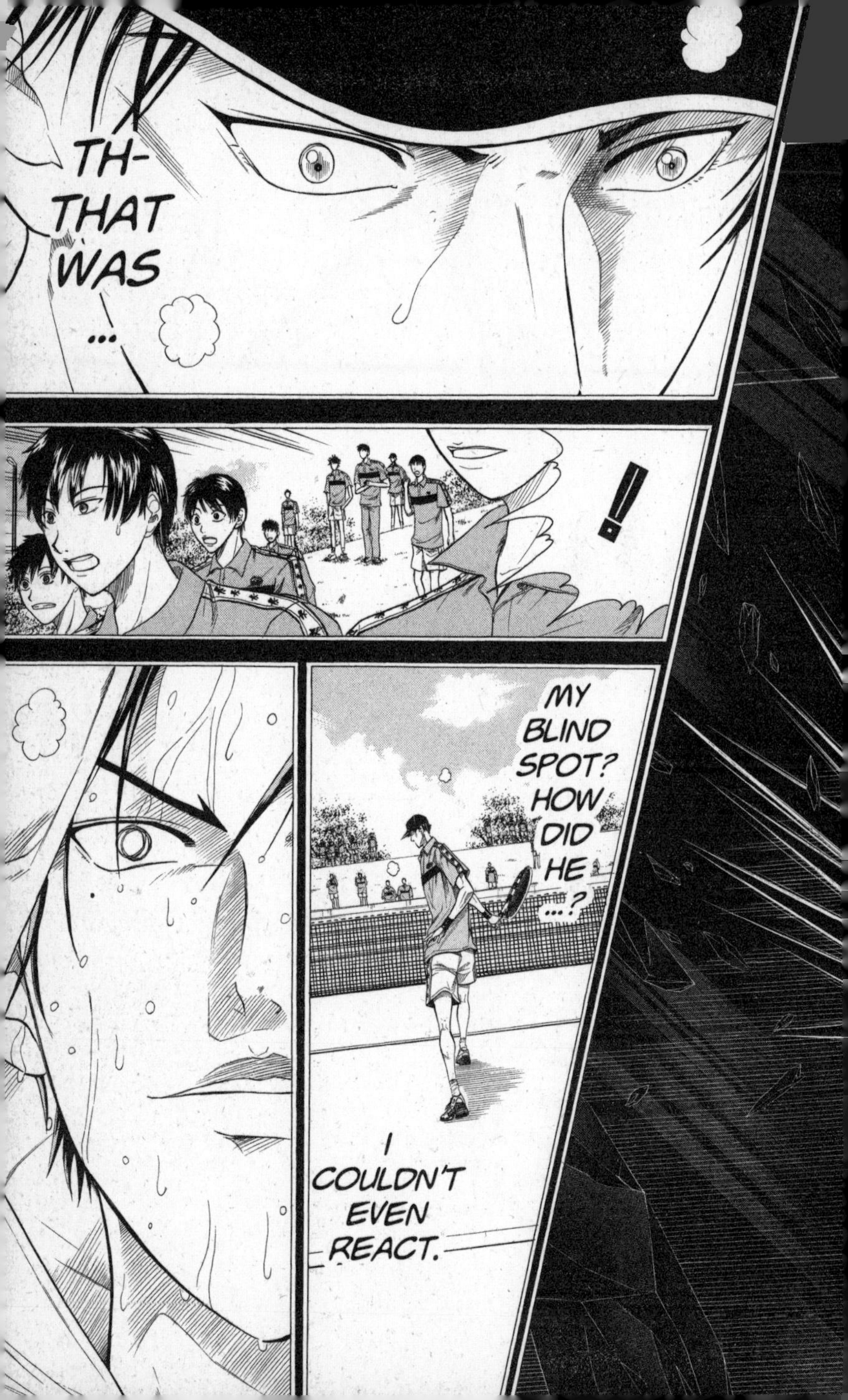
TH- THAT WAS ...
!
MY BLIND SPOT? HOW DID HE ...?
I COULDN'T EVEN REACT.

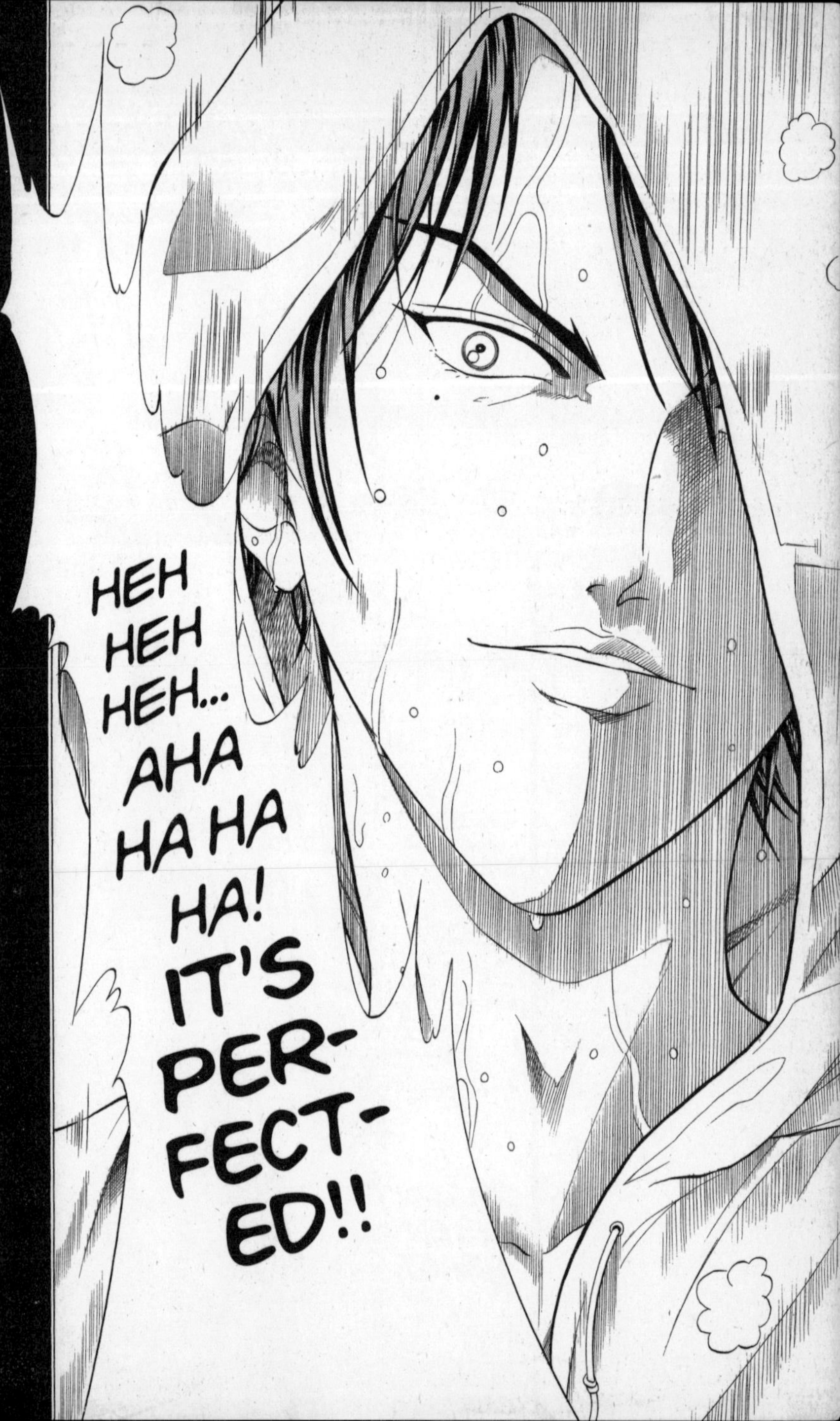
HEH HEH HEH... AHA HA HA HA!
IT'S PER-FECT-ED!!

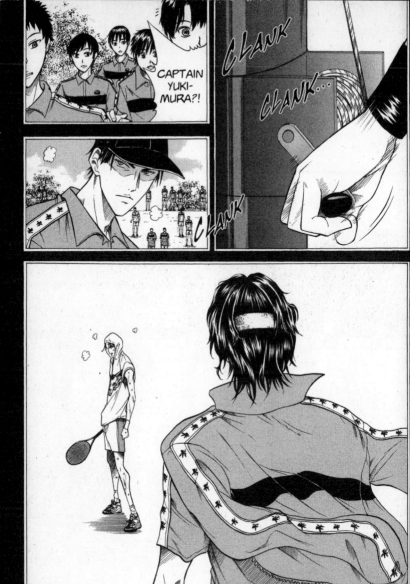

CAPTAIN YUKI-MURA?!

CLANK

CLANK...

CLANK

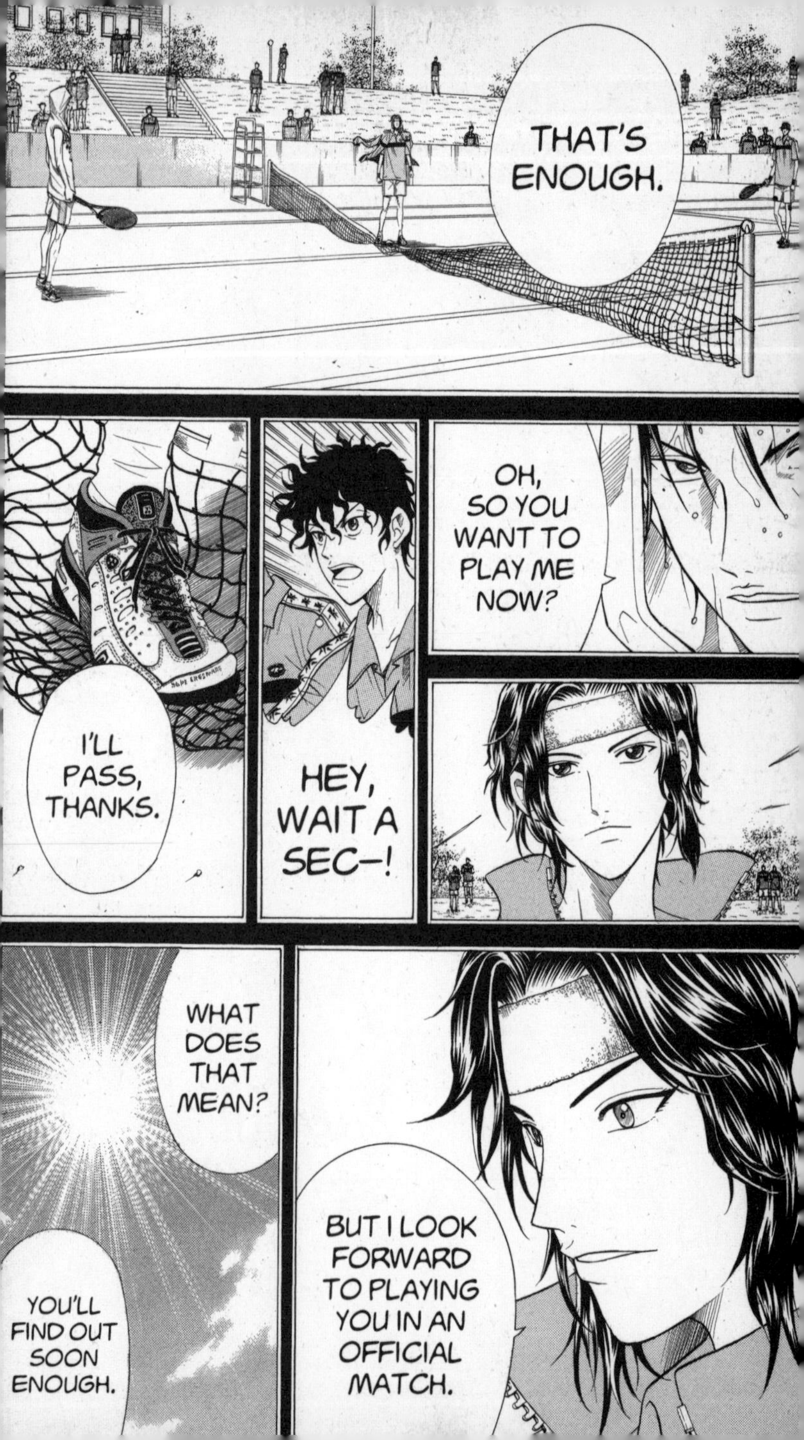
THAT'S ENOUGH.
OH, SO YOU WANT TO PLAY ME NOW?
HEY, WAIT A SEC—!
I'LL PASS, THANKS.
BUT I LOOK FORWARD TO PLAYING YOU IN AN OFFICIAL MATCH.
WHAT DOES THAT MEAN?
YOU'LL FIND OUT SOON ENOUGH.

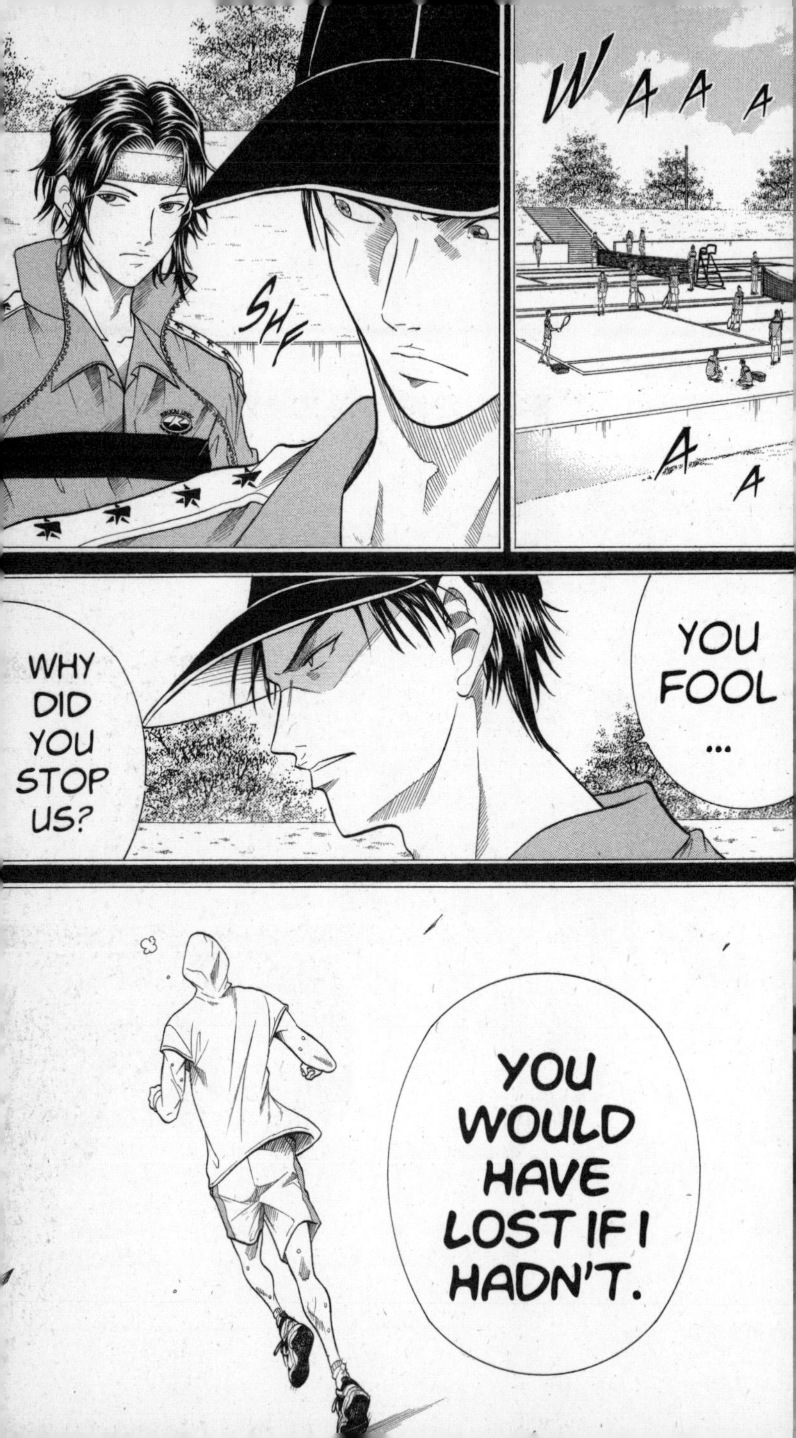

WAAA
A A
SHF
YOU FOOL ...
WHY DID YOU STOP US?
YOU WOULD HAVE LOST IF I HADN'T.

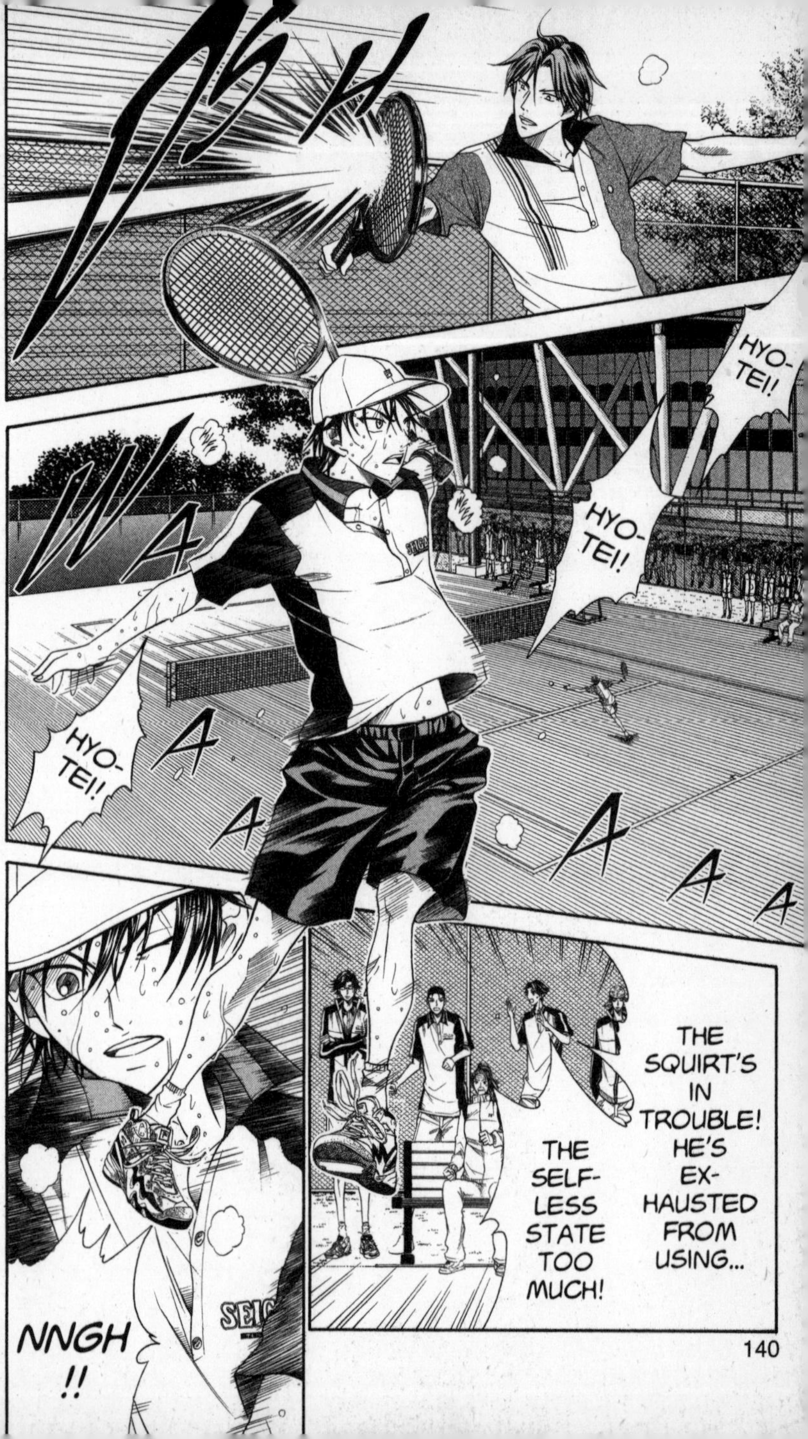

PSH
HYO-TEI!!
WAAAAAAAA
HYO-TEI!!
HYO-TEI!!
THE SQUIRT'S IN TROUBLE! HE'S EX-HAUSTED FROM USING...
THE SELF-LESS STATE TOO MUCH!
NNGH !!

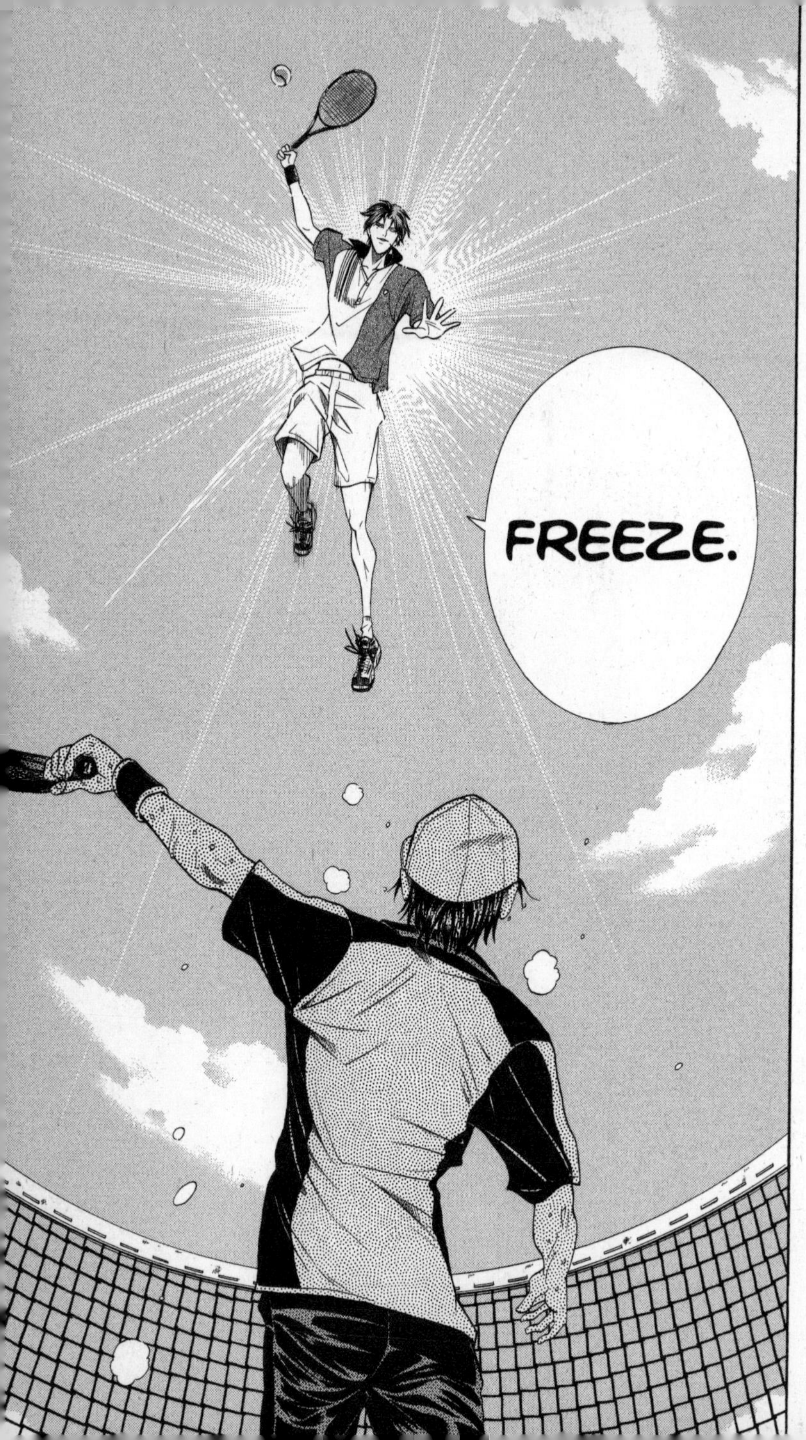
FREEZE.

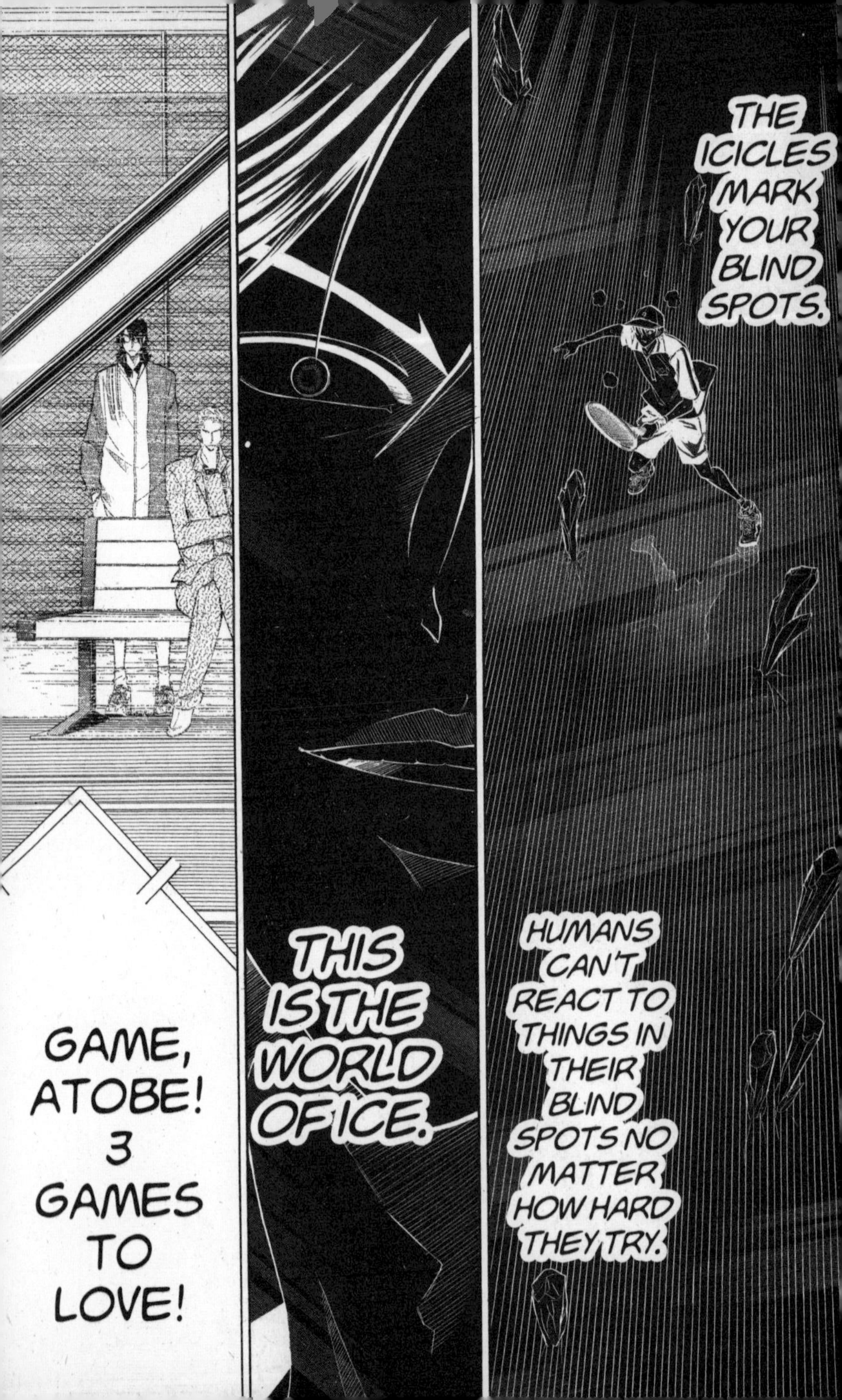
THE ICICLES MARK YOUR BLIND SPOTS.
HUMANS CAN'T REACT TO THINGS IN THEIR BLIND SPOTS NO MATTER HOW HARD THEY TRY.
THIS IS THE WORLD OF ICE.
GAME, ATOBE! 3 GAMES TO LOVE!

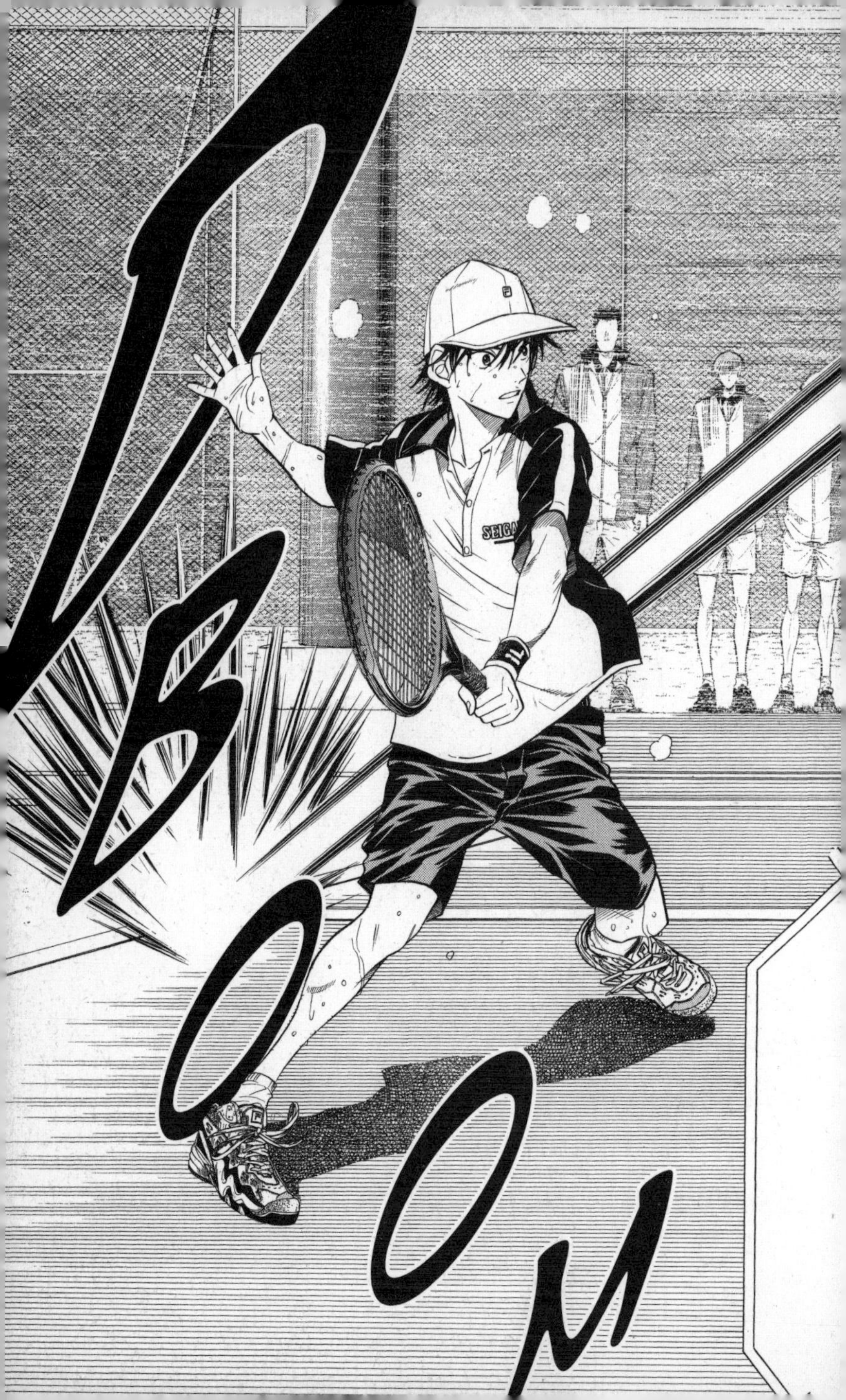
DBOOM

テニスの王子様

THE PRINCE OF TENNIS

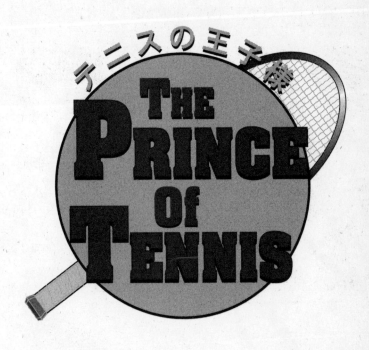

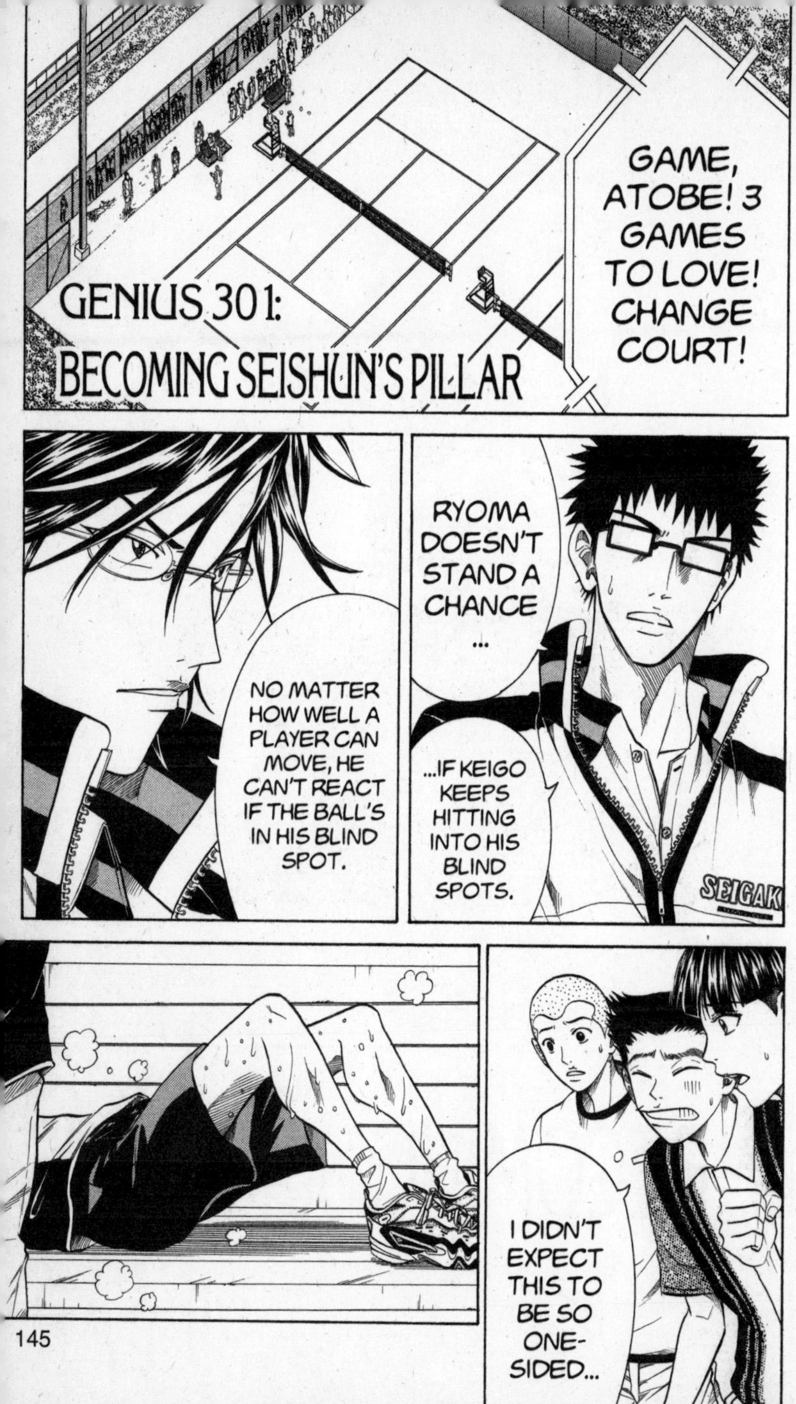
GENIUS 301:
BECOMING SEISHUN'S PILLAR
GAME, ATOBE! 3 GAMES TO LOVE! CHANGE COURT!
RYOMA DOESN'T STAND A CHANCE ...
...IF KEIGO KEEPS HITTING INTO HIS BLIND SPOTS.
SEIGAKU
NO MATTER HOW WELL A PLAYER CAN MOVE, HE CAN'T REACT IF THE BALL'S IN HIS BLIND SPOT.
I DIDN'T EXPECT THIS TO BE SO ONE-SIDED...

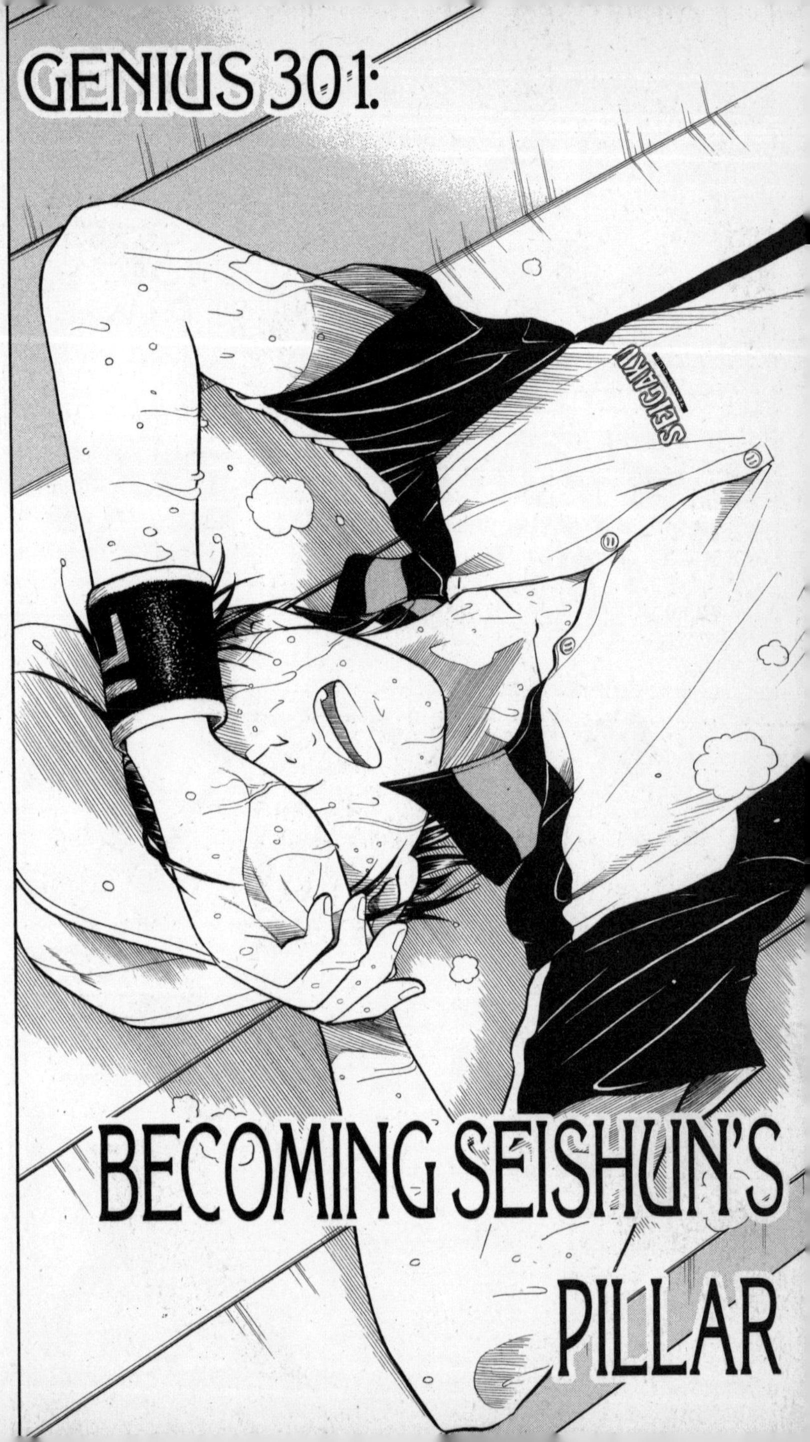
GENIUS 301:
SEIGAKU
BECOMING SEISHUN'S PILLAR

BEING HELPLESS LIKE THAT...

I FEEL FOR HIM.

HYO-TEI!! HYO-TEI!!

HE'S SPENT.

HYO-TEI!! HYO-TEI!!

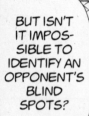

BUT ISN'T IT IMPOSSIBLE TO IDENTIFY AN OPPONENT'S BLIND SPOTS?

KEIGO'S MADE THE IMPOSSIBLE POSSIBLE.

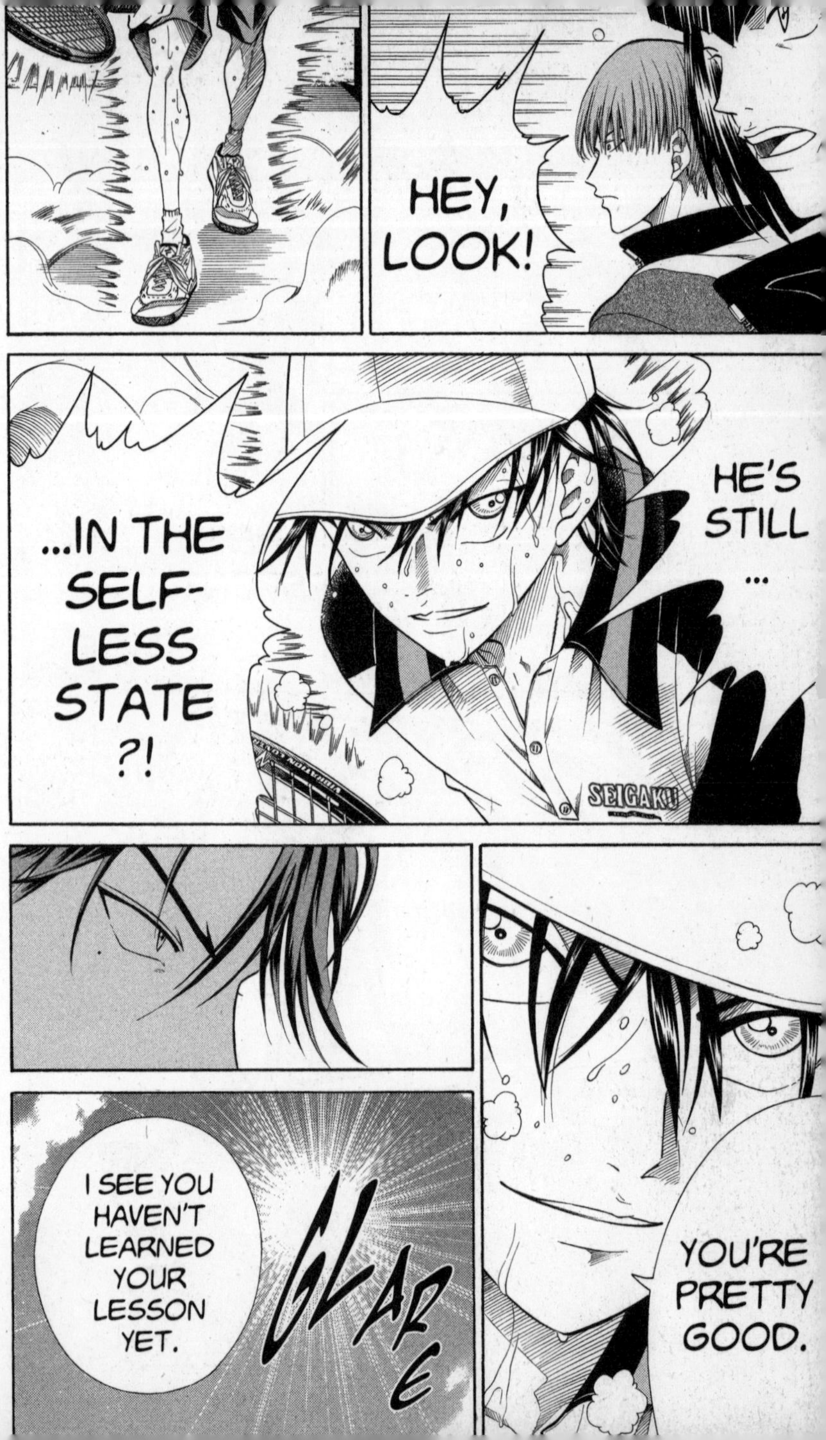
HEY, LOOK!
HE'S STILL ...
...IN THE SELF-LESS STATE ?!
SEIGAKU
YOU'RE PRETTY GOOD.
I SEE YOU HAVEN'T LEARNED YOUR LESSON YET.
GLARE

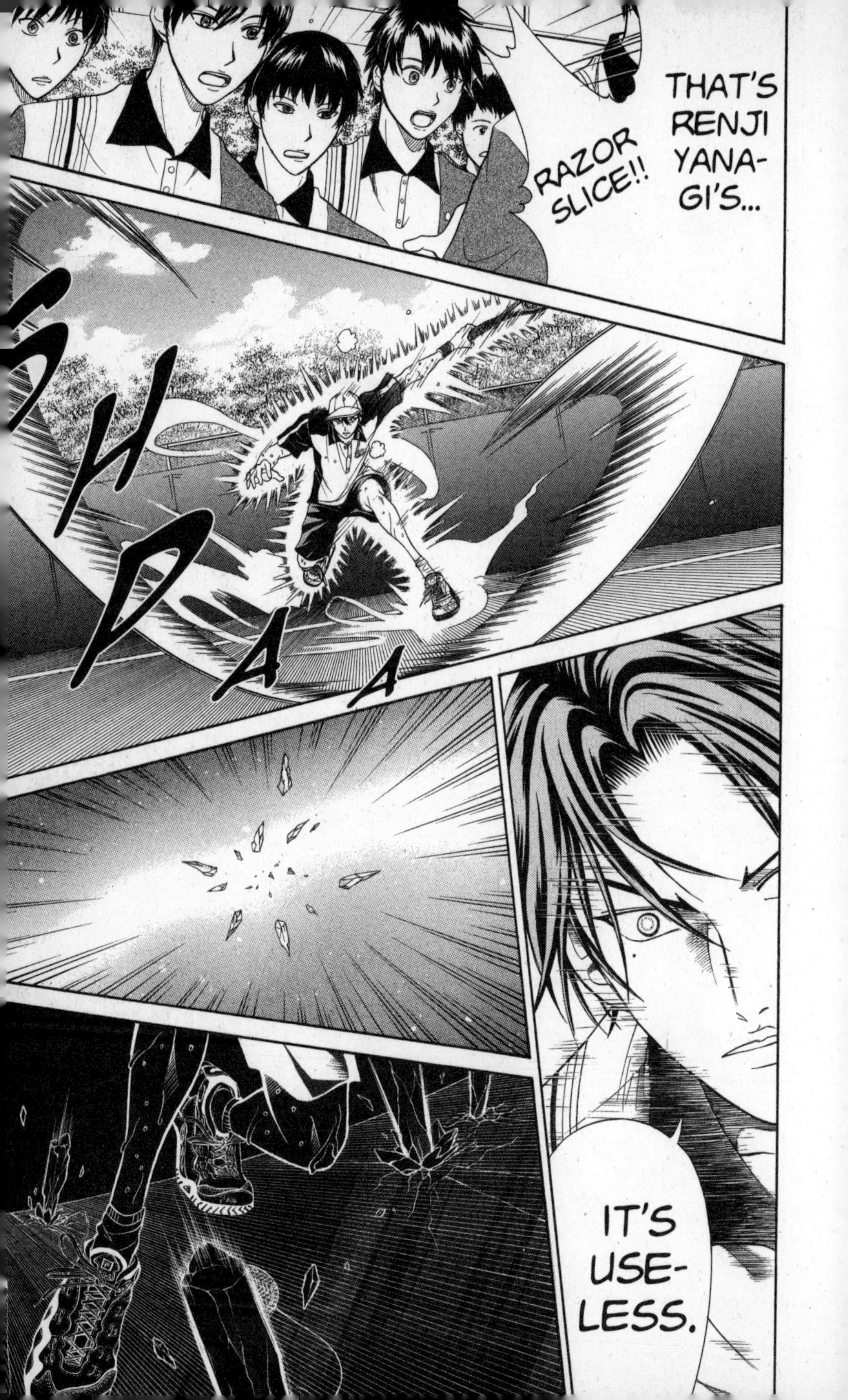
THAT'S RENJI YANAGI'S...
RAZOR SLICE!!
IT'S USELESS.

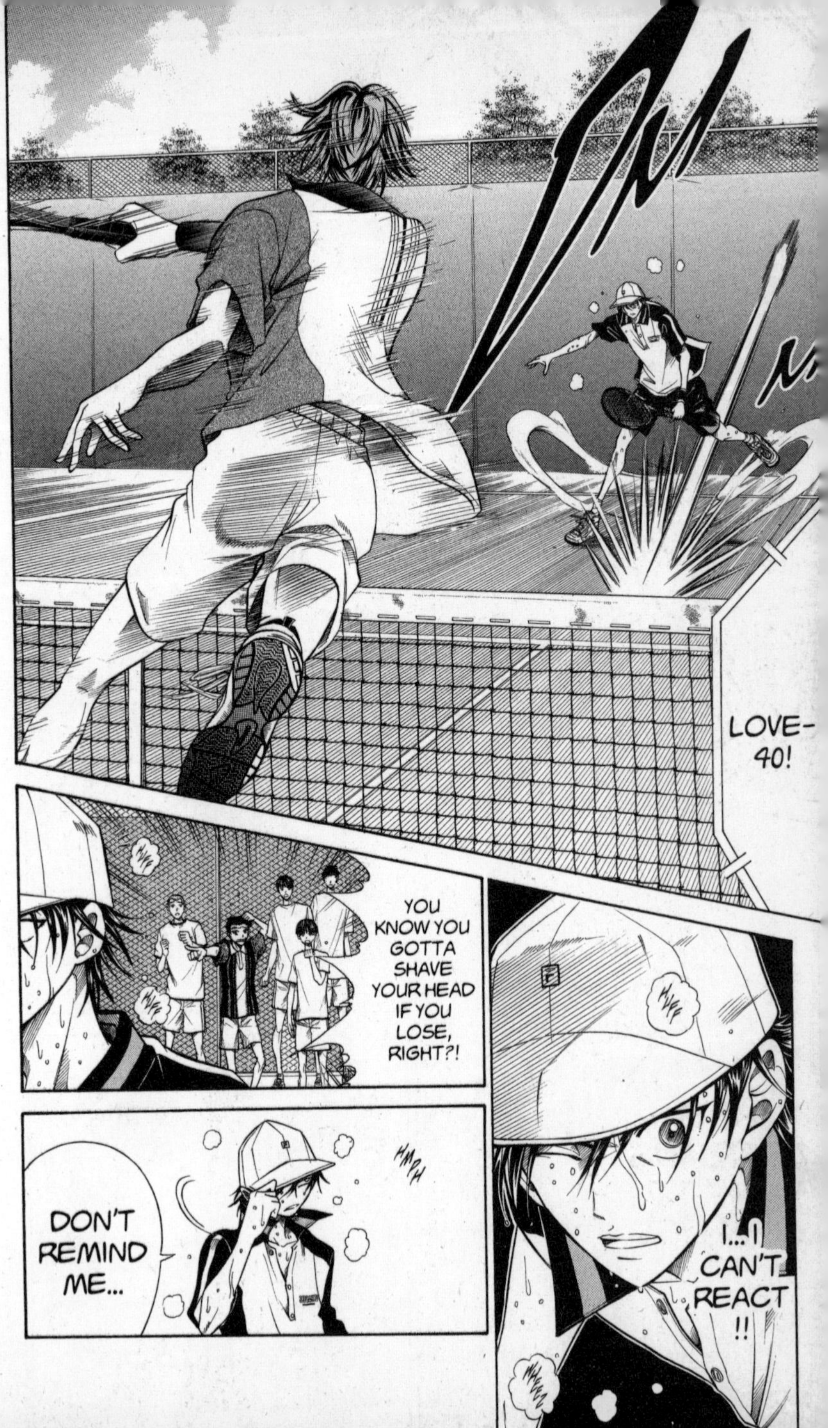
LOVE-40!
I... I CAN'T REACT!!
YOU KNOW YOU GOTTA SHAVE YOUR HEAD IF YOU LOSE, RIGHT?!
HMPH
DON'T REMIND ME...

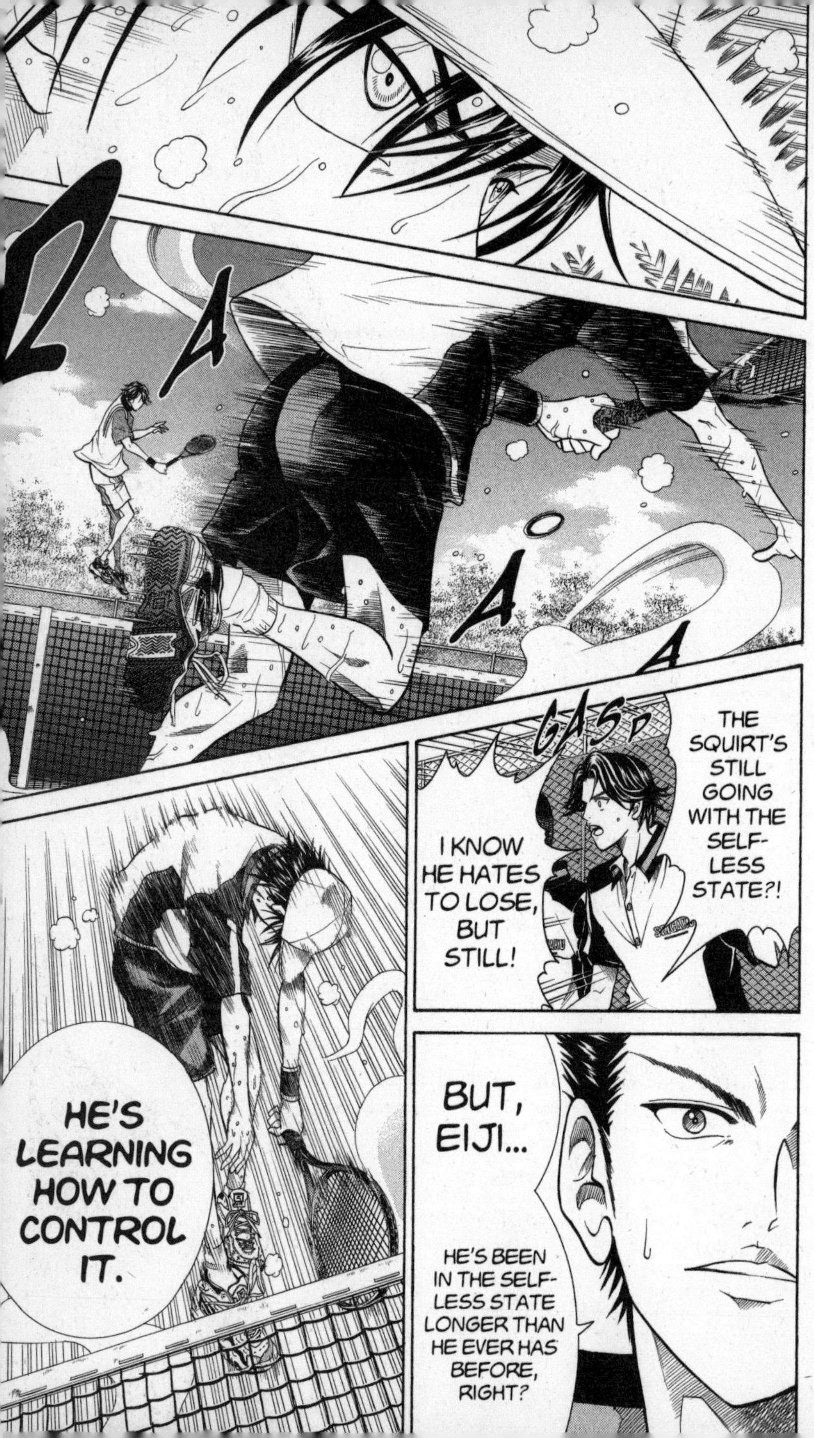
GASP
THE SQUIRT'S STILL GOING WITH THE SELF-LESS STATE?!
I KNOW HE HATES TO LOSE, BUT STILL!
BUT, EIJI...
HE'S BEEN IN THE SELF-LESS STATE LONGER THAN HE EVER HAS BEFORE, RIGHT?
HE'S LEARNING HOW TO CONTROL IT.

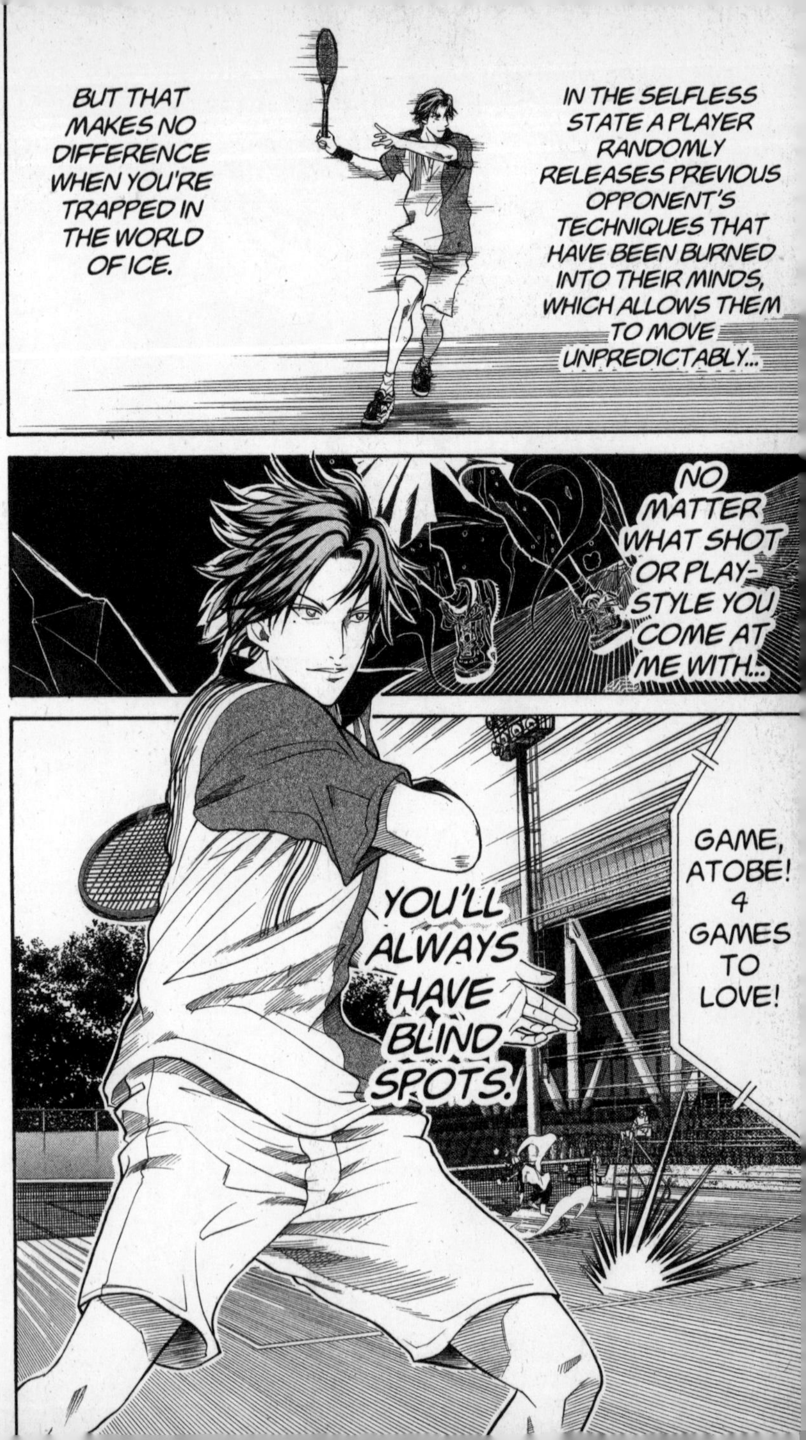
IN THE SELFLESS STATE A PLAYER RANDOMLY RELEASES PREVIOUS OPPONENT'S TECHNIQUES THAT HAVE BEEN BURNED INTO THEIR MINDS, WHICH ALLOWS THEM TO MOVE UNPREDICTABLY...
BUT THAT MAKES NO DIFFERENCE WHEN YOU'RE TRAPPED IN THE WORLD OF ICE.
NO MATTER WHAT SHOT OR PLAY-STYLE YOU COME AT ME WITH...
YOU'LL ALWAYS HAVE BLIND SPOTS!
GAME, ATOBE! 4 GAMES TO LOVE!

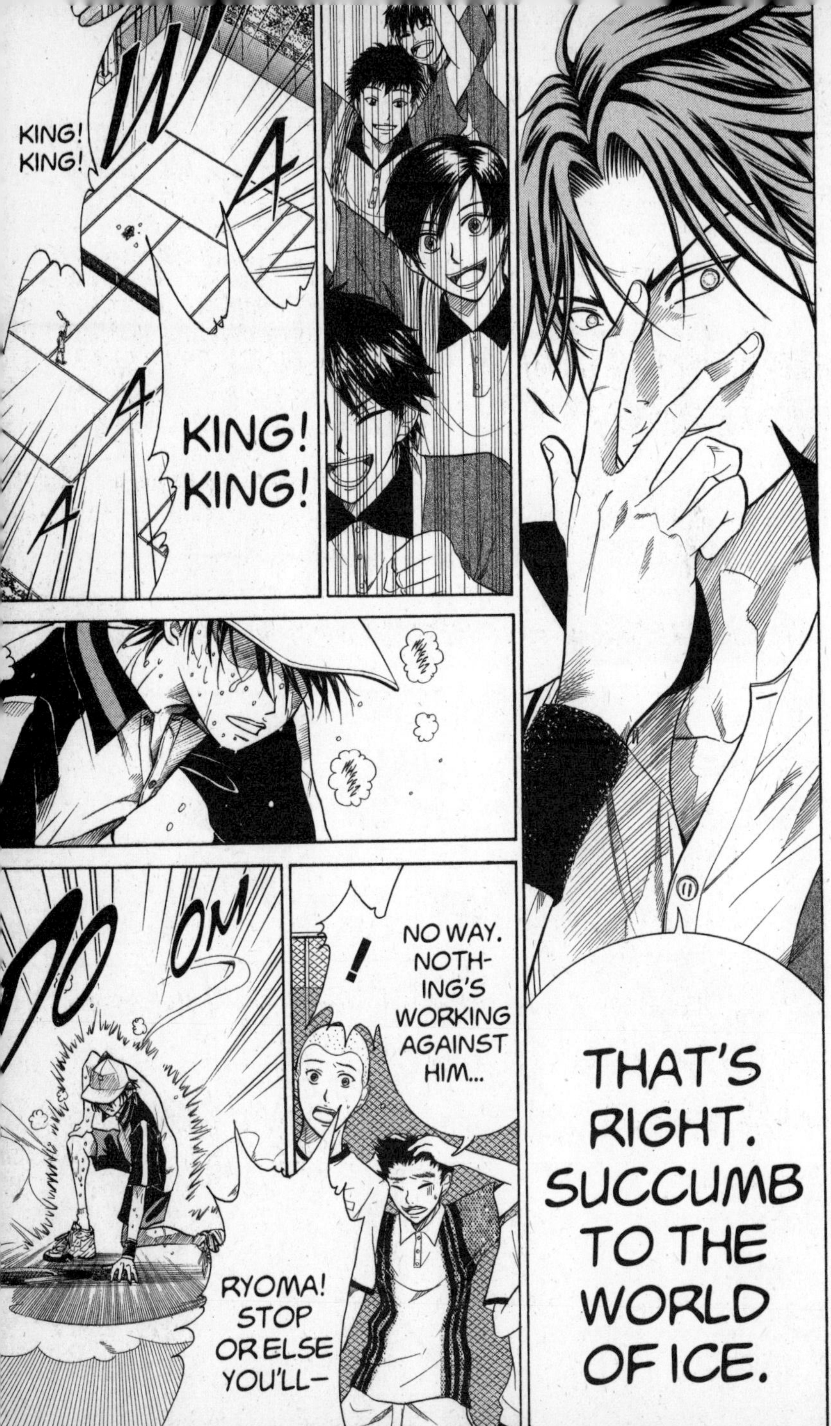
KING! KING!
KING! KING!
NO WAY. NOTHING'S WORKING AGAINST HIM...
!
RYOMA! STOP OR ELSE YOU'LL—
THAT'S RIGHT. SUCCUMB TO THE WORLD OF ICE.

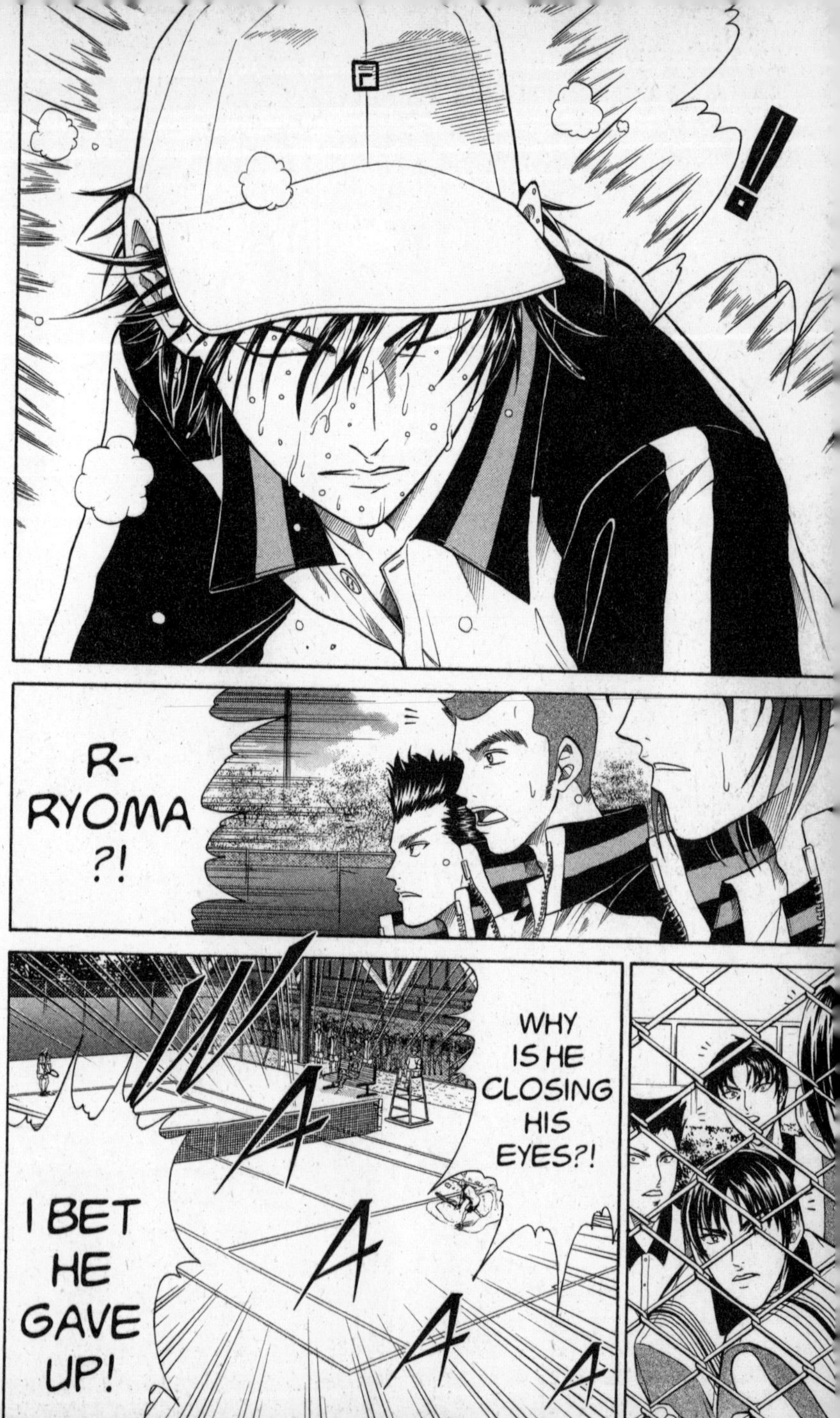
R-RYOMA ?!
WHY IS HE CLOSING HIS EYES?!
I BET HE GAVE UP!

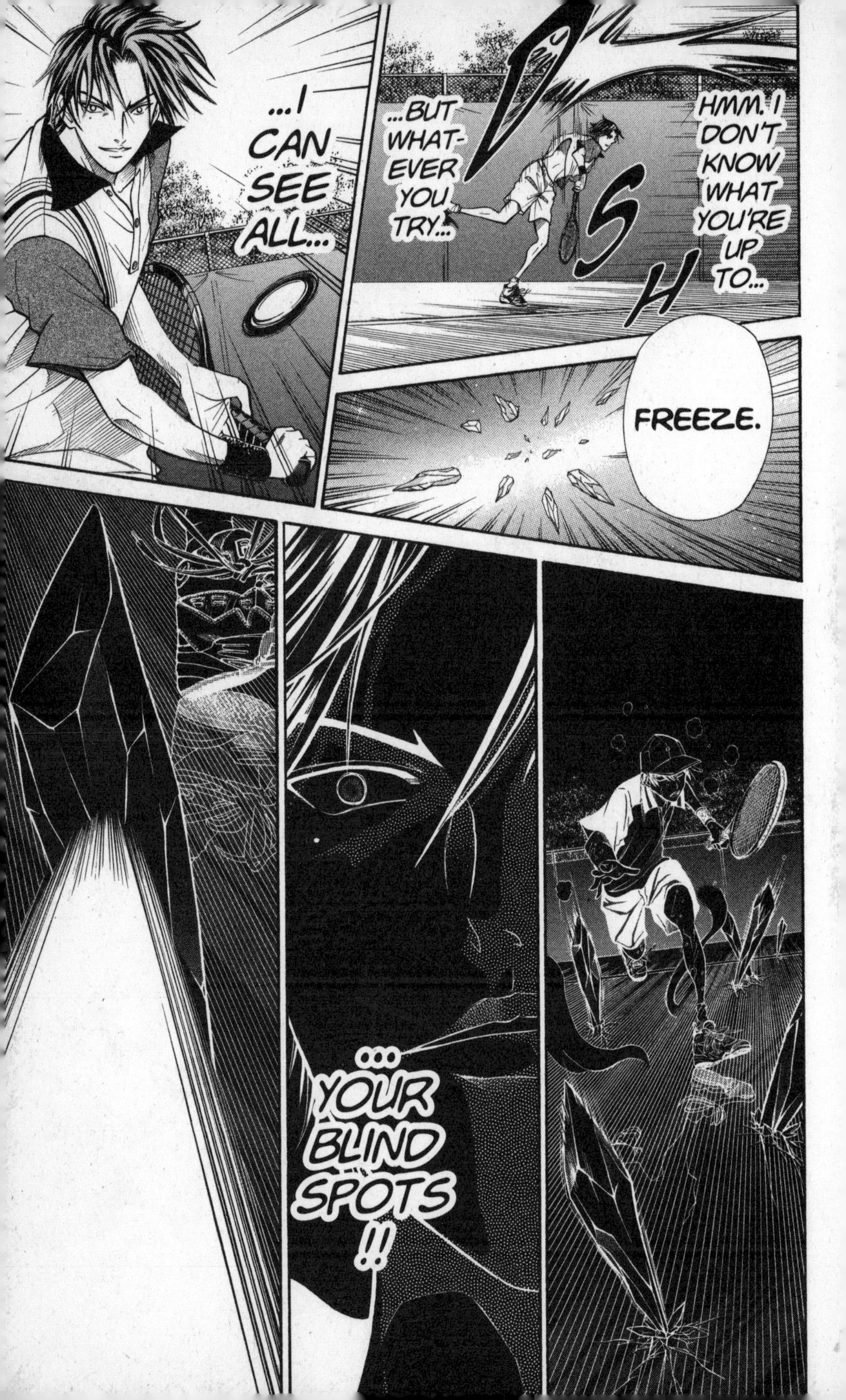
HMM. I DON'T KNOW WHAT YOU'RE UP TO...
...BUT WHATEVER YOU TRY...
SH
FREEZE.
...I CAN SEE ALL...
...YOUR BLIND SPOTS!!

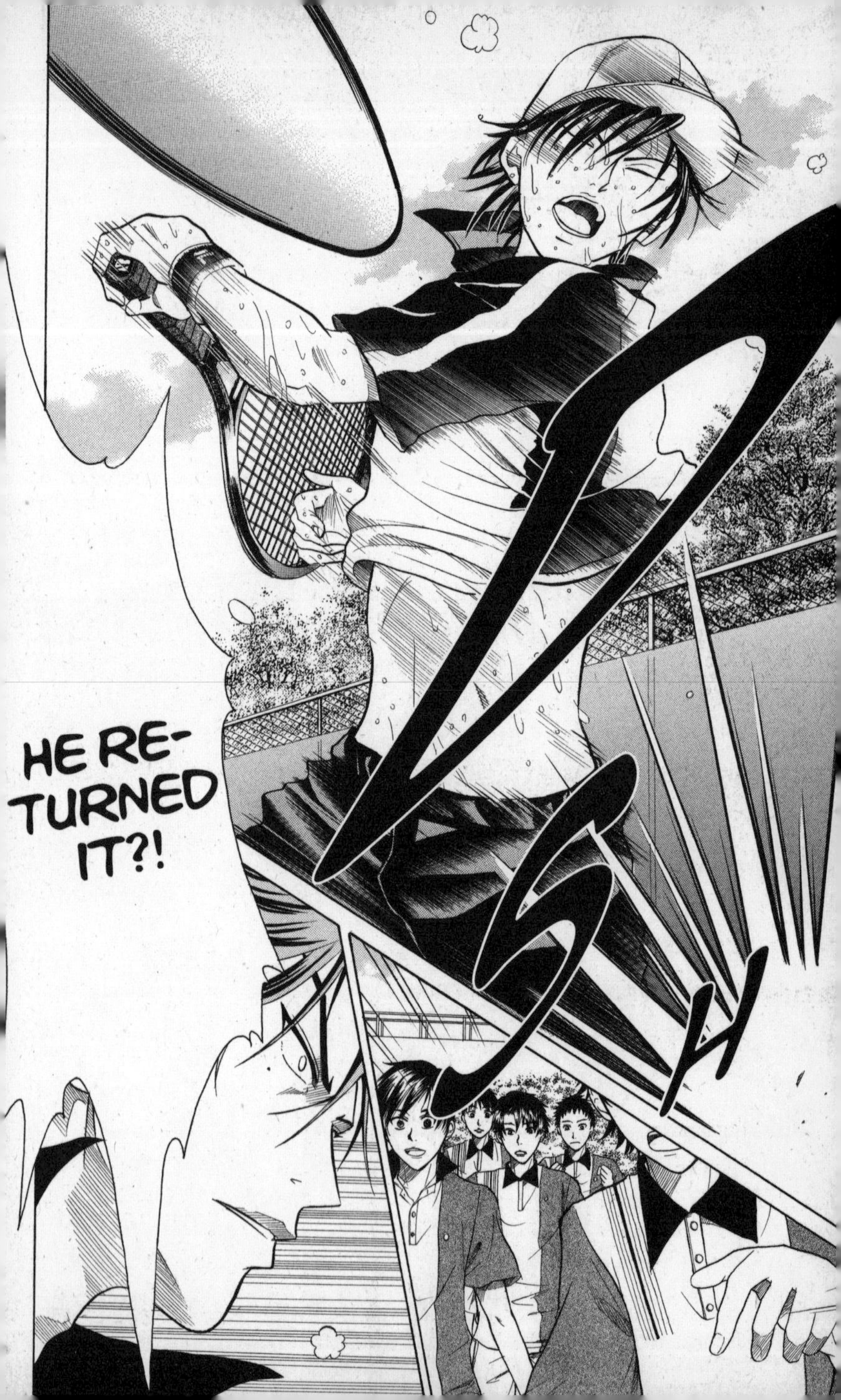
HE RE-TURNED IT?!

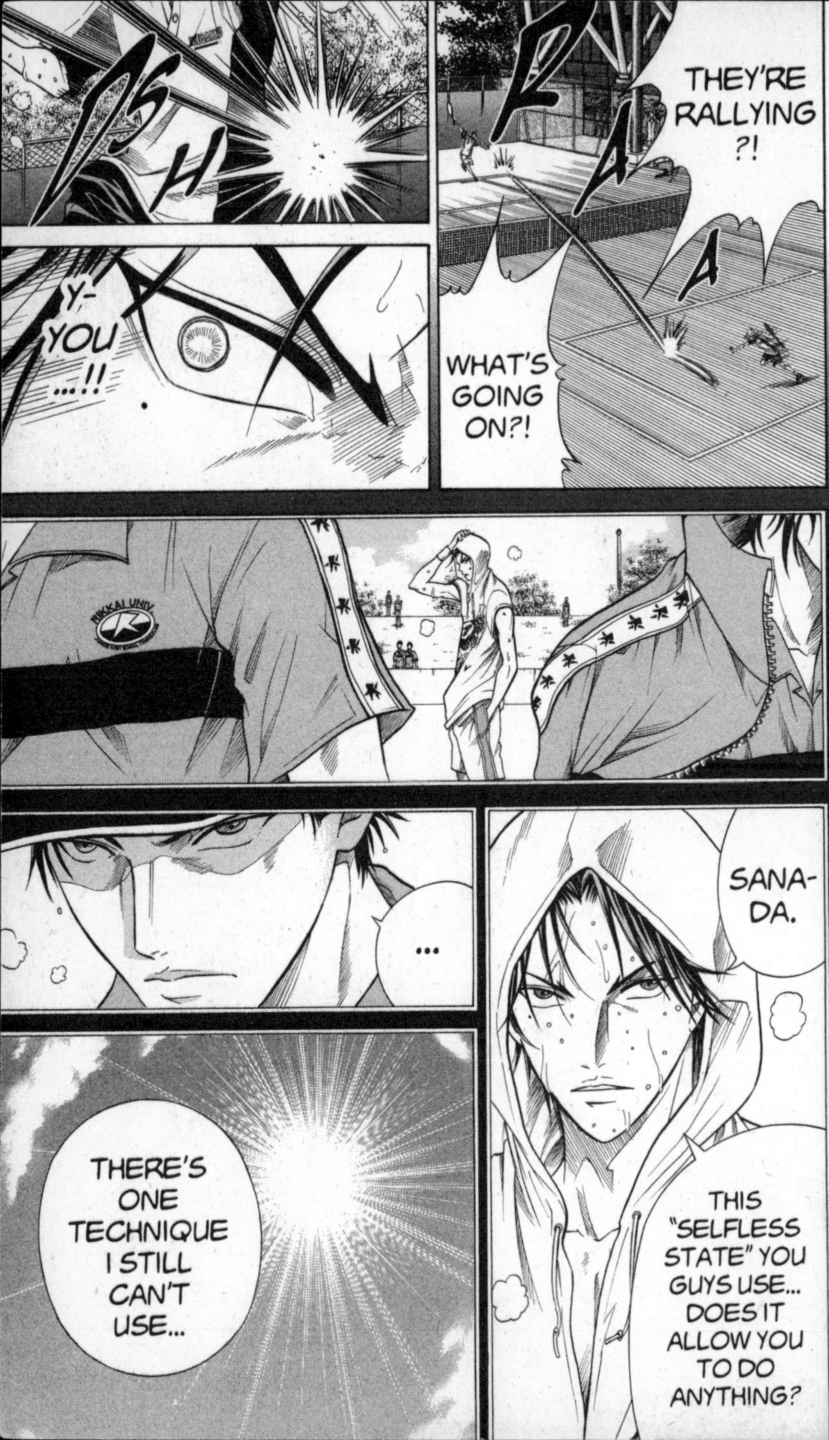
THEY'RE RALLYING ?!
WHAT'S GOING ON?!
PSH
Y-YOU ...!!
SANA-DA.
...
THIS "SELFLESS STATE" YOU GUYS USE... DOES IT ALLOW YOU TO DO ANYTHING?
THERE'S ONE TECHNIQUE I STILL CAN'T USE...

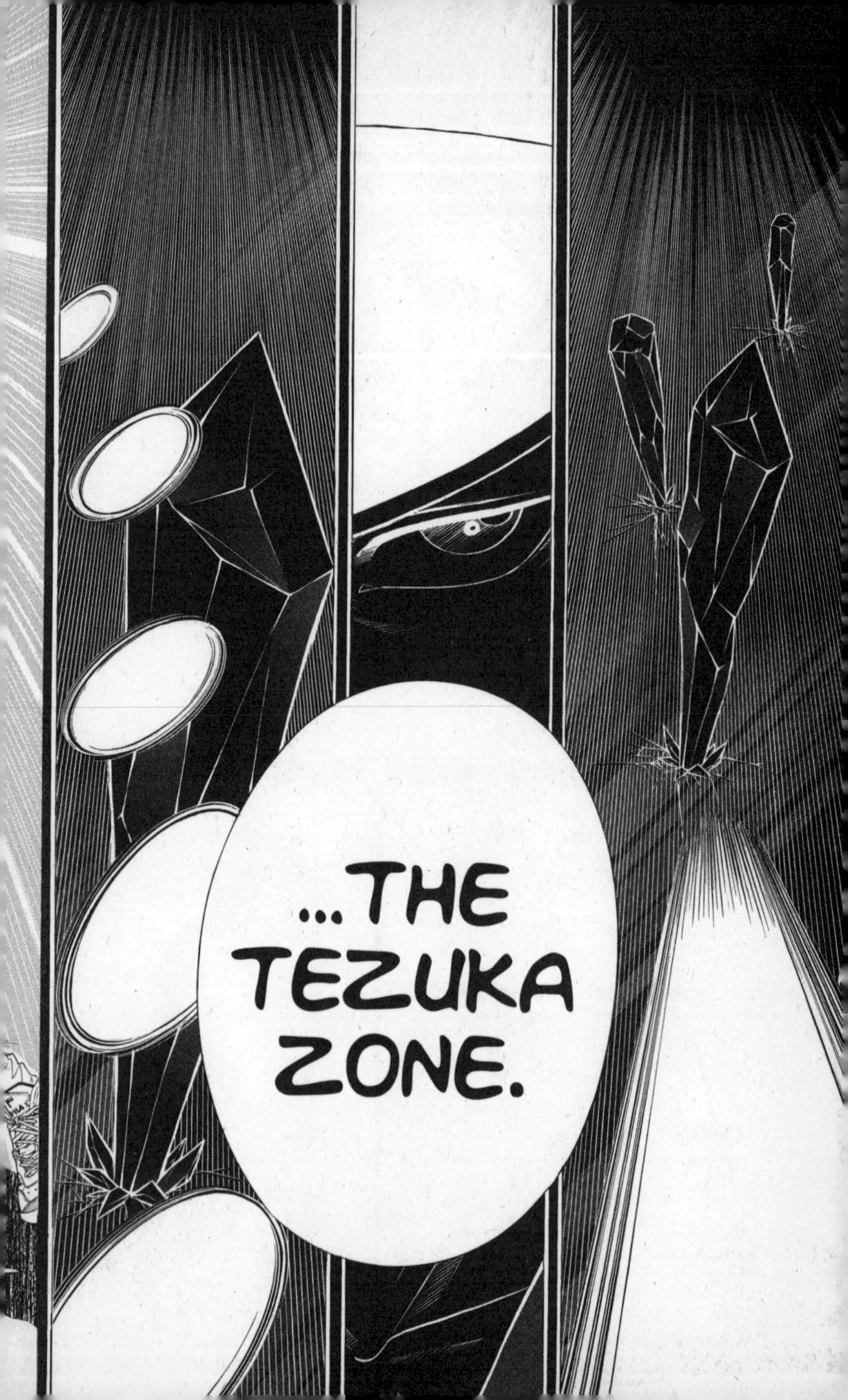
...THE TEZUKA ZONE.

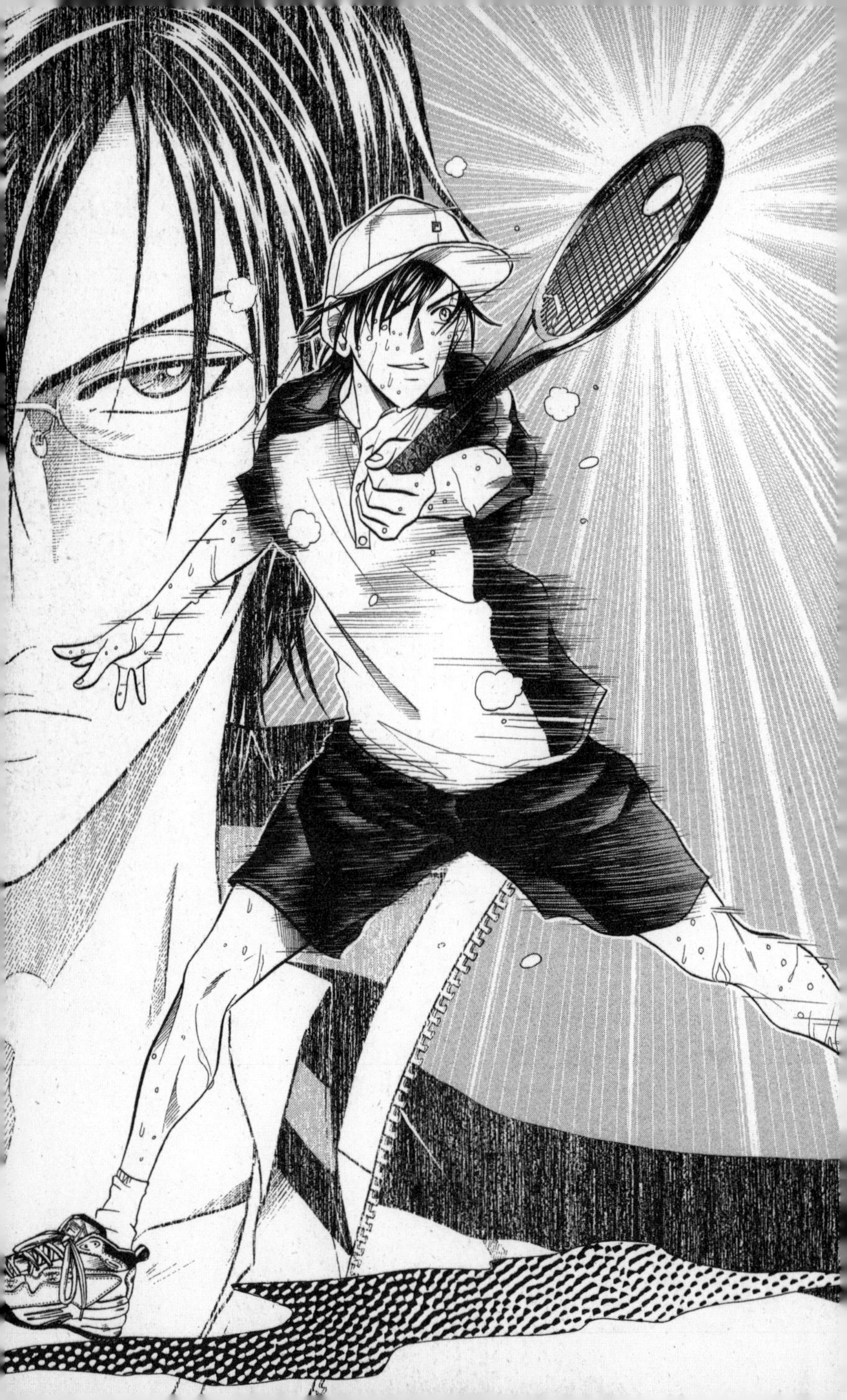

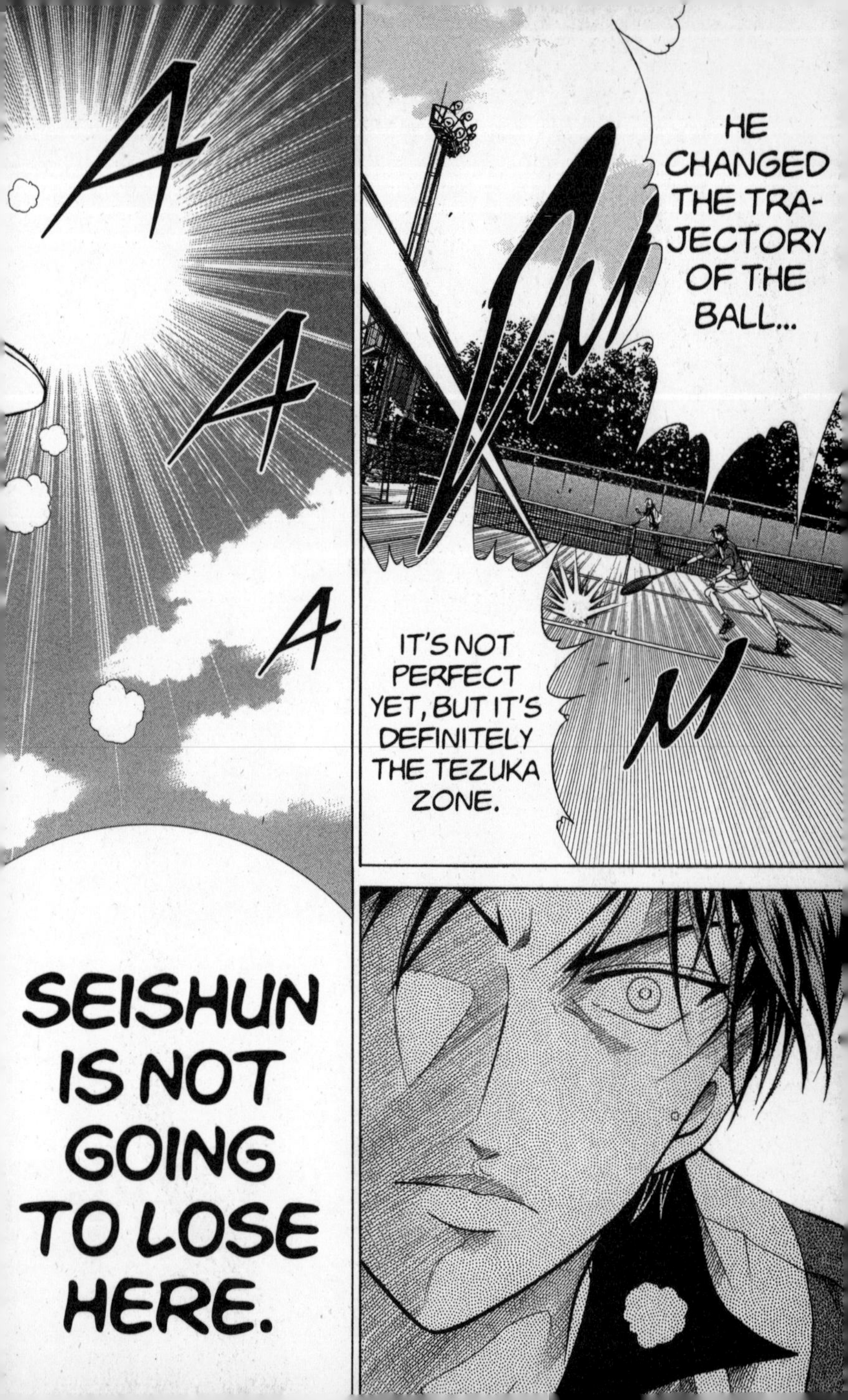
HE CHANGED THE TRA-JECTORY OF THE BALL...
IT'S NOT PERFECT YET, BUT IT'S DEFINITELY THE TEZUKA ZONE.
AAA
SEISHUN IS NOT GOING TO LOSE HERE.

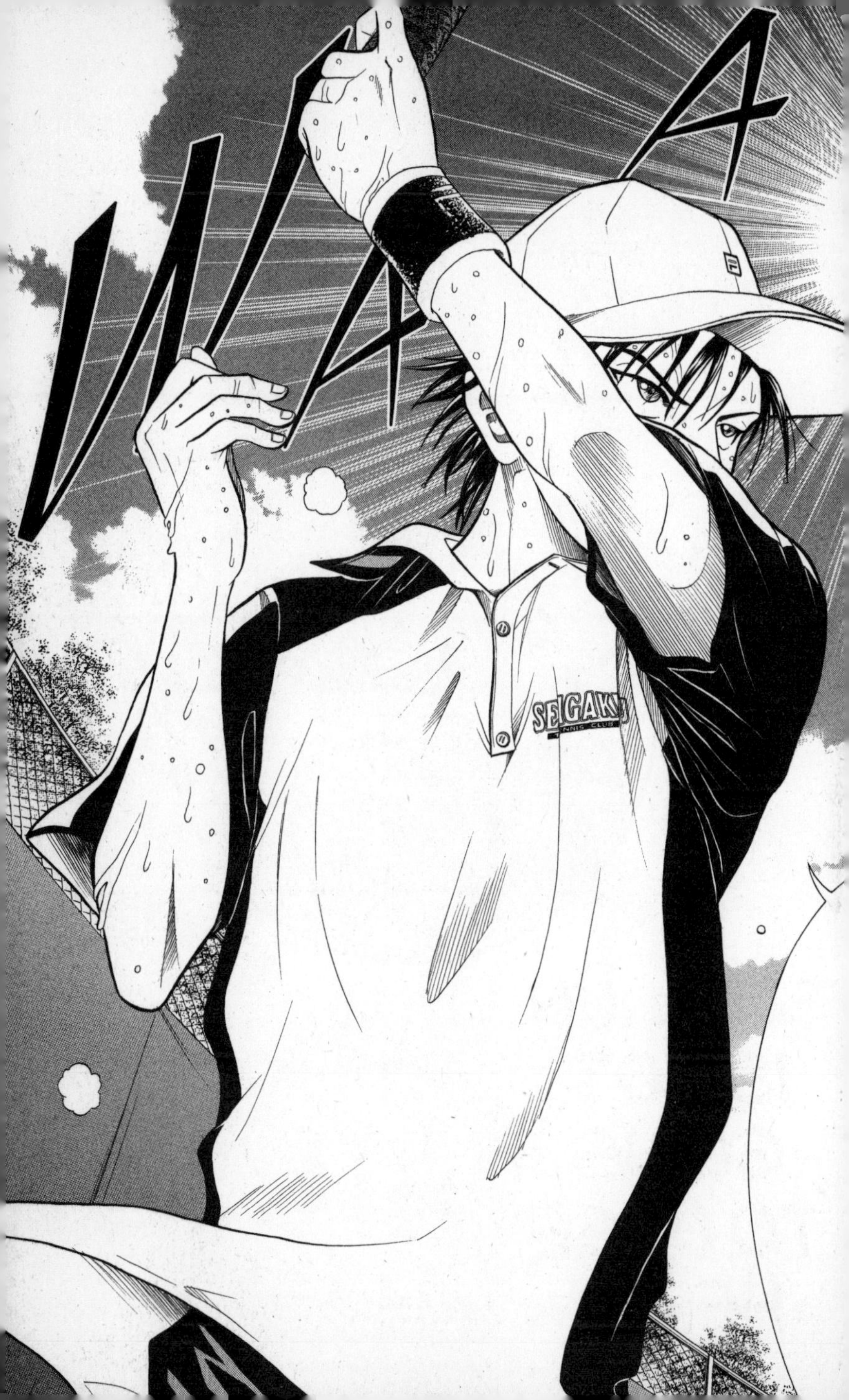
WAA
SEIGAKU
TENNIS CLUB

テニスの王子様

THE PRINCE OF TENNIS

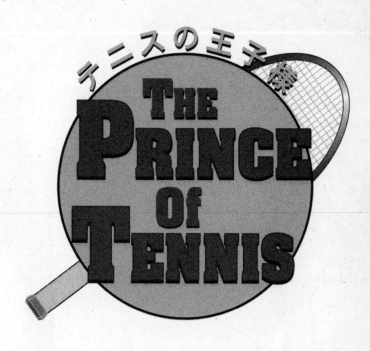

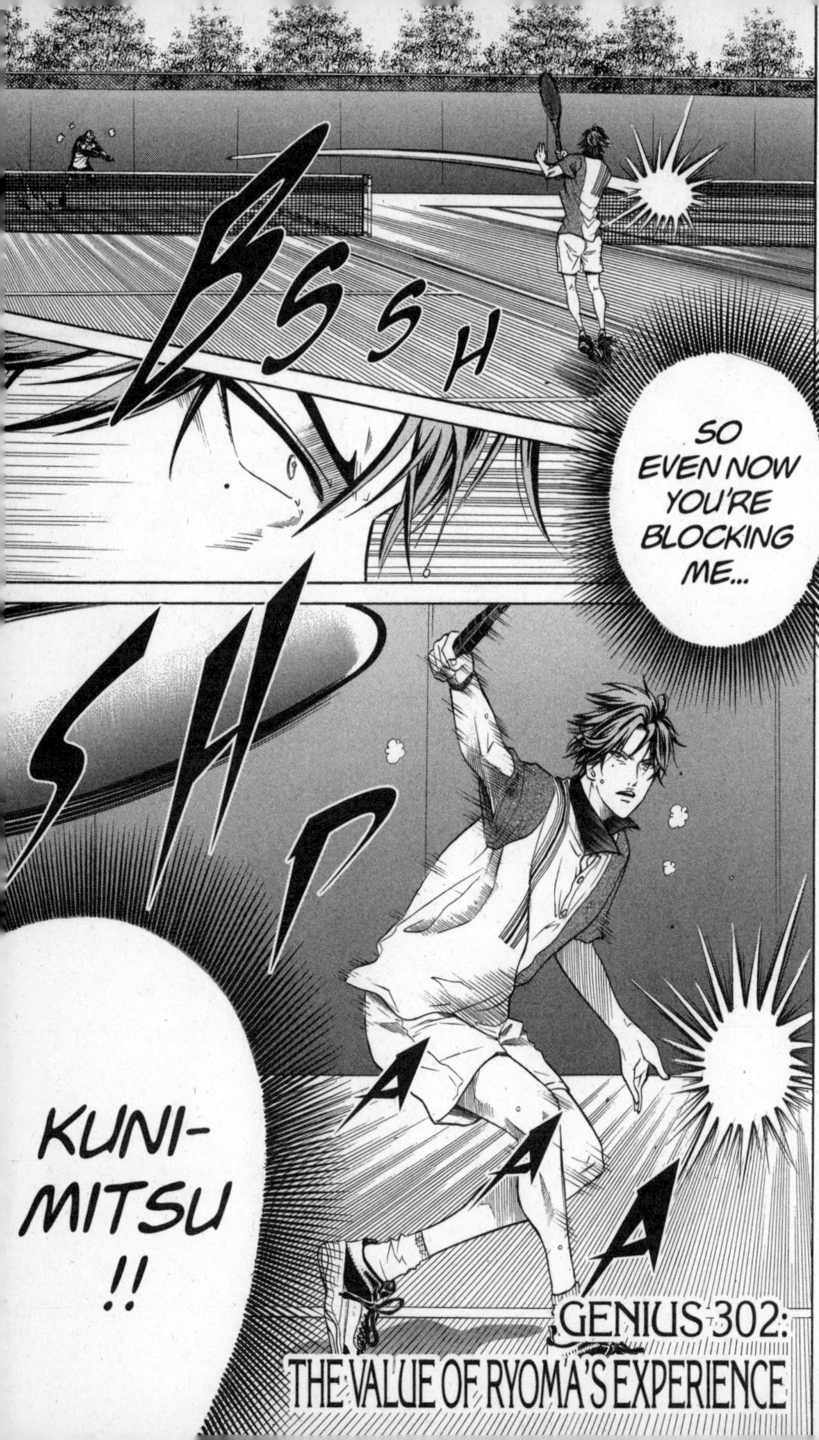
BSSH
SO EVEN NOW YOU'RE BLOCKING ME...
SHP
KUNI-MITSU!!
AAA
GENIUS 302:
THE VALUE OF RYOMA'S EXPERIENCE

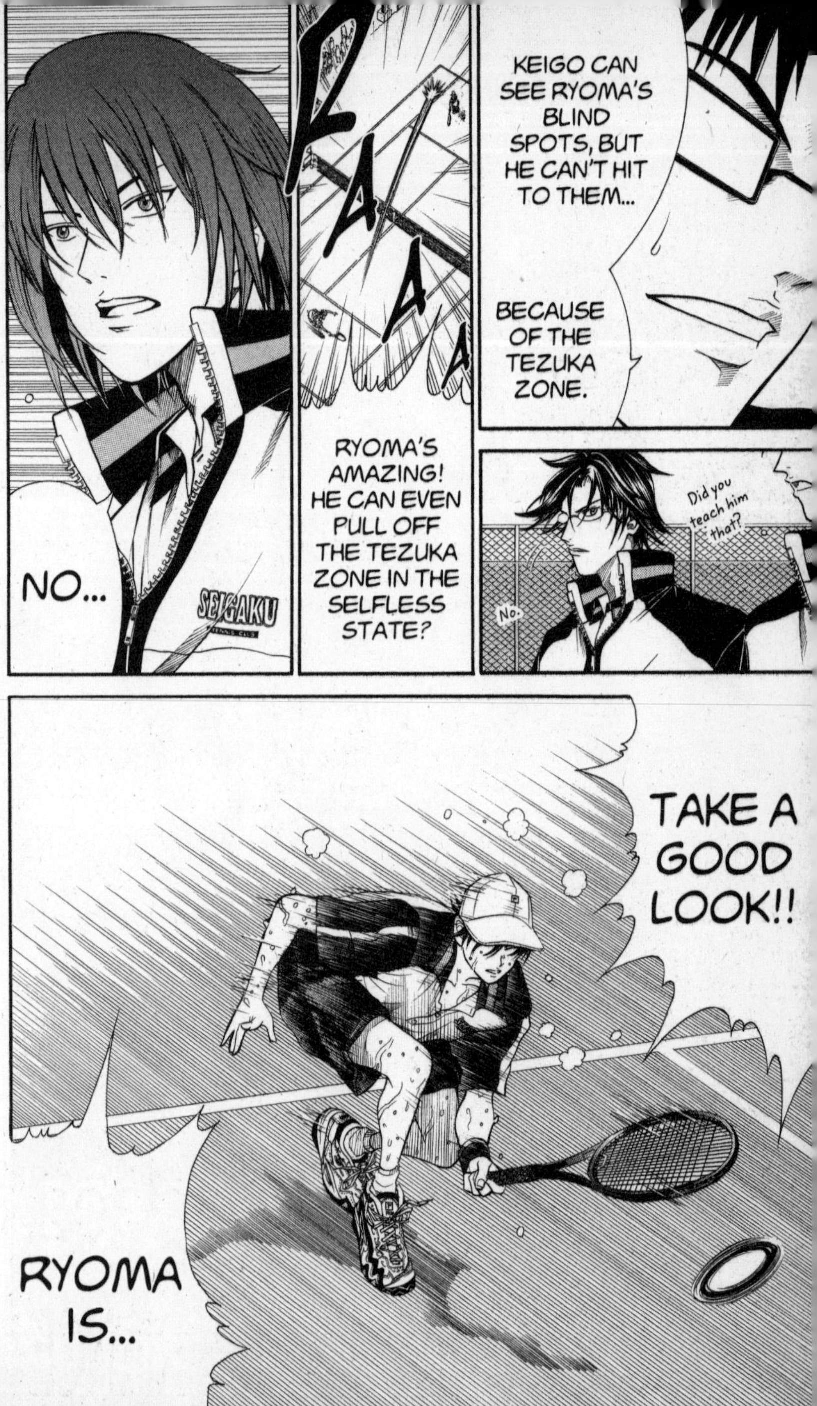
KEIGO CAN SEE RYOMA'S BLIND SPOTS, BUT HE CAN'T HIT TO THEM...
BECAUSE OF THE TEZUKA ZONE.
Did you teach him that?
No.
KAAAA
RYOMA'S AMAZING! HE CAN EVEN PULL OFF THE TEZUKA ZONE IN THE SELFLESS STATE?
NO...
SEIGAKU
TAKE A GOOD LOOK!!
RYOMA IS...

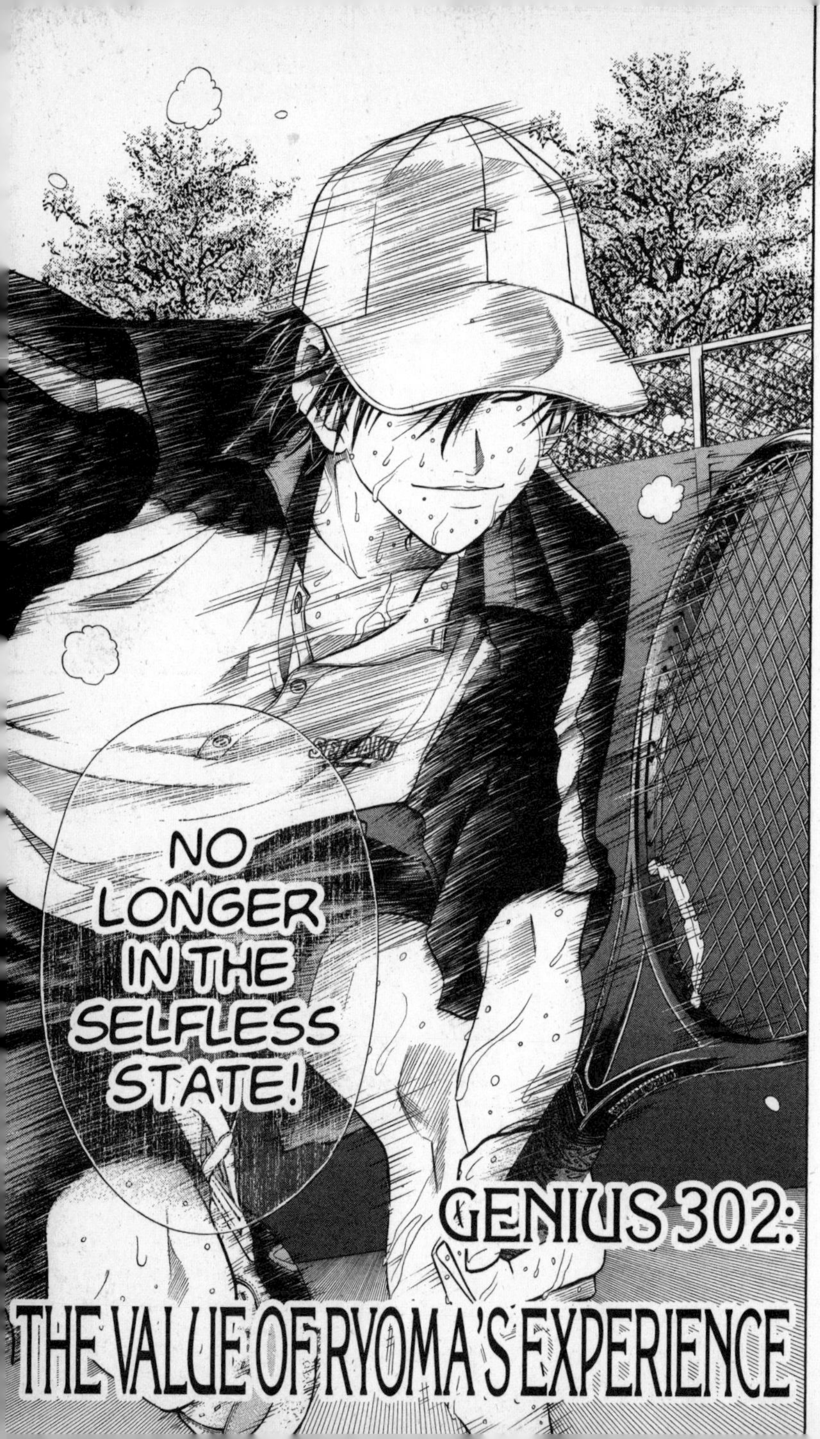
NO LONGER IN THE SELFLESS STATE!
GENIUS 302:
THE VALUE OF RYOMA'S EXPERIENCE

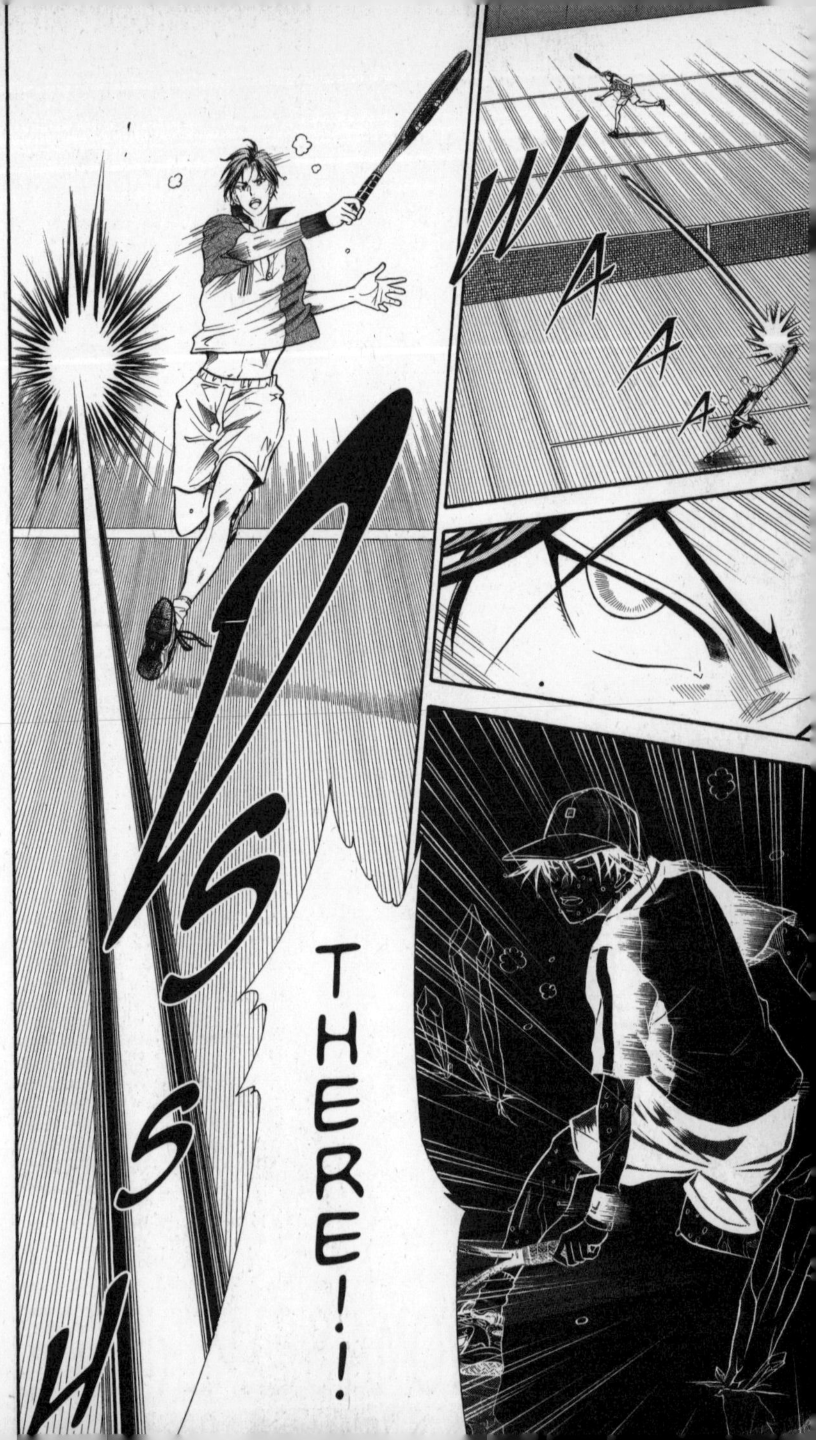
WAAA
THERE!!

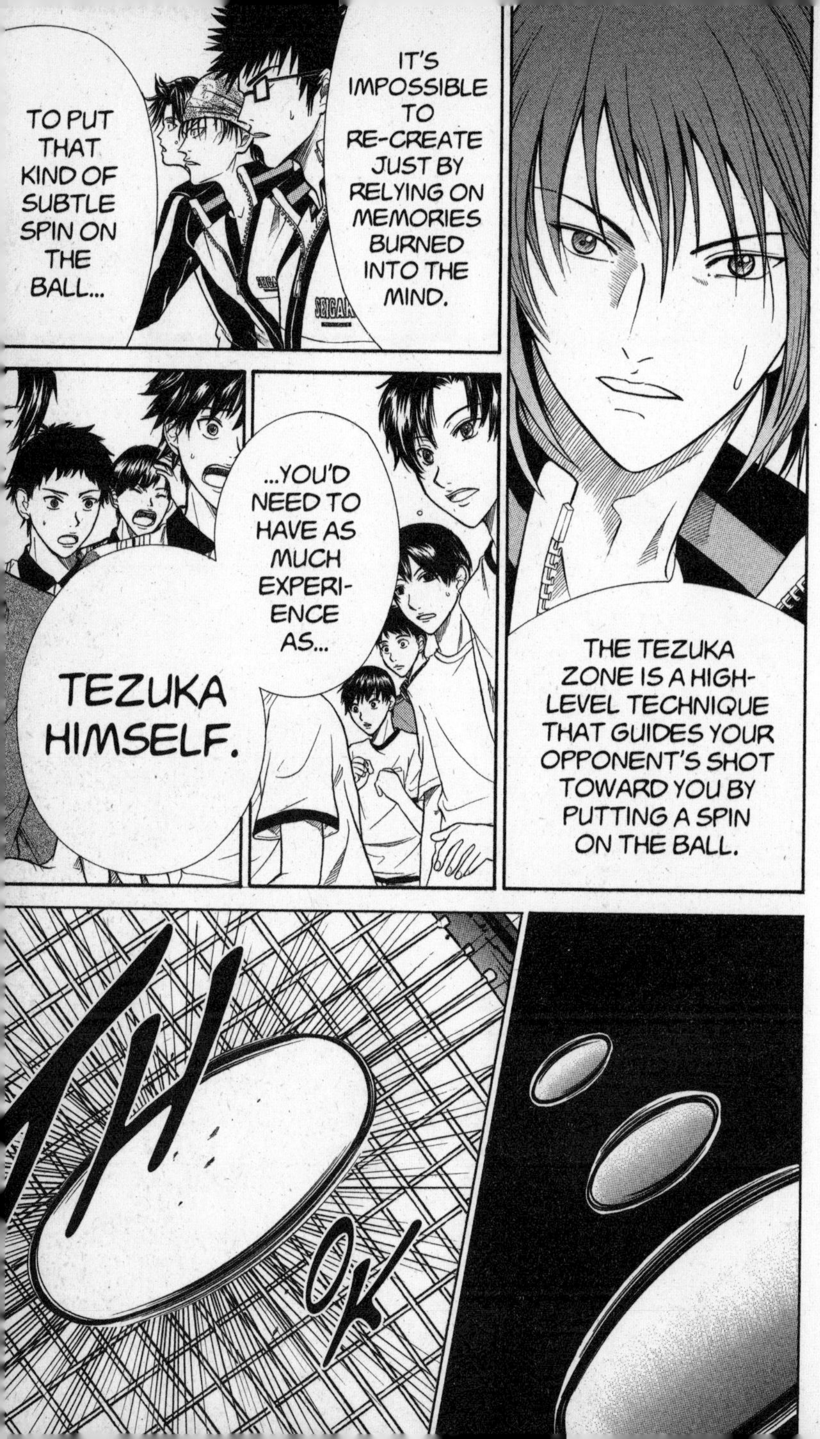
THE TEZUKA ZONE IS A HIGH-LEVEL TECHNIQUE THAT GUIDES YOUR OPPONENT'S SHOT TOWARD YOU BY PUTTING A SPIN ON THE BALL.
IT'S IMPOSSIBLE TO RE-CREATE JUST BY RELYING ON MEMORIES BURNED INTO THE MIND.
TO PUT THAT KIND OF SUBTLE SPIN ON THE BALL...
...YOU'D NEED TO HAVE AS MUCH EXPERIENCE AS...
TEZUKA HIMSELF.

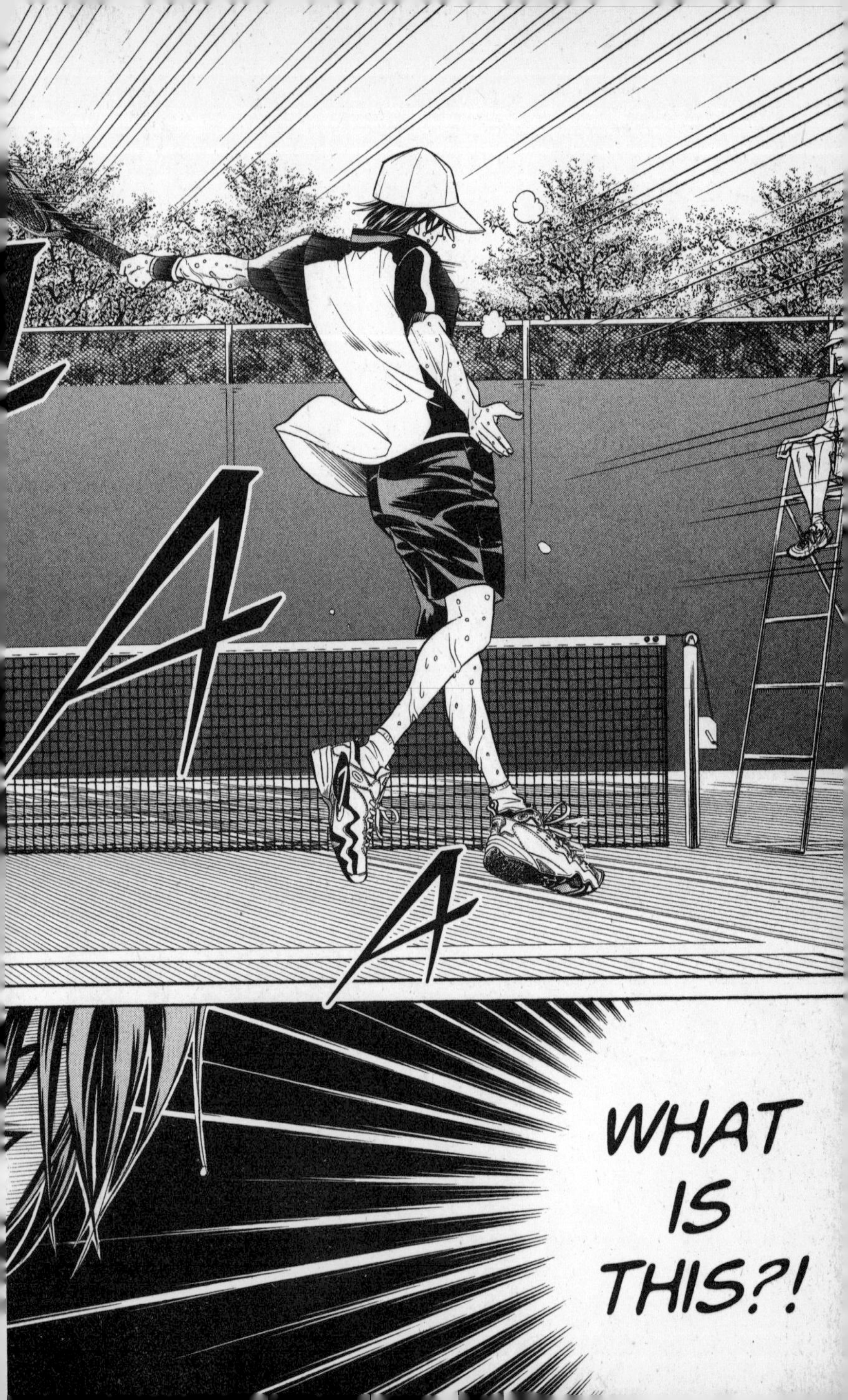
WHAT IS THIS?!

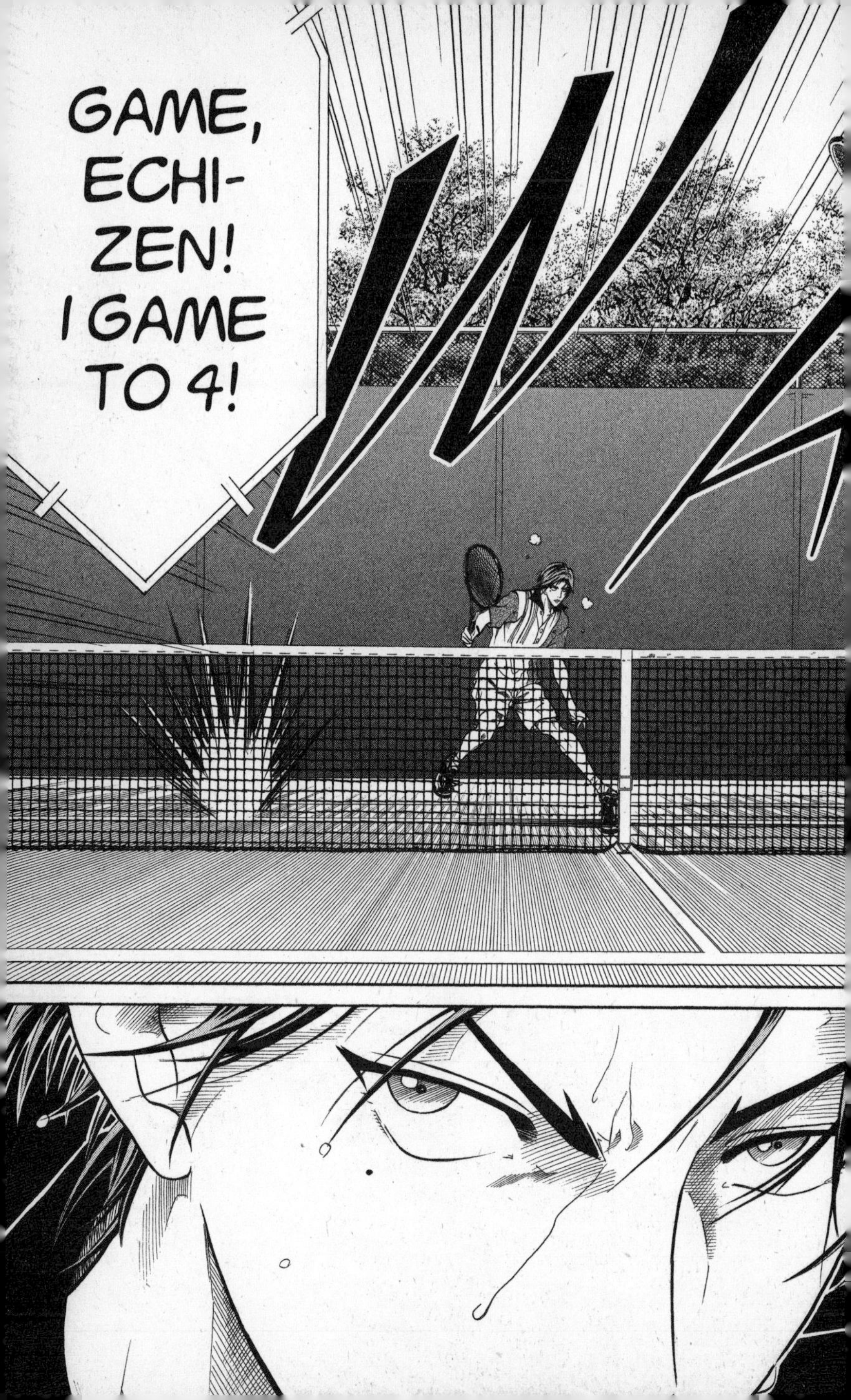
GAME, ECHI-ZEN! 1 GAME TO 4!

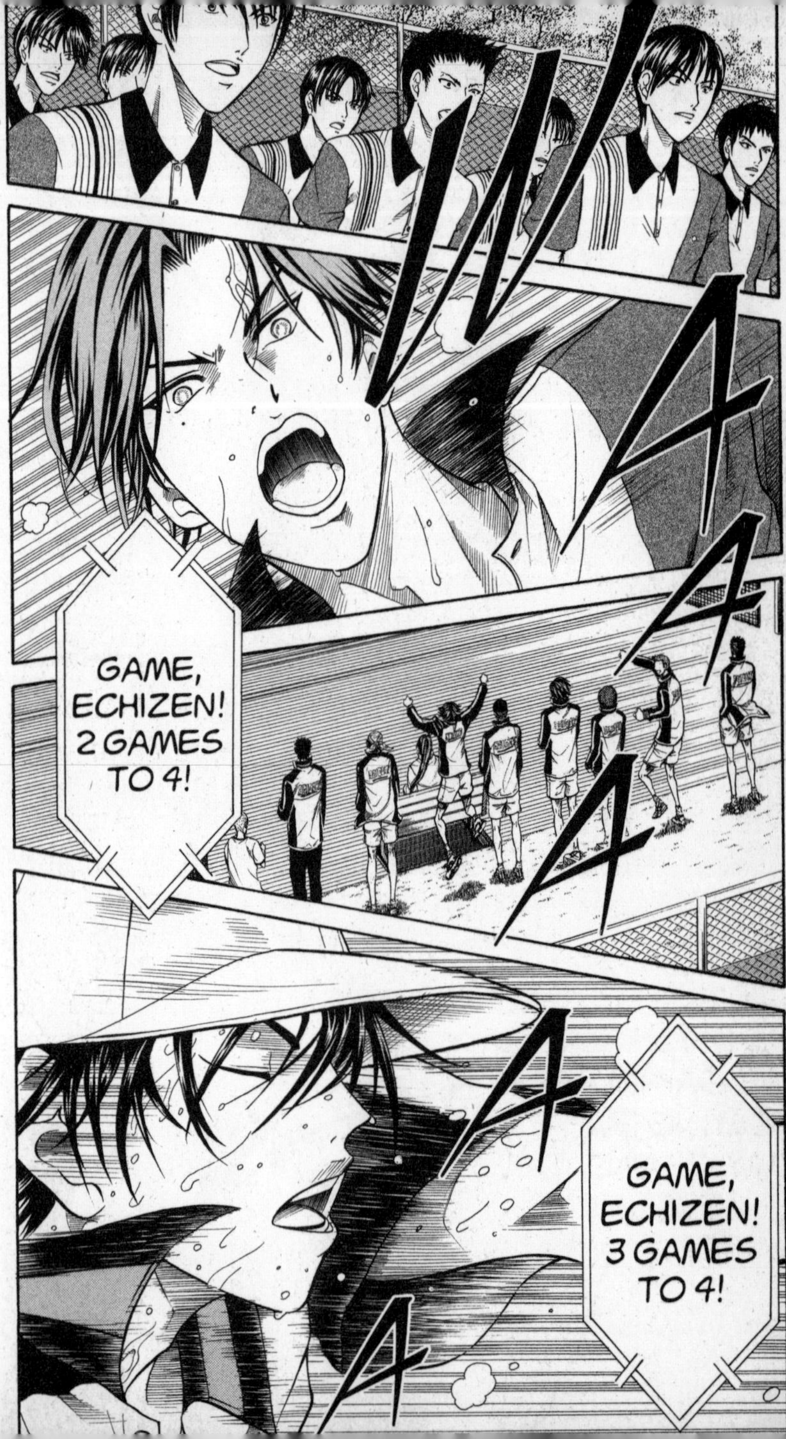
WAAAAA
GAME, ECHIZEN! 2 GAMES TO 4!
GAME, ECHIZEN! 3 GAMES TO 4!

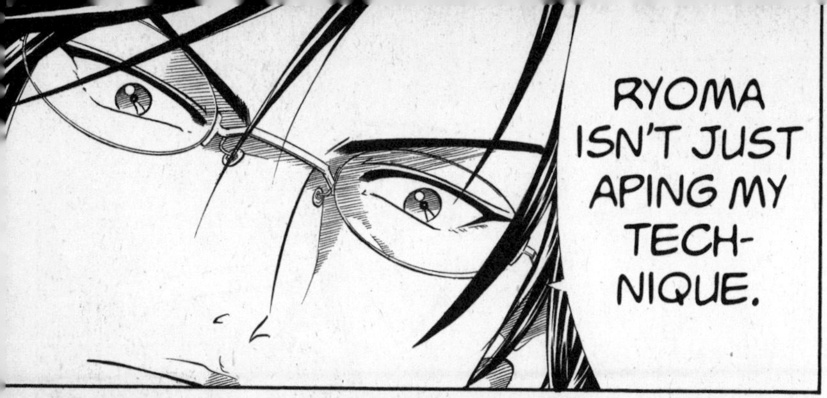
RYOMA ISN'T JUST APING MY TECH-NIQUE.

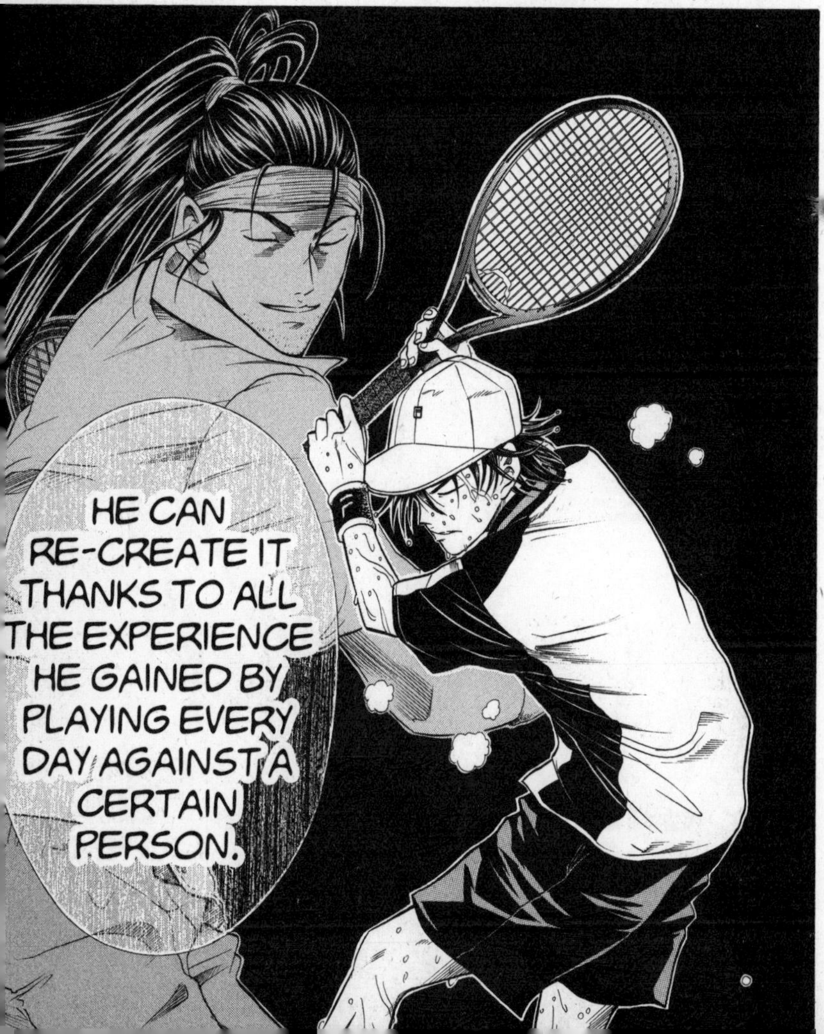
HE CAN RE-CREATE IT THANKS TO ALL THE EXPERIENCE HE GAINED BY PLAYING EVERY DAY AGAINST A CERTAIN PERSON.

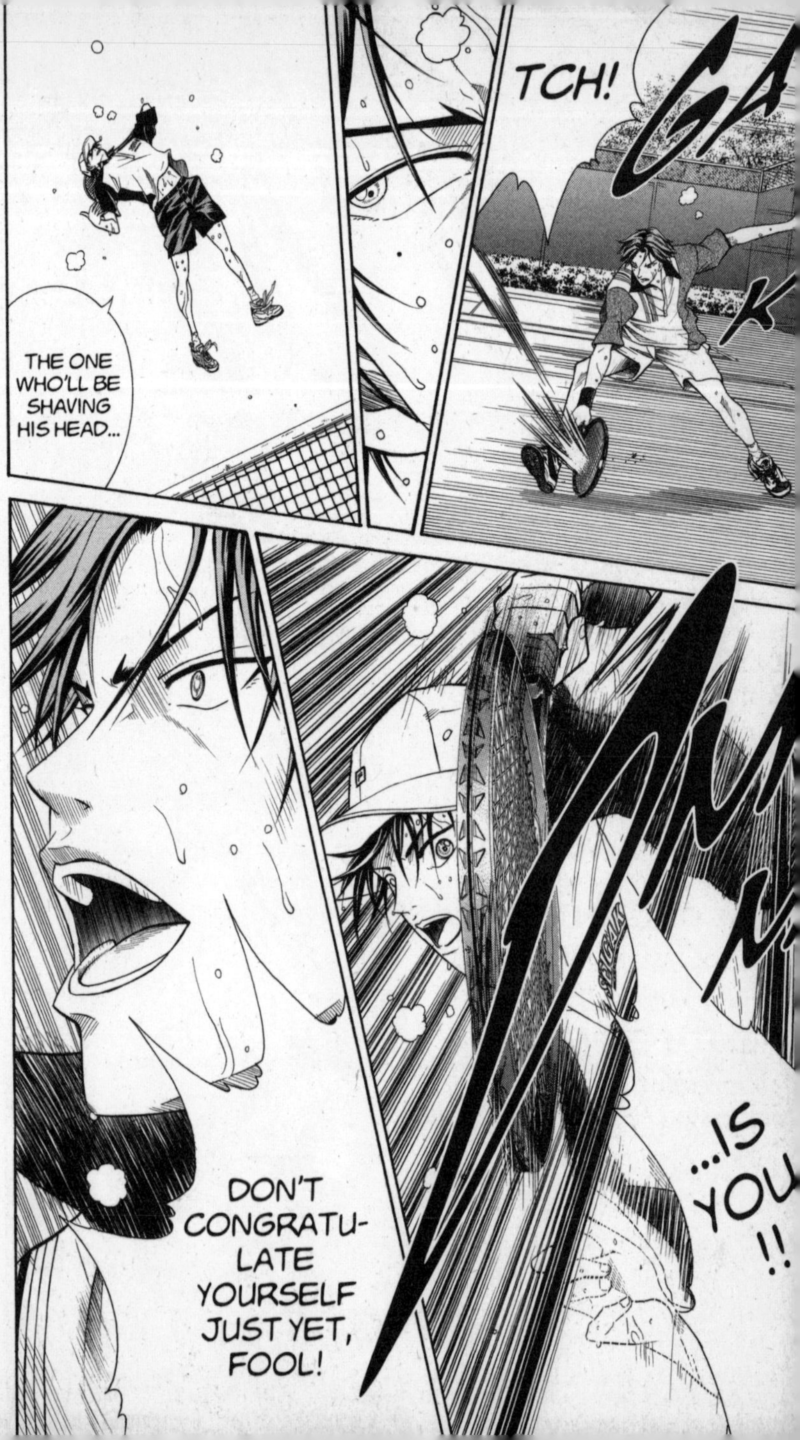
TCH!
THE ONE WHO'LL BE SHAVING HIS HEAD...
...IS YOU !!
DON'T CONGRATU-LATE YOURSELF JUST YET, FOOL!

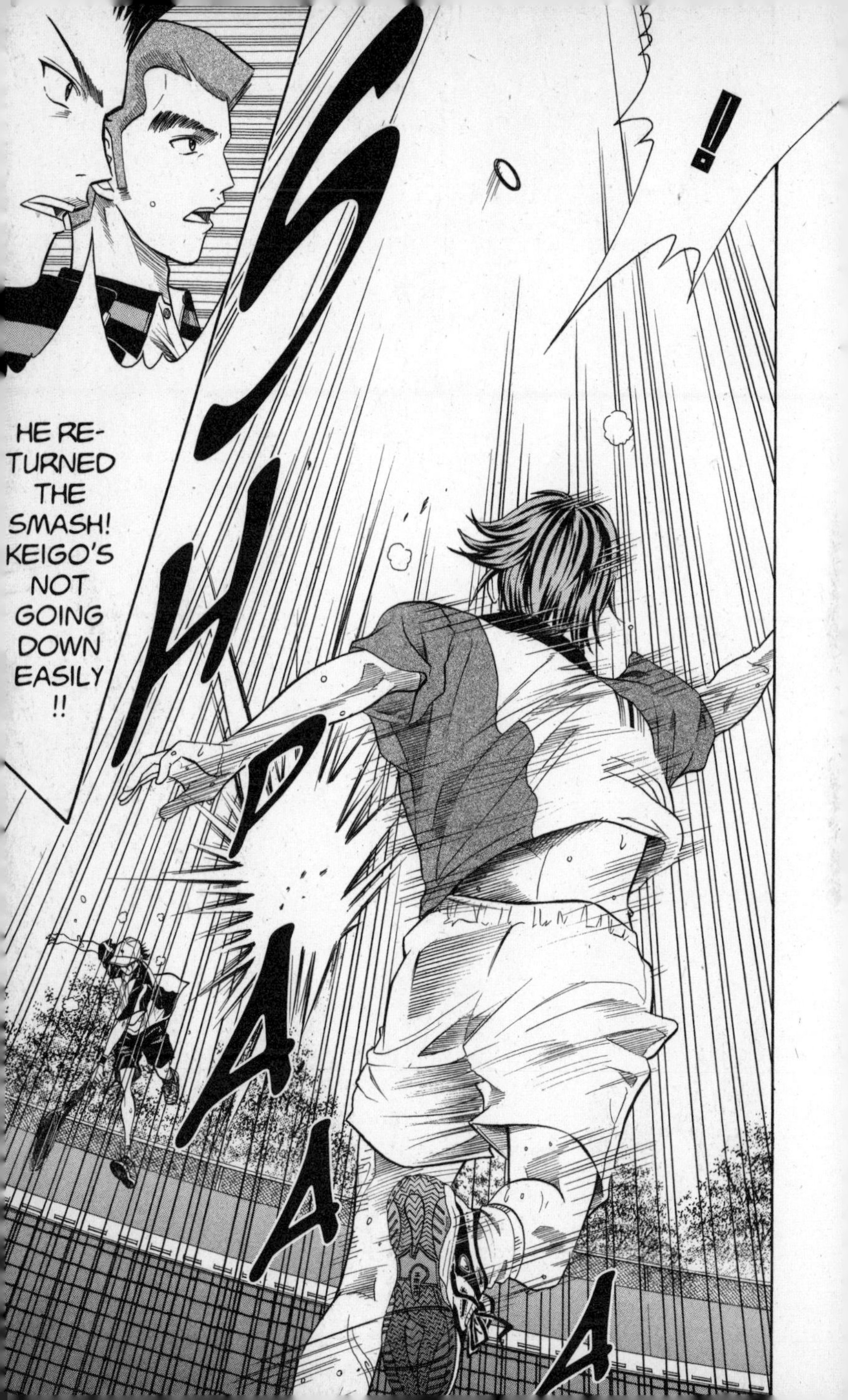
!
HE RE-TURNED THE SMASH! KEIGO'S NOT GOING DOWN EASILY !!

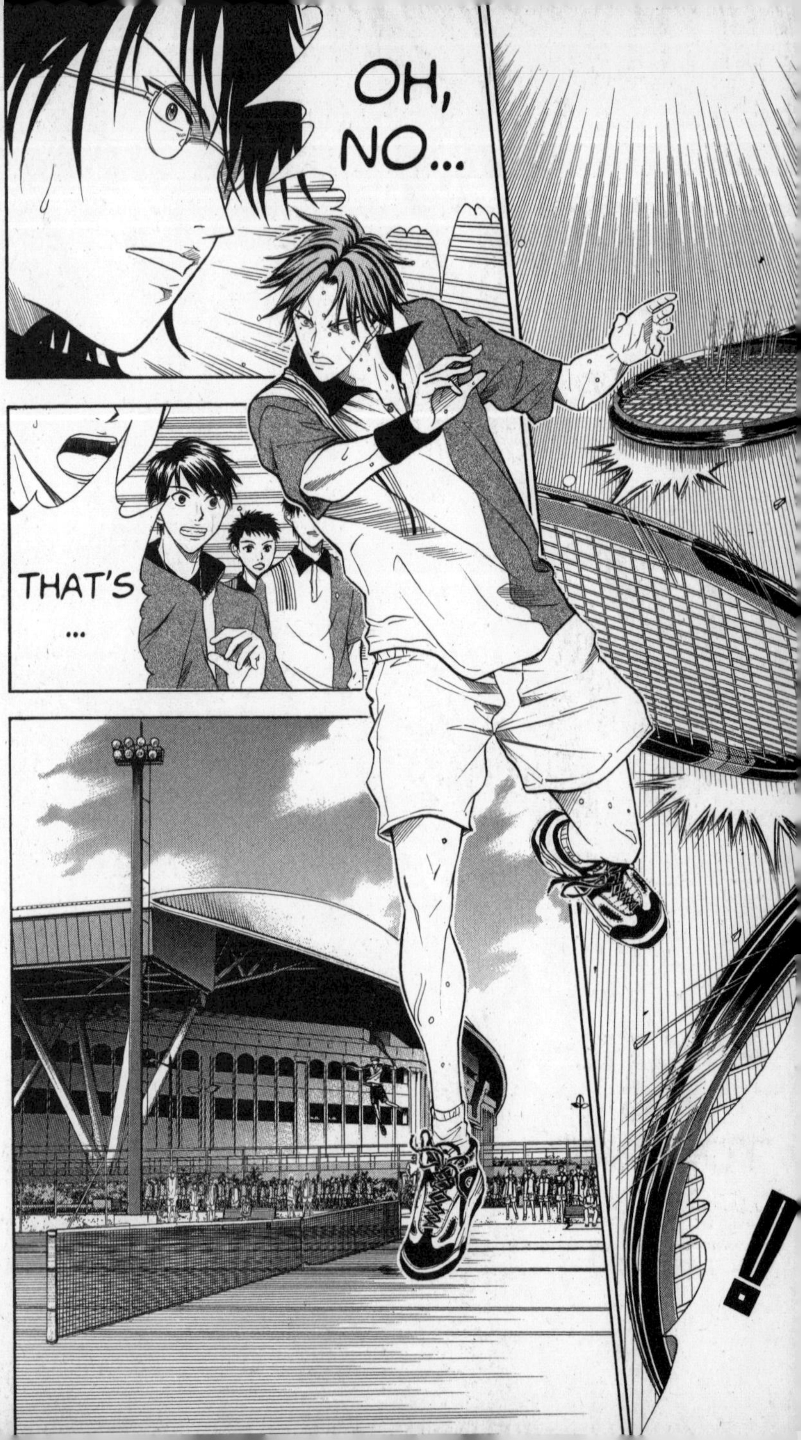
OH, NO...
THAT'S ...
!

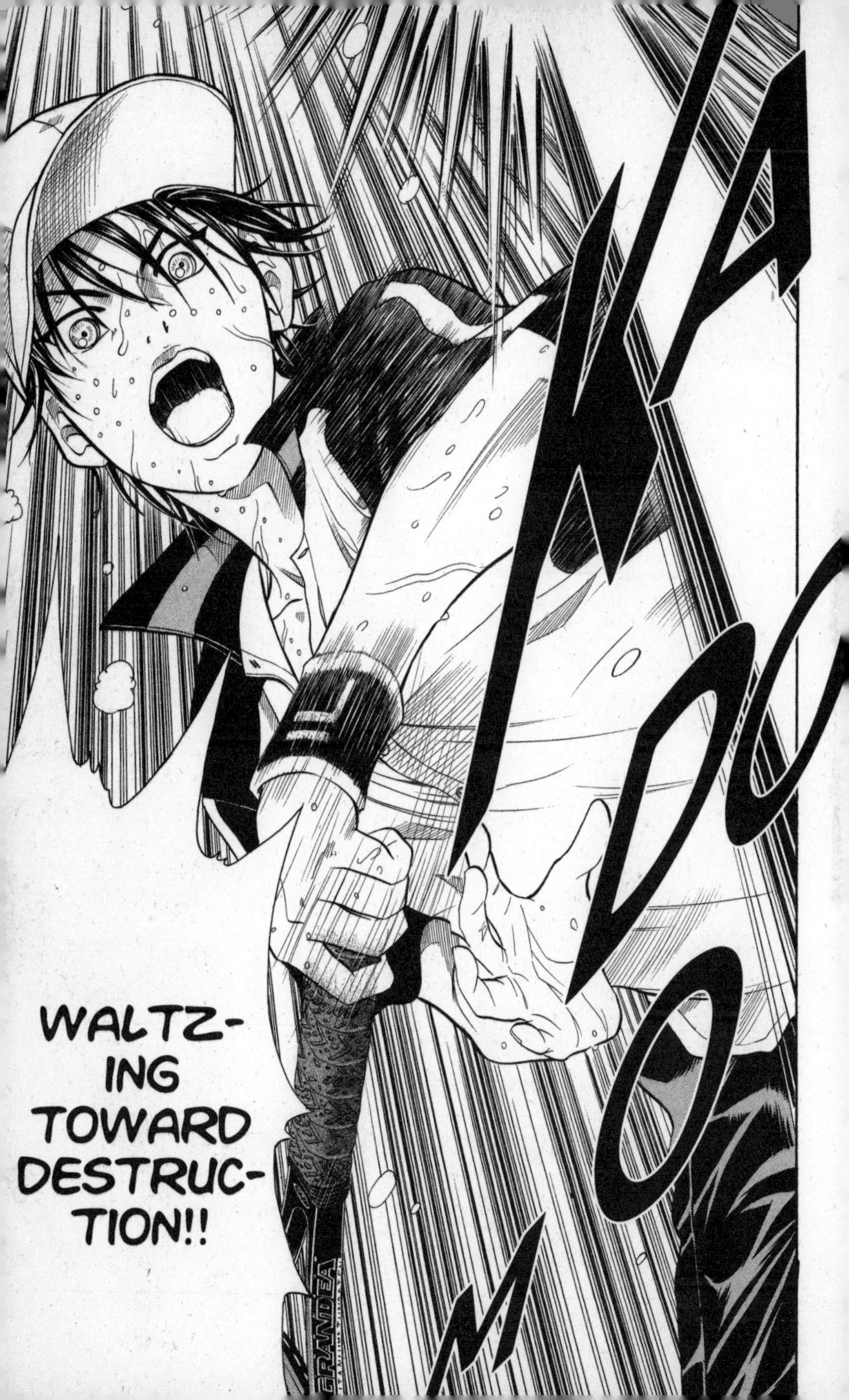
WALTZ-ING TOWARD DESTRUC-TION!!

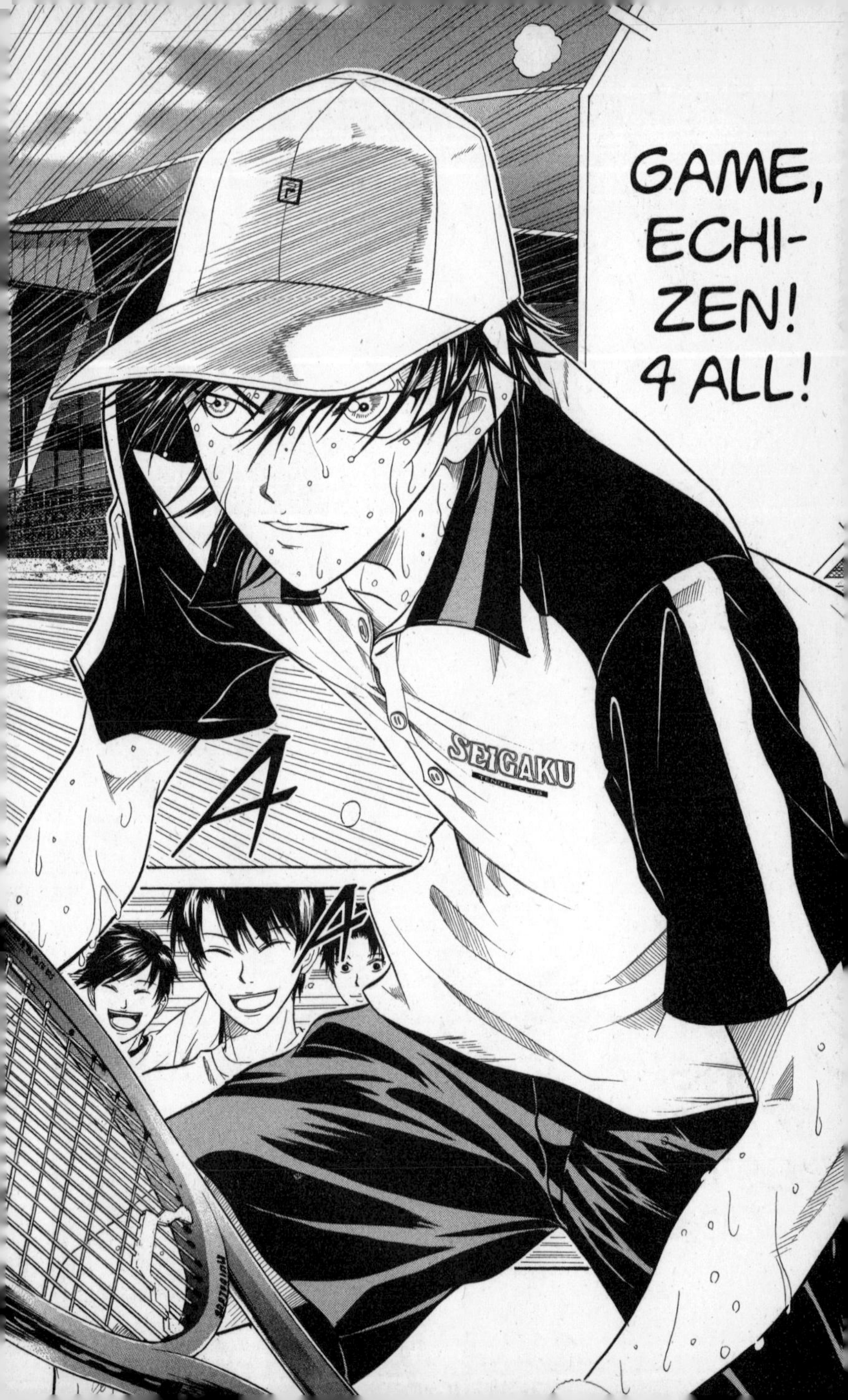
GAME, ECHI-ZEN! 4 ALL!
SEIGAKU
TENNIS CLUB

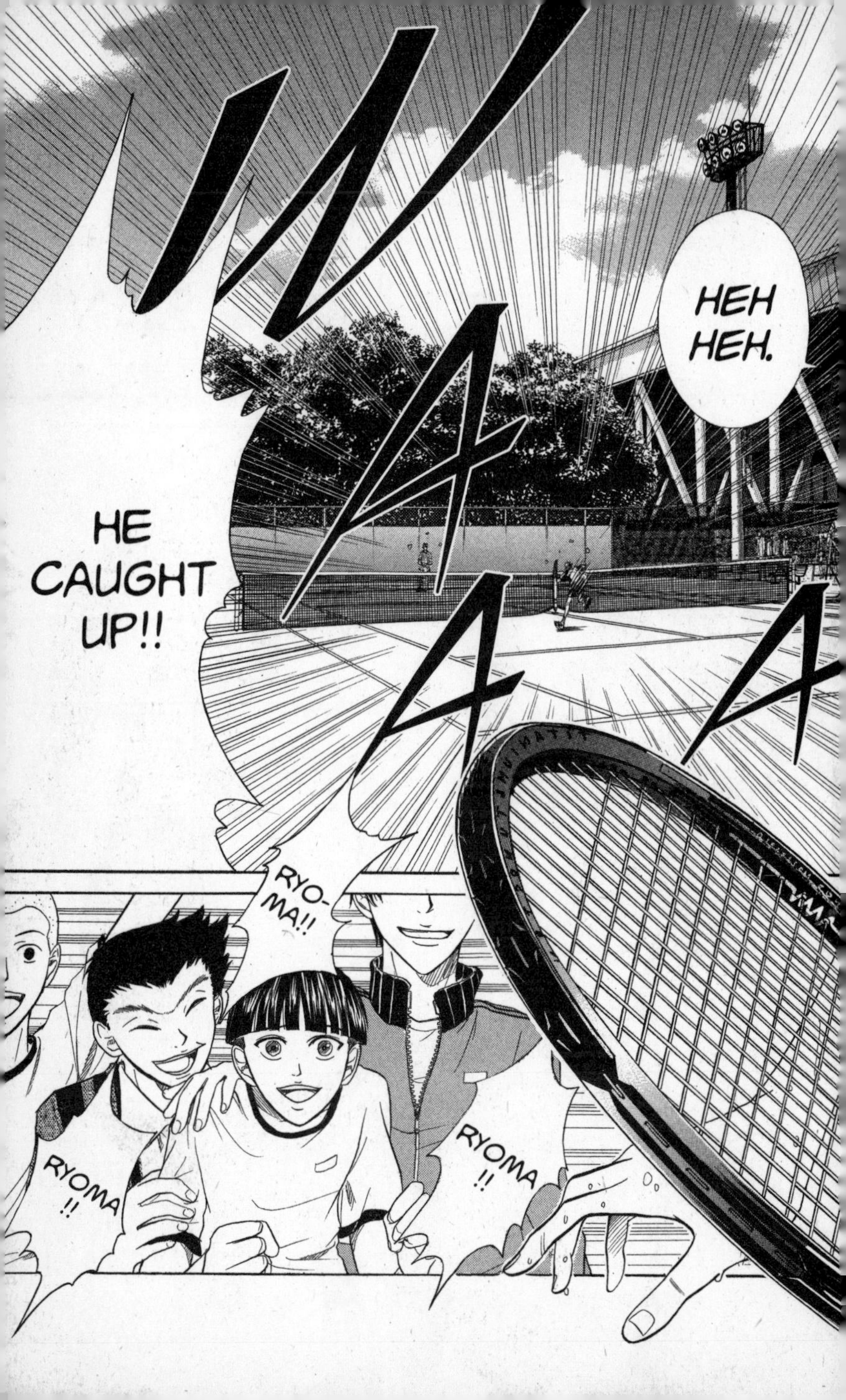
HEH HEH.
WAAA
HE CAUGHT UP!!
RYOMA!!
RYO-MA!!
RYOMA!!

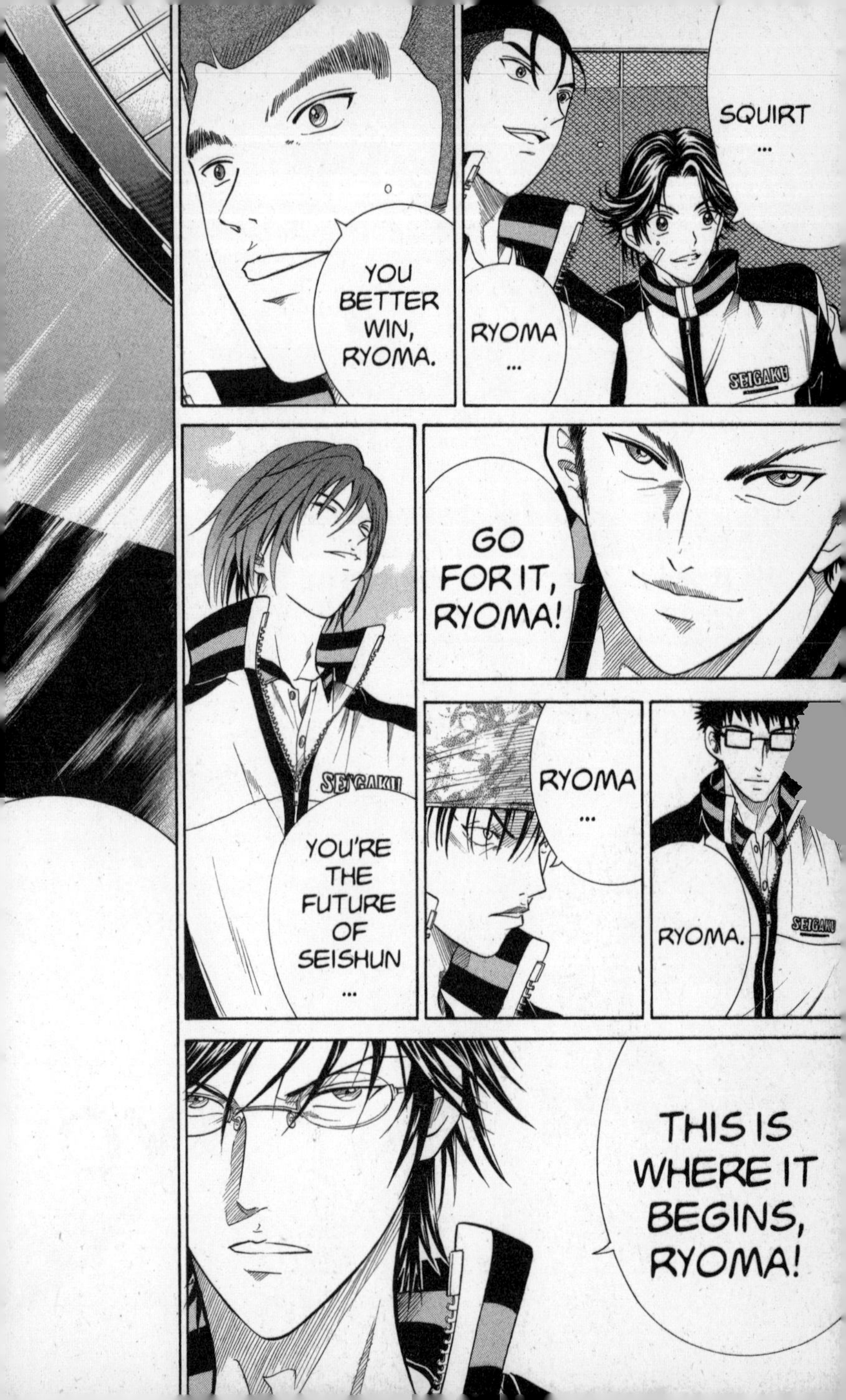
SQUIRT ...
RYOMA ...
YOU BETTER WIN, RYOMA.
GO FOR IT, RYOMA!
RYOMA.
RYOMA ...
YOU'RE THE FUTURE OF SEISHUN ...
THIS IS WHERE IT BEGINS, RYOMA!

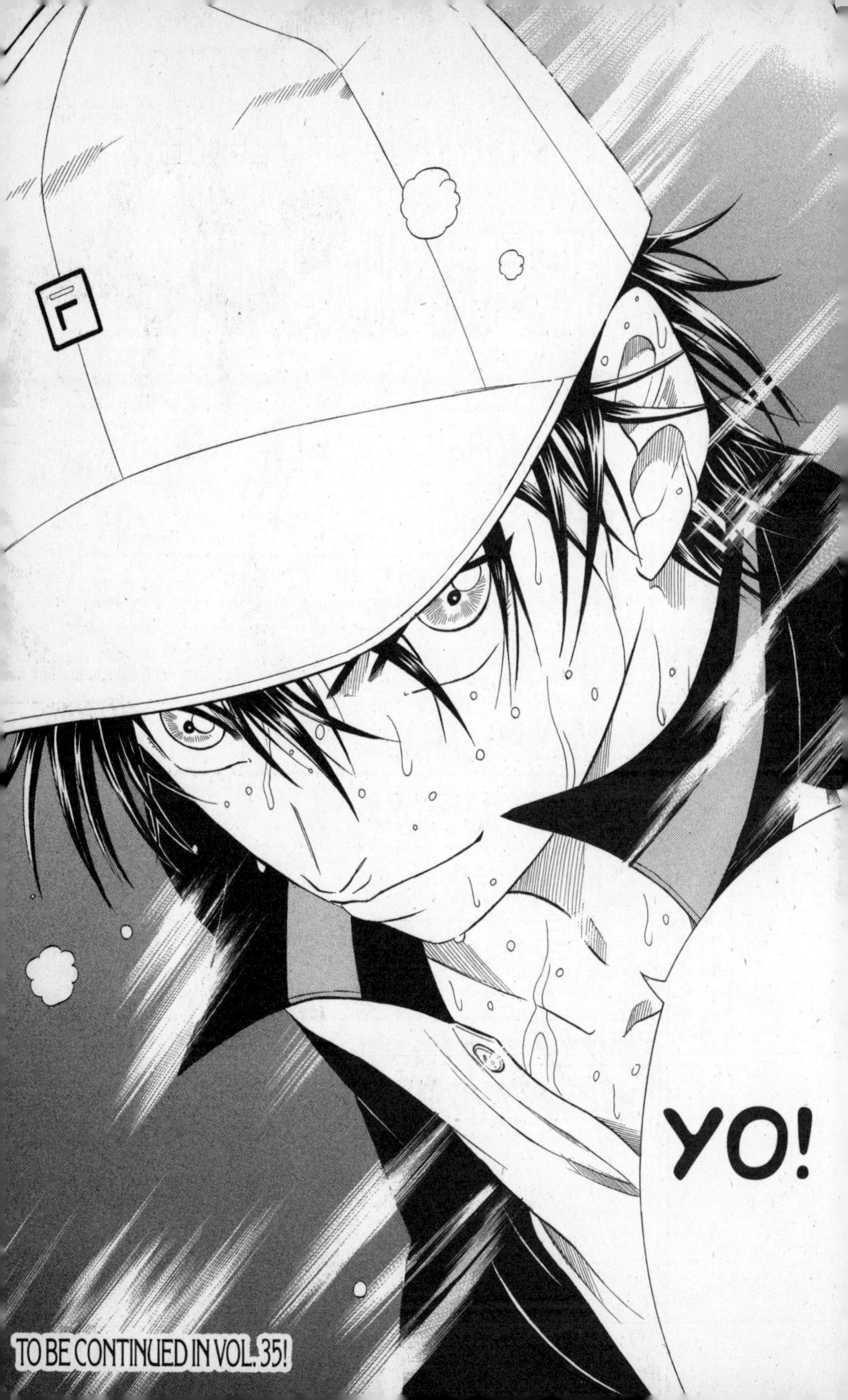
YO!
TO BE CONTINUED IN VOL. 35!

HYOTEI'S POPULARITY EXPLODES!!

THE 2006

VALENTINE'S DAY CHOCOLATE TALLY

1ST	KEIGO ATOBE	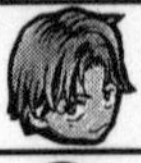	1,008
2ND	RYO SHISHIDO	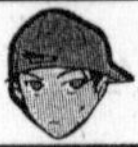	201
3RD	TAKESHI KONOMI	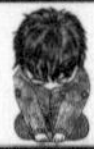	188
4TH	YUSHI OSHITARI	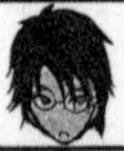	163
5TH	GENICHIRO SANADA	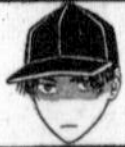	161
6TH	KUNIMITSU TEZUKA	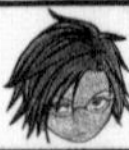	152
7TH	EIJI KIKUMARU	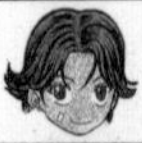	144
8TH	MUNEHIRO KABAJI	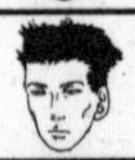	125
9TH	SHUSUKE FUJI	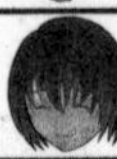	100
10TH	RYOMA ECHIZEN	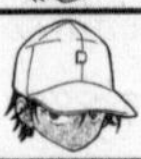	75

Rank	Name	Score	Rank	Name	Score
11TH	BUNTA MARUI	56	34TH	YUDAI YAMATO	8
	SEIICHI YUKIMURA		36TH	HIKARU AMANE	7
13TH	AKAYA KIRIHARA	53	37TH	KENTARO AOI	5
14TH	SHUICHIRO OISHI	48		SHINJI IBU	
	MASAHARU NIO			HARUKAZE KUROBANE	
16TH	RENJI YANAGI	39		KURANOSUKE SHIRAISHI	
17TH	HIROSHI YAGYU	31		KIPPEI TACHIBANA	
18TH	KIYOSUMI SENGOKU	29		TSUBAKI NISHIKIORI	
19TH	CHOTARO OHTORI	28	43RD	HAGINOSUKE TAKI	4
20TH	SADAHARU INUI	27		RIN HIRAKOBA	
	WAKASHI HIYOSHI			MICHIRU FUKUSHI	
22ND	GAKUTO MUKAHI	26	46TH	YOSHIRO AKAZAWA	3
23RD	KAORU KAIDO	25		KENYA OSHITARI	
24TH	TAKASHI KAWAMURA	23		KALPIN	
25TH	TAKESHI MOMOSHIRO	21		ATSUSHI KISARAZU	
26TH	JIRO AKUTAGAWA	16		EISHIRO KITE	
27TH	AKIRA KAMIO	14		TARO SAKAKI	
28TH	JACKAL KUWAHARA	13		KEI TANISHI	
29TH	KOJIRO SAEKI	12		KINTARO TOYAMA	
30TH	RYOGA ECHIZEN	11	54TH	KOHARU KONJIKI	2
	YUTA FUJI			MASASHI ARAI	
32ND	HAJIME MIZUKI	9		KYOSUKE UCHIMURA	
	KENTARO MINAMI			ICHIRO KANEDA	
34TH	JIN AKUTSU	8	58TH	OJI	1

(REST OF THE RESULTS OMITTED)

Thank you once again for all the chocolates!! They really make me feel everybody's passion for the characters. But chocolate is so expensive these days, so don't overdo it, okay?

T. KONOMI
2006. 6. 5

In the Next

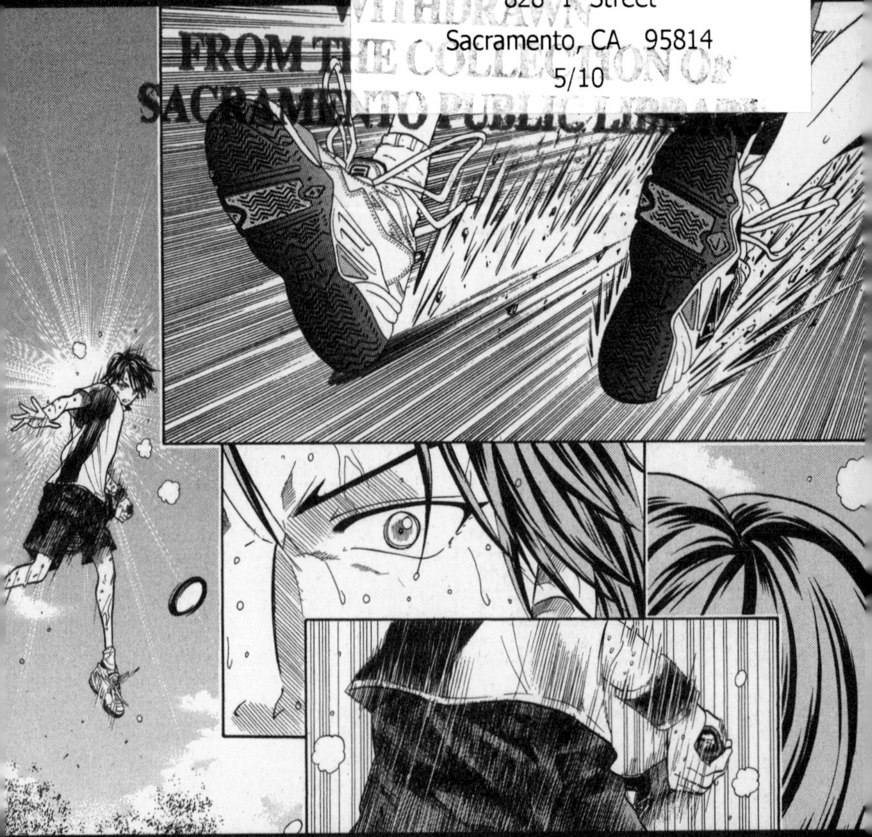

Farewell, Hyotei Academy

Ryoma and Keigo's incredible match turns into a battle of stamina and sheer will: whoever's left standing to make the last play will be the winner. Meanwhile, Fudomine's captain, Kippei Tachibana, plays his team's last quarterfinal match against Shitenhoji. His opponent is his ex-teammate, Senri Chitose. Can Kippei overcome the demons of his past and defeat his old friend?

Available January 2010!